THE FAMILY IN
GLOBAL TRANSITION

THE FAMILY IN GLOBAL TRANSITION

Edited by
Gordon L. Anderson, Ph.D.

A PWPA Book
St. Paul, Minnesota

Published in the United States of America by
Professors World Peace Academy
2700 University Avenue West
St. Paul, Minnesota 55114

Trade distribution by Paragon House Publishers

A Professors World Peace Academy Book

The Professors World Peace Academy (PWPA) is an international association of professors and scholars from diverse backgrounds, devoted to issues concerning world peace. PWPA sustains a program of conferences and publications on topics in peace studies, area and cultural studies, national and international development, education, economics and international relations.

Library of Congress Cataloging-in-Publication Data

The Family in Global Transition / edited by Gordon L. Anderson
      p. cm.
    ISBN: 1-885118-05-8 (Cloth) — ISBN 1-885118-06-6 (Paper)
    1. Family—History. 2. Family—Cross-cultural studies
  I. Anderson, Gordon L. (Gordon Louis), 1947-
HQ503.F3198   1997
306.85'09—dc21   97-2955
                                               CIP

TABLE OF CONTENTS

Acknowledgments

This book is the result of a major study on the worldwide state of the family which was begun in 1993 under the sponsorship of the Professors World Peace Academy. The project consisted of two phases. In the first phase, a major international conference on the subject was organized with a view toward the production of a book. The second phase involved selecting and honing the papers presented at the conference as well as the inclusion and commissioning of additional papers to make the book complete.

Recognition is due to those who helped to locate the paperwriters and organize the panels at the conference: Geoffrey Ainsworth Harrison at Oxford University for the historical papers; Bina Gupta at the University of Missouri for the chapters on the family in the major cultural spheres; and Nicholas N. Kittrie at American University for the papers related to public policy.

In addition to thanking the paperwriters who contributed chapters to the book, I would like to especially thank the Board of Directors of the Professors World Peace Academy for their financial support for this project, and I would also like to thank Rosemary Byrne Yokoi, who assisted with the correspondence, and Betty Lancaster for her work in copyediting the manuscript.

Gordon L. Anderson
April 1997

Introduction

Gordon L. Anderson

The Family in Transition

The family is the basic unit of human social organization and the basic institution for the socialization of young human beings into the world. Children mimic their parents and develop basic life patterns and attitudes before they enter school and the larger society. Recent studies in the social sciences have reconfirmed what most people know from intuition: without the love and care of a family, children are at a severe disadvantage for achieving a rewarding life. If the families in a society are dysfunctional, that society will become dysfunctional. If the families in a society are healthy, that society will be healthy.

The different cultures of our world have bequeathed to us a variety of forms of the family and specific roles that the family plays in society. Today these traditional cultures have all encountered modern life with its advanced technology, cultural pluralism, and globalism. Everywhere the family is in transition.

Transitions in human social life, and especially the family, are challenging and unsettling. As traditional families encounter the modern world they might fall apart, react with hostility and self-defense, or find some way to adapt to the new circumstances. Very few families in the modern world of today exist in the same way as the families of their grandparents or great grandparents. Everywhere families have been forced to change.

The twentieth century is littered with ill-fated attempts by societies to address the challenges of modernity through ideological and nationalist programs which attempt to replace or circumvent the family. National socialism and communism were extremely costly failures. Millions of people have died as a result of trying to impose a pure national or international culture by force. In such social systems, an individual becomes an impersonal statistic, a cog on a gear in a huge machine. Aristotle warned against the dangers of such a system in his *Politics*:

> There is a further drawback to common ownership: the greater the number of owners, the less respect for the property.... Applying this to the proposed communal possession of families, we might say that each citizen has a thousand sons, but these are not one man's sons; any one of them is equally the son of any person. As a result no person will concern himself very much about any of them (*Politics*, Book II, Chapter 3).

In a society where natural parental responsibility fails or is thwarted, it is inevitable that members of society will not develop the empathy, love and respect for life and property required to conduct orderly and civil affairs. Such a society is destined to collapse from within.

There has been a worldwide reaction to the modern secular nationalist and collectivist movements expressed in a resurgence of religious fundamentalism of all types: Jewish, Christian, Islamic, Hindu, and others. Members of these traditional cultures sense the threat to the family and attempt to protect it through the restoration of the traditional culture. However, these traditions are rooted in forms of social organization and systems of belief that make them ineffective in the modern world of global technology and pluralism.

It is our task, therefore, to understand how the family can best adapt to modern life and successfully rear children without succumbing to nationalist or collectivist temptations or reacting with the effort to impose old orthodoxies inapplicable to life in the twenty-first century.

This book is about the family, its historical role in human society, how modern life is affecting families throughout the world, and the challenges that families face. It describes how the various cultures of the world are responding to the forces of modern life and their affect on the family. It provides a global view of family life in the modern world. It shows which aspects of family life are universal and which are particular to a specific time and culture. In so doing, it is hoped that this book will leave the reader with an understanding of what the family is, and how families can best perform their role in this time of global transition.

The Family in History

The book is divided into three parts. The first part discusses the family in human history. Archaeological evidence suggests that in prehistoric times, human beings lived in small groups. However, Professor Knappert points out that there is no evidence to confirm that these groups resembled either the idyllic primitive communism described by Karl Marx, or the peaceful matrilineal societies of many feminist accounts. It is likely that prehistoric clans were more frequently ruled by a patriarch. Human social organization underwent a transformation with the development of agriculture 6000-7000 years ago, making it necessary to protect land and making it possible to feed cities and armies. The early empires were based on family dynasties, but the development of codes of law and the creation of geographic states made the organization of society in political units that transcended the family. The ancient Greek democracies were novel and family lineages dominated politics and economics in agrarian feudal society. The industrial revolution and urbanization it brought gradually shifted the center of economic and political power from old landed families to new centers of financial power. These changes in human social organization have required changes in family life as well.

Our examination begins with Elliott Skinner's examination of families which were organized in foraging bands, pastoral groups, and cultivating village communities. These families existed before the emergence of states and empires and still exist today in spite of state organization in many parts of the world. He examines differences between matrilineal and patrilineal societies, how these societies dealt with basic human needs and regulated sexual and other human impulses.

Next, Jan Knappert examines the family in antiquity, including Persia, Mesopotamia, Egypt, India, Israel, Greece and Rome. The whole of Sumerian and Babylonian marriage was monogamous. Hammurabi's laws governed ancient marriage contracts, which were necessary for inheritance from the father. Adulterers and rapists were punished with swift death. While some polyandry existed in ancient India, and powerful maharajas may have had many concubines, Indian philosophy speaks of the eternal marriage of one man to one woman which continues with their souls after death. The ancient Greek household contained a nuclear family, some of their relatives and a number of servants, yet a monogamous nuclear family was at the core of this larger "family." The breakdown of the monogamous family in Rome corresponds to the collapse of the Roman Empire.

The Christian influence on the transformation of the family in the Holy Roman Empire is discussed by Anthony J. Guerra, who argues that it took a millennium for the church to sacralize marriage in society and attack the widespread practice of incestuous marriages for the preservation of wealth. Charlemagne was the first emperor to extend legislation to the empire which was influenced by the Christian ideas on marriage. It was not until after 1000 AD that the Church's position on the sacredness of the monogamous marriage crystallized. It is a compromise between ancient Roman practices and Christian ideals which has led to the general conception of the family in the West which lasted until the mid-twentieth century, when the church began to lose its moral authority in modern society.

Chapter 4, by J. S. La Fontaine is an examination of the family in fifteenth through eighteenth century England, a period in which "modernity" was beginning to take shape. There is a debate among historians as to the extent the modern political, social, and economic conditions have had on the family. She argues that the structural form of the family was unaffected by these changes in the period investigated, however the nature of the relationships among family members was drastically altered. For example, arranged marriages have been gradually replaced by "love matches." Siblings are often found at great physical distance from one another, yet some network of relations called "family" persists. The early usage of "family" referred to what is today commonly thought of as a "household." The later use of family refers more specifically to blood ties. It is only in the twentieth century that "family" and "household" can be expected to be coterminous.

Part One concludes with a chapter on the modern crisis of the Western family by Jon Davies. In the modern era, the extended family moves off center stage, leaving the nuclear couple with all the responsibilities of nurture and maintaining a household. The sexual revolution of the 1960s began a deconstruction of the nuclear family and an individualist culture in which children are more than ever seen as autonomous agents and consumers. Religious authority and intervention in marriage has weakened, in part by the religious pluralism brought on by the Reformation and subsequent religious rebellions. We are left with men and women outside of marriage, on their own, called a "family" if they have children. Yet, these units are too small to supply the support for child-rearing traditionally found in the family. The logical conclusion for many people is either to stop having children or to have the state raise them through many daycare and public facilities.

If Davies is correct, then the family, and by implication the whole of modern society, is in serious trouble. A society of isolated individuals, whose accidental children are raised by the state, is not a society grounded in parental love and responsibility that can transmit patterns of great or self-sufficient character to the children. Such a society would be unable to produce the leadership it needs to maintain its existence.

Family Transition in the World's Cultures

Is the crisis of the family in the contemporary United Kingdom described by Davies a Western crisis or a global crisis? Certainly industrialization, urbanization, global communication and pluralism are becoming everywhere present. The collapse of the Soviet Union and single party states worldwide has removed the last barriers which kept people ignorant of modern civilization. Only a few isolated regimes remain, and the pressure on them to change is becoming unbearable.

Part Two of this book is a survey of how the families in the world's major cultural areas are responding to modern social conditions. This section contains chapters on the African family, the Chinese family, the Hindu family, the Jewish family, the Muslim family, the Latin American family, the former East Bloc family, and the Western family.

Gwendolyn Mikell observes that the family is in flux in many parts of Africa as a result of recent economic and political changes and crises. This is true whether the traditional society is matrilineal, patrilineal, or colonial. Three trends are emerging: people are accepting smaller family size, there are changes in gender roles, yet the language of familism remains intact. In rural areas, many households have no young men present and are dependent on distant wage earners. In urban areas alternative trends are developing. African states are being asked to initiate family laws once governed by local traditions.

Kate Zhou and Marion Levy note that changes in China began to occur when the decision-making of family patriarchs was turned over to younger party cadres during communist collectivization. However, the *baochan daohu* reforms beginning in 1978 returned control of farming to families. With these reforms came a wide variety of economic markets, jobs, and migrations. Children of farmers were sent to schools to gain greater knowledge than the head of the family—the member who was traditionally regarded as the wisest. Women became merchants and small rural industries led to an increase in independence from the land and the traditional family unit for everyone. Industrial jobs became an ideal occupation for young people. These young people migrating to cities, form new nuclear families independent of the traditional village kinship structures—and also an increase in the number of divorces and loosening of controls on sexual behavior. Older people cannot rely on the support of their distant children. These economic transformations have done more to dilute China's old patriarchal patterns than four decades of communist rule which aimed at destroying the old patterns.

The author of the chapter on Hinduism, Sushil Panjabi, believes that the traditional Hindu family system needs to be transformed to extend equal status to all, but that changes are taking place slower than elsewhere in the world due to an entrenched patriarchal caste system. In traditional Hinduism, marriage was seen as the second of four stages of one's life. There were eight types of marriage recognized by the Hindus, including low forms such as a woman being raped while intoxicated. These were recognized to assign responsibility to the father and legitimacy to the children. In actual practice, the Hindu family is patriarchal, controlled by the eldest male. Gender roles are elaborately constructed in Hindu society.

British colonialists and Indian reformers have tried, since the nineteenth century, to reform the traditions of caste and improve the rights of women, but most legislation has gone unnoticed and unheeded. Yet, the forces of urbanization and industrialization have, in India as elsewhere in the world, caused migrations away from traditional families and love marriages in the cities where both husband and wife work. In recent times, fundamentalist Hindu movements have reacted vociferously against modernization and the caste system has made life difficult for migrants through taxation policies. While many Hindus desire more freedom and modern life, they remain silent under the heavy hand of Hindu tradition with its gender-biases.

Rabbi Richard Rubenstein examines the Jewish family in both its ancient and modern forms. He notes that modern secular life after World War II has led to family breakdown, higher drug addiction and homosexuality in the West and in Israel, while there has been a strong resurgence of orthodoxy among the European Jews. Judaism is facing an internal division between orthodox, conservative and reformed Jews, which reflects the reactionary, transformationist and secular responses to modern life in general. He questions whether the family, as an institution, will survive among the non-traditional Jews, and doubts whether Judaism could survive without the family.

Armando de la Torre of Guatemala states that most Latin Americans think of the nuclear family as their primary under-standing of family. The more education a woman has, the fewer children she is likely to bear. On the other hand, the number of abortions and abandoned children is on the rise in Latin America generally. He predicts that a nuclear family—a product of long-term sexual bonding with one to five children and female domesticity—will successfully adapt itself to modern life. He makes this prediction based on the desire for mutual assistance and the survival of the species through reproduction and the nurture of children. However, modern forces, including the individualism portrayed in Hollywood movies, have been unleashed in Latin America and have proved a serious challenge to traditional Catholicism. He thinks that families will become smaller as the cost of childrearing increases and that a less authoritarian "macho" family style will emerge.

The "Former East Bloc" (FEB) nations, on the other hand, are marked with substantial diversity in family structure. These are the European nations which shared the experience of communist culture. During the last 20 years, the marriage rate in these countries has gradually decreased, while the divorce rate rose rapidly, especially the former USSR, leading to a high level of family instability. Global patterns, such as migration to cities and the increased economic independence of both sexes occurs in these countries as elsewhere. However, the post-communist conditions, especially the poor housing and wage opportunities, place severe burdens on young families. Many marriages are legalized after a child is conceived and, because of social immaturity upon entering marriage, many of these fall apart in the first five years, leaving the mother and baby to return to the girl's mother. Many children grow up primarily in daycare facilities and do not spend much time with their parents. The difficulties and disincentives of childrearing are leading to a lower than replacement level birthrate. Even though the author, Jaroslav Macháček, does not see a quick improvement in the family life of the FEB nations, he believes that the important role of family in the shaping of a child's character will become recognized and that social adaptations which provide more education and support for family life will develop in the future.

William Garrett's analysis of the Western family begins with a look at the widespread social and political debates over the "decline of the family." In the United States it is increasingly believed that the welfare system has created dependency and a rise in teenage births which is ultimately responsible for rising crime, drug addiction and illiteracy. Conservatives would like to see such welfare payments eliminated and those children placed in orphanages where they will learn traditional values. Liberals argue that cutting off welfare funds would create unacceptable social trauma. Large government deficits stemming from increased welfare payments are likely to cause such debates in other Western countries as well.

Garrett argues that because the family is going through a transition in the West, many problems, like rising divorce rates, are not wholly negative in the long term. Rather, second marriages in the middle classes, after an early divorce, are often entered into with more maturity, and a number of early first marriages would lead to long-term misery for all involved. The more serious problem, to which he does not provide a solution, is the high rate of illegitimate births in the underclass and how society can care for this group. As for the decline of family size and the fertility rate among the middle and upper classes, these are responses to population and financial pressures, and might be positively correlated with quality of life—including family life where children are very highly valued. While many of the functions of the traditional families are being replaced by other social institutions, Garrett does not think this will lead to an end of the family. The need for love, companionship, intimacy, and the rewards of childrearing will continue to fuel the formation of families; and these families will continue to search for ways to improve the quality of the lives of their members.

Family Change, Family Stability, and Public Policy

The third section of this book looks at issues which surround the changes in family life that are reflected in the public policy arena. Here debates are furious because they affect deeply held cultural beliefs, irreversible and global social changes, many people displaced and rootless in the modern world, and government taxation and redistribution of income.

The first chapter in this section is by Jean Bethke Elshtain, who emphatically states that in the midst of all the changes being made, we should focus on the raising of children. In the midst of the controversies over welfare dependency, government funding, violent youth, and absentee fathers, too often, especially in a democracy, debates revolve around the rights of adults who are political actors. Children, having no political voice, are often left out of the discussion. The truth of the matter is that fewer children are being raised amidst good examples of married life and family. It is among the unmarried and the underclass that most children are born. Excessive individualism has an unbearable social cost. She explains how modern social theory has aided these negative social trends; and, she emphasizes the need for social theory that emphasizes civic virtue and the social responsibilities of parenting and family life. Her paper, while emphasizing that we must restate the value of family and children in society, ends with more questions than answers.

Patrica Lança addresses the controversial issues of feminism and their relationship to modern family life. Is family life the joyful role of women or an expression of patriarchal dominance to be eliminated at all cost? Lança devotes considerable discussion to the distinctions of "gender-feminism," which she believes to be personally and socially destructive, and "equity-feminism" which views men and women with equal worth and dignity. Gender-feminism is portrayed as a women-centered, marxist-inspired movement of hatred which debases the nature of the female and is a method of achieving power and the redistribution of wealth for members of the gender-feminist movement. On the other hand, the equity-feminism with which she identifies, sees the family as the basic unit of society in which men and women can be loving companions of equal worth and jointly raise children that reproduce their joy. She believes that modern social conditions provide a great opportunity for the emancipation of women (and men) from drudgery of their traditional roles. Nevertheless, many of the traditional rules such as those which advocate pre-marital virginity and marital fidelity are necessary and worthwhile to protect young females from predatory males and create a stable social environment for children. Destructive views, like those of the gender-feminists, should be overcome, and a mixture of modern equity-feminist and traditional values be taught in order to create a healthy social environment for Western families.

The issue of the growing problem of fatherlessness is taken up by Mitchell Pearlstein. He documents the continuing increase of children who grow up without the presence of a father, a six-fold increase in 30 years, due to greater divorce and out-of-wedlock births. He argues that this problem is America's greatest social disaster. While politicians have previously worked to avoid addressing this problem, it now looms so large that it cannot be ignored, even if it is politically uncomfortable. The removal of social stigmas against pre-marital sex and divorce has provided an easy escape for men from their traditional obligation to care for families and children, and has led to non-formation and breakdown of families. He states that the Moynihan Report of 1965, which was accurate but politically ignored, is one of the best documents on the subject—and should have been heeded long ago. The growing Black underclass, outlined in that report, is now being replicated in a coming White underclass composed of children growing up without the presence of a father. While the author believes every child deserves to have both a father and mother present, none of the liberal or conservative policies proposals which he reviews have much chance of success in the current political climate. Thus he concludes that the problem of fatherlessness will likely continue until the situation becomes so severe that popular views, portrayed in the media on shows such as "Murphy Brown," become unpopular.

The next chapter looks at the greater openness toward same-sex and homosexual households in modern Western society and its impact on social stability. After an exercise in deconstruction of the terms, the author, Carl Pfluger, gets into the controversies surrounding the impact of homosexual parenting on development of children. He challenges conventional wisdom with the suggestion that, with the earth as populated as it is today, it may be appropriate for households to be based on sexual partnerships for pleasure which are not aimed at production of children—and this might be a positive development which others like Plato or Huxley have speculated about. While his arguments might be applauded by persons engaged in homosexual life, most of the authors of the other chapters of this book would argue that such a life-style is less stable and beneficial to the spiritual and moral development of the children raised in such households. As such, it is a lifestyle which should not be openly endorsed by society.

Twila Perry examines the public policy questions regarding race and gender issues and argues against the restoration of the traditional family structure which she associates with racism and sexism. She is a lawyer trained to defend the rights of the downtrodden. Many of her arguments echo the gender feminism decried by Patrica Lança. She also extends these arguments to racism. She attacks the misdeeds of patriarchy and racism and promotes the value of self-sufficient professional women. She applauds the efforts of communities of black single women to succeed in a society whose rhetoric seems to demonize them. Past injustices heaped upon the black woman in the traditional family are so serious that Perry believes the answer may be to eliminate all support for the family in general. She therefore adopts policies in which the larger society is formed of individuals, and that the larger community supports those individuals within it who are in need. She does not address the issue of how such groups of individuals, apart from marriage and family, can create the depth of social bonding and responsibility necessary to maintain society. Her critics could argue that the Soviet Union collapsed precisely because it was grounded in such a utopian mythology that a state could exist as a society of individuals, bypassing the intermediary levels. Most people today will sympathize with the historical plight of the Black woman and will argue that public policy should focus on the elimination of racism and sexism. However, this may require new attitudes towards gender and race taught within families, not the elimination of the family.

The following comments by Jerry Pournelle are critical of the perspectives of Pfluger and Perry. Citing Thomas Sowell's *The Vision of the Anointed*, he argues that the heterosexual family has always been the normal state of life, and that it is important in all aspects of civilization. The family is under attack today by government policies that support no-fault divorce, by programs that pay teenage girls for having babies out of wedlock, and for sex education in the schools which teaches alternative lifestyles rather than how to create a good marriage. Pournelle laments that much of the social science discourse on the family is not grounded in the real needs of human society, using communist ideology as an example that tempted so many academics in the twentieth century.

However, Pournelle sees the computer and information revolution as offering some remedy to the situation. First, the accessibility of information to all will counteract the elitist and totalitarian attempts to manipulate and control ideas. This process helped to bring down the Soviet Empire. Second, the information revolution might reverse the demographic movements from rural to urban life as people find it possible to conduct their business from more remote areas. Much of the business of the world can be conducted from anywhere, using fax machines, the Internet, and next-day delivery companies. The information revolution will bring changes to human society and the human family as radical as the industrial revolution.

The final chapter, by Nicholas Kittrie, looks at the relationship of law and cultural consensus to the policy issues which are so hotly disputed in the political arena. He notes that the traditional family was taken for granted by the framers of the United States Constitution and therefore not really addressed in the founding documents. The result is a lacuna in the legal system which has led to confusion in public policy regarding the family. Kittrie notes the unplanned consequences of legal decisions, such as *Roe vs. Wade*, in which the status of fathers or family has been undermined. He comments on other areas, such as tax and welfare policy, which impact decisions to marry and have children.

Kittrie does not outline specific policy because he believes that, in a democracy, sound policy must grow out of cultural consensus. However, he points to issues which need to be examined in a serious manner by the culture as a whole. It is hoped that this book will be a significant step in the creation of this debate.

In summary, this book describes the global transition of the family and the issues that challenge families today. It indicates that the family will be continually forced to adapt to new social and technological realities. Most of the authors believe that the family will continue to be small as the costs of raising children in the modern world are high. The underlying conclusions are that men and women will continue to form families, and that societies will always need responsible parents who understand the impact their actions have on the children they bring into the world. The more that the wider community, the schools and other social institutions support the family in this process, the better off the society will be.

Part One

The Family in History

Chapter 1

THE FAMILY IN
PRE-STATE SOCIETIES

Elliott Skinner

The human family had its origin quite early in the phylo-genetic record when the evolution of the mammals necessitated a longer bond between mothers and their off-spring. Since family organizations among contemporary lower primates have so many of the qualities found among *homo sapiens*, paleontologists have speculated that sophisticated social behavior must have already appeared among pre-sapiens such as *australopithecus* and *homo erectus*. It was therefore suggested that the bio-socio-cultural needs of *homo sapiens* stimulated the development of domestic groupings, chief of which was the family.[1]

George Peter Murdock defined the family as "a social group characterized by common residence, economic coopera-tion and reproduction. It includes adults of both sexes, at least two of whom maintain a socially approved sexual relationship, and one or more children, own or adopted."[2] He suggested that a group which he called the "nuclear family"—consisting typically of "married man and woman and their offspring, although in individual cases one or more additional persons may reside with them, it was "a distinct and strongly functional group in every known society."[3] For Murdock, then, the nuclear family (or better yet, conjugal family) was a universal human social grouping, being either the sole prevailing form of the family or the basic unit from which more complex family forms were compounded.

Anthropologists quickly pointed out that while the "nuclear family" was found in almost all human societies, it was not always the dominant social arrangement. They insisted that the nuclear family's sexual, reproductive, productive, educational functions, were readily satisfied by alternative domestic and non-domestic institutions.[4] For example, members of families were often found scattered among different domestic groups and husbands and wives often lived in separate houses; outside of the limits set by incest prohibitions, approved sexual relations were often extra-familial; marriage alliances differed widely and polygamous extended family groups of males and females often lived together. As far as educating the young was concerned, extended kin, age-sets and age-grades and other institutions performed this function and the young were often segregated from parents and adults. Given these exceptions, many anthropologists concluded that any review of ethnographic and historical records would show that many domestic forms could carry out the needs allegedly lodged in the nuclear family. Moreover, these domestic forms were constantly changing with no end in sight.

The nineteenth century anthropologists, such as Edward Tylor, Louis Henry Morgan and others, hoping to find sociocultural evolutionary laws comparable to reputed biological ones, postulated the evolution of the family from primitive sexual promiscuity of semi-animal hordes, through group marriage, matriarchy, patriarchy (in some polygynous forms) and culminating in the highest spiritual expression of the family, the Victorian monogamous family.[5] They were quite interested in how "consanguinial" or large family groups became transformed into "conjugal" ones, and how "polyandry" (a rare form of family in which a woman had many husbands, but in fact where a group of men, usually brothers, had one wife), became transformed into polygyny and finally into monogamy.

Later scholars successfully challenged these sequences as being ethnocentric, Eurocentric, ahistorical and imperialistic. Nevertheless, this debate provided the impetus for anthropologists and sociologists to examine family organization from various perspectives. These included: patterns of descent, kinship and marriage; psychological and developmental perspectives; from the point of view of economics and ecology; the use of structural functionalist theories; perspectives of feminism and modern critical theory; and political theories.[6] The ethnographies and theories that these approaches engendered provided scholars with a great deal of knowledge about the human family.

An early and still current debate about the family concerned its relationship to the state. Sir Henry Maine, in *Ancient Law*, divided human groupings into *Societas*, where kinship reigned and the family was the major institution, and *civitas,* the domain of the state or political society.[7] Edward Jenks, in *Law and Politics in the Middle Ages*, elaborated the difference between these two spheres. He observed that the family was constructed of principles diametrically opposed to those inherent in the state:

> The family originated as regulator of procreation and of all the consequences, social, economic, religious, of the assimilation of the young into the social order. The state, on the other hand, originated in war, more specifically, in the warrior chief and the war band that was mobilized whenever external attack threatened.

Not only did these scholars view the family as prior and different from the state, but some felt that primeval families often inhibited the evolution of the state—the highest form of human organization. In structurally dichotomous terms, they represented it as nature and the state as nurture. Nevertheless, it is still a fact that aspects of the family are anchored in the bio-socio-cultural characteristic of *homo sapiens*. The family has changed over time and has survived the evolution of the state. In the process of adapting to various natural and cultural factors, the human family took on many characteristics, but it still serves our species.[9] How did it do so?

Scholars may have been guilty of looking at family organizations through an evolutionary prism, with all that this implies for western bias, but there is no doubt that societies (and their component institutions) had to adapt to various ecological settings. These adaptations influenced and were influenced by the tools and productive equipment the humans had at their disposal. Walter Goldschmidt believed that there was a relationship "between the form of family organization and the nature of its basic food-getting techniques."[10] This relationship affected members of families because they first saw their cultures through the prism of family life. The organization of family institutions had a pervasive influence on the cultures and on the attitudes and values of societies.

Julian Steward believed that the interaction of natural conditions such as soils, rainfall, and temperature and with cultural factors such as technology and economy, led to cultural differences and similarities among human groups in space and time. He termed these "levels of sociocultural integration," ranging from "hunting bands or foragers," to pastoral groups, to village communities of cultivators, to states, empires and the like. Steward postulated that the observable institutional differences within these levels, such as family organizations, were often a function of specific histories.[11]

In presenting this synthesis of families in pre-state societies, I shall examine the sexual, reproductive, productive, educational functions of families that were organized in foraging bands, in pastoral groups and plant cultivating village communities in various parts of the globe. A necessary caveat here is that while most of the data were taken from ethnographies that were normally ahistorical, one should not assume that the societies they described had not changed since "time immemorial." Archeological and historical information often revealed that many of the societies described by ethnographers had changed their subsistence strategies, and what was described, may have come from earlier or later periods in their existence.[12]

Families in Foraging Societies

Family organizations in foraging societies often revealed by their institutional components, the difficulty of living in marginal ecosystems. Whatever their original habitats might have been, contemporary foragers like the San and the Australian aborigines lived in desert-like regions, the Inuit in the frozen north, and the Batwa and Siriono in dense forests. Many of these groups may have been driven or retreated into the areas where they were encountered, and had subsequently adapted to local conditions. For example, many of the hunters on the Great Plains of North America are believed to have been river valley cultivators before they became equestrian hunters of the buffalo.[13] Nevertheless, it is true, that the food producing repertoires used by foragers and consisting of fishing, hunting and gathering wild plant foods, were common to human beings for more than 99 percent of their existence. Moreover, such implements as the digging sticks, clubs, spears, bows and arrows, fishing devices, traps, fire and containers for food, permitted these families to survive. True, under normal circumstances, the sparse and often irregular sources of plant and animal food inhibited foragers from congregating in groups larger than fifty or one hundred persons, but fisher folk, on the Northwest Coast of North America, could, and did inhabit relatively large villages.[14]

Families in foraging societies were usually exogamous, meaning that they married outside domestic groups normally composed of near kin. Levi-Strauss noted the frequency of what he termed "restricted exchange" in band societies.[15] Men usually exchanged sisters as wives, or more usual, exchanged women between bands. Such marriages effectively supported incest prohibitions, but also extended the range for food collecting during periods of scarcity. Edward Tylor wrote that early human groups quickly learned that people had to "marry out or die out."[16] Band exogamy, when linked to frequent changes of residence and limited food supply may have facilitated the development of a bilateral kinship system where people traced their descent from both mothers and fathers, rather than almost exclusively either through males or females. The aboriginal Australians had complex rules of band exogamy and kinship terminologies, but this did not prevent persons from moving from place to place and finding relatives with whom they could live.[17]

Monogamy was the usual marriage rule among foraging bands. In some cases widows were inherited as plural wives, and high status men occasionally had plural spouses. But limited resources precluded plural marriages. Residence was normally virilocal, that is, with the husband, but as we have seen married persons often changed residence for economic or personal reasons. Without exception, the !Kung and San of South Africa required that all men spend several years providing "bride service" with the family of their brides. The reason they gave for this was that the parents of brides needed the proceeds from the hunting of their son-in-law.[18] The Inuit were normally monogamous, but exchanged wives when specific women were needed to perform particular domestic chores.[19]

While male dominance was usual in foraging societies, Kathleen Gough was basically correct when she asserted: "Especially lacking in hunting societies is the kind of male possessiveness and exclusiveness regarding women that leads to such institutions as savage punishments or guarding of female chastity and virginity, the denial of divorce to women, or the ban on a woman's remarriage after her husband's death."[20] !Kung, San and Inuit men did not have the power to brutalize wives, and could be sanctioned by male relatives or by the entire community. Unreasonable Inuit husbands were known to be the butt of ridicule when they were defeated in "song duels."[21]

Children were valued in foraging societies as replacements for the old and deceased. Twins and children born when siblings were still suckling were often suppressed. Twins were considered unnatural beings who overburdened mothers who could not provide enough milk for them. Children in foraging bands learned by doing. Boys were carefully trained to participate in the hunt, and girls were taught how to harvest plants, roots and berries. Yet even on this level, children acquired special knowledge during initiation ceremonies that marked puberty. Among the hunters of "great plains" in North America, young males were required to undertake vision quests to test their fortitude and to acquire "guardian spirits."[22] Successful youths often returned to camp filled with ambition to become great hunters and members of police societies that monitored the hunt. Failure to receive guardian spirits often indicated to the community that some youths had different religious, sexual and gender orientations. Such young men sometimes became skilled "medicine men" or *berdaches* whose life choice as female was respected by the band.[23] The most valuable lessons learned by children in many foraging societies was to respect and even support gerontocide, the killing of parents unwilling to permit illnesses to jeopardize the safety of the community.

Most foraging societies were egalitarian and did not posses the resources to permit stratification among families. The Kwakiutl of the Northwest Coast of North America was a much studied exception. Profiting from their ownership of clam-beds, sections of river banks and off-shore areas, and of hunting, berry and wild-root areas, some families were able to take titles and erect totem poles. Individual men and women were able to engage in elaborate gift-giving contests known as *potlatches*. Wealthy families often held chieftainships, kept slaves and boasted that they did not fight with weapons, but fought with property. Admittedly, this behavior was rare among foraging societies, and may have been due to contact with the West. Yet, the Kwakiutl indicated the social structure possibilities of foraging societies in favorable circumstances.[24]

Data about the beliefs of families of foragers, suggest people tended to identify with *zoomorphic* animals and plants. This was especially true among the Australians whose totemic beliefs and rituals linked families to mythical people and animals. As the worship of the sea goddess, Sedna, among the Inuit indicated, the hope was mostly to augment the food supply. But beliefs about "dream time" among the Australians may have represented an attempt to keep track of historical events.[25] Shamans, among the !Kung or Inuit employed curing ceremonies on behalf of family members. The Batwa Pygmies of the Ituri forests of Zaire held Molimo ceremonies to appease the denizens of their forest homes.

Families in Herding Societies

Herding societies often referred to as "part cultures" because they were often linked to plant cultivators, normally provided families with greater resources than did foragers. These families were usually embedded in larger social units known as lineages, clans or "tribes" based on actual or putative "genealogies." Generally, lineages viewed themselves as corporate groups possessing rights in persons and property, but these attributes were usually anchored in lineage segments that lived together. For example, the Somali dia-paying groups (used to pay the families of the victims of feuds), were said to be lineage-wide, but were really based on highly localized sub-lineages.

Undoubtedly, the genealogical structure of herding families was a function of their need to adapt to the transhumance needs of their livestock, and a corresponding need to protect their animals against both human and animal predators. Nomadic herders ranged far and wide to secure pasturage for their livestock, and they often developed protective or aggressive institutions to replenish herds depleted through raids and diseases.

Marriage alliances among herders were usually arranged by heads of extended families and lineage segments often without regard to the wishes of the persons to be married. Central to these marriages was the *bridewealth*, a customary gift from the husband and his group to the wife and her group, before, at, or after marriage. Ostensibly the gift was a compensation to the bride's family for the loss of her companionship and labor. It was not a "brideprice" since the bride could not be subsequently sold. Bridewealth was very much a "progeny price" that gave a woman's children full membership in her husband's descent group, even though she remained a stranger to that group.[26]

The bridewealth accomplished a number of ancillary functions. It tended to stabilize marriages and discourage divorce because persons who negotiated the bridewealth disliked haggling over refunding the gift in event of a divorce. Bridewealth also fortified group alliances because it was linked to the *levirate,* an institution in which the widow was inherited by her late husband's male relatives. A companion institution was the *sororate* in which families replaced a woman who died before bearing children for their husband's family or proved infertile, with another woman. It was not uncommon for men whose fathers had died before completely paying the gift, to finish the transaction to legitimize themselves.

Herding groups such as Arab or other Semitic pastoralists tended to be endogamous, that is, they approved marriages among persons with known genealogical relationships. Marriage with father's brother's daughter was not only permitted but was preferred.[27] Such marriage practices un-doubtedly served to preserve wealth within extended families or lineage segments, but they also solidified these units. The Somali and the Fulani of the Sudan further strengthened family bonds by adding a dowry from the bride's family to the new family. This gift included furnishings for the new household. Couples who received both parts of bridewealth and dowries, had an economic cushion when they established their house-holds.

Families in herding societies were frequently stratified due to the exigencies of raiding and warfare, or the health and increase or decrease of their herds. For example, Mongol families were socially stratified on the basis of wealth gained or lost as a result of raids. Poor families became dependent upon wealthy ones, but wealthy families kept few chattel slaves and massacred captives deemed useless or dangerous since they could decamp with animals. The Tuaregs of the Sahara and Fulani, on the other hand, sought and held captives from cultivators and used them to produce plant products, and to perform household chores.

The position of women in herding societies differed widely, and may have been conditioned by relations with agricultural societies with whom they were in contact. Wealthy men were permitted to have plural wives and concubines, but the exigencies of nomadic life precluded secluding women who often traveled with the herds. Tuareg women in the Western Sahara, had extraordinarily high statuses. Girls were permitted to indulge in a great deal of "petting" with young men, while friendships between married women and men were taken as a matter of course. How much of women's liberty was due their remaining at home while Tuareg men traveled widely, is open to debate.

While not as privileged as Tuareg women, Mongol women were fairly autonomous. They rode like men, and engaged in warfare when necessary. Each wife had her own "yurt" where she lived with her children and could acquire property on her own. The first wife in a Mongol's household was regarded as head of the establishment and took charge of her husband's herds while he was away. In marked contrast, the nomadic Arab family tended to be highly patriarchal with a corresponding diminution of the status of women. Men insisted upon of virginity of their brides at marriage, and often executed unchaste girls or an unfaithful wife and her lover.

There was a corresponding wide range of affective relations within the conjugal families of herders. Mongol boys were subject to their fathers and younger brothers to their elder brothers, but relations between Mongol mothers and their sons were close and persisted all their lives. They often formed an amiable conspiratorial group to circumvent the father.[28] In contrast, Arab fathers tended to be authoritarian within their families, and often invoked supernatural sanctions to control the sexual activities of their sons. It has been suggested that the combination of patriarchal suppression, and religious proscriptions often gave rise to homosexuality among Arab men, especially among boys and unmarried men. But this practice was usually replaced by heterosexual behavior when men married and became independent of their fathers.[29]

The education of the young in herding societies was primarily by emulation. Girls learned milking techniques from women when custom permitted, and how to care for their households, including erecting tents. Boys learned herding techniques from their male kin. In addition there were usually special institutions to train young males to protect their herds and to participate in the public affairs of their communities. Chief among these was the "age-set" system formed among boys who had been initiated, and who had jointly experienced the trauma of circumcision. They often received special instructions and were provided with a name to enhance their esprit de corps. Normally, such age-sets were formed during the period throughout the society, and even across ethnic groups. These age-set went through stages known as "age-grades." Thus a specific age-set would pass through the age-grade associated with herding, then through a grade known as junior warriors, then senior warriors, husbands, councilors, priests, and the ultimate, age-grade—the ancestors. Sometimes society-wide age-sets and those from neighboring societies were organized into regiments for warfare. East African pastoralists had cycling age-sets, that were revived every sixty or more years permitting new groups of men to serve the age-grades of their societies. Some societies had age-set and age-grade systems for females, but most of these were auxiliary to those of the males. Maasai girls formed a cohort to frequent the bachelor quarters of initiated men where they engaged in heavy petting.

Religious practitioners such as shamans in pastoral societies tended to invoke the supernatural for protection of families and their herds and were not above invoking supernatural sanctions against evil-doers. Shamans among the reindeer Chuckchee of Siberia were often curers who used ventriloquism to impress their congregations.

Family Systems in Societies of Plant Cultivators

Family systems in societies of plant cultivators, ranging from horticulture to agriculture, reflected the increasing control by human beings of their food supplies. This adaptive strategy permitted human beings to occupy a greater variety of ecological niches and to live in larger settlements.[30] This meant that their family organizations exhibited patterns of kinship, linearity, incest and marriage, locality rules, sex roles, stratification systems, and patterns of rearing the young, rarely found in other levels of sociocultural integration, including the early states.

There was a wide variation in the division of labor in food preparation, crafts, markets and trade, among families in plant cultivating societies.[31] For example, men among the Igbo of Nigeria, considered the yams they cultivated as the most important crop, whereas women cultivated the "small crops" such as maize, beans and the like. Mundurucu men of Brazil cleared the forest for manioc gardens, implanted the stalks, leaving women to harvest this staple crop and cultivate the lesser appreciated beans and squash. Besileo men and women of Madagascar jointly cultivated the rice fields, but the rice terraces were largely prepared by men. Tallensi men in northern Ghana proudly cultivated the millets and yams, their main crops, leaving women to cultivate the pulses and vegetables used as condiments. Nevertheless, a sample of 515 horticultural societies, representing all regions of the world revealed that women were the main food producers for their families. In 50 percent of the families women dominated cultivation, in 33 percent their contribution to food production was equal to that of the men. In only 17 percent of the families did men do most of the work. This, however, did not prevent male cultivators from pretending that they produced more food than did women.

A division of labor between men and women also existed in craft activities. Men and women might collaborate in cloth production, but women spun cotton into threads, men wove cloth, women dyed the cloth and men made the clothes. Only male smiths were permitted to produce iron hoes and other implements used for food cultivation and warfare. Their wives were often the potters. Men and women seldom sold the same products in the market places, and when they did so, they used different places. Extra-village and long distance trade usually were in the hands of males. Men were not invariably more successful than women in food production, in craftwork, on in commerce. Good luck and superior skills often resulted in females being wealthier than males. Nevertheless, men were judged the breadwinners.[32]

Anthropologists have long debated the reasons for the patterns of kinship and descent among plant cultivators, and especially the reasons for the high incidence of matriliny and uxorilocality (men living at homes of wives) within them. It is perhaps significant that in 64 percent of the societies in which women were the main food producers in the families, descent was reckoned through the female line (or matrilineally). In contrast, in only 50 percent of those cases in which males were the major food producers was descent traced through the male line (or were patrilineal). Does this mean that despite the ideology of men that they cultivated the major crops, people tended to live with the main food producers?

There is, however, less debate about the tensions between descent principles and locality rules in the families of plant cultivators. Conjugal life in matrilineal families was especially tense because the rights of women very often came into conflict with the more universal pattern of male dominance. Not only did women produce most of the food in such societies, but they frequently lived matrilocally and had relatively high statuses. Succession to political positions, allocation of land, and overall social identities were often based on links through females. Public authority was often assigned to men, but actual power and decision-making belonged to women.[33] In his description of what he termed, "A Woman-centered Family System," in a classical matrilineal society, Bronislaw Malinowski wrote:

> The typical Trobriand household is founded on the princi-
> ples of equality and independence of function: the man is
> considered to be the master, for he is in his own village and
> the house belongs to him, but the woman has, in other
> respects, a considerable influence; she and her family have a
> great deal to do with the food supply of the household; and
> she is—next to her brother—the legal head of her family.[34]

What intrigued Malinowski was the relatively equal division
of labor between females and males among the Trobrianders,
and that in this matrilineal society, "descent, kinship, and every
social relationship" was legally reckoned through mother only.
Women had a considerable role in the life of the community,
"even to the taking of a leading part in economic, ceremonial,
and magical activities—a fact which very deeply influence[d] all
the customs of erotic life as well as the institution of
marriage."[35]

While the Trobrianders had a well-established institution of
marriage, and the roles of "father" and "husband" were clearly
defined, they were inexplicably "quite ignorant of the man's
share in the begetting of children." A man was considered an
"outsider" in his family. Social positions were handed down in
the mother-line from a man to his sister's children, and
restrictions of marriage, and taboos against sexual intercourse,
the education of the young, leadership in both the political and
magico-religious spheres, followed from this custom. For
example, only persons related through the maternal line were
permitted to participate in funerals, mourning, that dramatized
the unity of the family and the kin group.[36] Parenthetically, one
of the few cases of "polyandry" or "group marriage" in the
ethnographic record comes from Melanesia. Men in matrilineal
societies who were wealthy enough to have plural wives were
permitted to give dependents access to these women.[37]

The family organization of other matrilineal societies such
as the Iroquois and the Zuni in North America, the Akan and

Thonga in Africa shared many of the characteristics of those described for the Trobrianders. Most of these families were monogamous, although polygyny was also found. Marriages were characterized as "brittle" and divorce was easy and frequent. Among the Hopi and Zuni of the Southwest in the United States, matrilineal women who lived matrilocally simply placed their husband's belongings outside the door, thereby initiating a divorce. Under the watchful eye of male relatives of their wives, husbands could do little but depart in peace. The situation was largely comparable among the Thonga of South Africa. Some men who uncharacteristically refused to live in their wives' villages after marriage, also uncharacteristically insisted that the spouses of their married daughters join them, as was the custom. Surrounded by male kin of wives, Thonga men who married into their wives' villages, had little control over these women and were easily divorced and expelled.[38]

The stability of marriages among matrilineal cultivator families was also affected by the absence of bridewealth which, as we saw above, enlisted both "wife-givers" and "wife-takers" in a conspiracy to prevent divorce with the subsequent return of the gifts. Again, the absence of bridewealth often meant the absence of the "progeny price" that transferred the control of a woman's children to her husband. The children belonged to their mothers' matrilineages, and men were responsible for the children of sisters.[39] Men, for their part, often resented passing on wealth and status to sisters' children rather than to their own offspring, and were not above subverting matriliny by attempting to create patricentric bonds with their children. This became more pronounced as the state emerged.[40] Whether because of these pressures or other requirements of their adaptive strategies, matrilineal societies disappeared from areas where they once existed or have left traces in societies that shifted to patrilineal family organizations.[41]

18

Family and marriage customs in patrilineal families of plant cultivators had many of the features of the families in patrilineal herding societies. Descent groups such as lineages and their segments, played more important roles in their family organizations than in matrilineal ones. Bridewealth was usually exchanged at marriage, and practices such as the sororate and levirate were also quite common. But although wives remained strangers in their husbands' families they were considered "our" wives by even female members of their husbands' families.[42] Also common were plural marriages such as polygyny, based, in part, on the belief of many cultivators that either they needed more help from wives, or more children to carry on their lineages. Infertility was very often the source of family tensions that led people to seek magical or medical help, or stimulated tensions that led to divorce.

Conjugal life presented fewer problems in patrilineal societies where women lived virilocally with their husbands after marriage.[43] It was otherwise, when in patrilineal societies, men attempted to live uxorilocally with their wives even though such locality rules existed. The issue here was that unrelated patrilineal men found themselves living with women who were related. The problem was not with the brothers of these women since those normally lived elsewhere. The issue was often solidarity among the women in the villages. As if to establish some kind of male solidarity in the face of such a situation, men among the patrilineal Mundurucu in South America who lived uxorilocally often inhabited "men's houses," where they spent most of their time together. They only went to their wives' long houses for food and sex.[44]

Men tended to dominate public roles in patrilineal families of cultivators. We are told that "In patrilineal-virilocal societies worldwide, men distribute prestige items, whether crops or animals, in alliance-forming marriages."[45] The men among the Afikpo Igbo, of Nigeria, a classic acephalous people, had three

values that dominated family and community life: attachment
to the land, the importance of strength, and a sharp division
between the sexes. Igbos men felt that farming was the best
kind of work and their contribution superior to that of their
wives. The importance of strength was demonstrated by the
determination of people to achieve their goals, by being
"pushy," "aggressive," and resentful of dictation of any kind.
The division between the sexes was marked by strong male
domination in almost all activities concerning males and
females from early childhood onward.[46]

Children were considered as great assets in the families of
plant cultivators and they normally had a greater number of
duties to perform. Living in settled communities, children were
useful in household cleaning, fetching water and fuel, and
performing other chores within their competence. Aboriginal
plant cultivators in North America educated their children by
"ridicule, praise and reward."[47] Hopi children of the American
Southwest were initiated into the *kachina* cult between the ages
of six and ten years old. They were not only expected to master
the "basic disciplines, the fundamentals of the kinship system
and the main tenets of the Hopi Way, but also to have become
a useful member of society with social and economic duties,
responsibilities and privileges, in accordance with sex and
age."[48] For Mundurucu youngsters in South American forest
cultivating societies, education was less formal and was by
emulation. Maturing Hanunoo girls in the Philippines learned
to abandon the activities of the young and learn adult tasks
such as weaving, and greeting visitors.[49]

African cultivating societies used a wide range of institutions to educate the young. For example, among the Nyakyusa
of Tanzania, six or seven year-old boys established play houses
on the outskirts of their villages, and these eventually became
full-fledged villages. Initially, the boys returned home for
meals, but spent most of the day "in good company" where

they educated each other. Later on, they slept in these villages while their mothers continued to provide food for them. Finally, the youth took wives to their villages and gave birth to the next generation.[50]

While the process of enculturation of boys among the Nyakyusa was gradual, age-sets and age-grades, marked by initiation ceremonies such as circumcision and clitoridectomy, transformed children to adults in most African societies.[51] While clitoridectomy was not as widespread as circumcision, age-sets and age-grades played comparable roles for girls as they did for boys. Among the Mande-related peoples of West Africa, age groups formed the basis of the semi-secret Poro and Sandwe societies for men and women respectively. These institutions, called "Bush Schools," educated their members to deal impartially in village affairs without undue regard for kin.[52] Such women's groups among the Igbo played Lysistra-like roles by forcing the men of the community to fulfill such obligations to the public as digging wells and building roads.

The families of cultivators used communal rituals to mark the stages of life or *rites de passage* of their members. The cults of the ancestors were almost universal in Africa. Ancestral spirits were venerated as benefactors by their descendants and feared as disciplinarians. They often appeared as masked figures at court trials. Spirit possession by gods in such cults as *bori* and *zar*, often permitted individuals to publicly reveal their desires or curse enemies.[53] In aboriginal North and South America, shamanistic figures using intoxicants were used to foretell the future, and to cure members of the community.[54]

Conclusion

Families in pre-state societies enabled human beings to live in domestic groups capable of dealing with the basic needs of our species. Although their organization differed widely as they adapted to various circumstances, they provided the basis for food production through division of labor without which life would be impossible. These families regulated sexual needs and curbed the disruptive force of sexual competition. Moreover, they guaranteed the protection of females during long pregnancies and during the months and years of lactation. Families were essential for enculturating the young, often providing various educational systems as vehicles for imparting knowledge to both sexes. Last, families served the function of maintaining order, both by coercive and supernatural means.

The family in pre-state societies relied upon the bonds of kinship or *gemeinschaft* to accomplish its tasks. Customs and traditions were its guide and authority was often exercised by older and presumably wiser persons in the community. The evolution of political society with its emphasis on *gesellschaft*, that is, contractual arrangements rather than on gemeinschaft, has increasingly usurped the duties of the family. This has been with respect to providing food for people, for regulating sex and marriage, for educating the young, for protecting life and limb, or even to appealing to the supernatural for aid. The emerging state gradually eroded the character and functions of the family, and contemporary political formations have usurped more of the functions of the family than at any other period in the history of our species.

It is widely believed that the political theorists of the twentieth century largely ignored the family as a central concern because they rejected the "concept of the primacy of natural order in human affairs."[55] Many modern thinkers have emphasized the contractual aspects of human societies, at the expense of those partly anchored in the bio-socio-cultural characteristic of *homo sapiens*. John Rawls believed that not only was the family not "essential for the just society," but that its benevolent characteristics permitted the toleration of economic and social inequalities.[56] For such thinkers, the human family was an accident of history that was not in the interests of society. Nevertheless, the biological features of humanity are not so easily dismissed. There must have been a reason why the families described above, emerged as served our species over the centuries. Moreover, concerns about the family, its values and its characteristics, are still with us as we approach the twenty-first century. Debates about its nature, structure and deep concern for its future are still the stuff of electoral campaigns in politically complex industrial societies. The family will continue to change, but until *homo sapiens* eliminate the biological bases for the existence of the species, some type of family organization will be with us.[57]

References and Notes

[1]Lancaster, Jane B, and Phillip Whitten "Sharing in Human Evolution," in *Anthropology: Contemporary Perspectives* (eds. Phillip Whitten and David E.K. Hunter, (Glenview, Illinois: Scott, Foresman/Little Brown Higher Education), pp.60ff .

[2]Murdock, George Peter, *Social Structure*, New York: Macmillan, 1949, pp. l-13.

[3]Ibid., pp. l-13.

[4]Harris, Marvin, *Culture, People. Nature*. New York: Harper & Row, 1985, p.261.

[5]Goode, William J., World Revolution and Family Patterns, New York: The Free Press, 1970, p. 3

[6]See chapters on "Kinship and Family in Preliterate, Peasants and Modern Societies," in *Anthropology Full Circle*, (eds.) Ino Rossi, John Buettner-Janusch and Dorian Coppenhaver, New York: 1977, pp. 294-313. See also introduction to *African Systems of Kinship and Marriage*, (eds.) A.R. Radcliffe-Brown and Daryll Forde. London: Oxford University Press for the International Institute, 1950.

[7]Maine, Henry S., *Ancient Law: Its Connection with the Early History of Society and Its Relations to Modern Ideas*. New York: Holt. 1873 (orig. 1861).

[8]Jenks, Edward, *Law and Politics in the Middle Ages*, New York: Henry Holt, 1898, pp. 308-09.

[9]Rensberger, Boyce, "On Becoming Human," in Whitten et al., 1990, pp.49-53.

[10]Goldschmidt, Walter, *Exploring the Ways of Mankind*, New York: Holt, Rinehart and Winston, 1960, p.226.

[11]Harris, Marvin, Ibid, p.520 and Julian H. Steward, *Theory of Culture Change*. Urbana: University of Illinois Press.

[12]Wilmsen, Edwin N., Land Filled with Flies: A political Economy of the Kalahari. Chicago: University of Chicago Press, 1989 pp.xi-xviii.

[13] See Fred Eggan's "Historical Change in the Choctaw Kinship System," and Edward M. Brunner's "Two Processes of Change In Mandan-Hidatsa Kinship Terminology," both of which was reprinted in Nelson Graburn's *Readings in Kinship and Social Structure*, New York: Harper & Row, 1971, pp.108-120.

[14]Benedict, Ruth, *Patterns of Culture*, Boston: Houghton Mifflin, 1934.

[15]Levi-Strauss, Claude, *The Elementary Structures of Kinship*, Boston: Beacon Press, 1969, p. 483.

[16]Tylor, Edward, Primitive Culture. London: J. Murray, 1871.

[17]See Claude Levi-Strauss, Ibid. pp.l46ff.

[18]Marshall, Lorna, "The !Kung Bushmen of the Kalahari Desert," in James L.Gibbs (ed.) *Peoples of Africa*. New York: Holt, Rinehard and Winston, 1965 p.261.

[19]Linton, Ralph, *The Tree of Culture*, New York: Alfred A. Knopf, 1957 pp.l50-169.

[20]Gough, Kathleen, "The Origin of the Family," in *Journal of Marriage and the Family*, November, 1971:767-69).

[21]Hoebel, E.A., *The Law of Primitive Man: A study in comparative legal dynamics*, Cambridge, Mass.: Harvard University Press. 1954.

[22]See Linton, 1957, Ibid., chaps.7 and 40.

[23]Lowie, Robert, *The Crow Indians*, New York: Farrar & Rinehart, 1935.

[24]Benedict, Ruth, op. cit.

[25]Linton, Ralph, op. cit., p.168.

[26]Skinner, Elliott P. cf. "The Mossi 'Pogsioure'," Man, vol. LX, no. 28:20-22. Reprinted in German as "Die Pogsioure der Mossi" (n.d.). This paper was updated as "The Mossi Pughsiure: An African Tributary Marriage System," at the American Anthropological Association meeting, November, 23, 1991. Although the Mossi had no formal bridewealth, their bride service had many features of the bridewealth.

[27]Linton, Ralph, op. cit., p.287.

[28]Ibid. p.274.

[29]Ibid. p.288

[30]White, Leslie, The Evolution of Culture, New York: McGraw-Hill, 1959, p. 286.

[31]Skinner, Elliott, See "West African Economic Systems," in Economic Integration in Africa, edited by Harwitz and Herskovits. Northwestern University Press, Evanston, Illinois. (Reprinted in Peooles and Cultures of Africa, edited by E.P. Skinner,1965.)

[32]Skinner, Elliott P. See"Trade and Markets Among the Mossi People," Markets in Africa, edited by P. Bohannan and G. Dalton. Northwestern University Press: Evanston, Ill., 1962, pp. 237-78.

[33]See Marin J, and B. Voorhies, Female of the Species, New York: Columbia University Press, 1975, cited in Kottak, p.244 and David Aberle, "Matrilineal Descent in Cross-Cultural Perspective," in David M.Schneider and Kathleen Gough, eds., Matrilineal Kinship, Berkeley: University of California Press, 1961, pp.655-727. There are no cases in the ethnographic record of matriarchy, a social system in which women totally dominated men, even though in many matrilineal societies women were often the basis of the entire social structure. Cf. A.I.Richards, "Some Types of Family Structure Amongst the Central Bantu in African Systems of Kinship and Marriage, (eds.) A.R. Radcliffe-Brown and Daryll Forde. London: Oxford University Press for the International Institute. 1950, pp.207ff.

[34]Malinowski, Bronislaw, The Sexual Life of Savages in North-Western Melanesia, London: Routledge and Kegan Paul, 1929: Chapter 1.

[35]Ibid.

[36]Ibid.

[37]Murdock, George P., op. cit., p.28.

[38]Cf. Murdock, Peter, *Africa its Peoples and their Culture History*, New York: McGraw-Hill,1959, p.377.

[39]Nanda, Serena, *Cultural Anthropology*, Belmont, California: Wadsworth Publishing Co., 1991, pp.238-240.

[40]Mikell, Gwendolyn, *Cocoa and Chaos in Ghana*, New York: Paragon House, 1989, pp. 92, 104, 121.

[41]Harris, Marvin, op. cit. pp.272ff.

[42]There are a number of cases of "women" marrying other "women" in the ethnographic record, but this did not involve sexual inversion. Melville J. Herskovits, reported cases from Dahomey (a proto-state) in which a woman may marry another woman or women, i.e., perform the same ritual—including payment of the brideprice—that would take place in marriage between a man and a woman; she becomes the father of children born of this union ("A note on 'Women Marriage' in Dahomey") *Africa*, vol. 10, pp.335-341, 1937.

[43]Skinner, Elliott P., See "The Effects of Co-Residence of Sisters' Sons on African Corporate Patrilineal Groups," *Cahiers d' etudes Africaines* 4(4): 467-478 (1962).

[44]Murphy Y. and Murphy R., *Women of the Forest*, New York: Columbia University Press, 1974. Families in a number of South American forest communities practiced the couvade, in which a man retired to his wife's hammock after she had given birth to a child, as though he was the one who had been through parturition.

[45]Kottak, Conrad, *Cultural Anthropology*, New York: Random House, 1987, pp. 246-247.

[46]Ottenberg, Phoebe, "The Afikpo Ibo of Eastern Nigeria" in Gibbs, Ibid., p. 611.

[47]Petitt, George A., "Educational Practices of the North American Indian," in *Exploring the Ways of Mankind*, (ed.) Walter Goldschmidt, New York: Holt, Rinehart and Winston, Inc., 1960, pp. 215-218.

[48]Goldschmidt, Walter, Ibid, p.191.

[49]Conklin, Harold, "Maling, A Hanunoo Girl from the Philippines," in *In the Company of Man*, ed. Joseph B. Casagrande (New York: Harpers and Brothers), 1960, pp. 115-116.

[50]Wilson, Monica, *Good Company: A Study of Nyakyusa Age-Villages*. Boston: Beacon Press,1951.

[51]See Ralph Linton, op. cit., 1957, especially "Historic African Peoples," ch.30.

[52]Gibbs, James L.,"The Kpelle of Liberia," in his *Peoples of Africa*, New York: Holt, Rinehart and Winston, 1965, ch.6.

[53]Lewis, I.M., *Islam in Tropical Africa*, see especially "Islam and Traditional Belief and Ritual," ch. v., Oxford: International African Institute, 1966.

[54]Linton, Ralph, op. cit., see especially ch. xl.

[55]Baumgarth, William, "The Family and the State in Modern Political Theory"in *The American Family and the State* (eds.) Joseph R. Peden and Fred R. Glahe, San Francisco: Pacific Research Institute for Public Policy, chapter 1, 1986.

[56]Cited from John Rawls, *A Theory of Justice*, Cambridge: Harvard University Press, 1971 by Robert Nisbet in foreword to *The Family and the State in Modern Political Theory*, in *The American Family and the State* (eds.) Joseph R. Peden and Fred R. Glahe, San Francisco: Pacific Research Institute for Public Policy, 1986.

[57]Skinner, Elliott P. "The Global Economic Order and the Poor Villages: The Issues of Mediating Structures," in the *Re-Evaluation of Existing Values and the Search for Absolute Values*. Proceedings of the 7th International Conference on the Unity of Sciences. New York: The International Cultural Foundation Press, 1979, vol. 1; pp. 347-357. See also "Anthropologists and the Rise of a Global Civilization," in Proceedings of the Eighth International Conference on the Unity of the Sciences. New York: International Cultural Foundation. 1979. vol. 1, pp. 279-86.

Chapter 2

THE FAMILY IN ANTIQUITY

Jan Knappert

Introduction

The first human beings on earth lived in very small groups. How were these groups structured? We know nothing about it, but many theories have been constructed to prove that human procreation took place promiscuously or that it was the result of a long-lasting, faithful family life. Sir Henry James Sumner Maine (1822-1888), a Cambridge law lecturer, was the founder of comparative jurisprudence. He discovered that ancient law systems took little notice of individual persons, but only regulated the relations between groups. He concluded that the earliest type of such groups was the clan, ruled by a patriarch; this conclusion may still be proved to be the correct one, as we shall see further down.

Johann Jacob Bachofen, a Swiss jurist (1815-1887), came to the opposite conclusion, based more on mystic intuition than on systematic research. His book *Das Mutterrecht* (The Mothers' law 1861) posited that the oldest political organization was the matriarchate or gynocracy, even though the evidence he adduced was scant. Yet to this day his book is a catechism for some feminist groups. He assumed that the first stage of the history of the family was a promiscuous free-for-all, which lasted until the women, disgusted with this immorality, punished the misbehaving men and instituted regular marriage. This female revolution heralded the second stage of human development, that of the matrilinear matriarchate.

Needless to say there is no evidence for such views. Modern patriarchic society, said Bachofen, began in Greece with the rebellion of the men who defeated the women in war. Curiously, though Bachofen was a conservative capitalist, his theory became received dogma for the Communists.

A third jurist, John Ferguson McLennan (1827-1881) was the first to point at the frequent traces of theft of women from other tribes, the best known example of which was the rape of the Sabine maidens. This collective crime was certainly commonest among the patriarchal tribes in the Middle East and Africa. The men of Israel were not allowed to take foreign brides (*I Samuel* 15: 3; *Ezra* 9: 2-12). Other nations however, such as the Arabs, the Turks, the Somalis and the Masai, take unto themselves the women of other peoples whom they have slain in battle. No doubt this has resulted in the miscegenation of races in Africa, as well as in curious types of mixed languages in tropical Africa. The necessity for this mass rape arises not so much (as McLennan supposes) from female infanticide as from the fact that the elder men hoard all the women of the tribe so that the young men have to steal women from neighboring tribes.

Unfortunately, McLennan's work suffered from a common defect of his days: lack of adequate data, which were generally inaccurate or insufficient, and often wrenched from the social contexts which alone gave them meaning; some facts were only superficial observations or prejudiced opinions. Even though McLennan was under no illusion about the value of his authorities, the travelers whose accounts were the only information most anthropologists had at their disposal, yet he could not avoid certain errors. Today we know that matriliny does not prevail amongst the Australian aborigines. Nor does it prevail among the existing "rude races" (as he called them). Furthermore, polyandry is extremely limited in extent and occurrence, and so, incidentally, is infanticide.

We could have done without these arguments, if they had not had such a strong and lasting influence on the Marxists who built them into their dogma which is still part of the creed of millions in modern times. They wish to believe that there were no rules in "primitive" times, no good and evil, only promiscuity, but careful research has refuted these ideas.

The most influential, curiously, of these early comparative evolutionists was Lewis Henry Morgan (1818-1881), an American lawyer who produced the most fantastic construction for his evolution of marriage and the family, in 15 stages, beginning with promiscuity and ending with monogamous marriage and the family in western civilization. This fanciful scheme of "progress" has been incorporated, through Engels, into the official Marxist doctrines of communism (Evans-Pritchard, p. 30). The Marxists added a chapter of their own, in which the proprietorial monogamy would be replaced by the good old promiscuity. A curious idea of progress this is; it should rather be called regress. There is no evidence that social structures succeed one another in a fixed order through history, on the contrary, each nation's history seems to follow a unique pattern of evolution. Nor is there a shadow of evidence for the primeval promiscuity. On the contrary, the farther we go back in history and mythology, the more it appears that men were very anxious to keep their wives to themselves, and women likewise wished to keep their men, as husbands whom they needed for protection, fertilization, as hunters of meat, as builders of huts and clearers of land.

The argument that animals are promiscuous, cuts no ice. Among the primates every species has its own typical courtship behavior. Every subspecies of baboons has its own social structure, monogamous or polygamous. So, what was man?

In the following pages some of the great civilizations of classical Antiquity will be studied from the point of view of what we know about marriage and the family in those countries before the beginning of the Middle Ages. This is a variable date: in Western Europe the Middle ages are usually reckoned to begin when the western Roman Empire expired in 476. For the Arabic world the classical period ended around the middle of the ninth century, when the Abbasid dynasty of the caliphs of Baghdad became gradually decadent. By that time the basic system of Islamic family law had been established. In India the classical period lasted until the invasions and conquest of Hindustan by the Muslims in the late twelfth century.

As for Iran, its long history permits us insights into the family systems of the Achaemenid period beginning in the sixth century BC until the end of the Sassanian period in 657 AD Here is the list of civilizations which will be briefly discussed in this paper; at the same time this is a table of contents:

1. Ancient Egypt
2. Mesopotamia
3. Hammurabbi's Laws
4. The Hittites
5. Ancient Iran
6. Ancient India.
7. The ancient Semites
8. Arabia and Koranic Law
9. Homeric Greece
10. Classical Greece
11. Ancient Rome
12. Roman Law.
13. Germanic Antiquity
14. Conclusion.

There is, it appears, a close relation between the family life of a nation, and the law. Time and again lawmakers endeavor to legislate for a stable family in order to maintain a stable social life in the whole country, which is finally carried to its downfall by the decadence of its own citizens. That is perhaps the chief result of this study.

Ancient Egypt

We are well informed about the life of women and their families in Egypt from the third millennium onward. Though women sometimes accompanied their husbands on tours of inspection, they normally stayed at home, not because of social pressure, but for their own safety. King Ramses III proclaims in an inscription: "I enabled the women of Egypt to go their way, without anyone assaulting her on the road." Without constant policing the roads of Egypt were, and are, unsafe. At home, however, the wives of civil servants lived in luxury. She had a splendid garden full of flowers, herbs and fruit trees (every single species is known to us). She had a cool and spacious house full of carved wooden furniture and beautifully decorated crockery, vases and jars. She had colorful clothes made of wool, cotton and linen. The women brewed their own beer, but the men made the wine. There were many servants/slaves who made bread, cakes and prepared dinner, cut meat, span, wove and sewed clothes.

Egyptians were mostly monogamous; both husband and wife brought property into the marriage; women could make a will and bequeath their property to their children or to others. By ancient law, a woman could marry her half-brother of the same father. Abraham did not lie, Sarah was his half sister (*Genesis* 12:13). Pharaohs too, married their sisters, so as to keep the royal blood pure. A son would be given his grandfather's name; many children were essential for the survival of the family. Most people were married before they were 20 years old, and many people died in their twenties or thirties. As a result, many persons had children by different spouses, so that wills could be quite complicated. In addition, a man of wealth (mainly the kings) could have concubines, usually the slave girls of the house, who were ruled by his wife.

Mesopotamia

Throughout the whole of Sumerian and Babylonian history marriage was monogamous, in the sense that a man might normally have only one woman who ranked as a wife and enjoyed a social status corresponding to his. One of the few exceptions to strict monogamy, provided for in the laws of Hammurabi, was that if a man's wife had a disabling illness he might marry a second woman, but the law gave protection to the disabled wife by providing that the husband might not divorce her but must maintain her as long as she lived.

Rich men could keep concubines if their wives did not object; some marriage contracts are known in which the wife stipulates that the husband shall take no concubine. Concubines were often slave girls and any children born to them also had the status of slaves unless their master accepted them formally as his own legitimate children. A man who heads such a household is reminded that "Where woman and woman agree that household will prosper." However, a household with more than one wife appears to be the exception.

Married bliss was no exception in Mesopotamia and there are references to love continuing into old age; one proud husband boasted that his wife was ready to give him their ninth child. However, there were also men and wives who deserted their spouses for reasons we can now only guess. Some men took concubines or visited prostitutes, and some women took lovers. In short, people were not very different from the people of our times. One Babylonian judge ruled against a wife after her lovers were brought in, all tied up.

Even so, there are very few records of divorce cases. No doubt the majority of marriages, then as now, lasted for life.

Although some Babylonian marriages were arranged by the parents, young people had plenty of opportunity to meet in public places, since the girls were not kept indoors as they are in modern Mesopotamia, under Islamic law. As a result they often fell in love and when love was not mutual, they resorted to incantations and spells in order to make the loved one reciprocate the love. Both young men and women made use of this mild form of witchcraft. The status of women in early Sumerian society was much better than in the later Assyrian period. In the Sumerian city state women could own land and other property, and if they could afford it, they could, it seems, take more than one husband, although some scholars maintain that the relevant passage refers to the permission to widows to remarry. Later, after the end of the Sumerian period, the unmarried woman was placed under the authority of her father, following the Semitic laws of the Babylonians-Assyrians. (*Deuteronomy* 22: 16). In Sumerian times women could own property, engage in business and be parties to contracts .

Children were desired and loved, but they were required to show love and respect for their parents; if they refused obstinately to obey their fathers they could be disinherited.

Women who had children were considered fortunate; they would suckle their infants for two to three years (cp., *Koran* 2: 233), so that few women had more than six children.

Very poor or deserted women might leave their children on the road and abandon them. Fortunately, some people who were anxious to have children would take these babies up and adopt them. Legislation for adoption occurs in the law codes, and numerous documents concerned with the rights and duties of adopted children have been found (Saggs, 155-161).

Hammurabi's Laws

Hammurabbi ruled Mesopotamia (now called Iraq) from 1792 to 1750 before Christ. He left us a major contribution to the development of human cultures the first code of law, engraved in cuneiform characters in the Babylonian language, on a stele, a diorite pillar, which was discovered in Susa in 1901, and made him famous.

Many of the king's laws are economic: sale and rent of land, gardens, houses; lending, debts and deposits, tax, inheritance, embezzlement, purchase or hire of slaves, and many other transactions are regulated equitably.

In Hammurabbi's time, the primeval society, composed of hostile tribes living as extended families, had already been dissolved as a result of the agricultural evolution. In the villages and towns that now housed the ever expanding bread-fed population of Mesopotamia, people lived in small houses, families together, parents and children. The patriarchal clan system of the ancient Semites had been replaced by a division of labor, since each village needed a blacksmith (i.e., a bronze smith), a potter, a carpenter and other "specialists," who enable the farmer to produce food, whereas the nomadic Semites only produced hides.

The sedentary population, born from the coalescence of many tribes (Accadians, Amorites, Sumerians, Elamites, etc.) needed a canon of laws that no longer belonged to one tribe as had been the case hitherto. These laws must be written laws, since the art of writing was already so well-known that all important contracts were written, signed and witnessed. Hammurabbi filled this need centuries before Moses or Solon. On the top segment of his stele, the king is depicted standing in veneration before the god Shamash who gives him the emblems of royal power: staff and ring.

Hammurabbi's laws divide society in three categories: free men, free women, and slaves. The family was patrilocal; it comprised a man and his parents, his wife and their children. If the wife was childless, the man would take a second wife. Without a written contract a marriage is void: they are not married, which meant that her children could not inherit from their father. Many marriage contracts have been discovered. If a man and a woman were surprised in flagrante adultery, they were tied together and thrown in the river to drown, unless the husband of the woman was ready to forgive them. A man who raped a virgin was also sentenced to death.

In case the husband was absent for a long time, e.g. on government business, the wife had to stay faithful to him as long as the means of livelihood which he had left at her disposal, would last for herself and her children; when she had nothing left, she was allowed to take another man. If her husband came back, she would have to receive him again as her husband and send the other man away, with the children she had born him. Many men died in the king's numerous campaigns, which lasted for years. What was a lonely woman to do except remarry?

If a woman wanted a divorce and spoke to her husband: "Do not touch me!" then the local official must examine her case. If her conduct is blameless, but her husband has humbled her and deserted her often, then she is entitled to take back her dowry and return to her father's house. If the husband wanted a divorce, then he had to return her dowry or give her a mina (500 grams) of silver. If she had born him children, he had to give her land to cultivate for their maintenance. Some marriage contracts have been excavated in which the conditions for a potential divorce are carefully stipulated to the wife's advantage. Such contracts were sworn and signed by witnesses. It was the best way to prevent a woman from losing her status.

The Hittites

The Hittites and allied peoples have left us inscriptions in eight languages on rock faces and clay tablets in central Asia Minor, most of them dating from the second millennium before Christ. One of the languages was called Nesitic by its speakers; it was related to Greek and Persian and it has yielded incredibly rich sources for the history and religion of the Hittite peoples in the area. One of the most valuable discoveries was the code of law, two large tablets inscribed in cuneiform with hundreds of laws; other smaller tablets contain later modifications of the legal system, since the wise Hittite kings knew the danger of stagnation as the result of codification of laws. Throughout this legal system it is implied that the clan structure is of the patriarchal type similar to the contemporary laws of Hammurabbi. This fact is illustrated by the rule that the father "gives away" his daughter in marriage to the bridegroom who "takes" her; if she is adulterous, he may decide her fate. At the betrothal ceremony the bridegroom gave a present to the bride's father, who gave her a dowry at the wedding. If she died the dowry would be inherited by her children. A man was prohibited from marrying his mother, his mother-in-law, his daughter or step-daughter. If a man dies, his wife shall be married to his brother; if there is none, to his father and if he too is dead, to his nephew. There is no punishment for a man if he has intercourse with his step-mother (i.e., presumably his father's second wife). This law implies that some clans still practiced the inheritance of wives by their husband's sons, as is still widespread in Africa. A man may not marry his sister (unlike the Persians) nor his wife's sister, as in the Koran. Marriages among slaves were also regulated by law.

Ancient Iran

Marriage was essentially monogamous in the Achaemenid Empire (539-333 BC), which at its apogee reached from Egypt to Afghanistan. Close relatives were encouraged to marry; the marriage contract already included features which have been preserved in Islamic law a thousand years later, for example, the formal meeting of the bridegroom and the bride's father, whereby the latter offers his daughter as a wife to the former who accepts formally. If a man wished to take a second wife, he was obliged to pay a substantial "fine" to his first wife, unless she was childless, in which case it was considered necessary to take an additional wife. If the first wife did have children, they would, when their father died, receive two-thirds of the inheritance, the second wife's children one-third. During the Parthian period (after 250 BC) it is reported that men could marry even their daughters and mothers, sisters and nieces. The emperors had large harems, which, according to the Greek authors, caused their decadence and fall.

During the Sassanian dynasty (226-656 AD), Zoroastrianism prevailed, though many old laws and customs remained.

Men could marry at 15 (as today), girls could be younger. Brothers and sisters could marry; a man could be legally married to two or more women with full rights. At the wedding, the bride was "given away" by her father, as in Roman law. The children inherited from both sides. Wives obeyed their husbands. Either party could sue for divorce; the husband had to pay 3000 silver drachmas for a divorce *sine causa*. If, however, his wife was childless or adulterous, there was no need to pay. When the husband died, the wife received a son's share, that is, a full share of the estate.

Ancient India

In contrast to the Africans, the Chinese, the Semitic and Turkic peoples, the Indo-Europeans seem to have been in general monogamous. The European peoples will be discussed in the next section. In ancient India, according to the abundant literature we possess from the early first millennium BC onwards, the maharajas were surrounded by concubines, but, it seems, the vast majority of the men lived monogamously.

There is one curious instance in the great epic of the Mahabharata, in which Draupadi, the strong-willed daughter of king Drupada, married the five Pandava brothers simultaneously, at the behest of their mother, Kunti. Theories of the occurrence of women's multiple marriage in ancient India have been based on this, but we have no record of this. Draupadi was a mythical character and her husbands were all sons of gods, so that we cannot draw any conclusions from this tale with regard to human manners and customs.

In the extreme north of India there are a few isolated peoples who do practice polyandry in the sense that two or three brothers may marry one woman who will "belong" to the eldest for as long as he is home, but when he is away, the next brother may sleep with her, until the senior returns.

One argument for the essentially monogamous structure of

the family in early Indian society is that all the prominent deities of the Hindu pantheon are depicted as couples, for example, Brahma and Sarasvati, Vishnu and Lakshmi, Krishna and Radha, Shiva and Parvati, and many others. Numerous romantic tales in early Indian literature, such as Nala and Damayanti, Shakuntala and Dushyanta, Rama and Sita, and many others, stress the love between one man and one woman, culminating in their marriage.

In Vedic times, around three thousand years ago and before, women enjoyed a great deal more freedom than they do in some circles today. First, women were well-educated and often capable of reciting the ancient poetry and even of composing hymns to the gods. "Where women are honored, the gods are pleased," wrote the great law-maker Manu at about that time. A few women are mentioned as having functioned as priestesses at the Vedic ceremonies for the gods; this was later abolished.

Well-to-do girls learned to read and write and to play the vina and other instruments, accompanying their own songs. When they had reached adulthood, they were allowed to select their own husbands (so there was no question yet of child marriages). For this purpose there was a very special ceremony which is described several times in early Sanskrit literature as an institution that even kings organized for their daughters. Princes from neighboring kingdoms were invited and the princess or princesses were asked to hang a flowery garland round the neck of the prince of their choice. It was expected that she would choose a prince not because he was rich or powerful, but because she had fallen in love with him. The standards of morality were high and the marriage was indissoluble. The vast majority of men in India were and are monogamous, but kings had concubines as well.

The wedding ceremony was and is very beautiful, and there were special songs which would be sung for the bride after the wedding, such as: "Go now to your husband's house, be the mistress of his household, and rule it all with wisdom. Be the queen of his family and influence your in-laws. May they be impressed by your wisdom."

The husband would take his bride home with the words: "By the right hand of happiness I take you, that you may reach old age with me."

In many Indian romances, a god and a goddess who are married in heaven decide to descend to earth and incarnate in two human beings, one male and one female who are just at that moment being conceived. When the two children are born, a boy and a girl, sometimes at great distance from each other, they are destined to marry one another, and they do find each other after many vicissitudes. Often each deity incarnates in more than one child, but always the boy meets the girl he is predestined to marry, so that a complex romance can be woven around the two or even four couples. A distant echo of these romances is to be observed in some of Shakespeare's comedies, which his Italian models had taken from Arabian tales, which in turn can be traced via Persia to the Indian originals. Each of these tales reinforces the ideal of the one to one marriage for love by couples who are predestined to become man and wife by the gods themselves.

Thus the ancient Indian myths combine the rules of lifelong monogamy with the concept of predestination and divine decree. Each and every human being has one and only one person of the other sex who is preordained by fate to become his or her spouse for lifelong comfort and happiness, and for the upbringing of children who will continue the family.

Polygyny was permitted under the Islamic rulers of India. When the Republic of India was established, it was made illegal in India but not in Pakistan. Of course the Indian Muslims do not regard themselves obliged to obey Indian family law.

Perhaps the most moving tale of the ancient Indian thesaurus is the one of Savitri who follows her husband when his soul is taken by the god of death. She never gives up until death grants her the life of her husband until she has given birth to the number of children she wants.

Marriage and the Family Among the Semites

In the beginning there were Adam and Eve. The famous French biologist Pierre Teillard de Chardin argues that Adam and Eve's existence cannot be doubted by biologists, since they and they alone had the unique combination of chromosomes which was responsible for the birth of human beings.

God's decree in *Genesis* 2:18 is commonly adduced as the institution of holy matrimony, when the Lord speaks: "I will make him (Adam) an help meet for him." In more modern English we might render it: a helper suitable for him. The Hebrew text says: *ezer kenegdo*, "a helper corresponding to him", or perhaps "to be present for him," the dictionaries and the translations differ concerning this word. The text seems to imply that a wife must be a constant helper, a helpmate who is similar and suitable and will always accompany him.

Thus God himself instituted marriage, according to those for whom the Bible is the fountain of morality, and this institution was confirmed by Jesus in *Mark* 10:6-12; *Matthew* 19: 4-11. We have to realize though, that the men of the Old Testament often had plural wives or concubines. Abraham had Hagar as well as Sarah (*Genesis*16:1); Esau had two wives (*Genesis* 26:34); Jacob had two wives and two concubines (*Genesis* 29:15ff.); David had several wives (*I Chron*. 14:3) and so had Solomon (*I Kings* 11:1ff.). Having more than one wife was taken for granted in *Deuteronomy* 21:15, and in 25:5: a man has the duty to fertilize his brother's widow irrespective of whether he already has a wife or not. This type of marriage, the so-called Levirate (from Latin *levir* "husband's brother") occurs twice in the Old Testament, in *Ruth* 4, and in *Genesis* 38. It is still widespread among the Bantu and other African peoples.

Genesis 38 seems to suggest that a father could act on behalf of his (dead) son in order to fertilize his son's wife; in Central Africa, however, it is normal for the son to 'inherit' his father's wives, all of whom will expect him to give them children, as long as they are not too old. In this way no young lives are wasted when an old man marries a young woman: his son will, after the father's death, make his stepmother(s) pregnant, thus "raising seed" for the patrilineage. This is the main metaphysical purpose of levirate marriages: to make sure that the patrilineage survives in an unbroken line of male descendants; originally the importance of this lay in the belief that the spirits of the male ancestors had to be "kept alive" by the regular "burnt offerings" of their sons.

This would also explain the curious behavior of the two daughters of Lot who "raise their father's seed" by lying with him on successive nights after making him drunk (*Genesis* 19: 52). Without this their father s lineage would have died out. When the levirate widow, after having her husband's brother "perform the husband's duty to her," bears a son, he shall succeed in the name of her husband "which is dead, that his name be not put out of Israel" (*Deuteronomy* 25:6). The primal reason, censored by later editors of the Torah, was probably that the spirits of the patrilineage can only be kept alive by the sacrifices of their male descendants in that lineage. Very similar customs have been recorded not only in Africa, but also among the (mainly Turkic) peoples of Central Asia. When, as a result of the frequent wars of those nomadic herdsmen, warriors were killed, their brothers had the duty to inherit their wives and raise seed for them. The result was that the distinction between brothers and cousins was often difficult to draw since many classificatory cousins were in fact half- brothers. Among the Arabs and other Muslim peoples the preferred marriage partners are parallel cousins of the patrilineage. This preference is already stated clearly in *Numbers* 36: 8, where the reason given is the wish to retain the land of the fathers within the patrilineage, resulting in parallel cousin marriages within that lineage. This Mosaic law, combined with the leviratic law, caused the indistinctness between brothers and cousins which appears to have been prevalent among the Arabs as well as many African tribes. It has been suggested by several distinguished authors (Th.W. Juynbol, G.A. Wilkes, W. Robertson Smith, J.Wellhausen) that in the primeval period the marriage of those peoples was not an individual wedding, but a collective acquisition of wives by a family of brothers and/or patrilinear cousins.

In some parts of Africa, sisters are married off together to one man, much as Jacob married two sisters (*Genesis* 29:27). Here, we may be on the track of one of the most ancient customs of the human species: married life as a pre-individual relationship, as a result of which fertility is maximalized. It may well be that in primitive times there were no individual marriages, but entire families concluded a concubinage, so that there was always a man to beget children, if the others were out hunting. The Tibetan type of polyandry by which one woman married two or more brothers may be a vestige of this collective marriage where several brothers married several sisters/cousins. In those days of high mortality through warfare and the hazards of the hunt, and for the women the hazards of childbed, offset by the absolute need to have children for an assured future of the tribe, these collective marriages were no doubt the most highly efficient type of union. Individualism had not yet been invented.

The family life and clan structure of the nomadic livestock breeders such as the Arabic speaking Bedouins, the Central

Asian Turks, the Somali and other East African tribes is remarkably similar to the life of those ancient Hebrew clans of biblical times. Their clans are all patrilineal with cousin marriages, a hierarchy of wives for a chief, with concubines, payment of bride-price, a low status of the women and a high status of the patriarch; the man can divorce his wife with little difficulty; the children belong to the father; widows are inherited by their husband's brothers. Marriages are patrilocal since the chief decides where the tribe will settle in times of drought.

Even details of family customs mentioned in the book of Genesis, tally with customs found as far away as southern Africa; for instance, the sons of the same father, but of different mothers have to go out and herd their father's animals; the eldest son is answerable to his father for the well being of the others (*Genesis* 31:21; 43:9; 44:32). When a man wants to marry two sisters (a common custom in Africa) he has to marry the elder one first (*Genesis* 16:3). The son of the first marriage is favored by his father above the sons of his concubines (*Genesis* 25:5-6). If a man's first wife dies first, the husband will keep her hut/house in good order, but build a new one for his next wife (*Genesis* 24:67). The son of the first wife inherits his father's estate, the sons of other wives get only presents (*Genesis* 25:6). The mother's brother had a certain authority over a young man, compare the relationship between Laban and Jacob, and between Joab and David. Bride price is paid by means of an intermediary (*Genesis* 24:53). A man with several wives gains prestige in his community anywhere in Africa.

In Africa, north of the fifteenth parallel, in most of eastern and southern Africa, the majority of the clans are structured according to the patrilinear and patrilocal system. Among the non- Muslim peoples this is based on the mythical concept of the ancestral spirits who still rule the clans of their descendants in the male line, through the mediation of the prophets or diviners, who possess an incredible variety of methods to learn the wishes or dissatisfactions of the ancestors and convey these to the clan heads. These clan heads are themselves the descendants of the ancestors in the patrilineage. Their male descendants in the male line will one day take over the leadership of the clan and perform the sacrifices to their fathers and grandfathers who by that time will themselves have joined their ancestors in the spirit world. They are invoked whenever an important decision has to be taken by the family. They are called by their names and on many compounds images or statues of the ancestors are kept, often in a shrine, and regular offerings are placed before them . Laban had such household gods (*Genesis* 31:34) and the Romans likewise invited their ancestral spirits to be present at their momentous family gatherings.

In all these communities, the belief that the ancestors still care for their descendants and have their well-being still at heart after death, keeps the family together. The belief that the ancestors will even punish those descendants who sin against the rules of good conduct, will uphold the morality of the living members of the clan. Thus disruption of the ancient beliefs invariably leads to immorality in our times.

There is good reason to believe that this clan structure was already prevalent in Africa in ancient times.

Koranic Law, Fiqh and Sunna

Islam introduced a minimum of changes in the customs of the Arabs of Antiquity. Especially Islamic family law is a faithful replica of the clan life of the heathen Arabs. Circumcision, never mentioned in the Koran, was made a *sunna,* required custom. Clans remained intact as patrilocal households, into which the sons introduced their brides. Bride price, *mahr,* remained a requirement to make marriage a valid institution; it is not mentioned in the Koran. The Koran does not forbid men to marry their brothers' widows, but it does prohibit a man marrying his father's wives, although it is not clear whether this refers only to the father's widows or only to the women he has divorced (4:22). Marrying two sisters together is forbidden, but full cousins and nieces are permissible for a man to marry (4:23).

A man may marry four wives at any one time; if one reads the passage (4:3) very carefully, this restriction appears to apply only to those men who are trustees for the property of orphans. Other men may marry as many wives as they can afford (physically as well as financially). Those men who cannot afford wives, are advised to take the women or girls "whom your right hand possesses" (4:25), that is, slave women. Slavery was taken for granted by Muhammad so that it is repeatedly mentioned in the Koran and is an existing institution to the present day. Slaves are made when Muslim slavers raid the villages of non-Muslims in Africa. The children of slaves are again slaves. A man has the right to have intercourse with his female slaves and breed with them. They may not refuse their master's wishes. Neither may wives refuse their husbands' desires (4:34) even though they be "free."

The children of a free man and a slave woman are free and may share in their father's inheritance; here the Koran has improved the conditions of the secondary wives' children referred to above (*Genesis* 25: 5-6), reflecting the older laws.

Note that the Koran addresses men only. It tells men whom they may marry and how many wives or concubines they may keep. The laws are there for men to observe; the women just obey (4:34). Nor do the women have a voice in their wedding or even the choice of their partners. In Islamic countries, the *wali* is the guardian of all the unmarried women in his household, even those who are majors, and those who were previously married. The bride is not present during the signing of the marriage contract; only the bridegroom, the bride's father and other male relatives and friends of both parties are present, as well as the imam who will conduct the proceedings. Recently a Turkish girl, Nazmiye Ilikpinar was murdered in Strasbourg by her family because she had gone in search of her own partner and refused to marry the one her father had selected (*Time*, Dec. 12, 1994). This sad event proves that in Islamic families the power of the father is still absolute; repeatedly do we learn of similar tragedies in Islamic families world-wide. The girl's father and, in his absence, his father, the girl's paternal grandfather, have by Islamic law the right of *wali al-jabri* "guardian of compulsion, of force," which means that they can force a daughter/granddaughter to marry the man they have chosen for her. The form of the contract is one in which the bride's guardian offers her to the bridegroom, who then formally accepts her as his wife. In practice this means that she is transferred from the authority (*tā'a* "obedience") of her father/grandfather to that of her husband. Asaf A. Fyzee (p. 200) distinguishes between Hanafis and Ithna 'asharis who regard a girl at the age of fifteen no longer as a minor, so that she may marry without a guardian. However, the Shafi'is, Malikis and, of course, the Hanbalis regard all unmarried women as minors whose wedding requires a guardian to be valid. A valid marriage can be concluded between minors: the minimum age for a boy to be married is twelve, for a girl nine years (Fyzee, p. 90), though Shafi'i law stipulates no minimum age (Juynbol, p. 189). Child marriages were no exception in ancient Arabia and Muhammad has not modified this rule. Indeed he himself married Aisha, his friend Abu Bakr's daughter when she was only six. She was not brought to his house, however, until she was nine, in 623, when Muhammad was 53. They never had any children. It is probable that the rule whereby a girl can be married at nine years is based on this first Islamic marriage. Evidently children cannot give their consent to their marriage so that such marriages are concluded for them by their two guardians, fathers or paternal grandfathers, who have the right to take the decisions for their charges. No other persons are authorized to join minors in matrimony.

A man may conclude marriages with four different women; a marriage with a fifth woman would be irregular but not invalid. A woman may be married only to one man at any one time; a marriage with a second man would be void and its issue would be illegitimate (Fyzee, p. 93). She would be a bigamist.

A Muslim woman may only marry a Muslim; a Muslim man may not marry an idolatress, even though the Muslim emperors of India often married Hindu princesses who gave them successors. (Fyzee, p. 95; *Koran* 2:220-1). A Muslim may marry a Christian or Jewish woman (*Koran* 5:7). A Hindu widow may not remarry, but a Muslim widow may remarry after the *'idda,* a waiting period of three months and ten days (*Koran* 2: 234-6).

Homeric Greece

Homer incorporated many wise lessons in his two immortal epics, since he was more of a moralist than modern literary critics want to give him credit for. In those days oral traditions were recited for the purpose of teaching the young. Among the numerous famous characters in Homer's great works there are two outstanding women, one steadfast and faithful: Penelope, and the other one shallow, weak of will, adrift: Helen of Troy, queen of Sparta. The great war begins because of the latter, and Homer ends his narrative with the former.

I have to assume that the history of the Trojan war is known. Paris, the handsome prince, gives the apple of contention to the goddess Venus when she promises him the loveliest woman on earth. It is clear that for the narrator of those days the moral of this episode is: either alternative would have been a better choice, but especially Hera's offer of royal power. Paris, whose stars foreboded that he would cause the ruin of his fatherland, visited the court at Sparta, while its king, Menelaos, was absent, he persuaded Helen to elope with him. Helen was the loveliest woman of the world, Venus could not refuse to help Paris and so, she made Helen fall in love with the handsome Paris. Again, the narrator implies clearly that fickle women cause ruin and disaster. Helen was a wicked wife!

Paris was later punished for his unfaithfulness to his wife Oenone whom he had deserted for Helen. He died of a poisoned arrow, after horrible pains. Helen had been his "wife" for ten years, during which Venus made their living together heavenly for Paris, but not for Helen, who protested when Venus called her to Paris' bed (*Iliad* 3:390):

> "Ominous goddess! Why do you wish to seduce me and trick me?
> "Will you marry me on to some country yet farther and farther?
> "Have you, there as well, a young man you love among mortals?
> "Is it, because, having vanquished my man, Alemandros.
> "King Menelaos wishes to take me home to his palace.
> "Me, a woman despised and hated and shunned by the others.
> "Is that the reason you come here to me with your tricks and your scheming?
> "Go, lie down with his body yourself and desert the immortals.
> "Worry about him forever and watch over him and protect him.
> "Until he makes you either his wife or simply his mistress.
> "I do not wish to go there for that would be shameful.
> "Servicing that man's bed! The women of Troy would deride me.
> "Afterwards. And I have unmeasured pain here inside me!"

Hearing such defiance the goddess was incensed and threatened the poor woman that her fate would be disastrous if she did not obey the goddess of love. Frightened, Helen followed her to Paris' bedroom. There she mocked him for fleeing from Menelaos, her true husband and a great warrior. Even so, when he summoned her to lie with him, she consented, probably still afraid of the goddess of love, who loved Paris.

In this brief episode, Homer the brilliant psychologist, paints in vivid colors the ambiguity of human motives. Helen did not love Paris, yet she let him make love to her, terrified by divine power, by the goddess of love, that is love itself. Or did Helen still love the admired Menelaos? Should she have done what she said and refused to go to Paris? It was too late; she had already caused the great war. We are all toys of the gods, and those of us who refuse to be so used, disaster will strike us. Helen had no strong character, unlike Antigone who defied the mighty Creon and buried her brother as her conscience dictated, then killed herself before Creon could have her executed. She had the true Greek character, for she accepted her fate, did what was necessary, and died for it.

In the Odyssey Helen reappeared, reconciled with her husband king Menelaos who is now very rich. When Telemachos, Odysseus' son visited Menealos she recognized him as the son of one of the great leaders of the Trojan war..." all for my sake, me dog-faced one"(*kynopidos*, usually translated as 'shameless') (*Odyssey* 4:145). Later on, she related how she recognized Odysseus when he had penetrated the palace of Troy, but she did not betray him. Later however, she devised a stratagem to lure the heroes out of the wooden horse. So, on whose side was she? She partly explained it herself, when she described how she woke up, as it were, from the spell that Venus had cast on her: "I began longing for home again, my heart had turned to nostalgia as the blindness cast upon me by

Venus, wore off, and I felt contrition that I had left my daughter Hermione at home alone as well as my husband, when Venus carried me away from my home."

Was she sincere when she confessed openly that she had had this change of heart? Homer certainly wants us to believe so.

Helen was not punished by the gods for her sin of deserting her devoted husband. He took her back from burning Troy and reinstalled her in his palace as his queen; there she will live with him until they are old, thus Proteus predicted. Helen was Zeus' daughter, so she lived happily ever after. There was only one shadow on their happiness: they never had a son, and every king must have a successor. So, Menelaos begot a son by a *doule*, a female slave whose name is not even mentioned. So, the divine Helen had to lie alone while her husband embraced a handmaid to gain a prince. When Telemachos arrived, that prince was just bringing a bride, the daughter of a king, to his patrilocal home, so he was recognized as the crown prince.

There were in those days, plenty of housemaids, *dmoiai* in the palace, whose task it was to wash the princes and rub oil in their skins (*Odyssey* 4: 49).

Classical Greece

The Greek family was monogamous and nuclear, being composed in essence of husband and wife with their children. Often, however, there were other dependent relatives staying in the house, and many people had live-in servants as well. The family was the source of new citizens who would have the right to membership of all Athens' democratic institutions. In order to qualify they had to be born of the legally recognized marriage between two Athenian citizens, who themselves therefore had to be the children of a legally recognized marriage between two Athenian citizens. So, when Pericles himself lost all his legitimate children to the plague, he had to ask permission from the city council for his other children to be legitimized. They had been born to him by Aspasia, his mistress who was from Milete on the coast of Asia Minor, undoubtedly Greek, but not Athenian, so her children by the great Pericles were classified as bastards who had no citizens' rights and could not inherit from Athens' leader.

At their parents' death, Athenian legitimate children inherited by lot, that is each one received an allotted share. For this reason, the Athenians kept their families small, so that each child would inherit a not too small "lot" of the property. This in turn led to middle class families dying out in a few generations, and so, to instability in the society. Young men were encouraged to find brides inside the extended family, so that the property would stay together. A woman could not own property of any size, only her personal possessions which included jewelry, slaves, clothes, furniture, utensils and so forth. If she was the sole heir after her father's death, her father's brother could claim her as his wife.

Every woman had to be in the protection of a guardian, *kyrios*, who was normally her father and, after her wedding, her husband. During the wedding ceremony the father announced: "I give this woman for the procreation of legitimate children." Then the bridegroom would answer: "I accept." The father would then hand over the dowry, *proix,* stating the amount and the bridegroom would express his gratitude. This formula was necessary to make the marriage legitimate. Without payment of dowry the marriage was not regarded as legal. The dowry was given to the wife by her husband when she had produced a legitimate child of the male gender. If the husband divorced her, her father would take her back, together with the dowry. In the upper classes of Athens all these rules had long since been relaxed, but the institution of democracy made life more difficult, because the majority imposed its rules, and the majority were peasants and artisans who regarded women with primitive suspicion.

No stranger was ever allowed to enter an Athenian house unless he was invited by the master. The latter would lead his guest to the men's side of the house where there was the *andron,* the men's dining room where wine was poured. The women had their quarters in the other wing, on the other side of the courtyard. If the house had two stories, the men would dwell downstairs, the women upstairs. In Islamic countries this social construction can still be observed. Women normally left the house chaperoned; only the peasants' women had to work in the fields without male protection. At the entrance of the well-to-do houses there was a porter, like the Indian *choukidar* who would make sure that the ladies received no male visitors except close relatives. The women kept themselves busy with spinning, weaving and embroidering.

Ancient Rome

Ancient Rome has a long history which we will follow from the early years of the Republic, founded in 510 BC until the sack of Rome by Alarik and his Goths in 410 AD, a venerable history of over nine hundred years.

It was Octavianus Augustus who transformed the Republic into the Empire and made himself the first *imperator*, "Commander-in-Chief, Emperor"; he reigned from 28 BC till 14 AD. In the early days of the Republic, the Romans were farmers at heart, devoted to their land and to its gods.

There are numerous names in Latin for the gods of cultivation who were worshiped at every successive stage of the process of agriculture through the seasons. Especially growing bread grain was a worshipful work, since many deities had to be propitiated during its ripening. The grain was a sacred, living being, treated with reverence since the life of the family depended on it. The Latin verb *colere* is to be translated as "to cultivate" and "to worship"; this is not a word with two distinct meanings, on the contrary, there is only one meaning, cultivating is worshiping the gods.

The Roman farmer was no less devoted to his family. His sons would one day inherit the farm, so they would have to worship the gods as well as grow the grain that would feed the family. Families were numerous as mortality was high and many hands were needed in the fields. Besides, many young men were needed as soldiers to defend Latium against the interminable attacks of other nations, the Gallians, the Etruscans and the Spireans, the Samnites and the Punians. The Roman soldiers were courageous and able to withstand hunger and cold. The farmers were pious, hard working, steadfast, patient and thrifty. These two classes of men created the Roman nation and kept it together for nine centuries. Their wives and mothers were the very backbone of the nation; they were willing to give birth to large families and to teach their children wisdom and endurance. Even those farmers who had become senators, consuls or administrators in the city of Rome, retained their farms where their families would live in the peaceful countryside. They would educate their own children since they considered education the best asset a person could acquire for his career. The content of their education was Latin grammar and rhetoric, often Greek as well; religion and respect for their elders.

By far the most essential virtue of all, according to those early Romans, was *fides,* loyalty to their families, to their brothers, sisters, wives and friends, and loyalty to *patria,* the fatherland, the Roman nation, the state of Rome in Latium, which protected them against their enemies because of its great strength, which was nothing else but the loyalty and devotion of its own citizens, who offered their lives in its defense. The family was united by its *genius,* the spirit of the ancestors as well as the living members. The family *genius* could perhaps be compared to our term team-spirit, a living but silent force that keeps a group of good friends strong in unison.

It is possible that this picture of life and work in the good old days of republican Rome has been idealized by the writers of the later, imperial period, when moral decadence had begun, according to their own works. It makes no difference however. Not all Romans were loyal to Rome; perhaps not all Roman wives in those early days were loyal to their husbands. What matters is that this loyalty to their religion, to their families and to their nation was the well considered ideal of those later writers, who were philosophers as well as statesmen.

It was in the second century after Christ that the morality of the Roman citizens began to decay seriously. Seneca already complains that the ladies of the senatorial classes "no longer blush" when they break up their marriages one after another. "They count the number of their marriages by the number of their adult years. They marry in order to divorce and they divorce in order to remarry," he writes. The Roman women were only adopting the bad habits of the men who had lost the ancient virtues of loyalty and love, and often married rich women in order to lead an easy life, making themselves—as the satyrical comedy playwrights said—the slaves of their wealthy wives' whims. If the men tired of these wives or if they met one even richer, they would have no compunction divorcing and remarrying.

The women who no longer had stable and lasting marriages to look forward to, imitated the men in other bad habits too: they participated in the lavish dinners so that some women became obese; they started drinking wine until they could no longer stand upright; and they used their money and relations to take part in the intrigues and corruption at court.

Wise rulers like Augustus and Trajan foresaw that the loss of morality in the daily life of the upper classes would lead to one great disaster for the Roman nation: the level of fertility fell dramatically in that period of Roman history, causing these provident emperors to worry that the senatorial classes would soon no longer produce a sufficient number of young people to fill the top posts in the administration and keep the Roman state alive and ticking over. They were right in their foresight, even though fortunately the disaster they had foreseen did not happen until after 400 AD when there were no longer enough men with good brains and strong will power to confront the enemies of Rome, so that it fell.

Roman Law

In ancient Roman law a married woman was equal in status to her children in that she owed obedience to her husband who managed her financial assets; if she had none, her *pater,* the man acting as her guardian, would give her a *dos*, dowry. The oldest wedding ceremony was the *confarreatio* from *far*, bearded wheat, of which cakes were made which were offered to the twelve witnesses; a sacrifice was made to the father-god, Jupiter. The *pater familias* "gave away" his daughter *in manus*, into the hands, that is the protection, but also the *potestas*, the authority, of the husband. If no proper ceremony had taken place, the law still recognized as married two persons of different sex who had lived together during one year: *in manum conventio usu* married status through usage. If the wife refused to be under her husband's *potestas*, she had to be absent during three nights per annum, *trinoctitio abesse*; then the *in manum* status could never be applied. This form of "free marriage" was already recognized during the Republic; it can be concluded without formality by mutual consent: *consensus facit nuptias*. Still, it was customary for the bridegroom to escort the bride to his house: *deductio in domum mariti*. Without this the marriage had not really taken place. Either party can terminate the marriage. This denunciation *repudium*, had to be conducted by means of a messenger, *nuntius;* since the cohabitation was also terminated: *verum divortium*. This free marriage maintained the woman in all her rights, *sui iuris* so that her property remained her own. In the days of decadence, under the later empire, the ladies used these easy marriages and divorces to enrich themselves, and so did the men. The moralizing writers are unanimous that the decay of marriage is the consequence of the crumbling respect for religion.

Germanic Antiquity

Concerning the peoples speaking Germanic languages in Antiquity, we possess written sources in the following languages: Anglo-Saxon (Old English), Old Icelandic, Old High German, Old Saxon, Old Friesian, Old Norse and Gothic.

From these sources, a rather grim picture emerges of the lot of women in northern Europe in late Antiquity.

At marriage, a woman is handed over ("given away" is the formula still used in English churches, now only a formality) by the father into the hands of her husband (as in Roman and Babylonian law). For this "gift" the husband has to pay a considerable sum. The wife lives under the protection of her husband (the Roman *tutela*) who is responsible for her and represents her in law. If she transgresses the law he may punish her. We know that the Friesians, in order to pay a particularly extortionate Roman tax, had to sell their cattle, their land and finally even their wives. The husband is the lord of the house, ruling not only his wife and children but also his younger siblings and the servants. Any men of substance had more than one wife. Usually the secondary wives were concubines over which the first wife had authority. It did happen that the first wife refused to allow a second wife into the house. Thus, in the course of the centuries the respect men had for their wives, grew gradually. For instance, in later times the wife was allowed to keep the bride price for herself.

Indeed the Roman historian Tacitus reports that the

Germans (meaning all the Germanic peoples) highly respected their wives and regarded them with reverence; the majority of the diviners and fortune tellers among them were women, demonstrating the women's close contact with the divine.

In later centuries the wife becomes the loved and trusted companion of the man whom she follows even on the battlefield, where she encourages him to fight on for his people. In some sagas the wife has more will-power and fortitude than her husband. One Icelandic woman found her house surrounded by the enemies of her husband who was inside; the enemies invited her to come out for they were planning to set fire to the house and burn her husband inside it. "So I will burn with him," she replied. "I was young when I was given to my husband, we shared life together, now we shall share death."

The wife was barred from membership of the *stureting*, parliament, nor did she have any political or legal power, but in the house she was the ruler, and many wives had to manage the farms while the husbands were away hunting or warring. This meant she was responsible for tending the animals, planting and harvesting, supervising the farmhands, for food and clothes. This made the wives independent and gave them character even in a patriarchical society. For the early Germanic peoples, as for the Romans, life was not "the pursuit of happiness," as the Americans formulate it, but it was a time to fulfil one's duties towards one's family, the clan, the nation, the king. Marriage was necessary for the continuation of the *folk,* the tribe or nation one was born into; therefore it was the business of the entire family that all its members were properly married. To "wed" meant "to pledge," to promise that one would keep the wedded one "to have and to hold," "until death us part." Instead of a "compensatory" sum of money for the loss of their daughter, the bridegroom's family preferred to offer one of their own daughters to a son of the bride's family, as a very ancient custom.

In the oldest days, the two families could constrain, or at least "lean on" their children to agree to marry each other, having selected fitting matches. Later, the bride was left free to marry the man of her choice. Divorce was not too difficult, provided the petitioner could adduce sufficient grounds for wanting it, such as repeated ill-treatment.

Although the children were essentially the purpose of life, the reason for the institution of holy matrimony, yet it has happened that the father was forced to sell them into slavery. As patriarch he had that right, which was laid down explicitly in Anglo-Saxon law a century after the Christianization of England. Similar rules are found in Babylonian law, always on condition that the father had no choice in times of famine or war. Thus arose the institution of the bondsmaids and bondsmen, who had become slaves to pay off their fathers' debts.

When a new baby was born, the father would place it on his knee and give it some food, signifying that he "took it as his own." Alas, poverty forced many to expose their children be their children were "taken up," thus making them foundlings. The father would also sprinkle some water on the child, the origin of baptism, signifying that he would look after it.

Germanic law did not provide for a will. A man's sons inherited the property, and looked after their aging mother. The daughters married "out of the house," taking their possessions. Although life in the harsh northern climate made them hard, the northerners loved their children very dearly, and gave them the best possible education. The daughters had to learn a hundred labors of the hand and to look after their younger siblings; the sons had to learn the art of warfare and weaponry, practicing the art of wrestling and fencing; blood often flowed during these rough sports. They all had to learn the ancient oral traditions.

Conclusion

It appears from our data that there are three stages of social evolution in the history and prehistory of humanity. The oldest stage seems to be the "family marriage" by which two groups of siblings marry, preferably cousins. The relics of this ancient system is the polyandrous marriage of the Himalaya tribes where one woman marries two or more brothers, and the patrilinear levirate system of the ancient Semites and of many African tribes where the surviving brothers or their sons, or even their father, inherit all the widows. Very ancient too seems to be the Old Iranian system, whereby two siblings are encouraged to marry, and where a man could even marry his daughter and his mother. All these systems of multiple marriages arise out of the need to provide seed raisers for the women as long as they are fertile, to replace the men who died in battle, while hunting, through accidents or disease. It must be pointed out that these family marriages were not promiscuous; on the contrary, there were strict rules which the family members observed for the sake of procreation.

The second stage of social development seems to be the over-indulgence of the men in their procreation for the patri-lineage, marrying and enslaving ever more women for their lust and their desire to father ever more children. The late king Abdul Aziz of Arabia sired 49 sons and an undisclosed number of daughters, in total well over a hundred children, by an undisclosed number of wives, who were at his beck and call. In such conditions there is never a real marriage possible, as some wives do not see their husband in months, while he is busy with others. There is no relationship, only a single fertilization when the wife's most recent baby is weaned.

The third stage of the evolution of human society becomes visible in the history of Greek and Roman civilization, where relations between men and women gradually become more equal, as there is a spiritual dimension added to the physical basis of the relationship. Among the ancient Indo-European peoples women enjoyed a far higher status than among the Semites or in Africa. We have seen how women in India learned to read the classical literature, likewise the daughters of the Germanic nobles. In the Middle East the status of women has badly deteriorated since antiquity.

In the Roman Empire the women finally become completely independent. The new affluence made it possible for upper-class women to move about freely and to control their own affairs. As early as 195 BC a women's organization marched to the Forum (the central city square), lobbied the leading politicians vigorously and even picketed the Senate. In spite of the eloquence of the conservative leader Cato, the women got their way and a very iniquitous law was abrogated.

As so often in history, a movement in the right direction continues past its optimal point and moves in the wrong direction. The equality of the women led to their imitating not only the good things men did but also the bad. Women studied and some became scholars, but they also took to drinking and eating too much, and they made a habit of divorcing their current husbands if they met a richer man. The resulting fall in the birthrate led ultimately to the downfall of the Empire and even the sack of Rome, since there were not enough able men to lead the once famous Roman army against the Vandals.

It was for this reason that the Christian church saw itself forced to prohibit divorce, as its leaders knew that only stable marriages create good homes for children. That was the lesson of the decadence of Rome.

Chapter 3

THE FAMILY IN THE HOLY ROMAN EMPIRE: CHRISTIAN INFLUENCE IN RESHAPING THE ANCIENT AND MEDIEVAL FAMILY

Anthony J. Guerra

Introduction

In popular consciousness, it is imagined that the conversion of Constantine the Great in 312 to Christianity bespeaks of the beginning of a soon fully realized transformation of the social order of the Roman Empire in late antiquity which endures throughout the Middle Ages only to be disrupted by the revolutionary periods of the Enlightenment and modernity. The magnitude of this mischaracterization of Christian influence on Western society is most clearly demonstrable with respect to the institution of the family. Indeed, Christian family values and practices in its early and formative periods were as much influenced by its social contexts: Hebraic and Hellenistic, as it influenced them. Centuries were needed before the distinctive emphasizes of the teachings of Jesus had measurable impact on European society. Second and third-century Christian literature staked out its position against the popular culture while relying heavily upon Cynic and Stoic marriage ideals. Even in its successful fourth and subsequent centuries, extant family traditions would be found resistant to Christian reforms. The monastic option, for instance, was utilized by the elite classes to solve their own family problems while the transformation of normative marriage and family patterns among these classes necessitated protracted warfare on the part of the ecclesiastical authorities. Coincident with emergent Papal civil authority, the Church began to succeed in reshaping the marriage practices of European society and eventually assumed the powers of legitimization for marriage.

The Mediterranean Family in the First Century: Jesus, Paul and Augustus

(a) Jesus and the Palestinian Tradition

The Hebrew Bible is both a record of the practices and attitudes of the Israelite people as well as a holy scripture that guided and reinforced the behavior of this people. These writings give unequivocal testimony that the Hebrew family type was patriarchal in nature. The importance of children and especially of the male heir is made abundantly clear in the story of Abraham. Both practices of polygamy and Levirate marriage, the obligatory marriage of a man to his brother's widow when the deceased leaves no descendants, are rationalized because of the necessity of producing heirs. There are indications of a monogamous disposition among the Hebrews early on which gradually asserts itself and becomes dominant leading to the disappearance of polygamy among Jews in the Middle Ages. All women and men, including priests, were expected to marry at an early age, shortly after puberty.[1] The parents, above all the father played the central role in the selection of spouses for the children although there is evidence that an exceptionally wilful son or even daughter (*Genesis* 24:8) might successfully resist parental persuasion. No doubt, however, in the overwhelming majority of cases the father's will prevailed in the selection of a bride for his son. The bridegroom's father paid a "bride price" finalizing the transaction in which the bride joins the bridegroom's family. A further feature of early Hebrew marriages was instant divorce effected simply by the husband telling the wife to leave.[2] At a later date, the formal procedure was set in place as indicated in *Deuteronomy* 24:1 whereby the husband is required to "write her a bill of divorce" stating the grounds before expelling her from his house.

Within this Hebraic context, the teachings of Jesus can only appear as quite extraordinary or even revolutionary. When confronted with the Mosaic allowance for men to divorce their wives, Jesus characterized the Deuteronomic law as a concession: "For your hardness of heart he wrote you this commandment." (*Mark* 10:5) Jesus provides a rationale from the purpose of creation for marriage relying on *Genesis* 1:27 and 5:2, "God made them male and female." Elizabeth Schussler-Fiorenza has correctly pointed to Jesus' use of *Genesis* 1:27 in *Mark* 10:7: "For this reason a man shall leave his father and mother and be joined to his wife, and the two shall become one flesh."[3] Here the man is called upon to sever his connection with his own patriarchal family rather than the woman being handed over to the power of man. Moreover, Jesus' admonition against divorce further emphasizes the notion of husband and wife as equal partners even though the latter part of the saying is inapplicable to women in Palestine who did not have the right to divorce their husbands: "Whoever divorces his wife and marries another, commits adultery against her; and if she divorces her husband or marries another, she commits adultery."[4] The radical nature of Jesus' saying on marriage and divorce can readily be seen by the Mathean revision, which against the Markan reading, allows the man alone the right to divorce his wife "for unchastity" (*Mark* 19:9). This crucial exception in the *Gospel of Matthew* seeks to place Jesus in respectable Jewish company such as the celebrated teacher Shammai (50 BCE-30 CE) who held to the same such exception against the equally renowned Hillel who taught that the man may divorce his wife whenever he so wishes. The central point of Jesus' understanding of marriage is its theocentric origin which both Mark and Matthew affirm: "What therefore God has joined together, let no man put asunder." It should be noted that Jesus is unique among the founders of the major world religions in advocating marriage as a lifelong monogamous commitment.[5]

By placing the authority of marriage beyond all earthly institutions including those of the patriarchal family and religion, Jesus proclaims a new standard of marital fidelity which is incumbent upon both husbands and wives. Jesus' revaluation of the marital relationship is also consonant with the radical reassessment of children, the poor and social untouchables such as prostitutes and Samaritans, a despised ethnic and religious minority of first century Palestine. Jesus' mandate for the individual to be concerned with his or her own purity of heart rather than condemning the other (*Matt.* 5:27; 7:1-5) provides the impetus to transform familial and other habitual social forms of behavior in ancient and medieval civilizations. In Jesus' "new family of equal discipleship" the little child becomes a primary recipient of the community's care and service (*Mark* 9:35-37; *Matt.* 18:1-4 and *Luke* 9:48). The early Christian Church quickly developed institutions of social welfare for its baptized children and widows that would distinguish it favorably in the eyes of even otherwise critical Romans. While *Deuteronomy* 21:18-21 gives parents the right to hand over a rebellious son so that "all the men of the city shall stone him to death," in the parable of the prodigal son, Jesus emphasizes the loving forgiveness of a father towards the son who has squandered his inheritance in irresponsible living and returns home empty-handed to the warm embrace of the father. The challenge of Jesus' familial ethics has never been fully met by the civilizations upon which it has been thrust. A part of the history of this encounter between the Jesus Marital Ethic and Western society will be examined throughout the remainder of the paper. But before proceeding to the next major Christian thinker on marriage, Paul, I will review briefly the concerns of the first Roman Emperor, Augustus.

(2) Augustus and Imperial Family Ethics

No doubt many today would question both the propriety and potential efficacy of legislating morality, particularly with respect to matters of private life. Many Romans including the brilliant Emperor Augustus, on the contrary, firmly believed that it was obligatory for government to guide the morals of its people and punish violators.[6] According to an older Roman moral code, it was a duty of the citizen to marry and bear children so as to replenish the ranks of Roman citizenry as well as to gain legitimate heirs to inherit estates.[7] Around 100 BCE, the Romans discovered romantic love with the result that young men, especially from the Roman nobility and the Italian gentry, looked upon the traditional values associated with respectable marriage and fatherhood with contempt.[8] Also in the last generation of the Roman Republic young women of the Roman aristocracy adopted these same new morals and became known "for their divorces, their adulteries and their reluctance to bear children."[9] It was against this threat to Roman traditional morality arising in the upper classes that Augustus sought to defend. In 29 BCE, Augustus introduced a law to penalize celibacy and require respectable marriages. However, the opposition was fierce enough to bring the astute young politician to withdraw the proposal. The poet Propertius railed against this proposed legislation in an elegy addressed to his beloved Cynthia. "Why should I provide sons to win triumphs for Rome? No, no one of my blood will serve as a soldier...you mean everything to me, Cynthia, more even than having children and continuing my line." (Propertius 2.7.13-14 and 14-20).

Augustus waited ten years and now with substantially greater political control after assuming the role of "supervisor of morals" in 18 BCE introduced a series of moral reforms. This new reform program included the lex Julia on adultery and the *de maritandis ordinibus*: "To encourage marriage by members of the various classes of citizens." Finally in 9 CE, the lex Papia-Poppaea was added and these three acts were the basis of Augustus' marriage legislation which remained in effect for three centuries until Constantine. This legislation made marriage a duty incumbent on all Roman men between 25 and 60 years of age and all Roman women between 25 and 50. Widowed and divorced persons within these age limits were required to remarry. However, citizens having met their quota, at least three children for a free-born person and at least four for a freed person, were exempted. Severe fiscal penalties were associated with the Augustan marriage laws affecting everyone of significant wealth. As his arch rival, Antony was fond of pointing out Augustus was of Italian origins, low social rank, both his father and grandfather engaged in banking. The rise of Augustan imperial power was coincident with the ascendancy of the equestrian class from which Augustus derived and the eclipse of the patricians who dominated the senate. Augustus' marriage laws were intended to promote the agrarian morality of the Italian hinterlands over that of the urban sophisticates. As might be expected both philosophy and religion were to have greater impact than imperial edicts in transforming the private lives of the Roman people.

(3) Paul and the Hellenistic City

Paul of Tarsus,[10] the self-proclaimed apostle to the Gentiles was a highly effective urban missionary and church administrator. Whereas Jesus and his disciples were rural Palestinians, Paul brought the gospel of Christ to several provincial capital cities in the Eastern part of the Roman Empire and shortly before his death was planning a major initiative in the West evidenced by his *Letter to the Romans*. Paul was widely conversant with Hellenistic ethical thought as well as rhetoric and literary conventions.[11] Most recently, Will Deming has convincingly demonstrated the Stoic-Cynic provenance of Paul's teachings on marriage and sex with reference to the locus classicus *First Corinthians 7*. In the first century, the question whether an individual should assume the obligations entailed in marriage and childbearing were openly debated not only by romanticizing poets as discussed above but also by renowned as well as mediocre philosophers and rhetoricians. Taking diametrically opposed positions, the Cynics and Stoics were two philosophical schools most deeply engaged in the ancient "battle" over the family. The Stoics initially were pro-marriage because they saw it as vital to the well-being of the city-state. Responsible married life is essential to the healthy household which is the basic unit of the city-state. The Stoics further favored marriage reasoning that married life and procreation were necessary for human beings to live in accord with nature, the defining criterion of Stoic ethics. To the contrary, the Cynics argued that by escaping marriage individuals preserved the free time essential to pursuing philosophy and attaining to the good or virtuous life. Deming notes certain Stoics developed a hybrid position wherein they argued that because of special or adverse social circumstances such as war or poverty, individuals should forgo marriage to pursue the philosophical life. Paul's own position in *First Corinthians 7* may be closest to this hybrid Stoic view.

The seventh chapter of *Corinthians* contains some of the

most often quoted early Christian words on marriage and sex: "To the unmarried and the widows I say that it is well for them to remain unmarried as I am. But if they are not practicing self-control, they should marry. For it is better to marry than to be aflame with passion." (vv. 8-9). At best, this and several other verses in chapter seven including v. 38 "So then, he who marries his fiancee does well; and he who refrains from marriage will do better" would seem to confer a begrudging second-class citizenship on married Christians as lacking greater self-control. Indeed, such a negative valuation of marriage and sexuality in the second century and till the present day has been affirmed by much of Christianity. The problem is that such a rendering of Paul's view neglects several other important elements of the apostle's conception of marriage and sexuality articulated in *First Corinthians* 7. Paul makes it clear that his admonitions against marriage derive from his eschatological conviction that the end time is present: "Yet those who marry will experience distress in this life, and I would spare you that. I mean, brothers and sisters, the appointed time has grown short.... For the present form of this world is passing away." (vv. 28, 29 and 31b). It is this apocalyptic element that is decisive in Paul's advice concerning the issue of assuming the responsibilities of marriage and family. Given the present "adverse circumstances " Paul recommends against marriage so as to avoid the burden that will distract the devotee from attending to the "affairs of the Lord" in what from his understanding are the final moments of fallen history.

Paul, in the opening verses of chapter seven, is opposing extreme sexual asceticism in the Corinthian community. He advises husbands and wives not to withhold conjugal rights from each other (v. 3) "except perhaps by agreement for a set time" (v. 5). Paul's advice reflects an egalitarian view of the relationship between husband and wife especially with respect to sexual relationships: "For the wife does not have authority over her own body, but the husband does; likewise the husband does not have authority over his own body, but the wife does" (v. 4). There is nothing squeamish here about Paul's advice on sex to the married couple. The anonymous *Letter to the Hebrews* transmitted as part of the Pauline correspondence by the early church pronounces: "Let marriage be held in honor by all, and let the marriage bed be kept undefiled" (13:49). The later *First Timothy* pseudonymously attributed to Paul explicitly condemns gnostic heretics who "forbid marriage and demand abstinence from foods" (4:3). Earlier in the same letter, conditions for those aspiring to the office of bishop include that one be the "husband of one wife" and "he must manage his own household well" (3:4). Nevertheless, the ascetic and celibate tendencies consciously subdued in the Pauline and Deutero-Pauline tradition soon will take center stage in church history.

The New Christian Society in a Hostile Roman Empire: Second to the Fourth Centuries

An array of articulate Christian spokespersons span the late antique period who directed their rhetoric not only at the emperors and all other outsiders but also inwardly as they disagreed with one another, often vehemently, about the meaning of the gospels. Such intra-Christian polemics were particularly intense with respect to questions of marriage and celibacy.[12] Although each represented widely diverse constituencies and perspectives, two major groups emerged in the second century known as the "Gnostics" and the "Catholics." The Gnostics embraced a radical dualism that denied value to not only the material realm but also the "God" who created this world. Thus for the Gnostics both marriage and procreation were part of the evil empire that evolved as a consequence of the fall of Adam and Eve. Catholics, on the other hand, acknowledged marriage and procreation as good, even though most tended to affirm that celibacy, or at least "chaste marriage" as a spiritually higher way of life. Justin proudly flaunts before his addressed Emperors, which included Antoninus Pius and Marcus Aurelius, the admirable self-restraint of Christians who engage in sex only to procreate while he calls attention to the sexual excesses of the Roman gods, people and even past emperors.[13] One's sense of the extraordinary moral austerity of early Christians can only be enhanced upon recalling that contraception, abortion, the exposure of unwanted infants and infanticide of slave children were "common and perfectly legal practices."[14] Moreover, there is ample evidence for the sexual use and abuse of both adult and child slaves by wealthy Romans. Christians, despite their internal differences, were widely recognized even by their opponents as exceptionally self-restrained in sexual matters.

It was not, however, the eloquent arrows of Christian apologists that brought the Roman Empire to its knees before the image of Christ but rather the battering ram of the burgeoning Christian community that developed its own unique social principles and infrastructure. Moreover, much of the Christian sexual ethic was not unique—even the restriction of sexual intercourse for purposes of procreation was a Stoic innovation. In the hands of the Stoics, the sexual ideal of self-restraint, family responsibility and the relative equality of husband and wife remained an elitist tradition that touched a small percentage of the upper classes including the Emperor Marcus Aurelius. The Christian leaders were able rapidly to democratize these ideals of sexual self-restraint leading, in the words of Peter Brown, to the "most profound single revolution of the late classical period."[15] Thus through Christian preaching and writings relatively rarefied philosophical notions of private spiritual life penetrated thousands of humble persons. From Paul onward the Christian movement was, in terms of class, a relatively diversified movement extensive with the social stratification of the wider Roman society. Unlike Judaism which offered its followers clear ritual boundaries through circumcision and dietary laws, Christians differentiated themselves from the pagan world in large part by adhering to an exceptional sexual discipline. Christians rejected divorce and disapproved of remarriage of widows. They practiced a marital ethic that followed the highest ideals of Roman morality.

Christian young people married early in order to avoid the temptations of illicit sexual liaisons especially with non-Christians. By avoiding remariage, the community could be assured of a supply of mature individuals able to devote their energies to the service of the Church.[16] Celibacy became the price of access to leadership in the Christian community; during the late antique period celibacy took primarily the form of postmarital abstinence usually adopted in middle age. This peculiar mark of the Christian leader emphasizing single-hearted devotion served to further distinguish the Christian movement from the wider society and its corrupted leadership. The tradition of caring for children and the poor, dating back to the earliest church, was critical in reinforcing the solidarity of the Christian community and, as I will explain below, was pivotal in its eventual success in gaining a privileged status in the Roman Empire. In the year 248 the Church of Rome had a staff of 155 clergy supporting fifteen hundred widows and poor in addition to the regular congregation. This was an enormous association by Roman standards of the time when the average cult group or burial club numbered in the scores, not in hundreds.[17] Although Christians experienced sporadic persecutions from the Roman authorities beginning with Nero, it was not until 250 that a Roman Emperor Decius ordered a systematic attack on Christianity which could now be considered a serious threat to the state.

Such attacks were renewed under Valerian in 257 and culminated in the so-called Great Persecution initiated by Diocletian in 303. This final persecution focused on destroying the leadership of the Christian movement and continued with varying degrees of ferocity until the victory of Constantine in 312.

Constantine, Augustine and Monasticism: The Potency of Celibacy.

It is probably impossible to discern the sincerity of Constantine's "conversion to Christianity." Certainly most of the contemporaneous sources extant were authored by Christian admirers whose literary efforts on the topic approach the hagiographical in character. In any case, as an emperor whose career proved him to be one of the more ambitious of this category, Constantine was, in my view, equally likely impressed with the effectiveness of the alternative society which Christians had constructed, particularly given the seemingly irreversible decline of the decurial classes who were responsible for the welfare of the Roman cities. The Christian community exhibited the will to order and great social consciousness that would appeal to an emperor wishing to shore up his own crumbling infrastructure in the face of unrelenting attacks from the Germanic tribes and the Persians who both had been for centuries enduring threats to the empire.[18] For our purposes, it is important to examine how the Christian understanding of the family and sexuality shaped and was shaped by the impressive emerging Christian organization.

After the conversion of Constantine, the Christian basilicas, perhaps now more numerous and often richly decorated as the result of imperial beneficence, remained the central meeting place for men and women of all classes, "equally exposed beneath the high chair of the bishops in the apse, to the searching eye of God."[19] In the fourth century the bishop was a powerful person politically, economically as well as spiritually; his prestige was based on his ability to care for multitudes of poor in the Christian congregation. As from the time of Paul not all Christians were poor; a significant group of influential women, mostly widows and virgins, supported the bishops' efforts on behalf of the poor. The bishop directed these women's energies and wealth in service of the Church and in turn protected them when necessary from exploitation of the male-oriented Roman system. Although the majority of Christians married, most Christians affirmed the primacy of renunciation. When Jovian, himself a celibate monk, argued that celibate persons are no holier than those who marry, he was attacked by the most prestigious Christian authorities of his time including Jerome, Ambrose and Augustine and was excommunicated by Pope Siricius, bishop of Rome.[20] The principle that the celibate way was spiritually higher than the married way was firmly, some may argue indelibly, imprinted in the Christian consciousness.

The Christian movement fulfilled a deep psychological need for order and self-control. Augustine pointed to the swamping of the conscious mind in orgasm for both men and women as evidence of the symptoms of original sin.[21] In his final theological dispute with Pelagius, Augustine argued that sexual desire and death are essentially "unnatural" experiences resulting from the sin of Adam and Eve.[22] Whereas earlier representatives of Christian orthodoxy, including Justin, Ireneus, Tertullian, Clement and Origen, affirmed the human person's moral freedom to control one's life including sexual life, Augustine denies the descendants of sinful Adam and Eve the free will to live in accord with God's will. The best one can do is to gain a battlefield advantage by abandoning the "world" and retreating to a monastic setting. During the century following the conversion of Constantine, the number of Christians grew from about five million to thirty million.[23] Unlike the Christians of prior times, there was no longer an instant social penalty to be paid upon being recognized as a disciple of Christ but rather Christian identity conferred preferential treatment. No doubt, many so-called Christians had mixed motives and lived their lives with far less distinctiveness from the pagans than had been the case in the previous era. Perhaps it was precisely this scenario that made Augustine's more pessimistic view of human nature and politics so compelling to leaders of the post-Constantine church. In this same century of rapid growth, Christians seeking high-intensity religion would and did opt for the monastic life; there were some thirty thousand monks in Egypt alone during this time. It would take centuries more for Christianity to domesticate men who would constitute the vast numbers of nominal believers in the families of the Holy Roman Empire.

The Frankish Family: From Clovis to Charlemagne

The Franks, a group of Germanic tribes were held in check by Roman legions for more than two centuries until Clovis took possession of Gaul expelling the last Roman governor in 486. Ten years later Clovis converted to Christianity at the prompting of his wife and a close relationship between the Frankish rulers and the papacy was initiated. According to Tacitus, the men of Germanic tribes were unique among the barbarians in living with only one wife. Because women did most of the productive work such as farming, a husband provided a dowry to his wife. Wives apparently accompanied their husbands to the battlefield where they tended their wounds as well as fed them. Within the confines of the Roman Empire, Frankish wives became more domesticated and were left at home on such forays. Clovis opened the door to direct Christian influence on the Frankish family which over a period of centuries was to have profound impact on Western standards and expectations with respect to family life.[24]

Around the time Clovis was establishing his kingdom, the churchman, Caesarius of Arles was castigating in his sermons the hypocrisy of men who expecting fidelity from their spouses indulged freely their own sexual whims.[25] The Church's impact on the ruling class's family practices is quite limited throughout the Merovingian period but Caesarius and other church leaders encouraged women to pursue monastic vocations which offered them varying degrees of independence from male domination. Caesarius also objected to the widespread practice among the nobility of procuring their wives through abduction and as victor's booty. When the Franks defeated the Thuringian king and captured his daughter Radegard, the sons of Clovis contested her hand in a judicial battle.[26] Desirable women were commonly abducted and were married against their wishes and more importantly the wishes of their fathers to these abductors. Given that the crux of Merovingian society was strong kinship groups, revenge was often taken directly by the blood relatives of the abductee. The chronicles record that Saint Rictrud's brothers killed her husband several years after her abduction, even though by that time several children had been born of the union.[27] Merovingian kings readily granted their most trusted servants permission to abduct girls from wealthy families. Ecclesiastical authorities opposed the Merovingians on this score and passed its own legislation encouraging women fearing abduction to take refuge in a church.[28] Not until 614 at the Council of Paris did Clovis renounce the practice of his predecessors ordering capital punishment for the abductors of women.[29] It would wait, however, several centuries before the Church's position on this matter would fully prevail in the wider society.

The Church also opposed incestuous marriages quite widely practiced by the wealthy in order to protect their possessions and strengthen kinship bonds. As in its opposition to abduction, the church argued that marriage should promote the cause of peace and that exogamous unions better served this end as they linked together the disparate kin groups of society. The Church's firm stand against incest by the end of the sixth century became effective making it difficult for kings to disregard the prohibition without consequence. Nevertheless, in the Merovingian period the marriage laws and practices of Frankish society were far distant from the Christian ideal of lifelong monogamy and coincided overtly only in the former's condemnation of abortion, abduction and female unchastity.[30] Four Merovingian kings indulged in polygynous unions and concubinage was rampant. Suzanne Wemple aptly characterizes the state of Merovingian marriage ethics: "the combination of Germanic polygamy and the Roman institution of concubinage gave almost complete license to men to be promiscuous, furthered male dominance, and accentuated sexual double standards in Merovingian society."[31] It was not until the rise of the Carolingian kings that the Church would begin to transform the accepted standards of family ethics. In Carolingian times, the indissolubility of marriage became a central issue. The insistence on the binding nature of marriage had both profound moral as well as social significance in Frankish and in European society. The initial impetus to embrace the reform ideas concerning sexual relations of Saint Boniface and other church leaders may have been largely political. As usurpers of the throne, the Carolingians needed ecclesiastical sanction for their new dynasty. Pepin also saw in St. Boniface's reform platform a weapon against "the widespread networks of alliances among the great families, which was formed mainly through marriages."[32] Also noting that incest remained unchecked among the Frankish nobility, St. Boniface enlisted the support of popes and Pepin readily responded by promulgating the incest prohibitions as part of his royal enactments. Pepin embraced less than wholeheartedly Boniface's views on the indissolubility of marriage which precluded second or third union while a previous partner was still alive. With Pepin presiding the Council of Compiegne in 757 stressed that both men and women were subject to the same laws but at the Council of Verberie (758-768), Pepin allowed divorce and remarriage "in the case of a man whose wife had tried to kill him or refused to follow him."[33]

Charlemagne was more hardline than Pepin, his father, in upholding Christian morality and in 789 prohibited the remarriage of any divorced man or woman. In 796, Charlemagne further proclaimed that "adultery could not dissolve the marriage bond."[34] Although a cuckolded husband could separate from his wife, he could not remarry while she lived. In 802, two years after his coronation as emperor of the Holy Roman Empire, Charlemagne extended this legislation to the entire Frankish Empire. Charles own life may give some insight into how at least some of the royalty and nobility coped with these stringent measures. Before his legislation on the indissolubility of marriage, Charles in his youth divorced twice but he lived steadfastly with each of his next three wives until their deaths.[35] After the death of his fifth wife in 800, Charlemagne did not remarry but enjoyed the company of four concubines. Nevertheless, the distance between Frankish customs and Christian ideas of marriage had been reduced. Louis the Pious, Charlemagne's only surviving son and the successor, was more ardent in pursuing these ideals both personally and in his role as ruler of the empire. He prevented bastards from succession to the throne and linked legitimacy to the validity of the parents' marriage.[36] After the death of his first wife, Louis married Judith who was accused of adultery but the king nevertheless refused to divorce her. This instance suggests that by this time the principle of marital indissolubility was widely accepted. In 846 and 847 bishops meeting at Meaux and Paris warned women and men to guard against adultery, concubinage and incest in their lives. With the exception of the principle of the indissolubility of marriage and the prohibition against incest, the Church, after Louis, accommodated secular customs in the second half of the ninth century. Yet Christianity had clearly defined the characteristics of an ecclesiastical model of marriage against the prevailing lay model. Although abductions, repudiation of wives and violations of incest laws continued, in the course of the next three centuries the ideals, now enshrined in secular as well as ecclesiastical legislation, would come to be accepted in the popular consciousness of Western Europe setting the new public expectations for marriage and family. Most importantly the emphasis on the indissolubility of marriage, elevated the status of the wife preparing the way for the conjugal family as the basic unit of society displacing the extended family as the dominant form of social organization.[37]

The Sacralization of Marriage:
the New Status Quo of the Family

A gradual process of sacralizing marriage began in Carolingian France and was not culminated until the thirteenth century. The Archbishop of Reims, Hincmar in 860 loudly protested King Lothair II's (the grandson of Louis the Pious) repudiation of his wife so as to marry a favored woman. Such practices, as well as that of abduction and marriage to near kin, continued as testified to by numerous treatises of churchmen condemning these practices in the centuries following that of Louis the Pious.[38] Moreover, marriage remained within the jurisdiction of civil law and priests were not closely involved in the marriage ceremony except in the case of queens.[39] Yet Hincmar and others like him were ready to stand steadfast for the evangelical law of one sole wife and against abduction and marriage within the seventh degree of blood kinship. The Church mounted its campaign against abduction and incest (in its wide interpretation as just mentioned) on the grounds that they violated the peace of society by setting families in conflict, seeking revenge for wrong done to their kin. Sound and wholesome marriage principles would promote the peace and welfare of society expanding the realm of amity, so argued the ecclesiastical reformers who sought to transform the Church as well as the wider society.

Around the year 1000, the Church was able to crystallize its position on marriage, effecting greater clarity in its own rulings as well as demonstrating its authority over family practices of even the royalty. Among the lower classes the Christianization of marriage practices was more readily accomplished as the Church's version of marriage quickly replaced concubinage.[40] King Robert of France and King Henry of Germany, at the beginning of the eleventh century, were to provide the Church an opportunity to exert its influence upon royal marital choices and practices. Having been brought up by churchmen and friend to the great monastic reformers of his time including Abbot Odilon of Cluny, Henry waited until his twenty-third year to marry and took as his bride a member of the lower ranks of the nobility so as to avoid "incest." Henry, who was caught up in the millenarian movement of his day, sought to restore order and peace to the world and also to purify God's people. Believing that he himself should be a model of a new purified people, Henry refused to repudiate his wife Cunegonde, although their union was fruitless. In biographies written after their death, the

Church portrayed the couple as living in absolute conjugal chastity and departing this world as virgins. Such literary inventions served the purposes of more austere ecclesiastical reformers at the end of the eleventh century. But between 1007 and 1012, Bourchard of Worms drew up a collection of texts known as the Decretum that was to have enormous influence on Germany, Italy and France. This Decretum devoted considerable attention to marriage; more than a quarter of the text dealt with marriage and fornication. Monogamy was its primary concern, prohibitions and punishments were much more relaxed as soon as the marriage bond was not in question. The Decretum condemns adultery by either sex but urges husbands to forgive adulterous wives, noting that women are reluctant to accuse their husbands while men habitually haul their wives before priests with such charges. The severest punishment was meted out for bestiality and also abduction and adultery. Bourchard could be lenient towards the sexual escapades of unmarried men but abduction and adultery were harshly condemned as he was more concerned with order and peace and less so with cleansing society of sin.[41] Bourchard still remains flexible with respect to remarriage and indissolubility allowing bishops to dissolve unions other than those deemed incestuous by the Church. Yet, there was lesser liberty granted to bishops in allowing those they had parted to marry again while their former partner was still alive. To put in perspective the limited authority of the Church over royal marital practices, one should look at the case of Robert the "pious." Unopposed by local bishops, King Robert pursued a bigamous relationship. Perhaps equally disturbed by the fact that Robert's third wife was connected to him by blood, the Council of Rome intervened and Robert was anathematized by the Pope. However, when his wife bore him a deformed child, Robert "got" religion and repudiated her. The Church exploited this "submission" and presented Robert as the repentant, pious sovereign indicating how tenuous a hold even at the beginning of the eleventh century the ecclesiastical model of marriage had on the European nobility. Nevertheless, Bishops continued to care for repudiated women, exhorted their husbands to take them back, and refused to give such husbands permission to remarry.

During the tenth and eleventh centuries as the feudalization of Europe proceeded, great, families emerged under the monarchial rule of a great founding figure and a sole successor in each generation. This sole male was in control of the wealth of the family and was responsible for arranging marriages for his children as well as the children of his sisters. By allowing perhaps only one of his sons legitimate marriage, the family estate was kept intact concentrating and centralizing wealth in the hands of a few feudal lords. This concentration of wealth was also furthered by a change in common practice occurring somewhat before the mid-eleventh century now excluding women from control over family property and rights. Meanwhile, the Church was winning its long fought battle for clerical celibacy in which it enjoyed the support of the heads of the great families. They were interested in limiting the claimants to inheritance and accordingly paid to stow away many of their younger relatives in monasteries precisely to prevent them from begetting legitimate children. From another quarter, the heretics attacked the Church's involvement in the sacramentalizing of marriage arguing that it was utterly inappropriate to pronounce a blessing on physical unions. The Church needed to establish a "pure," celibate priesthood in order to stave off the heretics while it continued to pursue its agenda to reform the laity primarily through the exercise of control over marriage. As the Church in the course of the eleventh century succeeded in imposing punishment upon such public crimes as adultery and abduction it de facto came to displace the secular authorities in such matters. In the last decades of the eleventh century, Pope Urban II and Yves of Chartres condemned the king of France, Philip I who abducted the wife of a count, his cousin, and lived with her while his first wife was still alive. The reforming prelates attacked the most prominent nobles in their relentless efforts to transform the marital practices of the laity. During this period the custom of involving a priest in the *desponsatio*, the ceremony placing the bride-to-be's hand in the hand of the proposed husband, as well as the nuptial ceremonies became fixed. A priest was also involved in the blessing of the ring before the mass as well as the blessing of the wedding chamber. These ceremonies effectively constituted a sacralization of marriage. Between 1093-1096, Yves of Chartres created a clear synthesis of all canon law on the topic of marriage. This work contributed greatly to the efforts of ecclesiastical reformers for whom a primary objective was to guarantee that the nobility accepted the need to submit all matrimonial problems to the Church for decision. Yves of Chartres affirms two primary principles with respect to marriage namely that it is indissoluble, and essentially spiritual. Instead of seeking to dissolve concubinage relationships, Yves equated it to lawful marriage and thus proclaimed such unions indissoluble making it no longer permissible for a man to dismiss a concubine in order to marry.[42] In this regard, Yves insisted that a girl whose father made a promise in her stead was entitled to decline such an arrangement. Here the advocates of reform were making a frontal attack on one of the main pillars of secular society "the right of the head of a family to dispose of its women."[43] Further, the emphasis on the *desponsatio* and consent by the couple provide the ethical as well as spiritual foundation for the Church's affirmation for the principle of the indissolubility of marriage as well as its

84

opposition to abduction. Most importantly, by the middle of the twelfth century marriage had come to be sacralized without being disincarnated.[44]

By the end of the twelfth century and early thirteenth century, husbands had accepted the constraints imposed by the Church and no longer repudiated their wives.[45] Young men were allowed a degree of sexual license for a time but only before marriage. Although violent abduction was no longer acceptable, the young men were allowed to joust in tournaments attended by maidens and their families and receive the required adulation for aggressiveness. On the other hand, modesty and virginity continued to be expected of women aspiring to marriage. In 1215, the Church lowered the degrees of consanguinity banning marriage and thus obliged a recognized marital strategy of aristocratic families. A compromise had been reached between two models of marriage: the secular and ecclesiastical and the result shaped the institution of marriage in the West until the most recent time.

Conclusion

In the last sixty years, the West has come rapidly to shed the restraints placed upon its marital practices by Christianity. Divorce on demand has become a common practice and the decline of the traditional family (i.e., father, mother, and at least one child) continues unabated. Although remarriage among the divorced is also common and the institution of marriage *per se* is not endangered, the percentage of children living without at least one of their biological has soared and threatens the health of the wider society. Moreover, individualism, which exalts self-interest over the welfare of the family and society, has displaced such Christian values as constancy, solicitude for the weak and the affirmation of an eternal spiritual relationship as the essence of marriage. Sigmund Freud, who may have unintentionally contributed to the "sex explosion"[46] in the United States, acknowledged that the attainment of civilization resulted in large part from the sublimation or redirection of the libido into alternative endeavors; Western civilization advanced by virtue of Christian asceticism and, I would add, its regulation of marriage and family life. As we have seen, the emergence of new norms and expectations for marriage and family life were wrought by the centuries-long struggle of Christian reformers and cooperating civil rulers with their own diverse motives. Once mainstream Christianity withdrew from asserting staunchly its spiritual ideal for marriage, the West lost an important foundation of its family and marriage traditions. Without the countervailing force of religion, it was inevitable that the overwhelming power of material culture would militate against the formation of families and a society in which equality, care and protection of the weak are the dominant values.

Notes

[1] Bernard I. Murstein, *Love, Sex and Marriage through the Ages*, (New York: Springer, 1974), p. 35.

[2] Ibid., p. 43.

[3] See Elizabeth Schussler-Fiorenza, *In Memory of Her*, (New York: Crossroads, 1983), p. 143.

[4] Mark 1:11; it should be noted that given the fact that Palestine is under Roman rule at this time and Roman law did allow for wives to sue for divorce, certain Jews holding Roman citizenry may have availed themselves of this right.

[5] See Geoffrey Parrinder, Sex in the World's Religions, (New York: Oxford University, 1980), p. 202. I am grateful to Stephen Post for this reference.

[6] See James Field, "The Purpose of the Lex Julia et Papia Poppaea," *Classical Journal*, vol. 4, (1944/45), p. 400.

[7]See Paul Veyne, "The Roman Empire" in Aries and Duby, *A History of Private Life*, pp. 35-37.

[8]See Richard I. Frank, "Augustus' Legislation on Marriage and Children," in *California Studies in Classical Antiquity*, vol. 8 (1975), pp. 41-43.

[9]Ibid., p. 43.

[10]A Hellenized city of Syria under Roman rule in Paul's time.

[11]See Anthony J. Guerra, *Romans and the Apologetic Tradition: The Purpose, Genre and Meaning of Paul's Letter*, (NY: Cambridge University, 1995).

[12]Elaine Pagel's description is most apt: "Like relatives in a large family battling over the inheritance, both ascetic and nonascetic Christians laid claim to the legacies of Jesus and Paul, both sides insisting that they alone were the true heirs." *Adam. Eve and the Serpent* (NY: Vintage Books, 1988), p. 25.

[13]See Anthony J. Guerra, "The Conversion of Marcus Aurelius and Justin Martyr," in *The Second Century*, 9:3 (1992).

[14]Veyne, op. cit., p. 9.

[15]See Peter Brown, "Late Antiquity," in Aries and Duby, *A History of Private Life*, p. 251.

[16]Ibid., p. 265.

[17]Ibid., p. 270.

[18]Note that the Christian sense of civic duty was restricted to their own community, from the perspective of the Romans, Christians could appear as lacking civic loyalties, the ostensible rationale for their persecution.

[19]Brown, op. cit., p. 275.

[20]See Pagels, *Adam. Eve and the Serpent*, pp. 91-95.

[21]Brown, op. cit., p. 309.

[22]See Pagels, op. cit., p. 130. Pagels also notes that many early Christians also believed that they could triumph over death not only in the future resurrection, but here and now, p. 128.

[23]Ramsey MacMullen, *Christianizing the Roman Empire* (New Haven: Yale, 1984), p. 86.

[24]See Suzanne F. Wemple, *Women in Frankish Society: Marriage and the Cloister*, (Philadelphia: University of Pennsylvania, 1981).

[25]Ibid., pp. 24-25.
[26]Ibid., pp. 33-34.
[27]Ibid., p. 36.
[28]Ibid., p. 55.
[29]Ibid., p. 158.
[30]Ibid., p. 75.
[31]Ibid., p. 38.
[32]Ibid., p. 76.
[33]Ibid., p. 77.
[34]Ibid., p. 78.
[35]It should be noted that the average age of women at death in this period is 36 years old.
[36]Wemple, op. cit., p. 79.
[37]Ibid., p. 105.
[38]George Duby, *The Knight. the Lady and the Priest: The Making of Modern Marriage in Medieval France*, translated by Barbara Bray, (New York: Pantheon Books, 1983), p. 32.
[39]Ibid., pp. 33-34.
[40]Duby notes that ninth-century inventories show peasants on large estates were firmly bonded in marriage—an arrangement benefitting, of course, the interest of their masters. See Duby, p. 48.
[41]Duby, op. cit., pp. 67-74.
[42]Ibid., p. 170.
[43]Ibid., p. 172.
[44]Ibid., p. 185.
[45]Ibid., p. 264.
[46]See on the term, Murstein, op. cit.

Chapter 4

THE FAMILY IN EARLY MODERN ENGLAND

J.S. La Fontaine

The nature of the family in early modern England has been a matter of considerable and continuing debate among historians. The period between the end of the fifteenth century and the beginning of the eighteenth, when historians consider "modern" England began to take shape, was a time of far-reaching changes, in population, in economic and political organization, in religion and currents of thought. However, historians, from Lawrence Stone to the present, have disagreed as to the effect these changes had on the family. Did they weaken a fundamental institution so much and so permanently that the family of modern times is merely the rump of the family of early modern England or did they, on the contrary, improve the nature of relationships that had been formal and lacking in affection, changing the role of parents from one of discipline to that of nurture? Economic changes took production out of the home but did they also erode family relationships and reduce the obligations that people felt to the old and weak among their kin? Historians may either stress continuity with the past (e.g., Macfarlane 1970, 1978, Houlbrooke, 1984) or emphasize the differences that divide the modern family from its immediate predecessor (Slater 1984, O'Day 1994). There appears to be no consensus on the matter.

These questions implicate theories of the family and are thus of importance to others besides historians. Examining how domestic life was affected by documented historical changes, such as those that characterized the early modern period, allows conclusions to be drawn about whether the family is the product of a particular type of economic and/or political organization or whether it is part of a complex of cultural concepts about relatedness that is more resilient and adapts to change. As this paper will argue, the historical evidence from this period seems to show that the structural form of the family was unaffected by these changes, although the relationships of members to one another became very different in content and the manner in which households were integrated into the wider political and economic systems of the nation was drastically altered. While the family is based on a set of resilient and adaptable principles, the human relationships involved have changed over time.

As an anthropologist and not an historian, I do no more here than consider the work of others. However it seems clear to me as a social scientist that much of the controversy about the early modern family depends on a lack of clarity about the object of study itself. If scholars identify different features of social life as critical to "the family," then it is not surprising that their conclusions do not agree. Moreover, a good deal of moral judgement may accompany analysis, as we shall see, and differences in what particular historians see as significant may result in quite different conclusions being drawn about the same material. However, the historians of today are agreed on two things: that the nature of the sources affects the way in which they can be used in evidence; and that the material must be contextualized before it can be considered either significant or reliable.

The Sources

The sources available to historians of the family in early modern England are agreed to be more plentiful than those for the medieval period, but historians emphasize that they are nonetheless limited in a variety of ways. Letters, diaries and biographies give an intimate view of relationships but they were produced by the lettered, which largely meant the elite, and hence reflect the way of life of a very small proportion of the population. Documents recording property transactions or the acquisition of skills have a wider relevance, but do not touch the unskilled and propertyless laborers who formed a large proportion of the population. Court records and administrative records, such as parish registers, tax assessments and the administration of the Poor Law have the widest coverage but have not always survived. Moreover, this last category of documents shows little of the attitudes and expectations of the people concerned, or how they behaved to one another normally. Litigation shows the breaches in relationships and in some cases what expectations of family conduct were, but as Amussen remarks: "The exigencies of the sources make it virtually impossible to find out how things worked when they went right" (1988:6).

The evidence for family relationships in the modern sense of the phrase, that is for their feelings, their thoughts about, and attitudes to, one another, is restricted to members of a small set of literate people, whose typicality cannot easily be judged. The behavior of the Verneys has been taken to show the authority of elder brothers and the manipulative, self-interested relations between siblings (Slater 1984) but other papers show a rather different picture (O'Day 1994). Given the chances the period afforded for upward mobility, there were literate men who also wrote about their childhood, offering brief glimpses of a different type of domestic life but they are even fewer. Where the evidence relies on small numbers of accounts, the range of variation cannot be known, and this type of material, although very valuable, may also be misleading. Too much weight should not be put on it.

Family and household—two different frames of reference.

A recent comparative study of family relationships remarks that while the term "family" was used by people in the early modern period "what they meant by it seems very foreign to modern developed societies. The term "family" was used to describe the household or domestic economy, the co-resident members of the biological family, and the wide group of non-resident kin"(O'Day 1994: xv). This is a good example of a stress on the differences that separate the past from the present and it is not, to my mind, entirely justified; none of those usages could really be considered "foreign" to modern English ears (see Harris 1983 esp. p. 30). "Family" is still used to mean "household" although in the twentieth century a normal household is expected to consist of "the co-resident members of the biological family." "Family" is still used in the wider sense of all relatives, and was also employed in the sense not mentioned by these authorities, and becoming obsolete today, that means birth or breeding and hence inherited rank. Another authority claims that the primary use of "family" in early modern England was for "the body of persons living in one house or under one head, including children, kinsfolk and servants" (Houlbrooke 1984:191). Servants were dependents of the head of the household and had the same status as children; they were, however, distinguished on many occasions by virtue of their birth. The family in this sense was a unit of administration defined by common residence, with the head being responsible for all members. Today it might more accurately be called a household.

It is important for analysis to keep distinct the notion of a household, defined by a common economy and common residence, and that of a family defined solely by ties of blood relatedness and marriage, whatever the usages of the time. Households contained varying numbers of people who were not related to the household head or his wife, or to each other. Household and family were not, and are not, coterminous. The extended family was not contained within any one household, as it is not today, but related individuals served as links between the several households they lived in, as they do today. The widest extension of the term family as it is used today includes all those recognized as related, wherever they live. The strength of kinship in this widest sense varied in the early modern period according to class and also geographically. It is difficult to draw conclusions about it that would be nationally valid.

In the late twentieth century, "family" (in the sense of parents and children) and "household" are often confused since they are expected to be coterminous, and historians may project this confusion onto the earlier period. O'Day describes a household that she describes as an "artificial family": it consisted of a bachelor, Leonard Stout, his mother and unmarried sister, Elin, and three of his brother William's eight children, one of whom was his apprentice (O'Day 1994:92). Relationships between the members of this household are of relatively close kinship but the assumption that parents and children living together form a "real family" is implied by the use of the term "artificial family." There is no evidence that the Stouts themselves were trying to pretend to be a family in the modern sense, or that the three children were in any sense the offspring of Leonard and his sister or mother. Besides, in the meaning given the term at the time, the fact of their living together made them a family without any qualifier being necessary.

This example demonstrates the importance of the historian's understanding of the data. O'Day sees the Stouts as an example of a close relationship between adult brothers, despite, I would add, their living in different households. Their mutual helpfulness is further demonstrated when William sends his daughter to take over the housekeeping for Leonard on the death of her aunt Elin. The practical benefits of maintaining relations with kin need not exclude affectionate relations with them, but an emphasis on one or the other may allow very different conclusions to be drawn. Slater seems to see similar exchanges among the Verneys as evidence of a manipulative and calculating attitude among brothers and sisters that, almost by definition, precludes affection. Any attempt to uncover what may be thought of as the "real" relationships, that is to say the reciprocal emotions of closely related people, seems likely to vary, not only with the example chosen, but with the historian's perceptions.

Historical Demography

The increasing sophistication of historical demography and the development of techniques of household reconstitution has made possible a greater precision in the estimate of population size, household composition, marriage and fertility patterns that can provide a firm context in which to consider the family. For example, it has been possible to show that not everyone in early modern England parried but that when they did they usually married late. This late start limited the number of births to any married couple. Child marriages were only to be found among the aristocracy, where marriage was a political as well as a domestic arrangement.

The popular idea that in early modern times households consisted of large extended families has been laid completely to rest (O'Day 1994:4-6). Many households were indeed larger than their modern counterparts but the difference is accounted for by the presence of unrelated people, such as servants and apprentices. O'Day has recently argued that a larger proportion of the population spent at least some of their lives in a large household, but even she does not claim that the larger households were so because they contained more kin or consisted of extended families (1994:13). The size of households varied according to rank or class, since it was largely determined by the amount of resources available to the household head and by the household's need for labor.

Households might be temporarily augmented in size by visitors, some of whom might stay for what we would consider long periods. The widowed matriarch Mary Ferrar had several members of her wider family living in her household, among them her great-nephew; in October 1630 he returned from a visit to his mother, accompanied by his aunt, another of Mary's nieces, who was proposing to stay the whole winter (O'Day 1994:270). Visitors seem mostly to have been relatives; the visits served to maintain relationships among close kin who had been scattered by their marriages and symbolized this closeness. The children of the elite were distributed among the households of their relatives to be brought up or to spend long visits. In emergencies, others might be sent to help out their elders by undertaking the household chores. The large house-holds of the wealthy aristocrats probably also received visitors whose connections with their hosts were political or a matter of business. These movements of people ensured that the household was itself rather fluid in membership, at least among the relatively wealthy.

Finally, it is essential and quite possible in this period, to differentiate between prescriptions for behavior and what actually happened. The further back in time one goes the more difficult this is, but the distinction must be born in mind, so that, for example, codes of law are not taken as descriptions of actual behavior. An important part of the data available to the historian of the early modern family consists of the wealth of contemporary writing on "the family," which was a characteristic concern to moralists of the period. It was seen as a microcosm of the State, the father of the family having the same relation to his dependents as the King to his subjects. As

William Gouge wrote in the early seventeenth century: "A family is…a little commonwealth…a school wherein the first principles and grounds of government and subjection are learned…,"(quoted in Amussen 1988:37). The authority of both king and father was supported by divine authority, although O'Day suggests that there was ambivalence about equating fathers with God (1994:37-8). Other authors have stressed that the similarity was more in the nature of an analogy or a metaphor, not an identity, and have noted that the period also included an effective revolt against monarchical authority. The theory of divine rule was not without its critics.

After the Reformation the churches began to interest themselves in the conduct of conjugal relations and the upbringing of children. Until then, continence had been seen as the most moral state and marriage merely the recourse of those unable to live up to this ideal. Relationships within marriage were little considered by the Church and the upbringing of children seen as merely a matter of containing their sinful nature. It is a matter of debate whether the change in attitudes to the family should be attributed to the Protestant churches, to the growth of humanism or to a current within the whole of Christianity. O'Day points to the absence of similar literature in Catholic France as indicating the role of the Protestant clergy, most of them married, in stimulating discussion of the Christian family (O'Day 1994:55). Be that as it may, a large amount of Christian literature on the subject of domestic life was produced during the early modern period, facilitated by the new technology of printing. In it marriage was represented in a mere positive light than hitherto and its role in ensuring the future was put forward as an additional justification for it. In particular, parents were to be responsible for bringing up their children as good Christians.

It is pointed out that this work concerned itself with the relations between spouses and between parents and children;

the family as depicted by the Church was the elementary nuclear family, not the wider circle of relatives (O'Day 1994:37). It is also important to recognize that this literature does not describe what actual relationships were, but what it was then thought, by various moral authorities, such relationships should be. It would be a mistake to consider, as some historians of the period and others seem to have done, that all husbands were stern authoritarian figures, with submissive wives and hardworking, obedient children. As in other societies at other times, there was an ideal which differed from practice. The records show that actual families, at least those who left records, varied in their behavior and the relationships among themselves, according to their circumstances and the characteristics and personalities of their members.

Variation

In fact, variability was a key feature of early modern England. Households varied according to the local economy and to their participation in any specialization that had developed in the locality. Local forms of landholding, inheritance patterns and forms of production for the markets that developed during the period, reflected the nature of the household which was still the main productive unit; the relationships of family members within it were greatly influenced by the division of labor that assigned tasks to them all. Children might be sent out as apprentices or servants as well as foster-children at a relatively early age; this was considered a means of educating them as well as ensuring their support. However, household demands for labor might encourage the sending of one sex rather than another; local craft specializations in one area might offer opportunities for apprenticeships that were absent elsewhere.

A constant and central feature of early modern society was its social hierarchy. Birth placed every individual in a ranked series of classes which affected the nature of its members' domestic life. The aristocracy and gentry were estimated by one authority as consisting of not more than two percent of the population (Houlbrooke 1984:23) and led a life that was partly urban, partly rural. Most other people lived in the country until the end of the period, during which time there was an immense growth in the size of towns. The smaller landholders and those large farmers who were not of gentle birth were labeled yeomen; middling and small farmers were referred to as husbandmen, while the laborers were referred to as such but might also be called cottagers. Rural craftsmen, who varied widely in wealth and status, might also be farmers and landholders. The urban classes consisted of merchants, some of whom equaled the aristocracy in wealth, and below them were the independent craftsmen, journeymen and lesser traders, with urban laborers making up the rest of the population. Houlbrooke considers that even in the early sixteenth century the majority of urban householders were employees and the proportion would have increased over the whole period. The newly established professions: administrators of the Crown and the Church, the legal and medical professions, linked town and country, and its more eminent members were recruited into the gentry. Within this complex hierarchy, there were different household patterns.

One significance of rank is shown by the size of households, which largely depended, as has been pointed out, on the presence of servants. Houlbrooke lists the average household size of the poorest as between three and four people; this low a figure implies the existence of some households of single people. Among those who were not gentry, merchant households were the largest: an average of just under seven and one-half, while the gentry averaged slightly fewer at six and two-thirds (Houlbrooke 1984:24). The households of the gentry were more likely to contain kin other than members of the nuclear family, than those of other classes. However the distinction between kin, especially more distant kin, and servants was not always clear, as kin might take on the role of servants in the households of richer members of their wider family. Presumably the presence of apprentices might have enlarged the households of craftsmen and merchants. The households of the great landed aristocrats were the largest of all, containing large numbers of servants, distant relatives who worked in the household, visitors and dependent children. As Houlbrooke has pointed out, the scale of such a household made for greater formality in relationships; "The more numerous servants were, the wider the range of intimate tasks they performed, the greater the constraints imposed by the need to maintain deference and decorum" (Houlbrooke 1984:25; cf. O'Day 1994:11).

There were two influences through this century that affected all families. The first was a rise in population, that was very rapid in the late sixteenth century but subsequently slowed to remain stable but at a higher level. The increased population put greater pressure on resources, swelled the ranks of the landless and poured into the existing towns. In 1600, five percent of the population lived in London; by 1700 the proportion had doubled to ten percent. Thereafter it was high mortality, particularly of the towns, and lower fertility that kept the population in check. The growth of the towns meant that the sons of landowners need not depend on land for their future, but could be established in a profession and in trade on the profits of the market in agricultural produce.

The demographic changes were accompanied by the second feature of the period: a rapid polarization in wealth. At one end of the scale fortunes were made in the new national market for food and in overseas trade. At the other, there was a great increase in the numbers of the partially employed who were unable to make ends meet, as well as in the numbers of complete paupers. High inflation and poor harvests completed the destruction of many small independent farmers. They, and many tenants, were driven off the land; wages were driven down by the excess of available labor. Private charity ceased to be able to support the needy and the new Poor Laws placed responsibility on the parish to support the indigent out of the rates. However, the parish only had a duty to those registered as settled within its borders; the landless migrants seeking employment were not their responsibility. The parishes were increasingly concerned at the numbers of the indigent they were having to support. In some places parish authorities refused to allow outsiders to settle, that is to marry and establish a household within the parish, even though they were employed, for fear that later their families might prove to be a burden on the rates. The poor were feared as a source of disruption. Amussen records that "the late sixteenth century saw an increase in prosecutions for all forms of disorderliness, including vagrancy, witchcraft and many other crimes, prosecutions directed at those whose behavior disrupted both families and villages" (Amussen 1988:31).

The structure of the household

Most English households were based on nuclear families. Houlbrooke states that, in an analysis of 61 population lists, 70 percent of households were shown to be based on parents and children; under six percent contained three generations and few of these contained more than one married couple, so that the senior generation was presumably represented by a widow or widower. These records covered a period from the late sixteenth century to the early nineteenth. The earliest census so far, that of Coventry in 1523, contained only three among 1,302 households of more than two related generations and only one in which there were kin of any other kind than the nuclear family (Houlbrooke 1984:20).

This state of affairs was brought about not merely by a conventional dislike of related couples sharing a house, although it was considered that a married couple should run their own household, but by demographic and economic constraints. Many children, in all classes, had effectively left home in adolescence or before. A young couple had to amass sufficient funds to start a household and this might entail several years of employment, or waiting for an inheritance. (Of course within a class what was considered "sufficient" varied; members of the aristocracy would consider themselves too poor to marry on incomes that would have seemed more than comfortable to those lower down the social hierarchy.) There were men and women in all classes who never married. For those who did, the age of marriage was effectively delayed for most until the middle or late twenties; often by this time the parents of one or both spouses might be dead. That the delayed age of marriage was largely economic can be seen from the fact of early marriages among the wealthy and in the earlier marriage of eldest sons. Aristocrats had a further positive incentive to arranging early marriages: the need to further political alliances or protect young heirs. Where they were very young, like Anne Fitton who was only twelve when she was married to John Newdegate, aged sixteen, the young couple continued to live with the parents of one of them until considered mature enough to establish their own household. In the case of the young Newdegates, this was not for nine years.

Aristocratic marriages differed from ordinary marriages in another respect: the wife might be very much younger than her husband, especially it he were marrying for the second time. Such age differences tended to reinforce the formal subordination of a woman to her husband. An age-difference between spouses might also be the case among wealthy, non-aristocratic couples but in some cases a young man might marry an older woman, particularly if she were a wealthy widow. For the bulk of the population, however, the pattern was the usual Western European one of marriages between equals in age.

The picture of households consisting of a simple family with (among the more prosperous) their servants and apprentices, has also been altered by taking into account an ever-present fact of the period: death. In all classes early death was not uncommon. The length of an unbroken marriage might be no more than ten or fifteeen years and the biographies of the gentry show men and women often making two or more marriages in their lifetimes. Even among yeomen the pattern was similar: Amussen records the marital career of Beatrice Barker who was married first in 1614 and fifteen years later, in 1629 was contracting her fourth marriage. This was to a man who had been married twice before, once to a widow (1988:74). This example may be unusual for the number of marriages but the authorities agree that death and remarriage was common. One local census in 1688 shows that nearly two in five couples living in the village included at least one spouse who had been married before. One historian states that in sixteenth century England, 30 percent of marriages were with widows (O'Day 1994:117). As a result of such demographic realities, the children in many households included the step-children of one or even both spouses, a situation that has led some historians to talk of the complex or hybrid nuclear family (O'Day, 1994).

Death was not the only means to break the ties of marriage and married people did not always stay living together. The rich couple who did not get on had ample opportunities to visit relatives, often for extended periods, or, when they owned more than one house, to establish a de facto separation. The majority of the population were constrained by circumstances to make the best of their marriages. Annulment could be granted by the church courts but in practice this strategy was available only to the rich. Such "divorces" were rare. At the other end of the socioeconomic scale, women and children were deserted by men unable to support them; a survey of the poor inhabitants of Norwich in 1570 showed eight percent of the married women had been abandoned by their husbands. Occasionally women too ran from their responsibilities, leaving their children.

Households were not static entities but changed over time. Although census data, parish registers and household lists have been the subject of innovative analyses in order to show the actual structure of households and provide insights into the demography of early modern England, they have a major disadvantage. They resemble snapshots, catching a household at one moment in time, but giving little understanding of the dynamic processes that shaped the institutions of household and family. Apart from individuals moving in and out temporarily or permanently, deaths and births altered the composition of the household. The newly-established household of husband and wife, with their servants or servants according to their rank was rapidly augmented by the birth of children. Although fertility was high in the early modern period, the mortality rate for children was also high. The average number of children born per couple was seven (O'Day 1994:10) although only four or five might survive. In the early part of the early modern period, Ralph Verney and his wife produced six children of whom only two survived (Slater 1988). At the end of it, in the seventeenth century, Ralph Josselin and his wife had ten children: two died in infancy and one age eight; a daughter, Anne, died aged 19, shortly after the death of the eldest son, Thomas, who had still been unmarried at nearly thirty (Macfarlane 1970:82). There were thus only five who survived to marry and have children. Many of the children who survived babyhood left the parental home, some as early as age eight. Children might be sent to live with grandparents when quite young and then at a later age, to live in another household as servants, for their education or they went to boarding school (Slater 1988:41). When widows or widowers with young children married again, their children were often sent to live with grandparents or other relatives, at least to begin with. The comments of contemporaries and the evidence of wills and records of litigation show that step-relations were considered to be difficult and actual relations among step-kin often lived up to expectations in this respect.

The numbers of children to be found in any household varied according to a number of factors, of which the fertility of the parental couple and their wealth was only one. One factor concerned the labor of children; they might be more or less useful to their parents according to the economic activities which supported the households. (O'Day 1988:22) Farmers, for example, not only kept their sons at home but might take in the sons of others as extra labor. The gentry, whose capacity to support their children was the greatest, might actually have very few of them living with them. Babies were handed over to wetnurses, many of them living in the nurses' own (poorer and probably less healthy) households; it was even said that it was better for their mothers not to see them until it was certain they would live (O'Day 1994:165). Wetnursing was one of the factors that seems to have resulted in a higher infant mortality among the aristocracy and gentry.

As has been mentioned more than once, the size of households varied with the number of servants they contained. Many of these would now be considered children: they were in early adolescence or even younger, and were often girls, for whom a period of service was considered a form of education. The apprentices in a household were boys; they were also there to learn craft or other skills to earn their future livings or to undertake the farming work that was considered would fit them for farming the land they might inherit. This period in service was considered particularly beneficial if it took place in a household that was wealthier or higher in social standing than that of the child's parents. If the system is considered as a whole, it can be seen as one which drew the labor of children out of their parental households to fulfil the labor needs of those, particularly the wealthier, who were prepared to pay their support costs. For very poor parents it deprived them of the labor of the children but might be the only way of ensuring adequate food and clothing for them. For the same reasons, stated an observer in 1601, poor children in towns might start work at the age of six or seven (Wilson, cited in Houlbrooke 1984:154). The English practice of sending their children away from home was commented on unfavorably by visitors from other countries. In 1500 an Italian observed: "The want of affection in the English is strongly manifested towards their children; for after having kept them at home till they arrive at the age of seven to nine years at the most, they put them out, both males and females, to hard service in the houses of other people, binding them generally for another seven to nine years. And these are called apprentices and during that time they perform all the most menial offices; and few are born who are exempted from this fate, for every one, however rich he may be, sends away his children into the houses of others, while he, in return, receives those of strangers into his house. And on inquiring their reason for this severity, they answered that they did it in order that their children might learn better manners. But I, for my part, believe that they do it because they like to enjoy all their comforts themselves, and that they are better served by strangers than they would be by their own children... That if the English sent their children away from home to learn virtue and good manners, and took then back again when their apprenticeship was over, they might, perhaps, be excused; but they never return, for the girls are settled by their patrons, and the boys make the best marriages they can" (Sneyd C.A., trans., cited in Macfarlane 1970:206). Same historians seem to have accepted this interpretation as an accurate account, but accounts from slightly later suggest that children were not always sent far away, might return to their parents for holidays and were sent home to be nursed when ill. Although modern theories of child development indicate that children treated like this would have suffered in their emotional development, it is going too far to refer to it as wholesale abuse of children. It may have been misguided but it seems to have been well-intentioned.

While all deaths affected the household to some degree, the death of the household head at any level above the very poorest caused a major reorganization of property and people, because the household depended on his particular combination of these that would now be redistributed. Although the household might continue in truncated form, the family relations within it suffered a major upheaval, because of the dispersal of property rights that followed. Among the poor the death of a major bread-winner was a catastrophe, reducing the surviving members of the household to complete indigence.

The characteristic feature of the English system of customary inheritance was primogeniture and this, of course, colored family relationships. However this referred to land rights and titles. In all but a few areas, where the system of partible inheritance known as gavelkind or borough English prevailed, the eldest son inherited any rights to land. Kent was the best-known of the exceptions but there were other small areas where partible inheritance was the custom (Amussen 1988:87). However, men and women in all areas were free to make wills disposing of property and these wills displayed a common concern for children other than the heir. Girls were given dowries and younger sons might be given money or set up in a profession or trade. Often the heir was burdened for several years with the payments to be made to his siblings out of the estate he had inherited. The mother's own property might be destined for younger sons, who might then have to wait longer for a share of the parental property. The detail of wills shows great concern for the equitable use of property to ensure the future welfare of all children. The obligation to carry out these dispositions fell to the heir, whose position vis-a-vis his siblings carried the authority of his position. However, many of these dispositions also made it clear that the interests of siblings were in competition with one another and the heir's control of the family assets gave his position a power which set him above the others. The Verney papers show the strains this might put on the relationships of a large group of siblings depending on an heir who clearly considered his property insufficient to meet their constant demands (Slater 1988). While the case of the Verneys may be extreme, property dispositions clearly affected relationships among siblings, giving the eldest brother a power and authority he does not have today.

Affective Relationships

A recent survey of the English family over four hundred years has argued that little attention has been paid by historians to the quality of family relationships as opposed to the demographic structure of households, the effects of property holding and the prescriptions to be found in the literature on the family (O'Day 1994). This approach would seem to assume, even if implicitly, that the "family" consists of sentiments. This seems a rather anachronistic view, one that risks interpreting the inhabitants of early modern households through the eyes of the late twentieth century. What people feel about each other is not more "real" than the facts of law and property. Relationships are built up out of rights and duties, material considerations are as intrinsic to them as the effect of birth order and parental preferences.

It is very difficult for historians to discover what people in general felt for members of their families; the diaries and letters in which such feelings may be expressed belong, as has been noted, to a small minority of the population, whose lives were hedged by different constraints from the rest. Houlbrooke has pointed out that it seems likely that the presence of servants, especially in large numbers, might have contributed to a greater formality of behavior between members of a wealthy or aristocratic family. However he also expresses doubt that much changed during the period, remarking that "the vastly increased quantity and quality of sources available from the sixteenth century onwards has led some to suppose that this period saw a revolution of sentiments and attitudes" (1984:254) and goes on to indicate that there is not enough data to decide this question.

The opinions of historians on the meaning of behavior may differ quite radically. Considering parents and children, O'Day takes the careful and detailed dispositions made in wills as evidence of concern for widow and children (O'Day 1994: 121, 123). By contrast Slater, considering the Verneys, states: "...Sir Ralph and Lady Verney's incessant concern with their children's training and socialization reminds us of the need to differentiate between devotion to one's children spurred by notions of duty and those feelings of parental affection which are the result of a perceptions of the child as a unique and irreplaceable human being"(1988:41). At this distance in time it is hard to tell who is right.

There has been particular debate in the historical literature over the question of the actual relationships between husbands and wives. Marriages in this period were not generally thought to be a matter for individual choice of partner, even though the Church insisted that a marriage must depend on the free consent of bride and groom (but see McFarlane 1986 for a contrary view). Most parents expected to arrange their children's marriages. The children of those who held land in knight service had least ability to influence their choice of partner; they were royal wards and the right to arrange the marriages of these wards was a prerogative of the guardian, the king. By the beginning of the early modern period the rights to the marriages of wards might be bought and sold, increasingly disposed of to relatives of the ward. (Formerly a knight's widow might equally have been disposed of in marriage by her late husband's lord, but by the sixteenth century this had lapsed.) For those who were not wards, freedom of choice depended on the rank and status of the individual as well as a variety of other circumstances, such as age and whether his/her parents were alive. Men seem to have had more freedom to choose than women and might even repudiate a marriage that had been made. Thus Walter Bagot married his ward Humphrey Okeover to his daughter when both were very young, but Humphrey repudiated the marriage when he reached the age of consent, that is, fourteen (O'Day, 1994:79). But not all marriages were arranged. The seventeenth century clergyman Ralph Josselin appears to have fallen in love with his wife at first sight and refused an uncle's offer of a living elsewhere in order to stay where he could continue his courtship of her. Macfarlane describes their long marriage as a "relationship that remained important and close." They shared decisions and responsibilities and discussed their problems together.

Even where there had been little acquaintance between the couples before their marriage, the relationships between husbands and wives were not always lacking in affection, just as the "love-matches" of the twentieth century do not necessarily ensure a happy marriage. Although formally a man was in a position of authority over his wife and was permitted to punish her if she disobeyed, there is much evidence that actual relationships were not as harsh as this might seem to suggest. The evidence from court cases may show relationships at their worst rather than displaying the normal range of relationships. While wife beating was not an offense in law, the customary norms of small communities, that were mostly quite close-knit and prone to gossip, put pressure on both spouses to keep discord from breaking out. The husband who beat his wife might be subject to village discipline. A wife might call on her relatives for help, even taking refuge with them when marital discord became unbearable; if these relatives were powerful and good relations with them important to her husband, it might do much to improve her position.

The authority of the husband/father was formally very great and he held legal responsibility for his wife and their children, although he was not liable to answer for their crimes. As head of household he held a similar position relative to the servants, for whom he was responsible. This did not, however, mean that servants were indistinguishable from members of the family. Children of "the family" had a higher status than the servants, even though these latter might have a good deal to do with their upbringing. Where servants were distantly related to the head of the family they might have a higher status but Ralph Josselin recorded in his diary that he must treat his sister, who was coming to them as a servant, as a sister and not a servant, implying some possibility of her position as servant eclipsing her sisterly role. While the Church viewed the head of the family as its priest, able to bestow God's blessing on his wife and their children, he was not necessarily treated with great awe on that account, even though his blessing might be asked. The custom of asking a formal blessing itself lapsed quite early in the early modern period. The control of property gave a father a power that in modern times, where individuals earn their own living, would be hard to credit, and a threat to disinherit could be used to discipline a disobedient child. However, there is at least one example of a case where this did not have any effect and in the event Ralph Josselin did not disinherit his son John, despite his faults and filial disrespect (Macfarlane 1970: 123).

Children were perceived as a form of continued existence after death and. more practically, as a possible support in old age. For those who were heirs to a famous name or great property, the duty to continue the line by begetting an heir was clear and failure culpable. For this reason children were welcomed, although there are hints that attempts to prevent conception or at least to space births were made by women. Nevertheless the high rate of infant mortality meant that many children did not survive to maturity and few parents would not have had to bury a child, mostly in the first year or so of its life. Houlbrooke records that "more than a fifth of all the children born under Elizabeth I, about a quarter of those born under the Stuarts probably died before reaching their tenth birthday" (1984). Of these, well over a half died in their first year and half of those in the first month. It has been argued that the high rate of infant mortality was evidence of parental neglect and lack of feeling. It is true that parental love, like conjugal love, was believed to grow with time so that the loss of a tiny baby was considered less grievous than the death of an older child but the evidence does not show such indifference to children that they might die of neglect. Wetnursing has been identified as a cause of infant mortality; the fact that the rate was much higher among the aristocracy, few of whom suckled their own babies, is some indication of this (Houlbrooke 1984:133). Yet it would be wrong to see the existence of wetnursing as indicating lack of parental care, or the resignation of parents to their children's deaths as showing indifference. It should be remembered that most parents firmly believed that their dead children were in Paradise.

Maternal love was expected to be stronger than paternal affection and some mothers appear to have interceded for their erring children with stern fathers. There is, however, the evidence of letters to show that many fathers were deeply fond of their children. Parental love was also thought to be stronger than the reciprocal love felt by children for their parents. (Modern readers might feel that this was a direct result of sending children away so young). Parents were warned, in printed works and by folk-stories not to trust to their children's care in old age and give over control of all their assets but to retain these in their own hands to ensure good treatment (Houlbrooke 1984:190). In fact, elderly widows or widowers might also have children or grandchildren living with them but only a minority lived with a married child as a dependent. Most of the elderly were householders and very few of them lived on their own (Houlbrooke 1984:208-9).

A rather pessimistic view of children's natures as inherently sinful underlay the strong emphasis on discipline and punishment which was to be found in many child-rearing manuals. "Spare the rod and spoil the child" was a maxim frequently reiterated to parents, just because it was thought likely that they might neglect this duty. For this reason, parents in the early modern period might consider it better to entrust the upbringing of their children to others who would not spoil them, as parents were thought very likely to do out of their natural affection. However, a more humanist and gentler view of how to bring up children was derived from the classics and this humanist view began to be more widespread, particularly among the educated. However, in all periods comments on the way in which parents departed from the written precepts showed that the literature of childcare is not to be relied on as a description of how parents actually behaved to their children. The relations between brothers and sisters form a relatively neglected subject, being passed over in most accounts. Moreover, it is only when siblings are adult men and women that there seems to be any information on their relationships. They appear to have often been separated when young and there is no discussion by historians of their relationships during childhood perhaps because parents were not sufficiently interested to record the information. The eldest son, when he inherited his father's property, seems also to have inherited his authority and his responsibilities; he may appear more paternal than fraternal in his relations with brothers and sisters. Among the gentry, children, particularly boys, were often sent away from home to learn manners and social deportment in another household, or in boarding school. This separated the older ones from each other and from their younger siblings who were still at home. Among those who were not gentry, girls and boys started working at an early age and even if they were still at home, they were given separate tasks to do. This might involve the older ones, particularly the girls, looking after their younger brothers and sisters. Whether this cemented relations between particular children may not be known, but it is not mentioned as a cause of close relations between particular adult siblings.

However, it is the links between siblings, ties with their children and with the siblings of parents that constitute the wider network of relations that can also be referred to as "family." Adult siblings seem to have maintained relationships, even if their motivation for doing so seems on occasions to be self-interested. Where the parents of a couple survived, then close relations were maintained between them and their parents. The evidence of the literate suggests that ties between mothers and daughters remained particularly close, although distance might prevent the less wealthy from regular visits. These "family" ties link households with one another in a series of different exchanges: of gifts, of visits, of children, of favors and even of money.

Brothers and sisters were clearly expected to help one another and even more distant kin would appeal to blood ties when asking for help. Sometimes the help might come in guises that would seem strange today: Ralph Josselin took his sister into his household as a servant. This arrangement obviously supported her but it lasted only eight months until she took a similar position with her brother's patrons, the Harlakendens (Macfarlane 1970:129).

While uncles, aunts and cousins are mentioned, ties with them are clearly weaker and depend on circumstances for their importance. The names of cousins' children may be forgotten, though doubtless when necessary even more distant connections could be, and were, revived. However, compared with many modern societies studied by anthropologists, the range of kinship ties recognized by people in early modern England is narrow. It seems to be restricted to the (adult) descendants of a common grandfather. In addition to its unusual custom of partible inheritance Kent had the reputation of recognizing a wide range of relatives, so that the term a "Kentish cousin" meant a distant relative. At the beginning of the period, on the Scottish border, men with the same surname banded together for defense against the incursions of the Scots and prosecuted feuds. The "surnames" had headmen who pledged good behavior to local officers of the Crown, ensuring royal toleration (Houlbrooke 1984:50-1). They endured for some time after the Union of Scotland and England but under changed political and economic conditions presumably the organization lapsed. Nowhere else in England is there any recognition of an organized group based on kinship that is wider in scope than the nuclear family, despite the recognition of a network of wider ties linking these families to one another.

Conclusions

To some extent historians have drawn different conclusions about the similarities and dissimilarities between the early modern family and that of the late twentieth century, according to whether they focused on residential patterns, inheritance or on personal relationships (O'Day 1994: xvii). The former have shown that the core of the household from the sixteenth and seventeenth centuries onward has been the nuclear family; the popular idea that in the past people lived in large households of extended families, in which the young and old were cared for by their kin, is a myth. A high proportion of all households contained resident servants, including in a few cases more or less distant relatives who acted as upper servants; they also might include apprentices and foster-children. The few households containing more distant kin than the nuclear family on a permanent basis, and not merely as visitors, were exceptions rather than the norm and occurred among the wealthier members of society. So in that sense "the family" has not changed: the household is still mostly based on a co-resident nuclear family.

The discovery that simple or nuclear family households were quite common in early modern England nullified the hypothesis that these had been the result of industrialization. Since it could be shown that this type of household preceded the Agricultural and Industrial Revolutions, it cannot be that the nuclear family form was their product. Yet it has been a revolution in work that has changed the nature of domestic life. The most striking difference between the households of early modern times and those of today is the absence of servants. While some domestic work is still performed by people employed for the purpose, it is now very rare to find domestic staff living in the household where they work. The whole range of tasks that are necessary to service the reduced modern household is now the responsibility of one woman, the housewife, a term which no longer means the senior woman of a household but the only one. In early modern England only the poor had no servants. The children of the better-off were also doing the tasks that servants did, but not for their parents; they were servants and apprentices in other households, until such time as they might establish a household of their own. Being a servant was often merely a stage in life, few servants were servants all their lives, although women might revert to being servants when widowed. This characteristic of young servants led Laslett and others to refer to them as life-cycle servants. Their status as legal minors gave them a similar status vis-a-vis the household head as the children of the household.

Children attended local primary schools in early modern England; they were also sent away to school. The richer their parents the longer they might spend being educated. Today, by contrast it is legally required that all children go to school and do not leave until the age of sixteen. Children are not considered the source of wage-labor, although the fact that they do undertake it is recognized in the regulation of their hours and conditions. The concept of childhood has changed. Children are not now considered a source of labor in the family enterprise, or as insurance for old age; they are seen as having value in themselves. The elements in the parent-child relationship that derived from participating in a common enterprise have largely disappeared and the affective element is now perceived as the sole content of the relationship. Since very few children today can anticipate living off an inheritance, they no longer depend on their parents for their future living and for the financial basis of marriage. They are independent of their parents in a way that in the sixteenth or seventeenth centuries was probably only found among the very poor.

The concern among historians (see O'Day 1994) to discover the affective relationships of members of the early modern family reflects another change. The modern family is characterized by "personal" relationships that are contrasted with the impersonal relationships of the contractual world of work. The former are expected to show a striving for harmony and emotional satisfaction; the latter are thought to manifest behavior which is self-serving and competitive. Indeed to many the feelings generated in families, what others would call the content of family relations, *are* family relationships. To some historians, such emotions are the result of the historical changes; to others they have always existed but it is only recently that the evidence for them has been sought out.

The problem of identifying any changes in the forms and nature of the English family from the early modern to the modern period results from an oversimplification of an historical process. It is clear that one cannot talk about "the" family; there were a variety of household forms that affected family relationships and these can only be understood by considering the relationship between domestic organization and other social institutions. Industrialization drew the majority of the population into wage-labor so that the connection between the household and the wider economy became the one familiar to us: the child bearing and rearing group, supported by the wage-labor of the father/head of the household, supplemented where necessary with that of his wife. However. as Harris rightly points out:

> It is absurd to attempt to understand the changing nature of a human group in terms solely of its place in the mode of production, or solely in terms of the structure of relations within it and between it and other groups or solely in terms of the cultural meanings generated by and attached to it. It is only by grasping the interplay of these different aspects of its being, that full comprehension can be achieved (1983:135).

Note

Harris (1983) points out that the dependent status of servants made it easy to assimilate the domestic group to the idea of a family, but this is only so if one assumes that there was an original separation between the two ideas (cf. Houlbrooke).

Bibliography of References Cited

Amussen, S.D., *An Ordered Society; Gender and Class in Early Modern England*. Oxford: Basil Blackwell, 1988.

Goody, J.,Thirsk, J., *Family and Inheritance; Rural Society in Western Europe 1200-1800*. Cambridge: Cambridge University Press, 1976.

Harris, C.C. and Thompson, E.P., "The Family and Industrial Society," *Studies in Sociology*, no. 13, London: George Allen and Unwin, 1983.

Houlbrooke, R.A., *The English Family 1450-1700*. Harlow Longman, 1984.

Macfarlane, A., *The Family Life of Ralph Josselin: A Seventeenth Century Clergyman; An essay in historical anthropology*. Cambridge: Cambridge University Press, 1970.

Macfarlane, A., *The Originss of English Individualism*. Oxford: Blackwell, 1978.

Macfarlane, A. *Marriage and Love in England*. Cambridge: Cambridge University Press, 1986.

O'Day, R. *The Family and Family Relationships 1500-1900: England, France and the United States of America*. London: Macmillan, 1994.

Slater, M., *Family Life in the Seventeenth Century; The Verneys of Claydon House*. London: Routledge, Kegan Paul, 1984.

Tucker M.J., "The Child as Beginning and End: Fifteenth and Sixteenth Century English Childhood" in L. de Mause, ed., *The History of Childhood*. New York: Peter Bedrick, 1988.

Chapter 5

THE FAMILY IN MODERN SOCIETY: FROM THE TYRANNY OF RULES TO THE WHIM OF RELATIONSHIPS

Jon Davies

"Ages" or "eras" are problematic concepts with fuzzy edges. Nevertheless, by identifying a set of practices that occur in this or that period in human history, archaeologists and historians have been able to specify clear time boundaries for periods like the Stone Age or the Iron Age. We live in what is called the Modern Age.

Typically, for a society to enter the modern era it must accept the mien of big cities, an industrial means of production, the rule of law, an intricate system of money and trade, a techno-scientific basis for education, and so forth—but along with these insignia of modernity comes the most important organization: the nuclear family. In the modern era, the extended family moves off center stage, as the process of social differentiation leaves the "nuclear" couple with specific and important nurturing tasks to perform, all other functions being taken over by the specialized institutions of civil society, state, or marketplace.

Over the years this version of family life has inspired an extraordinary amount of literature. To highlight what seems to be the distinctive style or features of the modern family in our age, we shall rely mainly on two books—David Riesman's *The Lonely Crowd* and Talcott Parsons' *Family Socialization and Interaction Process*, both written in the 1950s. It may be said that the modern family is like Janus— the Roman God of gates and doorways, which open both inward and outward, backward and forward—with one face looking toward the past, the other facing the terrifying possibilities of an uncertain future.

Two Models of the Modern Family

Parsons' book presents an intricate picture of the nuclear family in American society in the late fifties. He points out that "the nuclear family is never...an independent society, but a small and highly differentiated sub-system of a society."[1] It was, he felt, precisely this interdependence that made it likely that both the nuclear family and the larger society would remain relatively stable.[2] Such worrisome things like divorce were a temporary problem characteristic of childless couples: "Once people settle down to having children together there is a relatively high probability that they will stay together."[3]

At the time he wrote, the proportion of the population married and living with their spouses was the highest the census had ever recorded. New home-building programs seemed to overwhelmingly indicate the primacy of the single nuclear family residence. Parsons anticipated little change in the respective roles of women—"wife, mother and manager of the household"—and men, who were "primarily anchored in the occupational world."[4] In his most succinct description of the relationship between modern society and the family, he stated that

> it is because the human personality is not "born" but must be "made" that in the first instance families are necessary.... The basic and irreducible functions of the family are two: first, the primary socialization of children so that they can truly become members of the society into which they have been born; second, the stabilization of the adult personalities of the population.[5]

The key word is irreducible. Notwithstanding the functions lost by the extended family—defense, education, economic production, political power—the functions of civil society, marketplace, or state would never eclipse the parenting function. The two most important tasks of the family were systemically related— that is, that children can be socialized only in the company of, and under the direct care of, their parents, and that these parents themselves mature only in the nurturing of their children. For these reasons, Parsons felt the nuclear family would remain fairly immune to the caustic forces of modernity. Such an irreducible family, he noted, was small—small in the number of relationships operative within it, small in terms of the number of children within it, and small in terms of the number of adults interactively operational within it.[6] Like many scholars in our day, Parsons commented on and analyzed the way in which modern, or would-be modern, societies reduce the size of their domestic units over time. He observed that the nuclear family was a consciously self-liquidating institution that ended in its own intentional dissolution. Younger members are expected to leave home, having learned, both within it and as a consequence of its liquidation, the intricate mixture of collective altruism and individualized self-regard necessary for life in modern society.

It was from this axiom of the relatively unproblematic institutional stability of the small nuclear family that Parsons, the leading American sociologist of his day, approached the complex internal dynamics of modern family life. In *The Social System*, he attempted to articulate the "web of rules" within which the nuclear family operated. Parents are clearly super-ordinate to children, with husband and wife having complementary roles in a functioning family system. In the mid-fifties, the nuclear family was still firmly welded together.

Inner- versus Other-directed Persons

Six years earlier David Riesman had perceived the modern world, and its future, very differently. In what is an early version of "the end of history" thesis, Riesman argued in *The Lonely Crowd* that America, and to a lesser extent the other Western democracies, was triumphant in spreading capitalism over the entire globe because it was rooted in the Protestant work ethic, which stimulated the notion of individual achievement.[7] He commented on the "decisive importance" of the family in shaping America. The nuclear family, he said, "makes possible the bringing up of children with very intense identifications with parental models."[8] His thesis is that the dominance of the inner-directed type of American who founded the country is waning and that a new type of American, the other-directed, is emerging as the character figure of modern American culture.

By inner-directed person Riesman meant someone who early in life, under the guidance of parents and other socializing figures, develops goals and rules that direct him throughout life. The other-directed person describes one whose goals and rules are directed by and toward his peers and contemporaries, all new and endlessly renewed.

Riesman used the gyroscope and radar as metaphors to clarify the two styles. The inner-directed person possesses a psychic gyroscope that provides the balance and stability derived from the inner voices of parents and parent-like authorities. These voices provide a code of conduct that is singularly directive. The other-directed person, by contrast, is radar-like: He takes signals from and responds to a much wider circle of people—for example, personal friends or idealized figures in TV, sports, and Hollywood—who provide varied directions throughout his life. Guilt is the curse of the inner-directed, anxiety that of the other-directed. While the inner-directed person is rooted in the notion of the rugged individual who pioneered and built the country, the other-directed person is oriented toward the new American society composed of large government and business bureaucracies.

Riesman depicted a changing America in which a "characterological struggle" exists between these two types of social character. He felt that the inner-directed type would soon disappear from the American social landscape, to be replaced by the other-directed person. Inner-directed people were seen as hard, closed-minded types, with "definiteness of set and convictions."[9] Other-directed people were viewed as more open to change, tolerant, and sensitive to others.[10]

> The other-directed person wants to be loved rather than esteemed; he wants not to gull or impress, let alone oppress, others but, in the current phrase, to relate to them; he seeks less a snobbish status in the eyes of others than an assurance of being emotionally in tune with them. He lives in a glass house, not behind lace or velvet curtains. The problem for people in America today is other people.[11]

Riesman, perhaps realizing that the other-directed person might be lacking in popular appeal, looked forward to a third stage in which a truly "autonomous" person would bring about

> the liberation of men from the realm of characterological necessity. The power of individuals to shape their own character by their selection among models and experiences was suggested by our concept of autonomy...when this occurs, men may limit the provinciality of being born to a particular family in a particular place. To some this offers a prospect only of rootless men and galloping anomie. To more hopeful prophets, ties based on conscious relatedness may someday replace those of blood and soil.[12]

Like many writers of this optimistic era, Riesman assumed that the problem of wealth-creation would be solved, and, more amazingly, that human beings, once freed from the restraints of tradition, would act benignly. Clearly, the question of the family, and its nexus of sexual and intergenerational relationships, plays a central role in Riesman's analysis of modernity. The tacit assumption of the Parsonian model—that the nuclear family would, and should, retain a near monopoly of sexual and procreational activity—disappears in Riesman's model.

In a subchapter titled "Sex—the last frontier," Riesman predicts the sexual revolution of the sixties. Sex, he says, in the emerging other-directed person is not like politics. Politics can be simply avoided, but sex cannot.

> Though there is tremendous anxiety about how the game of sex should be played, there is little doubt as to whether it should be played or not. Even when we are consciously bored with sex, we must still obey its drive. Sex, therefore, provides a kind of defense against the threat of total apathy This is one of the reasons why so much excitement is channeled into sex by the other-directed person. He looks to it for reassurance that he is alive.[13]

Women will become, like men, "pioneers on the frontiers of sex,"[14] using it as a means of upward mobility in a male-dominated world. In this adult-consumer world, where everyone is a pioneer and marriage is no longer part of one's sense of self, society becomes a series of what Riesman describes as "adult self-exploiting peer-groups."[15]

This phrase occurs when Riesman describes the sun-tanning or sunbathing activities of other-directed Americans:

> In summer and even winter both men and women enter a beauty contest in which they can appraise their personalities and compare nuances in shade and hue of epiderm. Their taste buds, their taste, body image and skin, their "pep," "vitality," and intellectual and sensuous qualities are not exploited as avenues of ascent in a well-defined hierarchy. Instead, they are opened to inspection and introspection by

a desire to share in the leisure agenda of *the adult self-exploiting peer-group*[16] (my emphasis).

It is hard nowadays, looking at the human wasteland left from the social and sexual revolutions of the recent past, to understand why Riesman was, in the mid-fifties, so sanguine.

In the preface of the 1964 edition of *The Lonely Crowd*, Riesman expresses surprise about the public's hostile reaction to his book, mostly aimed at his rosy picture of the rise of the other-directed person. He seems to have realized that these psycho-social changes he predicted would bring with them "the dissolution of all distinctive practices, cultures and beliefs" of the existing world.[17] Yet he approved of the historical process, if only because the nonliterate cultures have indicated their preferences "to join the Big Parade—often meeting the more disenchanted Westerners going the other way."[18]

Along with other "deconstructions" of the sexual/procreational monopoly of the nuclear family, Riesman notes, parental authority will decline as the child's experience of his parents' incompetence increases. In another subchapter, "From bringing up children to bringing up father," Riesman foresees

an index of the new demands for sociability and leisure freedom of sensitive middle class couples [that] include the dynamic that each partner to a marriage expects the other to grow and develop at approximately the same rate as himself.... Any effort by the neotraditionalists to close the sex frontiers while it may restore the glamour sin had in the earlier era, would be irrelevant to the problems created by the greater demands a leisure-oriented people put upon their choice in companionship, sexual or otherwise.[19]

According to Riesman, children should become consumers in their own right. In the subchapter "Freeing the child market,"[20] he speculates on a "world's fair for children." Advertisers, who are seen as an extension of the educational system, would create a special currency "in a fund for experimental creation of model consumer economies among children."[21] Such a show-economy would expose children to "a variety of luxury goods ranging from rare food to musical instruments, thereby enabling us to see how children as consumers behave when they are free from the taste gradients end "reasons" as well as freedom from the financial hobbles of a given peer-group."[22]

After Woodstock

Be it academic or popular, written or musical, much of the literature of the late fifties reflects an enthusiastic rejection of the sexual and economic restrictions and repressions of hundreds of years of Victorian values. On both sides of the Atlantic, academics, poets, singers, novelists, and others called for *The Death of the Family*, to use the title of a book by David Cooper.[23] By the sixties, the basic values exemplified and expressed in the counterculture reflected a shift or a move away from the received notions of sex and procreation. Men and women no longer sought to follow the old rules pertaining to marriage and family— abandoning the "child-knowing" rules for "adult-regarding experiments."

Riesman—who sometimes sounds like a reporter, sometimes a pied piper—indicates that the modern world began with the collective murmurings of the self-generating, self-validating peer group. In the authenticity-mirroring infinitude of others, one is free to remake himself again and again. One simply rearticulates himself in each "new" interpersonal transaction. The self is fluid—value being found in the "activity" of negotiating and renegotiating one's self-image.

There is perhaps in Riesman's almost whimsical comment about "the Big Parade" a realization that the collapse into the postmodern world would not be problem-free. Certainly Parsons had not been impressed with Riesman's analysis of American society. In a rather laconic footnote, Parsons accepted that there was a cultural clash between the inner-directed and other-directed belief systems. But he felt "the strength of values in our society" would prevent the other-directed pattern from becoming dominant.[24] Parsons was wrong!

Throughout The Lonely Crowd Riesman hints that the nuclear family would be "improved" by these new cultural changes. He thought that in a self-directed value system people might find the fulfillment that the modern world opened up. This has proven illusory.

Today the contemporary family sits Janus like between two worlds: on the one hand facing a male-centered model of the family, perhaps repressive of women and certainly oriented to work and material achievement; on the other, a disassembled and reassembled postmodern world with congeries of sexual and procreational experimentations in human liberation—a world born of Woodstock at once more open and closed.

Riesman's perception of the modern world is closer to reality than is Parsons', although one doubts that the former's zeal for the future would be maintained in the face of so many demonstrable negativities. The question now is, What went wrong? Looking at the extraordinarily rapid decline of the nuclear family and its attendant authoritative buttressing of sexual rules, both liberals and conservatives today are beginning to sense that the modern experiment went too far. Worried neotraditionalists point to an overgenerous welfare state as an explanation for what has happened. In seeking to dismantle it, they speak of the restoration of "traditional family values," whatever that might be. Others see the fate of the nuclear family deriving from the very force—libertarian individualism—that gave rise to the nuclear family in the first place. A more radical explanation finds the problem to lie in Christian theology and its weak underpinning for heterosexual procreation. Since a "forbidden tree" stands between men and women, Christianity has attempted to regulate sex.

Christian and Secular Authorities

It is necessary at this point to go back to the early formations of Western sexual culture to see how we have arrived at
where we are. In pre-Reformation Christendom, premarital,
marital, and procreational relationships were regulated by both
ecclesiastical and secular authorities. Generally, the ecclesiastical
authorities were aware of the secular authorities' interests in sex
and marriage—whether these dynastic interests involved great
estates, nations, or small properties. In these matters, church
and kin usually came to a sensible working arrangement. The
kin would arrange the marriage of choice, and the church
would sanctify the arrangement—partly in response to intrinsic
spiritual reasons, partly to retain some material interest in the
various property settlements that attended marriage, birth, and
death. For common folk, the local priest with his confessional
and penitential powers, working in conjunction with local
courts of various types, set the context within which their
sexual life was consummated.

It should be stressed that this supervision *did not end at
marriage*. The ecclesiastical surveillance ignored what to us are
the private boundaries of married life and sought to control the
practices of the marital bed. Married people were expected to
engage in intercourse to have children, not to obtain sexual
pleasure. Again, there were little *principled* grounds for dispute
between the interests of the church and the interests of the kin.
In a marital-sexual system in which women were exchanged
between various groups of interested men, there was a common interest in the sexual purity of the women—the kin
because illegitimate children could complicate inheritance
patterns and the economic stability of the local community,
and the church because of the value it placed upon virginity.

To a large extent, the Reformation changed all this, not
because the reformers were sexual liberators, but because the
politically pluralistic world that resulted from their various

rebellions produced over many decades an insistence on, and gradual acceptance of, personal liberty. In sexual matters, this came to mean the privatization of sex, whereby "privatization" is meant the effective control of such matters by the male head of the household. The church father was eventually replaced by the father; the notion of kin was supplanted by the male parent. "All men are brothers" came to mean no one man is my brother. "My family" came to mean the family I create. Once "liberty of conscience" and personal "privacy" were introduced, they became integral parts of the "freedom" claimed by "all men." The Liberty Bell, once sounded, sounded for all, and attempts to exclude certain people have proven unsuccessful.

Men First; Women and Children Next

The story of *Robinson Crusoe* and its theological counterpart *Pilgrim's Progress* are mythical journeys of self-lonelied men. The leading figures—shipwrecked and thrown into a dark night of the soul—are outcasts from mother, father, wife, and children. The underlying theme is the conditional nature of domestic affections and the necessity of each man to find himself. The corollary for women is domesticity, the woman who awaits the return of her husband. For male children, the father serves as a role model who carries the obvious implication that the boy must one day leave home to find his way in the world.

In the endless versions of the Oedipus complex, which abounds in Victorian literature, it is clear that domestic structures work best when the sons "make their own way in the world" to become fathers of their own islands. Parsons' book, written in a rather dry, academic style, encapsulates this notion of Western individualism, born out of the child-centered home that expels into the world the children it so lovingly repressed.

Of course, this is the story of, and for, men. All this was soon to change, though. Where the history of the eighteenth and nineteenth centuries is about men claiming their rights, the twentieth century is about the liberation of women. "Votes for women" is an expression of enfranchisement of women in all areas of public and private life once occupied by men.

In domestic terms, this centuries long process—from the regulated sexual life of medieval Catholic ancestors to the family life of nineteenth-century men and women, to the nuclear family life studied by Parsons and waved "good-bye" by Riesman—might look something like this:

Figure A represents the earliest family structure, where the ego is transparent in family life. A man's relationships with his spouse and children are enmeshed within the mutually reinforcing regulatory systems of kin, church, state, and society. In such an arrangement, it would be hard for materialistic individualism to develop, because these systems' efforts are collective, and so too are their rewards. This, of course, is Weber's thesis, as well as Marx/Engels'.[25] But this process is much more complex than they understood. For example, Alan MacFarlane[26] and Peter Laslett[27] found in the case of England a capitalism property structure existing much earlier than previously thought.

Figure B represents the family at the start of the modern adventure, during the post-Reformation period. Increasingly privatized, the nuclear family is becoming free of external institutional constraints. The wife and children are more or less dependent upon the male head of the household. The bonding of the family over and against the rest of the world has as its corollary the restriction of sexual privileges and responsibilities to the husband and wife. When the classical economists talked about "the individual," they meant "the family"—or, more fittingly, "the individual and his family."

130

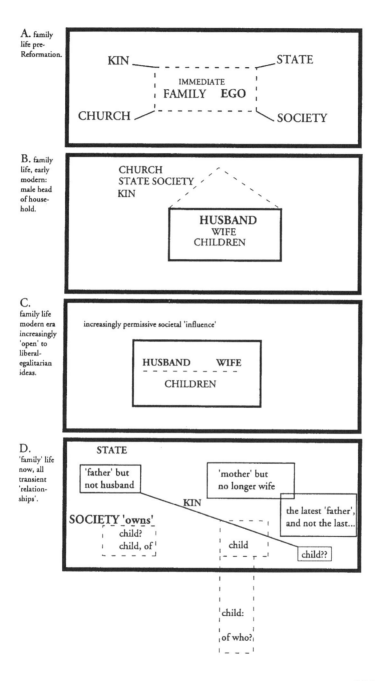

A. family
life pre-
Reformation.

KIN ──── ─ ─ ─ ─ ─ ─ ─ ─ STATE
IMMEDIATE
FAMILY   EGO
CHURCH ── ─ ─ ─ ─ ─ ─ ─ SOCIETY

B. family
life, early
modern:
male head
of house-
hold.

CHURCH
STATE SOCIETY
KIN

HUSBAND
WIFE
CHILDREN

C.
family life
modern era
increasingly
'open' to
liberal-
egalitarian
ideas.

increasingly permissive societal 'influence'

HUSBAND   WIFE
─ ─ ─ ─ ─ ─ ─ ─
CHILDREN

D.
'family' life
now, all
transient
'relation-
ships'.

STATE

'father' but
not husband

'mother' but
no longer wife

KIN

the latest 'father',
and not the last...

SOCIETY 'owns'
child?
child, of

child

child??

child:
of who?

F.A. Hayek, for example, is quite clear about this:

> In the language of the great writers of the eighteenth century, it was man's "self-love," or even his "selfish interests," which they represented as the "universal mover." ...These terms did not, however, mean egotism in the narrow sense of concern only with the immediate needs of one's proper person. The "self," for which alone persons were supposed to care, did as a matter of course include their family and friends.[28]

It is in the family that one learns to care for others, and where self-concern can be pursued without becoming hedonistic But in this household the father-child relationship is complicated. Their home produces the necessary constructive friction and insecurity that solidifies in the sons and daughters the values and experience necessary for the formation of their own nuclear family. As Michael Novak puts it:

> Insofar as democratic capitalism depends for its economic vitality upon deferred gratification, savings and long-term investment, no motive for such behavior is the equivalent of regard for the future welfare of one's own progeny.... This is the motivation that adequately explains herculean economic activities.... Through this regard for family the isolated individual escapes mere self-interest or self-regard.[29]

As any parent knows, concern for one's children in no way precludes the fact that they will someday leave home and create their own families. No other domestic system has been so persistently successful in establishing the basis for economic growth as the family.

In figure C the male-dominated nuclear family is depicted as moving toward a family that is still parent-dominated, but one based on equality, status, and increasingly, occupational competence between men and women. Women are more and more successful in claiming their independence and individualism. The diagram shows that this greater degree of equality and freedom carries with it an amount of "distance" between the spouses. It is worth noting that it is at this stage that Parsons observed a healthy egalitarian maturation of the nuclear family form. The context is set for the fission culture (described in Riesman's *The Lonely Crowd*) now sundering the family life of modern society.

Figure D represents a society where individualism and self-love are dominant. Responsibilities are seen as repressions. Liberty means freedom from the restraints of the family. Oddly, state, kindred, and society, though not church— which is by now a minority interest only—reappear at this stage. There are few distinct boundaries between who is, and who is not, a member of one's "family"—the very term has been stretched to include a variety of relationships well beyond its conventional meaning.

Unlike the eighteenth-century ideologues of individualism (and indeed many of their more socialistically inclined rivals), late-twentieth-century proponents of individualism push "personal liberation ideology." The world is populated by estranged adults who participate in "self-exploiting peer-groups." The language of contract—with its notions of caveat emptor, "arm's length" modes of relationship, calculation of advantage and disadvantage, time-limited and time-expiring transactions, along with litigious sophistries that make rational, if perhaps sordid, sense—rules society. The individual is the "prime mover" in modern society. Whatever public costs or disadvantages to a society that is "self-regarding" will supposedly be offset by the total amount of wealth created. But if one's wealth turns to ashes, freedom to loneliness, happiness to sorrow, and hopes to grief, to whom does it matter anyway? A society based on contractual relations between consenting adults cannot, when the contract fails, suddenly produce the gentle rain of altruism—and for adults perhaps does not have to.

Children are a different matter. By definition, they cannot be parties to a contract. Until recently, their precarious lives were underwritten by being born into a nuclear family where parents were unconditionally required to provide for their welfare. This task was made possible by following a highly institutionalized set of trajectories for men and women. Men became mature by becoming husbands and fathers. Women became mature by becoming wives and mothers. Marriage and parenthood was the maturation rite of the early modern era. The object of the rite, as seen in the 1662 Marriage Service of the Church of England, was the sustenance of children—not all children, or everyone's children, but my children, our children. Other children would not be neglected: They were the particular responsibility of like-minded adults. As the rite has been dismantled in the modern world, the truth of Parsons' comment on the "irreducibility" of the small nuclear family becomes clearer. What is left? A divorced mother "on her own," a never-married mother "on her own," a once-cohabiting man "on his own."

Such a "family" is simply too small an entity to provide sufficient altruism for child rearing. The "extended family" can provide little in the way of alternative support, because the extended family was itself an artifact of the nuclear family. Frenetic invocations of "community" in late modern society elicit scant response from a culture that has lost its sense of duty to the children.

There are three solutions to this problem:

1. **Stop having children**—and in every modern society the birthrate is now well below replacement level.

2. **Nationalize children**—or in the terms of economists, regard them as a public good, equipped perhaps with residual "biological-parental" support but essentially living in a kind of subsidized matriarchy. While exaggerated, this option looks forward to a time—for the United Kingdom predicted to be

2010—when the majority of births take place outside marriage. In effect, this would spell the end of marriage as the central expression of procreational concerns, just as it has already lost its role as the central expression of sexual concerns.

There are problems with this option. Child-rearing practices in a dedicatedly self-regarded society assume there will be enough reservoirs of altruism to pay for the upkeep of other people's children. Public facilities can take many forms, but they will have to be staffed at all levels by professional care-givers to prevent these repositories from becoming mere dumps. Such public child facilities would compete with public old people's facilities for limited resources, each facing a similar level of underprovision.

3. **Grant equal rights for children**—or confer upon children the benefits of full-fledged individualism. Complementary to the second, this option might be cheaper if the costs of the juvenile-criminal-management system are left out of the picture. Just as the twentieth century conferred upon women full individual freedoms, the twenty-first century—whether it is called modern, high modern, or postmodern—might confer fundamental rights on children, something Riesman foresaw and, to some extent, welcomed.

We are already moving into a situation where children are taking their places in Riesman's "world fair for children," as operational consumers and leaders of fashion in their own right. The typical "modern home" has within it highly differentiated private spaces that give children the same degree of autonomy that was once the preserve of adults. In fashion, music, drug, and media markets billions of dollars follow juvenile consumers. Every attitude survey shows that the young are less tolerant of restrictions on their right to consume, and more tolerant of "variety in relationship" and the freedom to experiment. The vast expansion of higher education has created great empires of the young who have left home to enter publicly funded pastoral-care facilities that offer endless opportunities for self-experimentation.

At the root of the debate over public or private systems of pension and health, one finds the older generation confronted with the invitation to provide for itself where it would have provided for the young. The generations are separating into different postures of bland and hardworking solitariness, following the patterns of separation already established between men and women, parents and children. The nuclear family, seen by Parsons as the irreducible expression of the relations between adult men and women, and the relations between the older and younger generations, is being swept aside by "the lonely crowd." The likely result will be a fission world composed of spuriously mature "children"—and, very likely, genuinely infantilized "adults."

Notes

[1]Talcott Parsons, Family: Socialization and Interaction Process (London: Routledge, Kegan Paul, 1968 edition), 35.

[2]Ibid., 9.

[3]Ibid., 4.

[4]Ibid., 14-15.

[5]Ibid., 16.

[6]Ibid., vii.

[7]David Riesman, The Lonely Crowd (New Haven, Connecticut.: Yale University Press, 1964) p. xx, iv.

[8]Ibid., xxv

[9]Ibid., xxv.

[10]Ibid., xvii.

[11]Ibid., xix-xx.

[12]Ibid., xlvii.

[13]Ibid., 154.

[14]Ibid., 156.

[15]Ibid., 157.

[16]Ibid., 157.

[17]Ibid., xxvii.

[18]Ibid., xxvii.

[19]Ibid., 331-32.

[20]Ibid., 338-341.

[21]Ibid., 339.

[22]Ibid., 340.

[23]D. Cooper, *The Death of the Family* (London: Penguin Press, 1971).

[24]Parsons, op. cit., 90.

[25]See Max Weber (1987)and F. Engels(1884).

[26]A. MacFarlane, *The Origins of English Individualism* (Oxford: Blackwell, 1978).

[27]P. Laslett, *The World We Have Lost* (London: Methuen, 1983).

[28]F.A. von Hayek, *Individualism and Economic Order* (London: Routledge Kegan Paul, 1949), 13.

[29]M. Novak, *The Spirit of Democratic Capitalism* (London: Institute of Economic Affairs, 1991), 163.

Part Two

Family Transition in
the World's Cultures

Chapter 6

MODERN CRISES AND THE RENEGOTIATION OF AFRICAN FAMILIAL RELATIONS

Gwendolyn Mikell

Introduction

In many different parts of the African continent today, relationships within the family are in flux, primarily in response to changing economic and political circumstances and the crises which have resulted. Thirty-five years ago, during the African independence decade, there was an expectation that modernization and advances in education, health, and social services would help to stabilize or diminish family size, and strengthen the roles and contributions of both parents. However, the expected transformations of African families from traditional to modern forms did not occur (Kayongo-Male and Onyango 1984). Many would argue that the "urban explosion," neo-colonial dependency, fluctuations in the global economy, national economic collapse and structural adjustment as well as the impact of political instability and military coups have taken their tolls on the African family.[1] Despite whether we talk about areas with large matrilineal structures (as in Ghana), areas with largely patrilineal as well as Islamic traditions (as in Nigeria or Kenya), or areas which had ambiguous/patrilineal systems resulting from the colonial/apartheid and traditional rapproachment (as in South Africa), some troublesome commonalities in family relations are emerging.

It has become evident that both men and women have been forced to rework many of their traditional familial relationships, albeit in differing ways. They are removing traditional family practices that are now out of sync with modern realities, although they often seek to retain the essence of important cultural norms and relationships. Three trends are evident among families across the Continent: 1) people are accepting a smaller size and breadth in the family, giving rise to a shrinking field of relatives to whom they have obligations; 2) there is change in gender roles and household form, resulting from diverging socioeconomic possibilities for men and women, and the emergence of the single parent household; and 3) there is a retention of the ideology and language of familism, although actual kinship behavior is changing.

Neither African individuals nor their states are rejecting the ideology of familism and lineage identity, although they are struggling to rework the concomitant marital and conjugal relationships, and how they interact with public and national structures. Rather, an intense process of negotiation of familial roles and statuses is initiated as people attempt to reconcile traditional expectations with modern realities. Anthropologists working within familial arenas will note that marital, household, and conjugal responsibilities (Mikell 1994a; Guyer 1981), transgenerational parent-child relationships (Oppong 1992), and inheritance or transmission of property within and between families (Mikell 1992b; Guyer 1987) are the three categories of relationships most affected by contemporary change. Given the phenomenal change in gender roles—often in responses to new modes of economic behavior and socioeconomic crises— some of the most important indices of change may be the new focus by the state as well as individuals on "conjugal" relations, and the heightened tensions about whether and how resources and property should be transmitted between husband, wife, and children.

Traditional Family Relationships

We must consider the traditional bases from which contemporary kinship negotiation proceeds. Although there is considerable variation in African traditional family structures and relationships (Radcliffe-Brown and Forde 1950), I have focused here on the classic patterns in the mid-range of the African family continuum, particularly those that developed in horticultural, complex pastoral, or urban areas of sub-Saharan Africa. Historically, the shape and complexity of the family correlated with the social and economic means that people used to acquire their livelihoods (whether in hunting-gathering bands, pastoral bands, horticultural lineages and clans, or nuclear and extended families within archaic or industrial states). When we look past the simpler band organized societies, we see that unilinear forms of family (patrilineal, matrilineal, and ambilineal) are widely distributed, each with discrete sets of gender roles and responsibilities within the family (see E.P. Skinner, Chapter 1). Caldwell and Caldwell have argued that despite the variation, families are largely shaped by one of two sets or productive relationships—family modes of production, or labor-market production (1992: 47-66). Today, as formerly pastoral and horticultural societies are become more complex, it is clear that preexisting forms of economy, family and social organization are being altered and superseded by the state and market based institutions. Nevertheless, for Africa, consideration must be given to unilinear kin relations since these were the predominant forms of family present in the midrange societies that persisted into the colonial and independence periods.

In traditional African kinship systems, males and females were members of their larger 3-6 generation descent groups, and remained so despite marriage. Primary loyalties to the kin group took precedence over loyalties and roles based on gender. However, dual-sex socialization existed, whereby males were organized in group activities and positions such as age-grades and other sodalities, quite separate from females' organization into such groups. Especially in the unilinear kinship groups, people had specific rights and obligations based on their sex and their age; but the subordination of persons to others of higher authority within the family as well as the predominance of the communal good over individual good, were fundamental principles. Since sociological rather than biological parentage defined lineage membership, adoption and fostering of children by other kin was an acceptable pattern in many African families.[2] Children were desirable because lineage members provided the labor that sustained family subsistence production, and that generated wealth in resources.[3]

Marriage had reproduction as its chief goal, and was the primary means by which a new generation of legitimate members of the descent group was produced. Most often this meant that the group, rather than the individual, exercised major authority in arranging marriages and deciding when and with whom marriages would occur.[4] In patrilineal systems, there frequently was an expectation of the bride's virginity at marriage, which occurred soon after the rituals announcing the girl's maturity although this changed as more girls entered schooling in the twentieth century. Given the strongly pro-natalist emphasis, the failure to marry was anathema, and sterility or barrenness were causes for divorce or polygyny. In patrilineal systems, the exchange of bridewealth from the family of the male to the family of the female, legitimized the marriage and gave the husband and his family control over the sexual and reproductive potential of the wife, while "progeny price" clarified that the offspring belonged to the patrilineage. Except during menstruation or during post-partum taboos on sexual activity, marital partners were expected to be sexually open to each other on a regular basis. However, variations in patrilineal descent existed, especially in decentralized areas or other areas strongly influenced by external factors such as pressures toward migration or Islamic conquest.

Among the Afikpo Ibo of Nigeria, men traced lineage through males, but combined this with matriclan affiliation which was traced through wives (Ottenberg 1969). The extent of control over the wife was often gauged by the amount of resources given by the husband upon marriage, particularly "bridewealth" [see Table I]. Virilocal (or patrilocal) residence was most common in patrilineages, causing women to be removed from their villages of origin. Marriage also entitled the husband to the labor or services of the wife on his subsistence farms, and often to the ownership of property which they jointly generated during the marriage. However, it also obligated the husband or his family to provide food, land for farming, maintenance and basic economic needs of the wife and children, despite any contributions which they themselves made to their own support. The ideal was to produce sons, since sons were the patrilineage heirs and custodians of patrilineal property while daughters married out of the household. Of importance was the exchange of symbolic or monetary bridewealth or progeny price which established the children's identity and right to property of the lineage. Spouses generally do not inherit under traditional systems, whether patrilineal or matrilineal. Therefore, the family as a group benefitted most from inter-lineage monetary transfers (Oppong 1994:74; Dolphyne 1991:28; Oloo & Cone 1966).[5]

Traditional marriage often contained possibilities of polygamy for the husband, but not for the wife; and although each wife bore responsibilities to her own children, the entire group of children of the husband were identified as sisters and brothers. In patrilineal systems, death of the husband need not necessarily have dissolved the union, because many patrilineages often utilized the institution of the levirate (or inheritance of the widow by another patrilineage male), which allowed women to remain with their in-laws and children. Although historical and situational change altered family and marital relations to some extent (sometimes increasing incentives for polygyny, delaying arranged marriage at other times, or allowing greater nucleation for short periods), these changes did not challenge the nature of these kinship systems. The couple, and what we call the nuclear family household, did not become separated out in most lineage contexts. Therefore, the parameters of conjugal life were supervised by the larger kin or residential group, leading to a greater sense of responsibility in the performance of family roles and obligations.

Table 1
MARRIAGE TRANSACTIONS AND KIN GROUPS IN AFRICA

	Type of kin group			
Marriage transactions	Patrilineal	Matrilineal	Double	Bilateral
Bride-wealth	154	22	12	7
Bride-service	10	8	0	1
Dowry	0	0	0	0
Gift exchange	1	0	0	0
Sister exchange	8	0	0	2
Token or absent	3	7	0	3
TOTAL	176	37	12	13

*Source: Goody 1973:50 Table 6, which is also reproduced in
C. Oppong 1992:73.

Many matrilineal societies predate and were transformed into patrilineal ones, although viable matriliny remained (Douglas 1971). But the category of "patrilineal" groups expanded considerably in the eighteenth and nineteenth centuries with the expansion of Islam from the Arabian peninsula across North Africa and Sudanic areas to the West African coast (Skinner and Chu 1965); with the expansion inland of East African coastal Muslim traders in the nineteenth century; and with the labor recruitment of Muslims from India and the Far East to work plantations in southern Africa. The expanding Islamic identity competed with preexisting African cultural identities, but ultimately fused in most areas. The Sub-Saharan Islamic families are predominantly patrifocal, and they were often shallower than traditional patrilineages since they acknowledged the authority of an alternative "power-oriented center"—Islamic or state leadership (Levitzion 1988; Eisenstadt, Abitbol, & Chazan 1988). These Muslim families usually retain many traditional African elements of ritual and lineage behavioral patterns, whether these were matrilineal or patrilineal. This is particularly evident in areas like Senegambia, where Islam penetrated after the late 1500s (Shaffer & Cooper 1987; Brooks 1976), and in Nigeria since the Fulani conquests. In these areas, negotiation of familial roles is not new, but has been continually changing.

Among the Muslim Hausa of Nigeria, about which many ethnographies, histories, and studies exist, the patrilineal *gandu,* is the major family institution (Smith, M. 1954:22-3 & 31-2; Smith M.G. 1960). The rural gandu once encompassed the extended family of brothers, at least two generations of paternal relatives and spouses, and the slave or client non-Muslim families who worked the fields. Arranged first marriages between parallel cousins (the children of classificatory brothers) gave some stability to the extended family, but second and other marriages, or gift and exchange marriages, established linkages between male friends and clients with different occupational and urban ties. Up to four wives per man was acceptable under Islamic custom and law, and this fused with the acceptability of polygyny in pre-Islamic traditions in the area. Pro-natalist attitudes also exist here, with each wife expected to bear sons for her husband, and sterility or barrenness was grounds for divorce.

However, gender roles within the Hausa family reflect the cultural fusion. Although men assume the primary responsibility for the family, for participation in public and Islamic rituals, for the family's economic maintenance, and its reputation in the eyes of the larger community, women also shoulder considerable economic responsibility (Coles and Mack 1991). Under Islam, women are thought to require the protection of marriage and some degree of seclusion, which varies according to class and rural or urban residence. However, the flexibility of dual-sex organization in African traditional cultures gives the woman among the Muslim Hausa considerably more flexibility, particularly in her movements within women's groups, in her supernatural activities outside Islam, in her ability to influence marriage arrangements, and in her ability to operate economically outside the household through the agency of her children. Fostering of children allowed the barren woman to still assume the status of mother and remain as a wife.

Traditionally, many Hausa women have been able to engineer divorce and remarriage in ways that meet their personal economic needs, and the needs of their own families of orientation. Alternatives also existed, so that divorced or unmarried women could engage in *Karuwanci* (courtesanship or prostitution) or in *bori cults* (traditional spirit possession) through which they earned money and were involved in a community of women (Dunbar 1991:76; Echard 1991; Coles and Mack 1991:7,9).

The support given by Islamic Shari'a law reinforced Muslim families and women's roles, although practice sometimes limited these. Male clerics who are acquainted with the family were called upon to mediate informal disputes, and the *Alkali's* courts—using legal texts and cultural experience—

existed to handle family conflicts, divorce, or other property issues (Christelow 1991; Rosen 1984; Smith MG 1965. The law mandates that fathers should continue to offer support for children, despite divorce; and in cases of intestate property settlement, the law specifies the ⅛ or ¼ share due to wives, and the ½ portions due to daughters (Mainaa, Muchai, & Gutto 1977: 195). Increasingly, it supports the nuclear family within the larger extended family, particularly in terms of maintenance of children, property, and wills.

In contrast, matrilineal systems, which today are fewer in number, focused structural attention on women and traced descent through them, although brothers were not ignored (Fortes 1950).[6] The classificatory separation of males and females (dual-sex socialization) expanded in state organized societies so that men struggled to create structures that paralleled and overshadowed female structures, but women competed equally with men for some positions (Mikell 1992; Wilks 1975). Nevertheless, women had greater rights of public and domestic decision making, property ownership and lifelong participation in lineage affairs in matrilineal systems than did women in patrilineal ones.

Women exercised some control over their sexuality, occasionally having births outside marriage, since the children born of women in the matrilineage were already legitimate members who had social, economic, and jural-legal rights within the kin group.[7] But, it was the father's recognition of paternity that incorporated them into his spiritual or clan group where such identities existed. The failure of fathers to do so cast a social stigma upon the individual, but did not affect lineage rights and responsibilities. Arranged marriages in the interest of the matrilineage were usually typical, although there are some groups where marriage is so tenuous that it is often called "recognized cohabitation," such as among the Senufo of Ivory Coast. More typical were brittle marriages and frequent divorces, such as among the Akan. But since the lineage retained jural authority over the individual and husbands received fewer rights, bridewealth among matrilineal populations involves less monetary value exchange. The symbolic ritual exchange was most important, and there was little financial loss with divorce (see Table 1).

Both women and men held positions of authority in the matrilineal family, but ofttimes men played more important roles in the dynamics of matrilineages than women did in patrilineages (Richards 1950). Sisters and brothers were linked together at each generation as important kin reference persons, since brothers often controlled resources and land of the matrilineage and passed it on to sisters' children, primarily their sons. Men acted as guardians for their sister's children, and exercised "jural authority" over the younger members of the lineage. They had the right to give nieces in marriage with the approval of the child's father; and often the chosen husband was the uncle's own son so that he could satisfy his lineage responsibilities as well as his paternal ambitions. Only if family matters regarding property, marriage, or misbehavior could not be adequately decided by the elders within the lineage, were cases taken outside to be aired before the chief or elders of the town. Such involvement of males in lineage affairs also contributed to what I have described as "patrifilial tendencies" within matrilineages—the privileged ability of men to marshall economic and human resources to their own personal benefit, rather than to the benefit of the lineage or women (Mikell 1992:92, 109, 121, 131).[8] Male control also extended into marriages, where husbands had the right of polygynous marriages, and residual rights of control over a wife's labor but not her property. Her property was to be inherited by her lineage members upon her demise.

Normally, matrilineal rights were exercised best when both males and females continued to reside in or near their ancestral villages (duo-locality) and family farms. Then, couples need not co-reside, since they could continue to retain residential rights in the lineage compound and establish a daily or regular visiting relationship with each other. The continued ability of both matrilineages to observe marital relations between the couple also encouraged the husband to be circumspect in his conjugal responsibilities, particularly related to subsistence and maintenance of his wife and children. As long as husband and wife fulfilled their responsibilities to each other, marriages could last. However, given the flexibility of residence, property ownership, economic activity, and individual choice that matrilineages allowed women, divorce initiated by women was a frequent occurrence—much more frequent than in patrilineal groups. The occurrence of nuclear households was rare, but periodic attempts to create male centered households occurred with considerable frequency (Arhin 1983). Among the matrilineal Bemba and the Thonga, these "patrifilial tendencies" were manifested by male attempts to create a virilocal residence pattern, or a pattern of patrilocal residence whereby a woman moved to the husband's village and he sought to encourage her brother or a section of her matrilineage to join them (Colson 1973). Among the Luapula of Zambia, they were often manifest in the father's attempt to encourage his children to come to live with him as they grew older and more educated (Poewe, I and II of 1978), and to participate through them in the modern economy. Although such creative attempts occurred throughout history, they increased with the penetration of market economies, wage labor, and cash cropping, and they moved in different directions depending on how national policies affected family and economic life (Mikell 1994b; and Colson 1980).

Among the matrilineal Akan, where rural families engaged in cocoa production for export, conjugal relations temporarily strengthened in the 1920s and 1930s as a man replaced the labor of lineage members with that of a co-resident wife and children who worked on the husband's cocoa farms. As early as the 1940s, the *Asantehene* (King) was recognizing that co-residence and marital/domestic labor increased the possibilities of individual men gaining wealth, property in land and farms, and achieving distance from his matrilineage. However troubling the issue of equity to wives and children, there continued to be opposition from among Asante chiefs to the notion of changing customary law so that rights of inheritance were extended to wives and children; and they only approved "gifts" of land during a man's lifetime. Such developments led K.A. Busia (1951:125-127), sociologist and former Head of State in Ghana to comment about the new divisions becoming evident within the Ashanti *abusua* (matrilineage) as a result of the cocoa cash-crop economy.

There are African ethnic groups that have variable sub-ethnic kinship patterns, and there are parts of the African continent where historical forces (colonization, missionization, and Islamic conquest) have resulted in mixed or ambiguous practices identified as "traditional." Many of these areas are nominally or largely patrilineal, although the lineage may have become shallow, extended kinship relations rather than lineage relations may have become the norm, or double-descent is present. Southern Africa is the area where a number of such ambiguity is found: 1) groups here often represent later waves of the Bantu Migration (Shapera 1950); 2) there were competing state expansions among Zulu, Xhosa, Swazi, and other Ngoni and Sotho speaking peoples in the seventeenth, eighteenth, and nineteenth centuries (H. Kuper 1986); and 3) the agressiveness of western Christian conversions coupled with colonial/apartheid expansion resulted in population dispersion and altered kinship dynamics (Comaroff and Comaroff 1992; Marks 1988).

However, what is noticeable about these areas is the strong

defense of what is designated as "traditional" African kinship, despite external pressures to relinquish it in favor of western family forms and relationships. Despite christianization and educational mobility in the twentieth century many Southern African groups exhibited the retention of identification to patri-kin units and their political leaders, retention of the notion of extended family, separate dual-sex organization of social life, female deference to males within marriage, and a tolerance for polygyny. In addition, brutal forms of European conquest and the movement into apartheid certainly intensified loyalties to traditional systems and relationships (Atkins 1993).

With the concomitant economic change, migration, and differential educational mobility for men and women, we see that in both rural and urban areas, men first and then women have adopted new residential patterns and male-female work patterns. These altered conditions have contributed to considerable ambiguity in the performance of conjugal, parental, and inheritance responsibilities. Perhaps most important has been the changing attitudes of women and of state leaders about acceptable conjugal, parental, and inheritance roles and relationships.

Conjugality

In large part, shifts have occurred in the nature of conjugal relations because modern economic forces and urbanization no longer support the separation of spouses or work against close-knit lineages or extended family groups (Caldwell 1992:5864; Abu 1983). Given the pressures on couples to retain kinship loyalties, there is some suggestion that married couples who move away from the wife's matrilineage area are more likely to co-reside and to have three or more children (Bleek 1972:54), whereas divorces occur with great frequency among couples with duo-local residence. Among patrilineal families, couples may have fewer divisive pressures, but many extrinsic economic problems exist. Today, few supports exist for the married conjugal couple, with the result that the nuclear family is a quite tenuous phenomenon in some areas, or a non-existent one in other parts of Africa.

Some of this is traceable to early twentieth century socio-economic changes, such as the provision of education for men, while education for females came much later. This removed men more quickly from rural communities through wage labor and urbanization. Alternatively, economic crises succeeded capitalist penetration (the Great Depression) and at these times families encouraged women to rely upon the resources of husbands to make ends meet. Other reasons include the increased christianization which denigrated polygyny, supported monogamous marriage and possible co-residence of spouses, but could not create conditions for stamping out informal polygyny. Still other reasons include the occurrence of traumatic national events which either removed men through migration or war, or provided economic and social dis-incentives towards marriage, but did not deter reproduction. Contemporary change has given increased flexibility and choice to men in domestic arrangements, but it has continued to restrict the choices available to women. With all these influences, male and female roles, in particular the roles of conjugal partners, and husbands and wives, have been in considerable flux, and African conjugal life has been altered.

Studies done in various parts of the continent now show that in rural areas, lineages and extended families are more compact than in the past. There are increased incidences of households of elderly, women, and children, in which there are no young men present. Alternatively, in rural areas, in many households which contain couples, the unions exist without benefit of the ritual or formal ceremonies of marriage which would have been required in the past. Much of this is traceable to the diminution in size and cohesion of lineages and other traditional kinship groups as a result of differential mobility and increasing segmentation within them. More prosperous branches of families appear to have hived off, and no longer recognize the communal obligations of counseling or reciprocity with distant kinspersons, so the recognition of lineage obligations takes place within smaller sub-units. It has therefore become more difficult for couples to obtain resolution to their domestic problems because of decreased felt responsibility or the diminished capacity for the family group to play this role.

In urban areas, whether among formerly patrilineal or matrilineal people, there are alternative class and culture-based trends occurring:

1) Among the educated and elite urban couples, there is now a higher incidence of co-residence of partners and spouses, with or without formal marriage, although some traditional rites may have been performed. The status of marriage has been retained, but the ability to achieve it has changed. These unions vary in their durability, depending upon whether they produce children, but in the 1970s and 1980s most women still retained a pronatalist stance and they endeavored to produce and raise the five or six children that husbands claim to desire (Lewis 1977; Oppong 1987). Generally after the birth and "outdooring" (public naming and acceptance of paternity) of one or two children, the couples may opt to cement the formal union through ordinance or church marriage, which is a major event for the family and the community. Where payment of bridewealth was traditionally required, the symbolic forms of it still remain as a major legitimating factor prior to ordinance or church marriage. Across the continent, these elites achieve the outer form of the western "nuclear family," although the dynamics differ. Using data from patrilineal groups in Nairobi, Kenya, Stichter (1986) suggests that monogamous married couples with co-resident spouses (nuclear families) and approximately 3.18 children are the predominant form of stable elite family there.

The major problems which confront these urban elite couples concern the divisions of household roles, family decision making, and the sharing of economic responsibility. Despite their education and modernity, many males still hold to traditional ideas regarding male dominance over the wife, male prerogatives of household decision making, and a gender based approach to household tasks which leaves housework to women. More problematic, however, is that although women are trying to negotiate for the establishment of a joint pool for household resources and income, men often have no such expectation. Men still expect women to contribute to food provision, furniture, maintenance of children, and other household expenses; but a man allows women few rights over his incomes, although he will often attempt to control her income (Schuster 1979; Oppong 1974). Stichter's data from Kenya, challenges this economic picture because middle-class couples are able to establish joint household accounts. On the other hand, many young Kenyan women continue to face pressure from parents who seek to control their incomes (Oloo and Cone 1966).

Often, co-resident partners fears the intrusion of the other's extended family or lineage into their affairs and the economic demands which these other relatives may make upon the household, so they protect their own money and resources. These tensions are exacerbated by the retention of informal polygyny. The man may be officially married to only one woman, but he may have dual families, which strains his financial resources and promotes tension within the household (Toungara 1996). With divorce, whether among matrilineal or patrilineal peoples, the struggle to decide about child support and property division becomes intense, and the wife may be summarily removed from the conjugal dwelling by the husband's family.

2) Working class and sub-working class urban families

engage in a joint cultural strategy, blending a larger range of rural domestic or marital practices with newer urban ones, and still they face crisis. Birthrates climb in this strata as women bear five to six children who can assist them with small jobs, trading, or sporadic urban gardening Fewer women have ordinance or religious marriages, and many are not even married under customary or traditional rites. Nevertheless, women still struggle to get male partners to marry or to acknowledge responsibilities to their households and biological children. In many cases, partners live separately and have a visiting relationship—a pattern which is necessitated by the heightened polygyny (informal or formal) among this group. Most women work since they must contribute in order to guarantee that children are fed and sheltered; but women's low incomes result in their increased dependency upon males. National economic decline, structural adjustment, the loss of a man's job, or decreased earnings by women in the informal sector, place enormous stress on these families, causing them to look to the state for alternative support. My work in the family courts in Accra, Ghana provides a profile of the characteristics and problems facing matrilineal women who seek assistance from the courts (Mikell 1994a).

Crises among these working and sub-working class urban families has been the major initiating reason for the expansion of new Family Laws, expanded Domestic Courts, and Family Tribunals in most African states since the 1970s. With the breakdown of lineage and extended family control, greater involvement of girls in education, and greater unwillingness of men to marry, births outside marriage now constitute a sizeable problem for women in this group (Dolphyne 1991). Girls and unskilled or uneducated young women are vulnerable economically. South Africa provides a special case because of the dynamics of mixed color and culture groups as well as African girls in this subset. Nevertheless, the emerging continental patterns of teenage pregnancy outside marriage is one that is also present elsewhere (Preston-Whyte, Eleanor and Maria Zondi 1989). Given the absence of other mechanisms to handle family problems, state welfare institutions and courts are inundated with demands from women for assistance.

3) Muslim families, both urban and rural, vary according to class and social status, but most continue to rely upon formal Islamic and community institutions to deal with their conjugal relations. Most of these couples are married under Islamic law, but where they are not married, the unions are often kept secret from other kinspersons and of short duration because of the stigma involved (Schildkrout 1975). Residence in mixed Muslim and non-Muslim urban communities can mitigate some of the social control which the Islamic community can exercise over individuals, primarily women. Therefore, one sees many cases of non-married women increasing their autonomy by insisting upon urban residence. However, for married Muslim women, some of the major problems relate to their desire to increase personal autonomy by working or finding economic means to earn income (Pellow 1991). Given the expectation of female seclusion in some communities, the permission of the husband is required for women to work outside their homes. In other situations, a husband's consent must be obtained before women can secure the facilities or space in which their children or other employees can engage in trade or commerce on her behalf. Among Hausa and other northern groups, I have heard women complain of the need to have community enforcement of the personal right to work and hold land or other resources—rights which Nigerian law gives to women as citizens, but which Muslim marital or conjugal relations may restrict.[9] During 1994 while in Kaduna, I listened to women from the Muslim Women's Organization talking about the need for women to collaborate in applying these pressures (Mikell 1995); and documentation exists of

women's organizations which have begun to be active on such issues (Imam 1993:134-6). Although the trend is still small, to a larger extent than before, married and educated Muslim women are residing apart from husbands and paternal families, while still maintaining conjugal relations that are acceptable to the family. This occurs more in places like Nigeria Senegal, and South Africa, than in places like Kenya and Tanzania.

In many ways, Nigerian Muslim women are considerably more liberal and aggressive on the issue of conjugal and family rights than are women in many Muslim communities, because in most places Muslim women have little contact with state institutions that regulate relationships of women and the family. In my work in Ghanaian family courts, Muslim women were virtually absent from the setting of the urban court cases (Mikell 1994a), but there are indications in higher court data that this may soon change.

Regardless of which of the three groups we examine, and regardless of whether we refer to individuals from patrilineal or matrilineal backgrounds, it becomes clear that single-parent households are becoming an increasing part of the African domestic scene. These are different from the traditional duolocal residence patterns for spouses, since those involved other lineage or extended family members.

Negotiation of New Parental Roles and Responsibilities

The socioeconomic and cultural desire for children has hardly lessened in Africa as evidenced by the high African fertility rate (6.1) in Table 2, by the still weak demand for birth control and abortion among African women (Kaiser Foundation 1993; Oppong 1987).

In a few countries like Kenya, Swaziland, and Zimbabwe, the fertility rate has fallen dramatically, but one wonders whether it will be long lasting. Oppong has stressed that the desire for children must be addressed not just by targeting women for birth control education, but also by educating men

Table 2
SUB SAHARAN AFRICA MALE-FEMALE DATA
(Percentages 1985-1991)

Country	Literacy Total & M/F 1991		Total Fertility Rate		Infant Mortality per 1000 Live Births 1991
			1985	1991	
Africa Total	50.0		6.1	—	—
Burkina Faso	(13)	28/09	6.5	7.1	138
Chad	(18)	42/18	—	5.3	139
Cote d'Ivoire	(24)	67/40	7.0	6.8	102
Ghana	(53)	70/51	6.5	6.3	68
Kenya	(59)	80/58	8.0	6.4	70
Niger	(86)	81/91	7.0	—	131
Nigeria	(42)	62/40	6.9	6.5	121
Senegal	(72)	—	6.5	—	130*
South Africa	(79)		[Bl 4.6/Wh 1.9]*		53
Swaziland	(67)	70/66	6.5*	5.1+	127
Tanzania	(85)	62/31	6.5	7.0	109
Zaire	(61)	84/61	6.7	6.2	107
Zambia	(69)	81/65	6.8	6.9	83
Zimbabwe	(76)	81/67	8.0*	5.5+	67

Source: World Development Reports 1985 and 1991 (World Bank, Oxford UP); and African Socio-economic Indicators 1986, ECA; and World Fact Book, Central Intelligence Agency 1986 1991.
*Data available only for 1986.

(--) Aggregate data in parenthesis, not male/female.

+ Indicates data from Reproductive Health Policy: Reflections on the African Experience. Harare: Henry J. Kaiser Family Foundation 1993.

to such options and choices. It appears that in the absence of marriage, childbirth and parenting continues, mediated now by socioeconomic ability to provide children with maintenance, education, and health. The reasons given for out of wedlock births vary. Preston-Whyte suggests that many South African girls see it as a way to experience motherhood even if marriage is not forthcoming; and in other areas it may be a means of demonstrating fertility so that marriage can occur. In Ghana, young girls may seek abortion as a means of preventing births that may stop their education, but most women still need encouragement from male partners to use birth control if women desire to lower fertility. Data from the Ivory Coast suggests that the fertility rate of educated, urban, working women may be only slightly lower (5.3) than the urban fertility rate, although it contrasts with that of low skilled, rural woman and with the national fertility rate of 7.0 (Lewis 1977).

On the other hand, parents are now responding to the new roles which they are required to play by modern social conditions or by state law, and are creating new parent-child relationships. Both males and females are forced to negotiate new relationships with each other as they play these parental roles, and one sees both successes and strains. Some of the negotiation between partners goes on internal to the couple as women attempt to force men towards marriage, or to "outdoor" their children borne outside of wedlock, or to shoulder newer types of maintenance costs for children which men would not have had to do in the past (education, health, etc.). Because men have tended to have more employment in the formal sector which brings with it more possibility of health and educational benefits, women feel justified in insisting that husbands and fathers play this role for their children. But during the economic collapses of the 1980s, many men's incomes fell and they could not provide children's maintenance, especially given their dual families.

Elabor-Idemudia shows that even in rural Nigeria, there were incredible stresses on women in single-parent households as they try various survival strategies to overcome their limited incomes. These strategies included reducing meals from three to two to one per day; eliminating chicken, eggs, milk, and beef from the diet; and finally borrowing money from relatives to buy food (1991:141). This was true in both rural and urban Ghana also, as the number of impoverished female-headed households rose during the 1980s.

But when informal strategies and negotiation fails, women appear more willing to enter the formal arena of state family tribunals and courts to legally encourage men to shoulder the new paternal role. Increasingly African states have accepted the challenge of providing legal measures to ensure the well-being of children within families, with particular emphasis on the paternal role. Particularly as economic restructuring limited the government's revenues for social services (World Bank 1994), it became essential for private citizens to handle new financial responsibilities. In Ghana in 1985, new family legislation required the formal registration of all marriages, entitled children to maintenance support from parents, established and authorized new levels of inheritance and property division for wives and children, and gave widows the right to request letters of administration over a man's intestate property (Mikell 1994a; Manuh 1996). Despite this legislation—and some would argue, because of it—the threat of sanctions was frequently necessary to get men to alter their behavior and accept new financial responsibilities. The profile of these Akan women and court cases appears in Table 3.

In my Accra sample from the courts, where there were both matrilineal and patrilineal female plaintiffs, women from patrilineal communities struggled to obtain visiting rights with children who had been taken away by husbands, or to get husbands to consent to custody of children who the wife could not support on her income. However, the major demands that matrilineal women made of men was to contribute mainte-nance costs, education, and health costs, because they accepted the fact of separate spousal residence and were generally unwilling to relinquish custody of children. In Table 3, I provide a profile of the matrilineal women involved in Family Court cases in Accra, Ghana.

Table 3			
DOMESTIC PROFILE OF GHANAIAN URBAN WOMEN			
*1990 Accra Court Sample			
WOMEN'S OCCUPATIONS		MALE PARTNER'S OCCUPATION	
Trading	37.9%	Trading	10.3%
Business owner	4.6%	Business Owner	6.9%
Blue collar	11.0%	Blue Collar	34.9%
White collar	17.0%	White collar	39.0%
Unemployed	19.6%	Unemployed	6.9%
Other	4.0 %	Other	2.0%
Not given	5.9%		
	100 %		100 %
WOMEN'S MARITAL STATUS			
Customary marriage	7.8%		
Ordinance marriage	3.9%		
Divorced (cust+ord)	26.2%		
Separated	2.6%		
Never married	32.7%		
Not given	22.9%		
	100 %		
MEAN NUMBER OF CHILDREN PER WOMAN = 1.93			
RESIDENTIAL STATUS OF PARTNERS			
Conjugal	5.1%		
w/ Lineage	7.3%		
w/ Ext. Family	13.2%		

Separate	72.8%	
Other	1.5%	
	100 %	

PRIMARY CONCERNS IN FAMILY COURT CASES		
Maintenance of chil-dren	58.8%	
Medical costs	27.1%	
Custody or Visitation	13.1%	
Other	1.0%	
	100 %	

OTHER FEES REQUESTED IN ADDITION TO MAINTENANCE	
Education costs	18%
Medical Costs	27%
Medical + Education	44%
Med. + Edu. + Job trn.	5%
Med. + Edu. + Other	5%
Other	1%
Total	100%

* N = 153. Source: Mikell sample of Accra Family Court Cases 1990.

Many of the women here have been or were currently heads of single-parent households which were suffering financially. There is evidence that young persons feel the absence of strong paternal relationships. In Ghana, some studies done in matrilineal areas suggest that young men are resentful of the refusal of fathers to shoulder financial aspects of paternal relationships (Aboagye 1979). Given the break-down of lineage responsibilities which Ashanti uncles should feel toward them, some boys and young men assert that "everyone has a father!" But socialization of children, particularly boys, to new paternal roles is also significant. African women are urging men to accept visitation rights with their children, even when they do not co-reside with them or choose to marry. They do not wish to break off relations with matrilineal relatives, but they know that they cannot depend upon them to support the conjugal family. Recent family legal change in many African countries tends to support and encourage these developments because it "recognizes the existence and importance of the nuclear family...," but it does not necessarily achieve these goals because the law has been hesitant to challenge customary officials and to challenge traditional law on men's rights and obligations. This means that socioeconomic circumstances have moved women further towards accepting new parental roles than they have moved men towards accepting them.

Male role resistance towards involvement in the female-headed household may be related to several factors: First, resistance is less in patrilineal areas where men would traditionally have "owned the children," and greater in matrilineal areas where the woman's brother would traditionally have been the child's primary authority figure. Second, a man's resistance is related to a desire to hold onto the privileges of polygyny, as well as to protect his public male image. Finally, men appear to interpret these demands as at odds with traditional behavior toward women once they are no longer wives or sexual partners. They see this as attempts to force upon them roles which would tie them more tightly to women with whom they no longer desire a conjugal relationship. However, there is also evidence that father-centered single-parent households are also emerging. Priso (1991:185) has hypothesized that instead of western style nuclear families:

> it is giving rise to single-parent families built around either the father or the mother. The movement towards individualization clashes with the need to be a part of a network of

solidarity which, for the most part remains the lineage.

Urban men who are financially stable are now more willing to accept custody of children, the responsibility for their mainte-nance and education, and to obtain the kinsperson or paid helper who assists with meals and caregiving. This is still not the major trend, but increasingly, such men appear in the courts, forcing legal recognition of these new attitudes when the court mandates custody and parenting responsibilities towards children. But since women, more than men, have been pushed towards accepting new conjugal and parenting, and household roles, the majority of these families are now female-headed.

Transmission of Property to Wives and Children

This category of kinship behavior is significant because it challenges lineage rules on property transmission by requiring new behavior on the part of men. This is not a new prob-lem--African women have faced the formal or informal restriction upon their receipt of inherited or transmitted property during pre-colonial as well as colonial periods. Whether because of Ethiopian state attempts to control land and bureaucracy (Crummey 1982; Berhane-Selassie 1996) or male attempts to profit from property transfers occurring related to Kenyan women's marriage or inheritance (Hay 1982), women's economic autonomy was being limited by the family. However, the consequences of the limitations on women's ability to receive property were more severe in the early twentieth century as capitalist ownership and individual property relations became crucial to economic development.

The movement towards legally empowering women regarding property increased slowly during the twentieth century with christian monogamous marriages which reinforce social norms of sharing resources within the conjugal family. In earlier times, when land was plentiful, it was labor—often the labor of wives and children—and not land or monied resources which had the greatest value (Mikell 1994b). The penetration of capitalist relationships in agriculture and in wage labor has altered this. However, the traditional notion that a man's resources belong to his lineage, not to his wife, is still generally supported by customary law, and only recently challenged by new family law in African states.[12] Many men resist making wills because, despite any loyalties to or sentiments for their wives and children, they do not want to alienate members of the lineage before death. Therefore, widows and children have often found themselves with no resources from deceased spouses, and with in-laws who feel no obligations to contribute to the maintenance of the family.

The new national concern for economic equity, combined with the state's concern to offset some of the negative effects of economic adjustment on women and children, has led to new laws which ease the task of transmitting property across lineage lines. In urban areas, such property may be houses, cars, furniture, and financial accounts. But the problems are even more significant in rural areas, because they involve direct income generating property necessary for economic livelihood of women and children—farms, land, animals, tools, and so forth.

In Ghana, new family legislation has altered traditional procedures by mandating that during intestate succession children receive the largest share of the deceased husband's property; that wives receive the next largest share; and that parents and other lineage or extended family members receive a very small share. Likewise, letter of administration can now be obtained by widows and children, so that they can benefit from intestate property. Yet, resistance from a man's lineage may frustrate this transmission.

Table 4 RURAL PROPERTY DEVOLUTION CASES IN THE HIGH COURT-SUNYANI, GHANA (1986-1990)*				
	APPLICANTS		CAVEATORS	
	Number	Percentage	Number	Percentage
LINEAGE+WIDOW	3	(12%)	0	0
LINEAGE				
Brother	4	(16%)		
Family Head	1	(4%)		
Sister	2	(8%)		
Niece/Nephew	2	(8%)		
WIFE ALONE	0	0	0	0
WIFE+CHILDREN	2	(8%)	1	(10%)
CHILDREN				
Son	1	(4%)	1	(10%)
Daughter	0	0	0	0
EXECUTORS OF WILL (all males)	10	(40%)	1	(10%)
Total	25	(100%)	10	(10%)
# OF WILLS	13 of 25	(52%)		n.a.
# OF MUSLIMS	8 of 25		2	(20%)

* Source: G. Mikell 1990. Data collected during August 1990 directly from individual dockets in the High Court, Sunyani Brong-Ahafo, Ghana.

Frequently, women must acquiesce to the threats of male members of the deceased husband's family, and join with them to obtain her letter of administration over property which the law has already given her the right to request.

In some cases, men have converted to another cultural system—Islam—as a means of guaranteeing that they could resort to Islamic custom to reinforce their desire to legitimize the nuclear family and transmit property to wives and children following their deaths. Table 4, with data from the high courts in matrilineal areas of Ghana, demonstrate these contradictions, because women were virtually never sole plaintiffs.

This is not solely a rural problem. There is other data still to be analyzed from Ghana's high courts in urban areas. But the urban data may also repeat the profile that has existed across the continent of the nuclear family of husband, wife, and children, struggling to negotiate autonomous roles and space outside the lineage, and of women and children seeking to obtain greater economic support for the family before the law.

Conclusions

Both matrilineal and patrilineal family dynamics are moving in directions which narrow and focus kinship roles and structures, initially exaggerating patrifilial roles, but ultimately creating new dilemmas for women and children. Conjugality is the recent focal point of modern African governments as they attempt to address the difficulties. But ultimately the problems come down to how to socially, and economically provide for the new forms of family, including how to make sure that previously male-controlled resources and property are available to address new family economic needs.

The challenges, as many modern judges, social workers, and women see it, is to convince men that the role and responsibilities of "father" are separate and discrete from those of husband, and that they should shoulder new responsibilities to the younger generation. But this leaves unaddressed the problematic trend of young girls who emerge as unmarried mothers and heads of households; and who, with little or no expectation that they will be able to obtain assistance from fathers of their children, must depend upon state social service for family support.

Despite the contradictions outlined above, there is now

increased incentive for men to transmit property to wives and children, and thereby guarantee the economic stability of the conjugal family. There are a number of questions which remain: how concerned are African publics about the new and economically vulnerable forms of family we are now seeing. How widely shared are these ideals of the new roles of father and provider, in relationship to traditional roles? If widely shared, how can they be supported and further reinforced in rural and urban areas throughout Africa without sacrificing important aspects of traditional culture?

Bibliography

Aboagye, Patrick Kofi, 1979. "Modern Attitudes Towards Matri-lineal Inheritance: A Survey in a Kumasi Suburb-New Tafo," Long Essay, Dept. of Sociology, University of Ghana, Legon.

Abu, K., 1983. "The Separateness of Spouses: Conjugal Responses in an Ashanti Town," in C. Oppong (ed), *Female and Male in West Africa*, London: Allen & Unwin.

African Development Bank 1990. The Social Dimensions of Adjustment in Africa: A Policy Aqenda. NY: United Nations, World Bank.

Arhin, Kwame 1983. "Peasants in 19th Century Asante," *Current Anthropology*, v. 24, no. 4, August-October.

Atkins, Koletso 1993. *The Moon is Dead! Give Us Our Money!* NY: Heinneman.

Berhane-Selassie, Tsehai 1997. "Ethiopian Rural Women and the State," in G. Mikell (ed) *African Feminism: the Politics of Survival in Sub-Saharan Africa*. Philadelphia: University of Pennsylvania Press.

Berquo, Elza and Peter Xenos (ed) 1992. *Family Systems and Cultural Change*, Oxford: Clarendon Press.

Bleek, Wolf, 1972. "Geographical Mobility and Conjugal Residence in a Kwahu Lineage," *Institute of African Studies Research Review*, vol.8, no 3, pp. 47-55.

Brooks, George 1976. "The Senaries of Senegambia," in N. Hafkin and E. Bay (ed) *Women in Africa: Studies in Social and Economic Change*. Stanford: Stanford University Press 1976.

Burman, Sandra and Eleanor Preston-Whyte (ed) 1992. *Questionable Issue: Illecitimacy in South Africa*, Cape Town: Oxford University Press.

Busia, K.A. 1951. *The Position of the Chief in the Modern Political System of Ashanti.*

Caldwell, John C. and Pat Caldwell 1992. "Family Systems: Their Viability and Vulnerability" in Elza Berquo and Peter Xenos (ed), *Family Systems and Cultural Chanqe*, Oxford: Clarendon Press, pp.46-66.

Christelow, Allan 1991. "Women and the Law in Early 20th Century Kano," in C. Coles and B. Mack (ed) *Hausa Women in the Twentieth Century*, Madison: Univ. of Wisconsin, pp. 130-144.

Coles, Catharine and Beverly Mack 1991. "Women in Twentieth Century Hausa Society," in C. Coles and B. Mack (ed) *Hausa Women in the Twentieth Century*, Madison: Univ. of Wisconsin, pp. 3-28.

Colson, Elizabeth 1980. "The Resilience of Matrilineality: Gwombe and Plateau Tonga Adaptations" in L.S. Cordell and S. Beckerman (ed), *The Versatility of Kinship: Studies in Honor of David Aberle,* NY: Academic. pp. 359-74.

_____ 1973. "Bemba" in Elliott P. Skinner (ed), *Peoples and Cultures of Africa*, NY: Doubleday.

Comaroff, John and Jean Comaroff 1992. *Ethnography and the Historical Imagination*. Chicago: University of Chicago Press.

Crummey, Donald 1982. "Women, Property, and Litigation among the Bagemder Amhara 1750 to 1850s" in Margaret J. Hay and Marcia Wright (ed), *African Women and the Law: Historical Perspectives.*

Dolphyne, Florence Abena 1991. *The Emancipation of Women: An African Perspective*, Accra: Ghana Universities Press.

Douglas, Mary 1971. "Is Matriliny Doomed?" in Phyllis Kaberry (ed) *Man in Africa*, NY.

Dunbar, Roberta 1991. "Islamic Values, the Sate, and the Development of Women: The Case of Niger," in C. Coles and B. Mack (ed) *Hausa Women in the Twentieth Century,* Madison: Univ. of Wisconsin, pp. 69-89.

Echard, Nicole 1991. "Gender Relationships and Religion: Women in the Hausa Bori of Ader, Niger," in C. Coles and B. Mack (ed) *Hausa Women in the Twentieth Century*, Madison: Univ. of Wisconsin, pp. 207 220.

Eisenstadt, S.N., Michel Abitbol, and Naomi Chazan 1988 "State Formation in Africa: Conclusions," in Eisenstadt, Abitbol, and Chazan (ed), *The Early State in African Perspective*, Leiden: E.J. Brill.

Elabor-Idemudia, Patience 1991. "The Impact of Structural Adjustment Programs on Women and Their Households in Bendel and Ogun States, Nigeria" in Christina H. Gladwin (ed), *Structural Adjustment and African Women Farmers*, Gainesville: University of Florida, pp. 128 150.

Field, Shawn 1991. "Sy is Die Baas Fan Die Huis: Women's Position in the Coloured Working Class Family," *Agenda*, no.9, pp. 60-70.

Fortes, Meyer 1969. *Kinship and the Social Order*. Chicago: Aldine.

_____ 1978 "Family, Marriage, and Fertility in West Africa," in C. Oppong (ed), *Marriage, Fertility and Parenthood in West Africa.*

Glazer-Schuster, Ilsa 1979. *New Women of Lusaka*, Maytield Publishing Co.

Goody, Esther N., 1973. "An Essay in the Family Sociology of Northern Ghana," *Studies in Anthropology*, no. 7, Cambridge: Cambridge University Press.

Gough, Kathleen 1961. "The Modern Disintegration of Matrilineal Descent," in D. Schneider and K. Gough (ed), *Matrilineal Kinship*, Berkeley: Univ. of California, pp. 631-54.

Gugler, Josef and William F. Flannagan 1978. *Urbanization and Social Change in West Africa*, London: Cambridge University Press.

Guyer, Jane 1987. "Women and the State in Africa: Marriage Law, Inheritance, and Resettlement," Women in International Development, Working Paper No. 129, East Lansing: Michigan State University.

_____ 1981. "Household and Community in African Studies," *African Studies Review*. African Studies Assn.

Harris, Betty J. 1997. In Gwendolyn Mikell (ed), *African Feminism: the Politics of Survival in Sub-Saharan Africa*, Philadelphia: University of Pennsylvania Press.

Hay, Margaret Jean and Sharon Stichter (ed) 1984. *African Women: South of the Sahara*. NY: Longman.

Hay, Margaret Jean and Marcia Wright (ed) 1982. *African Women and the Law: Historical Perspectives*, Boston University Papers on Africa, 7.

Kayongo-Male, Diane and Philista Onyango, 1984. *The Sociology of the African Family*. London: Longman.

Kenyatta, Jomo 1959. *Facing Mount Kenya*. London: JAI.

Kuper, Hilda 1987. *The Swazi: Modernization in A Southern African Kingdom*. Waveland.

Levitzion, Nehemiah 1988. "Islam and State Formation in West Africa," in S.N. Eisenstadt, Michel Abitbol, and Naomi Chazan (ed), *The Early State in African Perspective*, Leiden: E.J. Brill.

Lewis, Barbara 1977. "Economic Activity and Marriage Among Ivorian Urban Women" in Alice Schlegel (ed) *Sexual Stratification: A Cross Cultural View*, NY: 161-191

Lloyd, Peter C. 1969. *Social Change in West Africa*. NY: Penguin.

Maina, Rose, V.W. Muchai, and S.B.O. Gutto 1977. "Law and the Status of Women in Kenya," in *Law and the Status of Women: An International Symposium*. NY: Columbia University School of Law.

Manuh, Tekyiwaa 1997. "The Intestate Succession Law (1985) and Children in Ghana," in G. Mikell (ed)*African Feminism: the Politics of Survival in Sub-Saharan Africa*.

Marks, Shula 1988. *Not Either An Experimental Doll*.

Mba, Nina 1988. "Kaba and Khaki: Women and the Militarized State in Nigeria," Women in International Development, Working Paper #159, East Lansing: Michigan State.

Mikell, Gwendolyn (ed) 1997. *African Feminism: the Politics of Survival in Sub-Saharan Africa*. Philadelphia: University of Pennsylvania Press.

_____ 1995. "African Feminism: Towards a New Politics

of Representation," *Feminist Studies*, 21, no.2 (summer), University of Maryland, College Park.

_____ 1994a. "Using the Courts to Obtain Relief: Women in Family Courts in Ghana," in Fatima Meer (ed), *Poverty in the 1990s: The Response of Urban Women*, UNESCO & International Social Science Council, pp. 65-86.

_____ 1994b. "The State, the Courts, and Value: Caught Between Matrilineages in Ghana," in Jane Guyer (ed), *Money Matters: Instability, Values, and Social Payments in the Modern History of West African Communities*, Portsmouth NH: Heinemann.

_____ 1992a. "Cocoa Alters Kinship," chp 5, *Cocoa and Chaos in Ghana*, Washington DC: Howard University Press.

_____ 1992b. "Culture, Law, and Social Policy: Changing the Economic Status of Women in Ghana," *Yale Journal of International Law*, v. 17, no.1.

_____ 1989. "Peasant Politicization and Economic Recuperation: Local & National Delimmas in Ghana" in Journal of Modern African Studies.,

Munene, Fibi 1977. "Women in Africa: A Kenyan Perspective," *Africa Report*, January-February, pp. 18-19.

Oloo, Celina and Virginia Cone 1966. *Kenyan Women Look Ahead*. Nairobi: East African Literature Bureau.

Oppong, Christine 1992. "Traditional Family Systems in Rural Settings in Africa," in Berquo and Xenos (ed) 1992, pp.69-86.

_____ 1974 . *Marriage among a Matrilineal Elite: A Family Study of Ghanaian Senior Civil Servants*. Cambridge Studies in Social Anthropology #8, London: Allen & Unwin.

Ottenberg, Phoebe 1969. "The Afikpo Ibo," in James Gibbs (ed), *Peoples of Africa*, Holt, Rinehart & Winston.

Peden, Joseph R. and Fred. R. Glahe (ed) 1986. *The American Family and the State*, San Francisco: Pacific Research Institute for Public Policy.

Pellow, Deborah 1991. "From Accra to Kano: One Woman's Experience," in C. Coles and B. Mack (ed) *Hausa Women in the Twentieth Century*, Madison: University of Wisconsin, pp. 50-68.

Poewe, Karla 1978. "Matriliny in the Throes of Change: Kinship,

Descent, and Marriage in Luspula, Zambia," *Africa*, 48, 3: 205-19 and part II, Africa, 48, 4:335-65.

Preston-Whyte, Eleanor and Christian Rogerson (ed) 1991. *South Africa's Informal Economy*, Cape Town: Oxford University Press.

Preston-Whyte, Eleanor and Maria Zondi 1989. "To Control their own Reproduction: The Agenda of Black Teenage Mothers in Durban," *Agenda*, no. 4, April, pp. 47-68.

Priso, Manga Bekombo 1991 "Lines of Descent," in *Global Studies: Africa*, 4th ed, Guilford CT: Dushkin - Annual Ed.,pp 182-5.

Radcliffe-Brown, R. and Darryl Forde 1950. *African Systems of Kinship and Marriage*.

Rattray, Capt. R.S. 1923. *Ashanti*. Oxford University Press.

Richards, Audrey 1950. "Types of Family Structure Among the Central Bantu," in Radcliffe-Brown and Forde (ed), *African Systems of Kinship and Marriage*. pp. 207-251.

Rodney, Walter 1982. *How Europe Underdeveloped Africa*. Washington DC: Howard University Press.

Shapera, Isaac 1973. "Tswana Judicial Process," in Elliott P. Skinner (ed), *Peoples and Cultures of Africa*, Doubleday.

Schildkrout, Enid 1979. *People of the Zonao: The Transformation of Ethnic Identities in Ghana*. NY: Cambridge Univ. Press.

Shaffer-Cooper 1987. *Mandinko: An African Holy Land*, NY: Waveland Press.

Skinner, Elliott P. and Daniel Chu 1965. *A Glorious Age in Africa*, 2nd ed. Trenton: Africa World.

Skinner, Elliott P. 1989 *The Mossi of Burkina Faso: Chiefs Politicians and Soldiers*. 2nd edition, Waveland Press.

_____ 1973 (ed) *Peoples and Cultures of Africa*, NY: Doubleday.

Smith, Mary 1954. *Baba of Karo: A Woman of the Muslim Hausa*. London: Faber and Faber.

Smith, Michael G. 1965 "Hausa Succession and Inheritance," in D.J.M. Derrett (ed) *Studies in the Law of Succession in Nigeria*, Oxford: Oxford U.P., pp. 230-281.

_____ 1960 *Government in Zauzzau 1800-1958*. Los Angeles: Univ. of California Press.

Steyn, Anna F., H. G. Strijdom, S. Viljoen, and Francis J. Bosman (ed) 1987. *Marriage and Family Life in South Africa: Research Priorities*. Pretoria: Human Sciences Research Council.

Stichter, Sharon 1986. "Women, Employment, and the Family in Nairobi: The Impact of Capitalist Development in Kenya," Working Paper #121, Boston University, African Studies Center.

Thomas, Barbara P. 1988. "Household Strategies for Adaptation and Change: Participation in Kenyan Rural Women's Associations." Women in International Development, Working Paper #165, Michigan State U.

Toungara, Jeanne 1996. "Changing the Meaning of Marriage: Women and Marital Law in Cote d'Ivoire," in G. Mikell (ed) *African Women: States of Crisis*, Univ. of Pennsylvania Press (forthcoming).

Tsing, Anna Lowenhaupt and Sylvia Yanagisako 1983. "Feminism and Kinship Theory," in *Current Anthropology*, August-Oct., vol. 24, no. 4:511-516.

Walker, Cheryl (ed) 1990. *Women and Gender in Southern Africa to 1945*, Cape Town: Philip Curry.

White, Luise 1984. "Women in the Changing African Family," in Margaret Jean Hay and Sharon Stichter (ed), *African Women South of the Sahara*, New York: Longman, pp. 53-58.

World Bank 1994. *Adjustment in Africa: Reform, Results, and the Road Ahead*. Oxford University Press.

Notes

[1]Boahen 1987; Rodney 1982: 205-282; Gugler and Flannagan 1978; Lloyd 1969.

[2]Esther Goody (1973) has explored variation in parent-child relationships within Ghanaian society in Northern and Southern communities

[3]Oppong states that characteristics of these family systems were that: economic, demographic, and political spheres are congruent and associated roles are overlapping...the head of the kin group combines religious, political, and legal authority"...[and the existence of] the

"cooperative working group" (1992:71) .

[4]There were some exceptions. Kenyatta (1957) argues that among the Gikuyu, love and personal choice prevailed.

[5]Noteworthy is that Oloo and Cone say that many Kenyan women still support the notion of symbolic bridewealth because it legitimizes marriage, although they reject the idea of large monetary transfers which give the appearance of "purchasing a wife." They note that in 1966 many Kenyan women wanted to keep the celebrations and symbolic gift exchanges, but wanted to "have the Government abolish, or set a limit, on cash amount of the brideprice" (p. 19).

[6]The "matrilineal belt" in Africa extends in pockets from coastal West Africa (Senegal, Cote d'Ivoire, Ghana, Nigeria) through parts of Central and East Coastal Africa (the Congo Basin, Zambia, Mozambique). It is possible to document the transformation of many of African societies along the North and West African coast from matrilineal to patrilineal, particularly under the influence of external pressures.

[7]For example, Akan matrilineages were described as originally located in specific villages or towns where they had communal responsibilities, and perhaps held certain offices based on status differences between kinship groups. In these towns, kinspersons usually occupied a certain section of a ward, although family growth meant that relatives might live in other parts of town as well. Normally, these villages contained a graveyard where ancestors were buried (Busia 1951:3, 67). Rattray (1923) also spoke of Akan matrilineages as conferring economic rights upon its members, primarily with respect to access to land for farming. This "jural"-political dimension was later described by Fortes (1969: 60-86,158-170) as an important element which undergirded kinship identification.

[8]For the matrilineal Akan, men's superior ability to control and transfer lineage land among brothers had a negative impact on women within the matrilineage.

[9]Women refer here to international conventions which their countries have signed: the Charter of the United Nations, specifically the Preamble and Article 1, paragraph 3, as well and the Universal Declaration of Human Rights (1948) which guarantees "rights and

freedoms...without distinctions of any kind, such as race, sex, language or religion."

[10]Some have hypothesized that cultural lags exist, and because of sickle cell anemia and other childhood diseases, mothers are not yet confident that science and medicine can keep alive all children born to a woman, so they bear more children (Lewis 1982). Ali Mazrui, in the kinship segment of the film *The Africans* (1985), defends this pronatal attitude by saying that you will not have effective birth control until there is death control.

[11]The status of social services within the budgets of African governments was a controversial issue. By the 1990s, international policies were emerging to address it. See African Development Bank 1990, and Mikell 1992b.

[12]Mikell 1994b. Although Ghanaian women have contributed to the establishment and maintenance of men's farms, in the past they hesitated to challenge a male's insistence that her labor was simply conjugal labor to which husbands were entitled. New laws establish women's right to claim such property, but women do so over male objections.

Chapter 7

THE FAMILY REVOLUTION IN CONTEMPORARY CHINA 1979-1995

Kate Xiao Zhou
Marion J. Levy, Jr.

Families and Women in China

The startling political and economic changes of Chinese reform (1978 to the present) set changes in motion that altered the relations within families and the status of women in China. This paper argues that the post-*baochan daohu* (turning over production to the household) farmers' economic movement[1] (markets, rural industrialization and migration) is the primary cause of the return of the nuclear family to the center of the stage of rural social structure, and the changing position of women. Reform provided young persons, especially women, with new sources of economic power which they translated into increased status and power within the family.

This thesis represents a revival of ideas of Parsons and Levy that industrialization and urbanization were building up the nuclear family and women's status, in spite of their cultural heritage.[2] Thirty-two years ago, William Goode, in *World Revolution and Family Patterns*, revised the theory of Levy and Parsons' which made the family as the passive dependent variable and placed "the importance of independent influence of the family on the industrializing process."[3] Since then, social scientists have criticized Parson's theory as a Western model imposed upon non-Western societies.

Recent development in China seems to support Parsons, Levy and Goode. While the change of family structure (*baochan daohu*) led to the dramatic proliferation and variation of markets, rural industrialization and migration, increases in the prevalence of the nuclear family and increased equality for rural women have accompanied those related economic changes. In other words, the independent family control over economy in the context of the period brought about incentives to people leading to the rise of markets, industrialization and migration which in turn brought about increases in nuclear families and changes in women's position. In what follows, we briefly examine the Chinese family structure and women's status in the status quo ante and the advances and disappointments of the Mao period before moving on to our main focus on changes brought about by recent reforms.

Curiously, scholars in the West have concentrated onesidedly on the negative effects of reform on the status of women.[4] Scholars in China link the rise of kinship and lineage networks to the rise of patriarchal value in the countryside. To some extent the reforms, by loosening social control, allowed ancient practices such as ancestor worship, tomb building, big weddings, and lineage organizations to revive. But these phenomena did not spring back into place unchanged from the day before the revolution. New kinship relations have accommodated many changes initiated under Mao, reinforcing rather than negating the changes in women's status. One may now hear someone refer to a woman as "xiaojie" (rather than "tongzhi"), but no one's going to bind her feet! While women continue their collective disenfranchisement under the communist system, economic reform has empowered them individually and locally, and they have not shied away from using that power.

Before the Revolution

In the traditional Chinese society, increasing age was accompanied by increasing higher status. The ideal image of women was *sancong side* (three dependencies and four virtues): *sancong* suggests that a woman depended on her father as a child, on her husband as a married woman, on her son as a widow.[5] *Side* required a woman to be virtuous in morality, speech, manner and hardworking. The ideal family structure was that of an extended family though actual families often fell short of that ideal. Typically, Chinese farmers ran independent farms in an open class system, granted the system often got clogged. Ideally speaking, however, it was an open class system for over 2000 years. In the villages, family heads, who knew farming, managed the farms. A civil service selected bureaucracy governed Chinese society, but officials rarely intervened directly beyond the *xian* (the county) level.[6] Still and all, roughly 85 percent of the population, the farmers of China, kept themselves and the urban Chinese alive by farming that was planned and directed by family heads, not by government officials or overlords. The leadership of the People's Republic of China (PRC) changed those social structures radically, including some that had remained stable for over 2000 years.

Central Planning and Collectives

The Communists criticized the traditional kinship structure family farming system and set about to replace it with a purely political hierarchy. After the Communist revolution in 1949, profound changes occurred in the position of the rural family and the nature of society, the most profound of these, perhaps, associated with collectivization.[7] The changes affected the source of farming decisions directly and decisively. The Communists set out to remove the Chinese family from the nexus of local organization and decision making. The party organization represented by cadres took over control of farms and farming. The commune and later the production teams replaced the family as the basic social unit of farming.

Collectivization of farms succeeded in reducing the influence of lineage. With cadres taking responsibility for farming, traditional relations lost legitimacy relevance. Age-specific precedents changed: older men were not necessarily respected for their experience at farming. Younger people, especially those with party connections, often had more control in village life.

Kinship as welfare

Hukou (household registration system determining grain rationing to each individual) and the rationing system (subsidized grain distribution for urban people and producer grain allocation for rural people) curtailed social mobility for rural people.[8] The new closed class system that tied people to the land and subordinated them to their cadres narrowed the choices for all members of the family and frustrated hope for social mobility for every member of the family. That hope, however slender, had been a hope for Chinese farmers since Chin Shih Wangti, i.e., for more than two thousand years.

The family head lost major decision making power in the family in terms of marketing, production and labor allocation.

The patriarchial and patrilocal patterns, though frustrated, still dominated rural life because the state did not provide a comprehensive welfare system for farmers. As a result, the lack of material resources from the state meant that local people had to depend on their kin for support in times of sickness, death, birth, and hardship. As a result, the ideal type of lineage was broken down but the actual pattern was that kin provided the only non-state shelter upon which each villager depended.[9] Kinship remained the source of welfare for farmers though such networks were condemned by the cadres.

Despite the government's ideological protestations about independent women, the closed nature of its social structure provided little potential for women to achieve independence. There was no vehicle for women to go beyond the confinement of the patriarchal village.

Increased life expectancy

The People's Republic of China also increased life expectancy.[10] The longer life expectancy and social immobility brought about the possibility that several generations of the family might live in close quarters and for a longer time than ever before. The problems of the aged were no longer taken care of by short life expectancy.

Lower wages for women

Finally, the closed class pattern also created problems for the position of women. Although Communist ideology made sexual equality an ideal pattern, the actual patterns for rural women were quite different. On the collective farm, women everywhere were ranked as lower-paid workers because they were regarded as "weaker bodies."

Incentive to have more children

Farmers were motivated to have more children in order to gain a larger share of grain because the collectives allocated grain on the basis of the number of mouths in a family. Under such circumstance, women's ability to bear children and to work in the collective farm were continued important considerations.

Paying a bride price continued as the dominant pattern because the groom's family gained an economic advantage by having a working woman coming in. Despite the state propaganda, most marriages were arranged by parents while the future bride and groom were still young (early teens).

Gains for urban women

Chinese working women in the city gained a certain degree of independence in marriages and work. As most urban women worked in the factories and other non-farm related work, most married women were able to live in nuclear families.

In short, the result of feudalization of Chinese farmers greatly altered the basic structure of Chinese family without rapid improvement of women's lives.

Baochan daohu

In the late 1970s and early 1980s, farmers cut themselves loose of cadre control using the knife of *baochan daohu* (the practice of turning over production to the individual household). Families began to contract for control of the farming of specific land. After providing a grain quota to the local government at the controlled price and a payment to the village cadres to "look the other way," they kept the surplus themselves or sold it on the market. Above all, the planning of farming was returned to family heads even though land ownership was not. By so doing, collective "peasants" reclaimed their status as farmers, setting off a chain of events that were startling in their implication for agrarian productivity and economic reality. These included increased family income and autonomy, a revival of kinship, and the laying of groundwork for markets, rural industry, and migration.

Increased family income and autonomy

The surplus gave families a source of income other than the state. Their contract with the cadres freed them from the collective, returning a degree of autonomy in the form of decision power over production.

Young people with more education and knowledge came to have more power in the family because they had more knowledge of technology and markets. Their schooling also provided them with extra-village ties that enable them to take initiatives whereas in Imperial China, the knowledge of older farmers was highly valued because the main source of knowledge was farming experience itself.

Baochan daohu provided conditions, institutions and new opportunities for each individual member of the family. Without a direct assault on the patterns of the collective, members of the family escaped political and economic constraints. The family began to orient itself toward making money not just from farming but from markets, rural industry and other opportunities as they arose.

If *baochan daohu* had achieved nothing more than increasing family autonomy and income, no changes in family structure or women's status need have followed apart from those of prosperity. But by increasing productivity, *baochan daohu* also led to the spread of markets and rural industry. Hands that were no longer needed on the farm could work in markets, rural industry, or migrate to the city.

Increase of lineage and kinship influence post-*baochan daohu* saw a rapid increase of lineage and kinship influence in rural China. Ancestor tombs, lineage temples and kinship networks boomed when the political control began to loosen up as the result of family farming. Other aspects of lineage in rural people's life declined as profit making and mobility increased the opportunities open to rural individuals.

Markets

Baochan daohu gave farmers the surplus they produced above the government quota. Farmers' efforts to sell this surplus I led to the formation of markets. Markets gave young persons, especially women, a chance to get out of the village and establish ties with the outer world, while making money.

Women merchants

When rational calculation in a broader sphere became the most important basis for family decision making, other non-economic considerations became less important. Even though local custom regarded it as inappropriate for women, especially young women, to travel long distances, it is now common for young women to engage in long-distance trade. More and more rural women are becoming merchants. In recent years, tens of thousands of Chinese rural women are either directly or indirectly engaged in international trade. The post-*bacchan daohu* market activities directly changed the position of women in rural China.

Rural women have played an important role in creating and expanding markets in China. Throughout the 1980s, they occupied a conspicuous place in *jishi* (farmers' markets) of all sorts. In many local and intermediate *jishi*, there were often more women than men. Life as a merchant became a significant alternative for rural women as a result of the increases of markets.

Rural men tended to take responsibility for transporting goods to markets. Selling did not require a lot of strength and thus was regarded as more suitable for women. But more importantly, women were thought to be good at human relationships such as selling and dealing. There was a rural couplet in Hubei to express this new division of labor: *"Maolü lamo niu geng tian, nanren lahuo nü shugian, qe you benshi"* (Men transport goods and women count money; donkeys grind and oxen cultivate, each according to its nature).

This new form of sexual division of labor may come from gender stereotyping. In an era of trucks, carting goods to market may not be a matter of brute strength beyond the strength of women. A greater obstacle may have been the fear of women out on roads alone. But the presence of rural markets did provide many rural women new ways of life that were not possible under the collectives.

In Imperial China and under collective farming, only men were barbers. In fact, it was considered bad luck for a woman to touch a man's head. Since barbers went from door to door to provide their service, no women were allowed or willing to become barbers because a proper women's place was at home. Now, it is fashionable for a man to have a haircut by a female barber. Rural women constitute the main body of barbers and beauticians.

Similarly, in traditional China and under the collectives, there were no women butchers. Slaughtering pigs was an important male ritual in many villages in China. The cooperation of several men during the process showed a strong male bonding. Women were not even allowed to cut meat for sale at the market. But now, it is very common to see female butchers at markets both in the city and in the countryside (what caused this change?).

Another common way for rural women to gain independence is to open small restaurants along the road where they can get away with it. Many rural women become owners of those small businesses.

Markets expanded opportunities for women, increasing their economic power and giving them chips to bargain for family status. Rural industry added further opportunity. The greater the opportunities for women become, the greater became the task of supervising and controlling them; when women are off on their own and supporting themselves, patriarchy is weakened.

Rural Industry

The rapid increase of agrarian productivity released labor from farming. After *bacchan daohu*, both men and women were able to leave the land due to increasingly high agricultural productivity and to their increased political independence.

Once the family submitted the quota grain and paid the cadres their due, they could do pretty much what they wanted. With the government restriction on rural-urban mobility, factories boomed in rural China. Industrial jobs became an ideal occupation for rural youth. These took them out of the household, giving them a separate income. As more and more rural people became involved in industrial jobs, income from the factory often mattered more than agricultural work, because the income is higher and the work load is less.

Women as factory workers

Rural women actively participated in the process of rural industrialization. Tens of millions of rural women, especially the young and the unmarried, became workers in local rural industries or migrated to find employment elsewhere.

Women's contribution to rural industrial development was great. According to the official statistics, by 1989, 40 million rural women, one-fifth of the female labor force in the country-side, were employed by rural factories. By 1993, 50 million female workers, one-fourth of working women in rural China, worked in rural industry, making up 42 percent of the entire rural industrial labor force.[11]

These women are not necessarily "sending their wages home," although they may buy gifts for their relatives when they go back to visit their relatives in the village. This is especially true for migrant workers in South China. For most of those migrant working women, the most important thing is to secure their urban employment. They need savings to prepare themselves to find other alternatives since they do not have secure work. Their reference group now becomes coworkers in the factory. Most of them are young. Fashion is more important in these new groups than filial piety.

The separation between work and home produced a fundamental change in all aspects of those working women's lives. The new female factory workers had a degree of personal autonomy their sisters in former Chinese society lacked.

Women's participation in industrial work affects their position in the family. Working couples tend to form nuclear families. In most nuclear families, women, especially young married women, have more responsibility and power than their counterparts in the extended or stem families because of lack of in-law control.

Separate unbiased income

When a female worker's income is separated from that of the rest of the family and is to a high degree under her control, every member of her family knows very clearly how much she earns. "How much money do you make a month" has become a standard greeting in the countryside nowadays. There can be little doubt that the clear knowledge of a woman's economic con
tion enhances her social status at home. Women become increasingly autonomous in the factory as well as at home.

They also develop greater self-confidence. Many women work in light industries and assembly lines making toys, shoes and clothes. Since many rural factories pay piece rate wages, *women in light industries often do as well as or even better than men.* This increases their self-confidence and gives them a sense of pride in their labor. It also gives them whatever increases in power go along with the control of money. Patriarchy is extremely vulnerable to the control of money.

The independence of women can be expressed as women's four new serfs: *zizun* (self-respect); *zixinq* (self-confidence); *zili* (self-reliance); *and ziqianq* (self-improvement).

More importantly, the scale of income earning of rural women is no longer constrained by institutionalized gender inequality like that in the collective. Some women make more than men within the same village, although on the whole rural women still make less than men.[12]

Migration

Just as rural industry brought more opportunities for rural women, so did the rapid increase of rural-urban migration make more choices available to women. Migration provided women with opportunities that were never before possible in Chinese history. In Imperial China, the major employment for women outside the village were prostitution and concubinage. Although prostitution also exists in today's China and is increasing, it is far from the main employment opportunity.[13] For most rural women, their life cycle had for a long time focused on two villages, the village of their parents and the village of their husbands. In each village, the social circle was perhaps 200 to 500 people. A woman spent most of her life working and socializing in contact with those people. Although this closeness did provide some solidarity and networks of social relations, village communities also stultified individual empowerment and controlled women. In many villages, the punishment for adulterous women was stoning or drowning. Village gossip was sharp as a knife, able to kill any individual initiative (especially among women).

For two thousand years, almost every member of any Chinese village spent most of his or her time working and living within eyesight or earshot of other members of his or her family or other villagers. For women this was particularly true. Never before the past decade and a half had so many women worked outside family and village context.

Now rural women leave villages to work in various kinds of non-farm related jobs in rural industry, joint-ventures, foreign enterprises, or private service (restaurants, maids, nannies, and cleaning ladies).

Migrant women increased their power in the family

Under the collective arrangement, almost all rural women were completely denied the opportunity for non-agricultural work. Their few chances of upward mobility (joining the army and party promotion) were almost completely reserved for men although a few token rural women were regularly presented as showcases. Rural women also contributed to the rise of free labor markets in China. As more and more women migrate, leaving the land for alternative employment, the occupational choices became more complex. Migration also has important implications for women's autonomy.

Now outside their village, women could do things that would be impossible in their villages. There is no one gossiping about them. For women who do not have sons, migration provided a way out of discrimination. As one migrant told me in a 1986 interview in Guangzhou: "I was a damned woman in the village because I failed to have a son. Villagers with several sons would always make fun of me. Now I am a migrant. No one knows that I do not have sons. I no longer feel sad." Although rural migrants still prefer to have sons, their social status is no longer determined by their ability to carry sons when they interact with new people.

In short, migrant husbands have less reinforcement from their kin network in villages and hence have less control over women.

Cost of migration

On the one hand, migrant women seem to have little to lose by relinquishing or weakening village and kin ties. On the other hand, it is simplistic to say that women gain without any loss. Migrant women also have to care for their children without the support of other kin as they would have in villages. When family disputes occur, the wife has no kin network to smooth things out. Both men and women miss important village events, marriage, birthday celebrations, funerals, holidays, mutual aids and feasts. They are lonely in new lands.

The increase of nuclear family

Both men and women, especially the young, go where opportunities lead. The rapid increase of geographical mobility makes it hard for migrants to retain their kinship network. Their relations with village kin become less important in life, though they make the best use of old kinship ties to pursue those opportunities. New *quanxi* (relationships) are more important than the kinship network. Many migrants travel long distances. Many of them cannot even write to their kin, forcing them to make it on their own or depend on their small nuclear families.

Other migrants have replaced kin as the main external force in family life.

Migration reduced the control of kinship and village influence

The new migration patterns in rural China differ radically from the old migration patterns in which some men would leave their villages and families for some time. With low levels of industrialization, there existed few opportunities for rural people. In many cases, to leave the village meant a life of devastation as beggars, or hooligans although a lucky few may have become small scale merchants. More importantly, the goal of migration is different. In the old days, migrants would try to save money and send their savings to the villages to get married, to buy land and to build houses for the family. Now farmers look for a way out of rural life altogether. If they are married, they try to establish themselves and send for their families. If they are single, they will try to find spouses and to marry migrants. They often choose their own spouses or ask friends and relatives (migrants) to introduce someone to them. Even when migrants send money home to build houses, the new houses are more of a security against an unknown future fate. If they fail to set up a life, they will at least have a place to stay when they get back to the village.

Extended kinship ties weaken when couples work outside the village. The moral controls of village elders and village customs regarding intimacy between unmarried young and married couples are greatly weakened. It is very common to see husbands and boy friends carry wives and girl friends on their bikes to go to markets, shopping, and movies. Such public intimacy would have been regarded as bourgeois under Mao, and simply scandalous before that.

From Imperial China to Communist China, the interest of the group, kinship, village or state took priority over the wishes of the individual. This ideal pattern is less and less relevant to everyday life of most Chinese people, especially among rural migrants.

No mother-inlaw

The rapid movement of rural people and the rapid development of rural industrialization also means that more and more couples live their lives apart from their in-laws. The nuclear family was the dominant pattern of rural migrants throughout the 1980s. *For most Chinese women, that in itself is a liberation.* The period of subordination as a daughter-inlaw has been regarded as the most stressful stage of a woman's life. The rapid development in the countryside achieved without effort a feat that neither the PRC nor the Republic states had been able to achieve in 84 years. All these were achieved with little or no assistance from the government.

Divorce

The relationship between couples has become more important and more intense while at the same time the intensity of the relationship also leads to unstable marriages. Moreover, without kin to interfere and to mediate in the family's disputes, conflicts may also become intensified. Migration is linked to rapid increase of divorces, especially among migrants. Indeed desertion via migration becomes, in a sense, the divorce of the poor!

New China

The components of reform mentioned above (*Baochan daohu*, markets, rural industry, and migration) combine to produce general effects not mentioned above. By generally increasing the income opportunities and autonomy of persons, they enabled broad family and gender changes. These changes concern arrangement of marriages, the sharing of authority between husbands and wives, attitudes concerning sexual desire, timing of family division, the eclipse of kinship by *guanxi* networks, the changing of old virtues, and the rural resistance to the one-child family policy.

Marriage decision making

With the rise of female factory workers and with strong emphasis on wage earnings, women workers began to have more control in their marriage decision makings. Arranged marriages are decreasing. According to a 1990 survey by the *Journal of China's Women*, 74 percent of new marriages in China are not arranged marriages.[14] Personal involvement in marriage decision making is enhanced. Eighty percent of marriages are formed through "introductions." Total free marriage reached 13 percent while old fashioned parental arranged marriage constitute only seven percent.[15]

Many young women wait to get married. They try to save up enough money to buy the necessary household goods (furniture, televisions, washing machines, tape recorders). For them, it is very important to establish a stable economic position before having a family. When women contribute a substantial amount to the new family, their status in the family is very different; patriarchy is weakened.

Since young people are believed to have more knowledge about the new trend of markets and opportunities, young people have new veto power. Some women would convince their parents to allow them to make their own choice. Sometimes, those women already have pretty good knowledge of some men and would even suggest several possible choices. Some even have personal contact with those men before the formal arrangement is made public. It is obvious that at the root of material consideration for marriage choices also lies a consciousness about the persons involved.

Current marriage arrangements come more from friends and coworkers than from kin in the village. Dating has become a norm for young migrant girls. Since many of these young girls do not have a permanent urban residential card (*hukou*), some may have to return to their hometown. It is crucial for them to find men with permanent residence or to be able to have other job opportunities. This pressure forces them to become resourceful and aggressive both in finding jobs and in finding husbands.

Qunxueniu (snowballing) marriage network

One of the amazing developments in rural China is the rise of cross-provincial women's marriage networks. Women from poor areas migrate to rich areas to find husbands to be resettled. According to one survey in the rich area of Zhejiang, more than 100,000 women from other provinces had married Zhejiang farmers. The main motivation for the migration of those rural women was to "find a rich husband" and "live a better life."[16] This pattern of marriage was suppressed under the collectives. The growth of markets, rural industrialization and rural-rural as well as rural-urban migration diversified marriage alliances, and the marriage base of farmers has broadened as well.

Although migration was always a way out for women in poor areas, the new marriage migration is radically different from the old one both in numbers and in quality. First of all, many women themselves initiated migration marriages while in the old times, parents and relatives found partners for them or sold them to men in better areas. Although traffic in women persists in some poor regions, most migrant marriages have been initiated by the women themselves. It is under such circumstances that *qunxueciu* marriage network took shape.

Some women would go where they think opportunities are and ask door to door about the eligibility of bachelors in villages. When a woman migrated to a rich rural area and settled with a family, she would write or send home information about life in the new land. She may ask her sisters, cousins or other friends to join her. In many cases, she would help those female relatives and friends to look for marriage partners. When those friends come, they may inform others. The information circle enlarges whenever a new migrant marriage takes place. As it so happens that women from one county tend to get settled down in one rich area. In this *qunxuegiu* marriage network arrangement, women themselves are the major players.

Those migrant wives are not just parasites. They are good workers and carry with them their local skills in production and netting, providing important income for the family. In more developed regions, markets and rural industrialization are better developed and women have better chances.

A typical example of marriage arrangements among migrants is that of Zhou Xianhua from rural Hunan. Beginning in 1980, Zhou was on the road, falling in love three times before she was finally married to a migrant worker in Yuanjiang, Hunan. She met all those three men through her migrant friends.

Wives take part in decision making
Baochan daohu made the family responsible for major economic decisions. Wives began to share in making many of those decisions. It is easier for rural women to share decision making with their husbands than with cadres who were almost

all men, too. In many cases, women became an important source for family income because they were engaged in sideline production (raising chickens, ducks, and pigs). This role expanded as families became involved in marketing or rural industry.

Attitude toward sexual desire

Migration is also linked to the rise of companionate relationships between couples. Away from home and watchful eyes of their fellow villagers and inlaws, couples enjoy more time together and pay more attention to the husband and wife relationship including sexual relationship.

The loosening of community control over sexual behavior weakens traditional moral restrictions that limited couple's (especially young women's) sexual behavior. This lack of community control gives much freedom to young women while at the same time contributes to the rise of prostitutes. Now prostitution has become a voluntary occupation for some rural women.

With the rise of prostitution and other sexual activities, sexually transmitted diseases are also on the rise. Many private snake oil sellers try to sell drugs to cure these diseases, while ads on sex-related treatment cover telephone posts and other public places.

Early family division

One strong indicator of increasing independence among the young is that almost all young couples will begin *fengjia* (family division) as soon as they get married. If a family has only one son, *fengjia* does not take place. If there are two sons, *fengjia* is the norm. The new *fengjia* is different from the old in that older parents are often split up during the division. Since older people are considered economic "burdens," brothers have to share the cost of taking care of the aged. In many cases, formal arrangements are made between brothers to indicate who is responsible for which parent.

The Xian brothers in a Tongxing family will help to illustrate the "fengjia." The Xians have four children (two boys and two girls). Both daughters married out. As soon as the elder boy got married in the 1980s, the new couple moved out (traditional *fenqiia*). When the younger son got married four years later, the brothers got together and split their responsibility between them for the future care of the parents. The elder brother became responsible for the mother while the younger brother took responsibility for the father. As soon as the decision was made, the older couple lived separate lives. The father helped the younger son in production and ate with the young family while the mother helped out with the older son (raising chickens, cooking and cleaning). The older couple might sleep together at night in the same bed, but they lived separate lives the rest of the time. *More importantly, in both families it is the young men who are the family heads not the older parents.* This new form of stem family is very common in most of rural China, creating new and clear boundaries. Given the fact that parents may be only just over their forties, the new *fenqjia* means that the older man loses his status in an early age.

In many other cases, the older parents live separately by themselves while sons negotiate among themselves how much each should provide for the older couples. While in the old way parents tended to stay with at least one son, the family head relinquished his power at a much later stage. The young married woman often gains from the early division. She is no longer under the watchful eyes of her inlaws and sisters. The early family division is also directly responsible for the rise of the nuclear family in the countryside.

Nanyü tonggong (both husband and wife are factory workers)/the rise of the companionate marriage

The spread of rural industrialization was important for the rise of the nuclear family and even the companionate marriages, especially for couples who both work in rural factories. There are several reasons for such social phenomena to occur.

Chores

At home, even though working wives are still responsible for childcare and household chores, husbands also help.

Wife-beating

For husbands and wives, emotional satisfaction became increasingly important. Wife beating decreased.

Mothers' burdens

Kindergarten became more popular after the economic change in the countryside. For the first time in the history of China rural parents and grandparents are no longer the sole care-takers and educators of the children. Women have more time to engage in outside activities. Still, rural women are the main transmitters of social values to the young, but the changing role of women is associated with the disruptions or weakening of patriarchal order.

Guanxi: the transformation of kinship networks

Some try to use the rise of *guanxi* (persona connections) to illustrate the cultural resistance to social change. We shall use *guanxi* to indicate the transformation of kinship networks. From the transformation of *guanxi* we can see both the change and uniqueness of Chinese social relations. *Guanxi* are now so fundamentally different from the old kinship network that it may be the indicator for social changes. First of all, the old network enhanced kinship cohesiveness and served as security against unexpected events. The new *guanxi* network serves the interest of the nuclear family with little broader kinship interest, although kin may be part of *guanxi*. Second, the social ties in *guanxi* networks function ideally as an instrumental resource for each member while the kinship ties contain more or less some elements of affective ties. Third, *guanxi* is more flexible while kinship ties are more or less permanent. The flexibility of *guanxi* also dictates that *guanxi* ties are now often short-term arrangements while kinship networks focus on long-term investment interest. Fourth, the *guanxi* resources are not limited to kin. In fact, many of *guanxi* resources came from contacts an individual has through work, school, and economic activities. The distinction between the new *guanxi* and the old is not clear cut but is a continuing spectrum, varying from region to region.

The rise of local financial *hui* also illustrate the change of kinship network. The new *hui* is radically different from the old kinship network. It is a community of neighbors and acquaintances. The membership of a *hui* is determined by the available resources rather than by kinship, although kin also may become members. The family financial situation, not the family blood relations, is the key determining factor. Since women are believed to have a deep knowledge of the family economic situation and are in many cases in control of financial matters in the family, they are of great importance in the formation of financial *hui* in rural China. Although *hui* as informal financial organizations have existed for hundreds of years, the profit-motive in some of contemporary *hui* suggests that it is resources that matter not kinship.

The weakening of the old virtues for women and the rise of the new sancong side (three obediences and four virtues)

The post-*baochan daohu* economic developments in rural China alter the value system and bring a new ideology for rural women. For thousands of years, Chinese women tried to follow the code of women's behavior codified as *sancong side*.

Although not many women in the past fulfilled those codes, *sancong side* was the ideal code for women. Rapid social change also altered this gender-specific code. The new ideal code is radically different from the old one. The new *sangtong*:

1. *shuncong siji de yiyuan* (obey one's own will);
2. *gencong shehui de jiaobu* (follow the steps of society);
3. *bancong airen zinü* (be a companion to husband and children);

And the new *side*:

1. *chuanyi yao shede* (spend money on clothes);
2. *chifan yao tiaode* (be picky in food);
3. *jiashi yao fangde* (go easy with housework);
4. *yanzui yao bide* (care little).

Although many women may not have lived according to the new *sancong side*, the new code has become ideal for them.

Rural resistance to the one-child family policy

The structural change of the family economy enables many to have a relative degree of freedom even under strong government one-child family rule. The government was not able to enforce one-child policy in the countryside although it was able to bring down the fertility rate. The main reason is that autonomy of the family provides space and ability to evade the governmental coercion. Many farmers are able to bribe their way out of the one-child law. The rural resistance not only provides for rural people to have at least two children, urban people are also increasingly able to get around the state restriction to have a second baby. The one-child family is an imposed ideal pattern; it has never been an actual ideal pattern for either rural or urban people in general. It has approached an actual pattern in the urban but never in the rural setting.

Internalization of smaller family size

But the combination of rural resistance, governmental coercion, and economic development have fundamentally altered the way farmers think about family size. The main decisive factor is no longer "more children, more happiness" (*duozi duofu*), though most farmers would like to have a boy baby to carry out their family line. So long as one boy comes, a farmer may prefer to have a small family because having children would cost the family since women are now important income earners for the family. As the result and interdependence of those variables, small size families have become an ideal and even an actual pattern for most Chinese families, the norm for most Chinese families. A recent survey in many provinces indicates that without governmental coercion, a substantial number of farmers would prefer to have two children.

How many children do you prefer to have without the constraint of the state policy? (percent):

sex	one	two	three	four
male	5	44	22	16
female	7	49	19	16

Dai Kejing, "Zhongguo shisishengshi nongcun funü jiben zhuangkuang jiqi shenghuo jianxi," (Position of Rural Women in Fourteen Provinces an of China), *Shehuixue yanjiu* (Sociological Studies) (July 1992)4:104-109.

This change towards small family ideal may also influence other aspects of rural life. For example, the culture of small family size may mean that sexual activities may be associated less with reproduction than with pleasure for many rural couples.

Farm women

This comparison is most salient for those farm families whose husbands work outside doing non-agricultural work.

Despite the fact that many rural women work in rural industries, the sex ratio of industrial workers still favors men. Since each farm family had to produce a grain quota for the state, more men quit agricultural work leaving the farming to women, because women have to take care of young children at home.[17] A recent social survey from China suggests that farm women occupy between 60-70 percent of the agricultural labor force.[18] In a cross-provincial study, Barbara Entwisle et al. found that "working-age women are more than twice as likely as men to work exclusively in agriculture (including agricultural sidelines)."[19] In Imperial China and under the collectives, the gender pattern in Chinese villages had been either *nan geng nü zhi* (men farm and women weave) or *nannü gong geng* (men and women farm together). Now two new patterns—*nan gong nü geng* (men work outside and women farm) and *nannü gong gong* (both men and women work outside) begin to take root in rural China.

In those families where the husbands have left for non-agricultural work, wives are responsible for almost all production and marketing decisions. In fact, women become the actual heads of the households. This is especially true for those women whose husbands work in other regions. Those "holiday" husbands (many of them construction workers and rural merchants) come home only once or twice a year. The new female heads not only have to work hard physically as laborers but also have to plan for their family's affairs on their own. They hire farm hands to help out during the busy seasons. Since crop surplus and sideline products are sold at the market, women's agriculture activities are directly linked to market activities. The long absence of the male family head leaves him ill-equipped for major family decisions even though he may continue to enjoy patriarchal social status. Sometimes, farm women have to support their husbands when those men fail in their businesses or are not able to find jobs in the cities.

The new female family heads have decision power to buy whatever they deem important for the family.

Although a Chinese woman in Imperial China could also become a family head by default, she could never become one ideally even after the death of the family patriarch, not even Mother Jia in *The Dream of the Red Chamber*, who had age and generation to support her role. The new female heads assume family responsibility when they are in their twenties, thirties and forties.

They are more prominent in less developed regions with fewer rural factories. But in other places, women also gain more control in family decision making, as Ellen Judd's study of North China suggests:

Women—not simply as laborers, but as especially skilled or able persons—are often decisive in enabling a household project to flourish, either by virtue of their own particular abilities or by virtue of their capacity to act as effective partners.[20]

Graham Johnson's research in Pearl River Delta, a region with strong rural industrialization, also indicates that rural women dominate the agricultural economy.[21] Moreover, most farm women are not subsistence farmers. They are small-scale commercial farmers. In Shandong alone, out of 14 million working rural women, 12 million participated in commercial endeavors of all sorts (grain production, handicrafts, animal husbandry, garden economy).[22]

Women's economic roles have important other social implications for family relations in rural China. Although sexual inequality still exists, women's status in the family has risen greatly. According to the government news agency, Xinghua, a recent survey shows that more than 47 percent of rural couples share economic responsibility for the family.[23]

While specific aspects of development have specific effects on family structure and women's status, their greatest influence flows through the general economic power they gave young couples and women. For women it meant income, mobility, and opportunity. They use their economic power to improve their status through: markets, industrialization and migration.

Conclusion

Several key features of the new Chinese family begin to take shape in China:

1. The relationship between husband and wife is intensified at the expense of kin and villages;

2. The increase of individual autonomy and personal pursuit of economic opportunities alter the function of kin and village ties.

3. Rural women have achieved more equality than ever before. It seems that women's new power and independence, including their powers of marital decisions, is also linked to their improved living standard and to alternative outside opportunities.

Of course, China is so huge that there are many regional differences in terms of the degree of those changes. And not every woman is able to use the opportunity to leave farming. The majority of farm women still live in villages and still spend much of their time in agricultural production. But farm women also experience changes both within their own home and in the village communities. Indirectly, farm women themselves gain from non-agricultural opportunities available to others.

Baochan daohu, markets, rural industrialization, and migration are providing a necessary, but certainly not a sufficient, cause for the weakening of lineage ties, the rise of the nuclear families and the increased relative equality between the sexes .

It is also important to stress that those changes are not necessarily "good" for every member of the rural society. The older men may resent the progress women make. Even women themselves have gained much and lost some in those changes.

THE FAMILY IN GLOBAL TRANSITION

Despite differences in the contemporary Chinese family revolution, the Chinese case seems to confirm hypotheses proposed by Parsons. Levy, and Goode.

The libertarian context created in the last decade by the Chinese farmers' spontaneous, unorganized, leaderless, nonideological, apolitical movement (SULNAM) has, unintentionally, done more to dilute China's age old patriarchal patterns than has the political leadership of the PRC in more than four decades.

Notes

[1]Kate Xiao Zhou, *How the Farmers Changed China: Power of the People* (Boulder, CO: Westview Press, forthcoming, 1995).

[2]Talcott Parsons and Robert F. Bales, *Family, Socialization and Interaction Process*. Glencoe, Ill.: Free Press, 1955. Marion J. Levy, Jr. *The Family Revolution in Modern China,* (Cambridge, MA.: Harvard University Press, 1949) and *Modernization and the Structure of Societies* (Princeton: Princeton University Press, 1966).

[3]William J. Goode, *World Revolution and Family Patterns* (London: The Free Press of Gelncoe, Collier-Macmillian Limited, 1963). [4]See gender inequality in post-Mao rural China in Barbara Entwisle, Gail E. Eenderson, Susan E. Short, Jill Boura, and Zhai Fengying, "Gender and Family Businesses in Rural China," *American Sociological Review*, vol. 60, no. 1 (Febuary, 1995), pp. 36-57.

[5]Marion J. Levy Jr., *The Family Revolution in Modern China* (New York: Atheneum, 1948).

[6]Fei Hsiao-Tung, *From the Soil: the Foundations of Chinese Society* (Berkeley: University of California Press, 1992) and Maurice Freedman, *Chinese Lineaqe and Society: Fukien and Kwanotunq* (New York: Humanities Press Inc., 1971).

[7]For a good discussion on the family social structure prior to communist China see Marion J. Levy Jr., *The Family Revolution in Modern China* (New York: Atheneum, 1948).

[8] As far as farmers were concerned, the most important aspect of hukou was its control over grain rationing. Therefore, I shall use hukou to refer to both control of mobility and of food. The residence registration system also monitored the identity, social status, party status, and residence of all mainland Chinese. For a good description of Chinese hukou system see Cheng Tiejun and Mark Selden, "The Origins and Social Consequences of China's Hukou System," *China Quarterly* 139 (September 1994):644-668.

[9] William L. Parish, Jr. and Martin Ring Whyte, *Village and Family in Contemporary China*, (Chicago, University of Chicago Press, 1978).

[10] Mark Selden, *Political Economy of Chinese Development* (Armonk, New York: M. E. Sharpe, 1993).

[11] Quanguo funian Nongcun chu (Rural Work division, Chinese Women's Federation), "Zhongguo nongcun de 1.8 yi" (Chinese Rural 180 million), *Zhonqquo Funu* (Chinese Women), 11, (1993), p.23.

[12] See gender inequality in post-Mao rural China in Barbara Entwisle, Gail E. Henderson, Susan E. Short, Jill Bouma, and Zhai Fengying, "Gender and Family Businesses in Rural China," *American Sociological Review*, vol. 60, no. 1 (February, 1995), pp. 36-57.

[13] The new prostitution may also be characterized by less patriarchy than was commonly the case for China (most other societies as well). The emergence of call girls in China is a case in point.

[14] Wang Jian, "Shuju Xianshi Zhongguo Funu Shehui Diwei." (Data Reveals Social Status of Chinese Women," Zhonqquo Funu (Chinese Women) 1 (1992), pp.24-25.

[15] Dai Rejing, "Zhongguo shisishengshi nongcun funu jiben zhuangkuang jigi shenghuo jianxi," (Position of Rural Women in Fourteen Provinces and Cities of China), Shehuixue Yandiu (Sociological Studies) (July 1992)4:104-109.

[16] Wang Jinling, "New Characteristics of Marriages Between Zhejiang Farmers and Women from Outside the Province," *Social Sciences in China*, (Summer 1994-), pp.59-64.

[17] Laurel Bossen, "Chinese Rural Women: What Keeps Them Down on the Farm?" Paper presented at the conference, "Engender-

ing China," February 7, 1992, Wellesley College and Harvard University, Boston, MA.

[18]*Zhongguo Funü (Chinese Women)*, no. 390 (1991), p.8; no. 392 (1991), p.13; and no. 402 (1992), p.2.

[19]Barbara Entwisle et al. 1995.

[20]Ellen R. Judd, *Gender and Power in Rural North China*, (Stanford, CA: Stanford University Press, 1994), p.159.

[21]Graham E. Johnson, "Family Strategies and Economic Transformation in Rural China: some Evidence from the Pearl River Delta," in Deborah Davis and Stevan Harrell, eds., *Chinese Families in the Post-Mao Era*, (Berkeley: University of California Press, 1994), pp.103-136.

[22]Quanguo funian Nongcun chu (Rural Work division, Chinese Women's Federation), "Zhongguo nongcun de 1.8 yi (Chinese Rural 180 million)", *Zhongguo Funu* 11 (1993): p.23.

[23]*Shijie Ribao* (World Journal), June 26, 1995.

Chapter 8

THE HINDU FAMILY: CONSTRAINTS OF THE PAST, STRAINS OF THE PRESENT

Sushil Panjabi

The Hindu family today is a collage of contrasting and conflicting images embossed on the canvass of a tension ridden society. The post-independence strains of a technological onslaught, cross-cultural currents and communal discord, and of the more recent media explosion of the nineties have all drawn up against traditional Hindu value systems to give rise to these tensions. In fact, the contemporary realities of a multireligious and multicultural Indian society in transition are such that they completely undermine the monolithic notion of an unvariegated Hindu family.

The approach to the Hindu family in this paper is not based on any particular "ism" or ideology, but is an attempt to understand it as a signifier of a particular social order with a certain ideal, in the context of its own religio-philosophical and social setting.

Deeply entrenched in a tardily changing social matrix in the midst of globalization and the information explosion, the Hindu family faces the challenge of retaining its specific cultural identity even as it participates in the process of a contemporary homogenizing globalization. On the one hand the tyrannical backward pull of the *samskaras* (early impressions/realization of past perceptions), impedes this onward march; and on the other, the revolt against authority and subjugation necessitated by the demands of a rapidly changing economy raises its head, and the need for self-expression and self-assertion often takes aggressive forms, more so in the younger generation. As a result the unquestioned security and protection provided by the family is endangered.

In addition, the Hindu is traditionally supposed to follow a path to the spiritual goal in which the family is but a stage; but in post-independence modern India, with its insurgent multicultural currents, the emphasis shifts, and the Hindu family is thrown in the travails of questioning its own identity. This study is framed as follows. It first delineates the concepts of family and marriage, the power and position of man and woman, and the sex and role relationships as envisaged in Hindu philosophy and scriptures. Then, at the level of social practice, it analyzes the subjugating strategies and the apparently arbitrary social and emotive constructs of men and women in a "traditional" Hindu family. The next section discusses a few important aspects of the social reform movement in India. Finally, in the context of the changing contemporary reality, this paper examines the relation of modern patriarchal practices to the politics of social change; the exigencies of the rights and freedom of the individual that underlie the recasting of male and female roles, with respect to social and moral responsibility; and the strivings of modern Hindu families through the strains of experienced reality, towards renewed identity.

* * *

Hinduism is a way of life, permeated with the spiritual outlook rather than conformity to a particular concept of religion; for a Hindu may be an atheist, an agnostic, a mystic, a pantheist, a dualist, or a monist. Allowing full liberty in thought, Hinduism enjoins a strict code of conduct in social life. Accordingly, *dharma*, or right action is a very important concept. As A.B. Creel puts it, "...any genuine understanding

210

of Hindu culture will necessarily involve considerable attention to the life and thought structured around dharma" (Creel, 1). So comprehensive is the concept that P.T. Raju, in his glossary of Indian philosophical terms, gives the following list in equivalence of dharma: "Law, nature, rule, idea, norm, quality, entity, truth, element, category" (Raju, 445).

Dr. Radhakrishnan too brings out various aspects of dharma: "Dharma is right action. In the Rig Veda, *rta* is the right order of the universe. It stands for both *satya* or the truth of things as well as dharma or the law of evolution. Dharma formed from the root *dhr*, to hold, means that which holds a thing and maintains it in being. Every group of life, every group of men has its dharma, which is the law of its being. Dharma, or virtue is conformity with the truth of things; *adharma* or vice is opposition to it. Moral evil is disharmony with the truth which encompasses and controls the world (Radhakrishnan, 77-8).

In addition to the ontological, natural, social and moral aspects, dharma also implies a stress on the preservation and continuity of society and conformity to old customs. S.N. Dasgupta maintains that the motive of dharma is "essentially of the nature of social preservation and the maintenance of social solidarity" (xxii-xxiii). Along with this, the central norm was the preservation of *sanātana dharma*, or eternal dharma.

Dharma is closely related to the concepts of *moksa* (salvation) and *karma*, with the latter both in the general sense of action or activity, as well as the specific sense of the law of karma as determining one's present character and status or the duties of one's station in society, that is, one's dharma.

While each individual is born with certain innate tendencies and dispositions according to his karma, and the present is determined, this determinism however, is not irremediable. For the future, though conditional, depends on one's present karma (activity), and dharma consists in the proper functioning of one's life, nature or constitution.. Hence the faithful performance of dharma may lead not only to the improvement of one's present position, but through a series of incarnations, also supply a motive for moksa or salvation.

The twin aspects of karma—the social and the individual are highlighted by the theory of *varna* (profession or caste), which emphasizes the social aspect, and the theory of *āsramas* or the four stages of life, which lays down the individual aspect. Accordingly, the four castes are: *brāhmin*, whose function is the study of religious texts, reading, writing, teaching, and training the young; *ksatriya*, invested with the responsibility of protecting the community and the state by means of valor or warfare; *vaisxa*, entrusted with the job of carrying out trade and commerce; and *sudra*, alloted the task of serving the three upper castes. And the *āsramas* or the four stages, taking up approximately one-quarter of the life of a man, or twenty-five years each, are: *brahmacarya*, the period of celibacy, training and education, during which there is complete emotional and financial dependency on the parents; *gārhastya*, the stage of a householder with involvement in family life; *vānaprasthya*, the period of retreat for detaching oneself from social bonds; and finally *sānñyāsa* or renunciation.

The above scheme is a system of interrelationships, and is hierarchically structured with the provision of differential noms for the proper functioning of society. Dharma in this context is social regulation. And besides the universal dharma—the norms and duties equally obligatory for all human beings—is the doctrine of the *varnāsrama dharma*, comprising the differential norms corresponding to the different norms and stages. As Surama Dasgupta observes: "In case of conflict between the *sādharana dharma* or universal duties and the particular caste-duties the latter are to prevail, for example, the *ksatritya* may violate the principle of non-injury in times of war; and this has been emphasized in the *Gitā* and the *Mahābharata* as well"

(p. 15). And she stresses the point again: "If ever there is any conflict between the *sādharana dharma* and the *āsrama dharma*, the latter should prevail" (p.91).

The Hindu concept of the family accordingly cuts across both caste and the different stages of life with four supreme ends or motivations. These are dharma or righteousness, *artha* or wealth, *kāma* or artistic and cultural life, including desire and pleasure, and *moksa*, which is spiritual freedom or salvation, as the ultimate end. These four motivations provide a link between the realm of desire and that of spirituality, between the temporal and the eternal, indicating that the former is not to be condemned as it is a road to the latter; nor is the latter ever to be lost sight of, for that is the ultimate spiritual realization. *Artha* and *kama* answer to the demands of material reality, while the aim of *moksa* is the final release from the influence of worldly bonds through the pursuit of dharma.

Though Hinduism emphasizes the social system with the individual members subordinated to it, yet there is a realm beyond this one in which society and dharna become unreal, and the individual finds his true being in the spiritual reality. The link is provided by the *Bhagavad Gita* in the doctrine of *nishkama karma*, that is, dharma or duty for the sake of duty, whereby the individual in performing the duties of his station, without desire for the fruits, attains mastery over himself and puts himself on the path to salvation.

* * *

Against the background of such a scheme, we are concerned mainly with *gārhastya*, or the second stage of the *āasrama dharma*, that of the householder. With *kāma*, or the desire for pleasure or cultural life being one of the accepted ends, monastic tendencies are discouraged in this stage. The individual is encouraged, after a period of *brahmacarya*, to enter into family life through the institution of marriage.

While eight kinds of marriage were recognized by the

Hindu law books, the marriages in which personal inclination is subordinated rank higher. The marriages by choice are regarded as low, the lowest being when the woman is purchased, or her modesty is ravished without her consent, in sleep or in the intoxicated state. But even these low forms of marriage are regarded as valid in order to grant the status of wives to women, and legitimacy to their offspring. And while polygamy was traditionally tolerated, monogamy was regarded as the ideal. With the ideal of marriage as a spiritual union in view, the relation of marriage was regarded as sacred and indissoluble.

In Hindu mythology the gods are also married, and the highest of the religious icons are worshipped along with their consorts: Lakṣmī with Viṣṇu, Śiva with Pārvati, and Rāma with Sītā. Besides the image of Śiva as *ardhanārīśvara*—half man, half woman—signifies both masculine and feminine functions of the supreme being. Ideally therefore, marriage implies a relationship of cooperation and complementary functions in the joint missions of procreation, ensuring continuity, and maintaining the solidarity of the society.

In actual conventional practice however, the scenario is very different. The family is controlled by the eldest male member as the kartā or the swāmi (lord) of the family, who also provides for it. He wields the ultimate power over the women, children, and servants. The woman is regarded as *ardhāngini* (half body) and *sahadharminī* (one who helps in observing dharma), implying a man-centered society, with the man as the doer, and the woman as a helpmate with a secondary role to perform. She is supposed to have special functions and duties. She is the *janani* (progenitor) who gives birth to and rears offspring, and performs all the domestic chores. As such she is relieved of the economic burden. But the woman's dependence on the man in the initial division of labor takes on pivotal significance in determining the roles man and woman play in the family.

With patriarchal and patrilineal practices prevalent in most parts of India a male child is much coveted, for it is the son who has to feed the funeral pyre of the father. This is regarded as indispensible in the father's journey to the other world. This is also reflected in the central role the son plays in the *śrādh* ceremony (salutations to the dead), "hereafter he takes on the hardship of the family and is responsible for ensuring the solidarity and well-being of the family. So great is the importance of having a male child that even the second marriage of a man could be justified on grounds of the need for a male heir.

Gender roles are very deliberately and painstakingly constructed in Hindu society. A boy, from his very childhood is conditioned into believing that he is the future lord of the family. Accordingly, he is encouraged to develop certain attitudes towards his female siblings and view the latter as being in need of his protection and support. He is given to feel superior on the basis of his physical strength. Certain traits like valor and manliness are encouraged in him, and the self-assertive, acquisitive and aggressive tendencies are condoned to a certain degree. Also, he is allowed to express himself more openly than the girl child. He is trained to shoulder the responsibility of the family in terms of economic provisions, protection, marrying off his sisters, and taking care of old parents with the help of his wife. He is further expected to keep the name, honor and prestige of the family intact, and if possible, enhance it. The burden of his responsibilities is lightened by making certain concessions to him. His occasional incursions in the field of sex are ignored. Marrying another woman while the first wife is still alive is not strictly condemned, and widower remarriage is unambiguously encouraged. In general, it is taken for granted that he have greater freedom of expression, assertion and action than his female counterpart.

The birth of a girl is borne with equanimity, but if more

than one female child is born into the family it is often considered a misfortune. The unscrupulous custom of dowry lurks in the minds of the parents, the fear being that the dowry for the daughter's marriage could deprive the family of its prosperity, if not ruin it altogether.

As the girl is to be given away in marriage, she will have to adjust to a changed environment. Hence she is trained to be compliant, conform to the established order, and be submissive and obedient. Forbearance, self-control and self-denial are encouraged in her. She is made to cultivate the virtues of sacrifice and service to the family, disregarding her own comfort and convenience. Further, she is supposed to be modest, and safeguard her chastity at any cost, lest the family name be soiled.

Apart from the strict moral codes prescribed for a woman, there is also a definite stand on the status of the embryo and abortion. The embryo enjoys a special moral and spiritual status meriting respect and protection. The traditional medical texts state that the descent of the *jiva* (soul) in the individual abode of consciousness coincides with conception, the killing of a pregnant woman is considered equivalent to the killing of a Brāhmin which is regarded as a heinous crime. As such, abortion is traditionally unacceptable to the classical Hindu view on spiritual, moral and social grounds, except in cases where the mother's life is endangered (Lipner, 41-69).

A widowed woman, in complete contrast to the widower, is ordained to live a simple and austere life of rigid self-control and non-indulgence, and to follow a strict moral code of self-denial at the material, social and physical levels, even to the extreme extent of abstaining from foods that are said to arouse the passions. Woman's sexuality is thus controlled through such social codes of conduct. Not only is her identity as a partner in the family, property, and power, refused to her, her very individuality as a human being is denied to her.

There is also the gender based division of work. A boy is educated and trained to be part of the productive process, or to join one of the various services and make a living for the family. He is relieved of the domestic chores. A girl is trained to do all the household work which is never acknowledged as real work. Often she is deprived of a formal or higher education on the grounds that ultimately she has to take care of the house and look after the children. In the lower classes, where she is also involved in industrial or agricultural labor, her work is doubled. She has to face exploitation within and outside the family.

Eulogizing practices often become veiled strategies for the subjugation of women. An unmarried girl before she attains puberty is made an object of worship on *Kumāri pujá*, on the eighth day of the famous festival of the goddess Durga, and is also regarded as *śudha* (pure). The woman is often compared to, or even given the status of a *devī* (goddess), as *Saraswatī*, the goddess of learning, Lakśmī, the goddess of wealth, or Durgā, the embodiment of *śaktī* (power). These practices reinforce the "ideal" of womanhood and serve to legitimize the strict moral codes to which women are expected to conform.

These moral codes, thus firmly entrenched in family and society, are based on the subjugation and the submission of women. The emphasis on virginity, on a girl being *śudha*, is so strong that it has also given rise to the practice of child marriage; the girl is married off before she attains puberty. Such a marriage of course closes off all avenues of choice and freedom for the woman.

While being unmarried is a social stigma for a Hindu woman, a married woman too is conventionally denied any autonomy whatsoever. According to the *Manu Samhita*, upon which much of contemporary Hindu Law is still based, a woman is, before marriage, the property of her father; after marriage she is regarded as her husband's property; and after her husband's death, as that of her son (218). The father has the right to give away a daughter in marriage as charity or *dāan*; one of the marriage rituals is *kanyādaān* or the giving away of the daughter. And the extent of the husband's right over his wife is exemplified in the famous gambling episode in the *Mahābhārata*, when Yuddhiṣthira, having lost all else, even stakes his wife Draupadī in the game. Very often a marriage is merely a means to improving the prosperity of the groom's family, for along with the bride comes the dowry—comprising exorbitant gifts and cash for the groom and his family. This dowry system, though illegal now, continues unabated in actual social practice. A young woman is thus treated not merely as a commodity that can be bought, but who is given away too along with the gifts.

After marriage, a wife is to be a *patīvratā* (dutiful and faithful to her husband). And Manu lays down the duties of a wife thus: "Even if he is destitute of virtue, seeks pleasure elsewhere, or is devoid of good qualities, yet a husband must be constantly worshiped as a god by a faithful wife" *(Manu Samhita*, 220) [translation mine]. As for a man, it is not a serious problem if he is not inclined towards his wife, for he may seek satisfaction elsewhere, or marry another woman. Again, though bigamy has been outlawed for more than forty years now, the practice of taking on a second wife is far from uncommon for a Hindu man. The woman, on the other hand, is bound to the life of her husband—and sometimes to his death—as his deathmate or as *satī* by burning herself upon her husband's funeral pyre.

* * *

With this traditional background, several attempts were made in nineteenth century colonial India by Indian social reformers to reconstruct the past, and modify traditions to make them more suitable to the demands of the changing times. And the need to confront the onslaught of the dominant western culture, which posed a challenge to the Indian value system, proved to be a catalyst for the reform movement in India.

Europeans in India engaged themselves in the rediscovery of India's past, and the Orientalists like William Jones and H.T. Colebrook highlighted the notion of a golden age which had existed in an unspecified period of India's past. This served the purpose of "reintroducing the Hindu elite to the impenetrable mystery of its ancient lore" (Chakravarty, 31) from the western point of view. Colebrook's researches also focused on the question of women. He cited Gārgī and Maitreyee as examples of the glory of ancient India's womanhood and highlighted the duties of the faithful Hindu widow. One of the most influential Orientalists was James Mill. The criterion by which he judged the level of civilization was the status it accorded to its women. On grounds of the degradation of women in the context of *sati*, the denial of education and property rights, and their subservient position in relation to men, he termed Hindu culture to be a "barbaric" culture (Chakravarty, 35). As Uma Chakravarty observes, these Orientalist attitudes served not just to establish the notion of British superiority, but also to provide a justification of colonial rule in India:

> The degeneration of Hindu civilization and the abject position of Hindu women, requiring the 'protection' and 'intervention' of the colonial state, were two aspects of colonial politics. The third aspect was the 'effeminacy' of the Hindu men who were unfit to rule themselves. On all three counts British rule in India could be justified on grounds of moral superiority. (35)

The indigenous intelligentsia were not watching the scene passively. The status of women, and Hindu culture itself became the site of struggle between the British rulers and the Indian leaders, and this had far-reaching consequences for the Hindu family with the introduction of new legislation. In order for Indian culture to survive it had to legitimize itself in terms of the reinterpretation and authority of its scriptures and the law books. Rājā Rāmmohan Roy's researches found the alternative to the "degenerate" Hindu civilization in the form of the *Vedās* and the *Upaniṣads* as the core of Hindu tradition, and chose the elements relevant to the requirements of the then social and political needs. The impartation of divine knowledge to Maitreyee by Yājnavalkya was used by Rāmmohan Roy to show that women were not inferior to men and that the pandits had given distorted versions of the shastras. He fought against the practice of *satī* and equated forcible concremation of a woman with her dead husband to murder. He rejected the arguments of the advocates of *satī* by pointing out that the Vedas upheld the superiority of knowledge over rites and the ultimate goal of all Hindus was seeking oneness with the divine reality which could not be attained by the practice of *satī*.

Rājā Rāmmohan Roy also fought against the evils of polygamy and caste based marriages. With the prevalence of the rigid caste system, a high-caste Hindu would rather marry his daughter to a high-caste Hindu man having many wives than give her in marriage to a bachelor of a low caste. Roy vouched for women's rights in the ancestral property as well as the property of her husband, by quoting from the different law-givers like Yājnavalkya and Manu.

Like Rāmmohan Roy, another powerful social reformer from Bengal, Íshwarchandra Vidyāsāgar raised his voice against the evils of child-marriage and polygamy. "But his memorable stand," says Susobhan Sarkar, "was in 1855, when he caused a sensation by his outspoken advocacy of widow remarriage in the teeth of the deepest social prejudices. Like Rāmmohan Roy, he made out his case by a parade of scriptural authority to silence his critics.... Legislation was secured for the reform, though the upper-class society was hardly convinced of the need for such a reform" (Sarkar 35).

In the context of the nineteenth and twentieth century nationalist ideology, one of the most significant changes in ideological configuration took place in the context of the nationalist glorification of motherhood. As Jashodharā Bāgahi states,

> The masculine occident conceived the orient as a feminine image. Ironically the nationalists conceived their own country as the great mother figure in keeping with the sanction derived from the religious practices of Hindu Bengal (66).

By representing the country as a Hindu mother/goddess the nationalist culture

> created a political image that resulted in a composite, often self-contradictory image of the mother. The human ideal was one of the all-suffering mother....As the stable centre of a fragile colonial society, she provided constant solace to the humiliated son; on occasion her heroism acts as an inspiration to lift up the downtrodden spirit of the son. But she is also the divine ideal. In her divine form she is the destructive Shakti, ready to destroy the demon of evil.
> ....motherhood is made to stand for the sacrosanct space not sullied by any petty influence. Even in the sphere of education mothers were valued as the wholesome agents of education who will not allow a drastic reversal of indigenous values (Bāgahi, 66).

Thus, thanks to nationalist politics, while the mother was eulogized as a goddess, and raised to sacrosanct levels as the inspiring muse of nationalist spirit and the preserver of indigenous values, this was simultaneously successful in containing the woman within the household, keeping her subservient to the menfolk for all practical purposes, and denying her desires and aspirations as an individual.

Has the Hindu woman, wife or mother, really benefitted from the ideological reconstructions and the reform movements? As Uma Chakravarty says,

> The nation's identity lay in the culture, and more specifically in its womanhood. In the changed political and social environment the image of woman was more important than the social reality. Historians and laymen would complete the process by ensuring, through continued writings in the twentieth century, that the image also came to be perceived as a reality (78).

And in the context of the reinterpretation of the ancient scriptures also, Chakravarty rightly points out that

> No one tried to read the ancient texts to see what rights the Vedic dasi (woman in servitude) and others like her had in the Vedic golden age. Recognizing her existence would have been an embarrassment to the nationalists. The twentieth century has continued to reproduce, in all essentials, the same kind of womanhood that the nineteenth century has so carefully, and so successfully constructed as an enduring legacy for us (79).

* * *

In the latter part of the twentieth century of post-independent India, a number of developments have created cracks in the firm foundation of the Hindu family. The exhilarating speed with which technological changes have been taking place, the media explosion, multiculturalism, the supposed newfound freedom of the individual on the basis of humanistic philosophy, and the erosion of established values have all contributed to the reassessment of one's relation to the society and the family as its nuclear cell. Why should one be enslaved to traditions and be bound by social and familial regulation? The connotation of freedom as *mukti* or salvation has lost its relevance. The mundane meaning has its tangible references: freedom from oppression, from exploitation, from the yoke of rotting institutions, and from encroachment on the privacy and dignity of the individual. Thus the question of individual happiness is foregrounded as against the familial values.

As such, the modern family is passing through the vicissitudes of the security-insecurity paradox. Traditionally the family is supposed to provide the maximum security on various fronts—love, home, interaction, nurturance, support-systems and crisis management. With the growing consciousness of the rights of individual members, the questioning of the fundamental Hindu family, greater love of adventure, and fundamental urges, have facilitated great flights of freedom with hardly any branch to hold onto. The insecurity has seeped into the interpersonal relations of the adults for lack of mutual trust and the conflict of egos. The children are the victims of the fallout of this warfare, and experience the pressures of finding their own proper place in the family. The conflict between the old values and the demands of the fast-changing global society have created tensions which make the task of accommodating oneself to the mechanical, technological and electronic texture of the material circumstance a major challenge.

On the social front, the tensions are even more accentuated. Steeped in traditional morality of familial relations and archaic beliefs, caste-discriminations still persist in the Hindu society. Though in big cities the attitude towards caste among the highly educated Hindus is generally in favor of its abolition, the system is still prevalent in orthodox families and continues to be quite tyrannical in the small towns and villages. Inter-caste dining and inter-caste marriages are not happily accepted. The increased awareness among the lower castes of their oppressio by the higher castes, and the avowed superiority of the latter create inter-caste tensions. As Kuppuswamy observes, "...though social life in India has been revolutionized, still one cannot say with any confidence that caste is not with us. It is there and probably will continue to be there in the foreseeable future" (190).

Despite the ostensible improvement in the status of women, the actual family scene is a trying situation for a Hindu woman. Many women easily succumb to the arbitrary eulogizing constructs, internalize the images so presented as ideals, and try to conform to them. Moreover, the majority of women lack consciousness of their own status as individuals and their rights due to the lack of education. Very often they shun the courageous pursuit of their own objectives due to the fear of being discredited in society. The limited opportunities for improvements are within the periphery of patriarchy. Gerda Lerner's observation in this connection is very relevant to the Hindu family and society:

> The system of patriarchy can function only with the cooperation of women. This cooperation is secured by a variety of means: gender indoctrination; educational deprivation; the denial to women of knowledge of their history; the dividing of women, one from the other, by defining "respectability" and "deviance" according to women's sexual activities; by restraints and outright coercion; by discrimination in access to economic resources and political power; and by awarding class privileges to conforming women (217).

The practice of patriarchy, in addition to the old ways, has found new modes of exploitation. Kumkum Sangari and Sudesh Vaid, in *Recasting Women*, also point out that the social developments of the past two decades have shattered the postcolonial complacency about the improving status of women. They talk about the pressing urgency to analyze the interrelation of patriarchal practices with political economy, religion, law and culture, in view of women being pushed to the margins of the production process, escalation of communal conflicts, and politicization of religious identities (p.2). Where the core of society is fraught with the domination of the one and the subordination of the other in terms of family, caste and class, social democracy is a hypocrisy and the political advocacy of it only an eyewash. Justice in familial relations is relegated to laws based on ancient scriptures and their biased interpretations, often in the interests of the stronger.

While this is the social situation, women themselves are not mere passive victims of these practices. As Leela Dube asserts:

> ...Hindu rituals and practices set certain limits in terms of the dispositions they inculcate among women and the different kinship roles with varying status which they assign to them within the family. The rituals and practices and the social system are, moreover, imbued with a certain givenness and appear as a part of the natural order of things. It is within these limits that women question their subordination, express resentment, use manipulative strategies, often against other women in the family, carve out a living space and collude in their own oppression. All this is informed by what we call after Gramsci, a contradictory consciousness (181).

Women deal with such tensions by manipulating the restrictive situations in both positive and negative ways. They often become well-versed in traditions, manage the. affairs of the family efficiently, and control the younger members, thus creating a position of authority for themselves, though in the ultimate analysis they may well be subordinated to their husbands or to the eldest male member of the family. Sometimes their resentment is expressed in the outbursts of rebellion against the control over their lives, particularly when they see their daughters suffering the same kind of fate.

Manipulations that could empower women often ironically result in the oppression of women by women, too. Greater consumerism and the desire for more and more material goods lead the inlaws of a woman to make greater dowry demands. The mother- inlaw, who may have been subjected to torturous treatment in the past, often turns upon her daughter-inlaw and oppresses her in collusion with the other members of the family, including her son. Thus she empowers herself with the patriarchal power which was the cause of her own oppression.

Recently there has been a rise in fundamentalism, both Hindu and Muslim, in India. Linking of Hindutva politics to family ties can also be seen in the functioning of a fundamentalist Hindu organization, that was banned for some time after the demolition of the Babri Masjid in Ayodhyā in October 1992, the Rāshtrīya Swayam Sewak Sangh. The RSS likes to be popularly known as the Sangh *parīvaar* or the Sangh family, implying not only that the RSS is one large family that demands family loyalties within its organization, but also connoting the fact that it has located the Hindu family as the site of political training for its members; the fundamentalist values of the RSS have to permeate the very family itself.

The Hindu fundamentalist drive to create a privileged space of Hindu culture has also taken a nasty turn in instigating forced cases of *satī*, and the controversial sati of Roop Kanwar of Deorala in Rajasthan in 1987 is an important indicator of how fundamentalist Hindu patriarchal power can still force a woman to burn on her husband's pyre in the name of preserving Hindu culture (Sangari, 1987, Sunder Rajan).

On the other hand, the rapidly increasing industrialization, urbanization, economic pressures, globalization and the media explosion have brought tremendous changes, and the monolithic notion of the Hindu family has been ruptured.

Large-scale industrialization in the post-independence era has forced the villagers and the poor to migrate to industrial centers, giving rise to slums in the cities and larger towns. Extreme poverty, and the hardships of slum life often lead men to drinking, as a consequence of which they often beat up their wives, and commit adultery. The women, though not very conventional themselves, ultimately shoulder the burden of supporting the family. Though in many cases there is a reversal of the economic role, there is hardly any change in the power relations.

In the more affluent circles, while on the one hand the joint family had begun to give way to nuclear families with the younger generations desiring greater freedom, or because of the mobility demanded by transferable corporate jobs, on the other hand, the desire for the nuclear family has also received a blow due to the economic pressures of inflation, and the boom in the prices of real estate, making the small joint families more economically feasible.

A peculiar feature of a large number of Hindu families is that even where there are nuclear households, the family still remains a joint family in spirit, with the elders and influential members of the joint family often continuing to make the crucial decisions on behalf of the nuclear units.

The modern joint family is characterized by generational strains of various kinds. Fraught with the contradictions in consciousness of tradition and modernity, the middle-class family lives in stifling conditions and finds it difficult to come out openly and acknowledge its desires and cravings relating to the choice of profession, of the marriage partners and living a life of freedom according to its own tastes and inclinations. The media, particularly television, which now carries a large number of foreign serials like Santa Barbara and The Bold and the Beautiful, in addition to the indigenous ones, and films, both foreign and Indian, project conflicting ideologies. These contradictions are apparent not just between the foreign programmes and the Indian ones, but even within the Indian programmes themselves. On the one hand, epics like *The Rāmāyana* and *The Mahābhārata* are serialized, perpetuating conventional familial values, reinforcing the Hindu cultural identity, and the ideals of *Sītā* and *pativratā*, and on the other, serials like Dard, portraying extra-marital affairs, highlight the outbreak of rebellion against traditional Hindu norms in the more permissive pockets of contemporary society. The strains thus created breed contradictions in culture. Often in the same family the elderly people have one kind of culture, living and thinking in the old ways, and the younger generation another kind, succumbing to the multinational corporate and individualistic culture, fashion, novelty and consumerism. For example, in one room the Sanskrit hymns may be chanted softly with utmost religious devotion by the aged, while in the other rap and pop music may be played at deafening volumes. Caught between the two, the middle-aged group keeps wondering about questions of adaptability versus the validity of cultural traditions.

In the cities the family pattern varies across different classes and sections of society. In some elite pockets the mores are openly flouted on the grounds of individual liberty. It is not uncommon in these circles for man and woman to live together without being married. Nor is marriage indispensable to grant legitimacy to their children. In such circles a child born outside of wedlock is known as a "love child." Illegitimacy which is still associated with severe social stigma in most of Hindu society, hardly invites any social censure in these cosmopolitan pockets, where the individuals have the advantage of wealth, position and power.

With the increase of individualistic lifestyles there is a perceptible rise in the number of single parent families due to separation, divorce and desertion. Most of these families are headed by the female parent. And while the excessive premium placed on motherhood in Hindu culture often acts as a restrictive force curtailing a woman's self-fulfilment in other spheres of life, it often plays a positive role in the case of children from broken homes. The values of motherhood and nurturance still take precedence over individual desires with most Hindu women, so as a result there are fewer cases of emotional breakdown among children of single mothers than among their counterparts in highly individualistic cultures.

Economic pressures that necessitate both husband and wife

to maintain jobs even at the cost of living apart or the wife's desire to fulfil herself through work of her choice, have given rise to the commuting or long-distance family. The fact that such decisions are often mutual decisions shows a shift in power relations within such families. It is significant that this is in contradistinction to the prevalent Hindu marriage laws which grant the husband the restitution of conjugal rights, force the wife if she has chosen to stay away from her husband to cohabit with him.

Through the media explosion, the increased communication between different cultures, and the rise in the exchange of international students, the influence of the gay rights movements in Europe and North America has made an impact on Indian society. The critical need to increase awareness about aids and modes of preventing aids, especially among the gay community has been another important factor responsible for gay men coming out of the closet as activists and starting up a dialogue on this issue with other gay men.

The predominant view of homosexuality as a social taboo, and the active suppression of it to the extent of encouraging homosexual men to marry women and continue with their homosexual activities under the cover of a "respectable" heterosexual marriage is now being challenged. This is evident in the formation of gay and lesbian associations such as Red Rose and Sakhi in Delhi and Khush in Bombay, the publication of gay magazines like *Dost* from Bombay, and also in the first national gay conference held in India in January 1995. As a result the larger cities like Bombay and Delhi are now witnessing the presence of the first openly gay and lesbian families, few though they may be in number.

The various strains of contemporary reality thus threaten to fragment traditional notions of the family. Amidst all this however, the Hindu family has largely retained its integrated character. The family as a basic conjugal unit along with its immediate offspring has not been substantially challenged so far. Love as the basis of interpersonal relationships is still regarded as being of prime value.

The close bond is illustrated by the weekly interviews with prominent personalities conducted by a popular weekly, *The Telegraph Colour Magazine*. In answer to questions regarding the most important influences in their lives, most of these personalities refer to their fathers or mothers, and children are usually cited as their most precious possession or the love of their lives.

One may wonder about the sustaining sources of this strong bond. One answer may be found in the traditional notion of the *āsrama dharma*, specifically the stage of *brahmacarya*, the first-quarter of one's life, which involved dependence of the young on the parents during this period of training and education. Though *bramacarya* is not generally practiced in its original sense today, it is still conventional for daughters to stay with their parents till they get married, and for sons to live with their parents for at least the first twenty-five years of their lives and perhaps even more if they continue to live in a joint family after marriage. This calls for a lot of sacrifice on the part of the parents, not only as a matter of duty but also as an expression of love and affection. This is responsible for the formation of stronger bonds within the Indian familythan in cultures where children tend to go away from home earlier.

The residues of nationalist ideology regarding the family and motherhood could also be responsible for the strong bonding in the Hindu family. The demarcation of the family as the sacrosanct site for the cultivation of spiritual, ethical and nationalist values, and the role of the mother in ensuring both the cultivation and the preservation of these values even at the cost of great personal sacrifice, lends not just social, but also ethical, and spiritual force to the family, inextricably linking an individual's sense of being, and sense of social, material, ethical, and sometimes even spiritual achievement with the well-being of the family.

In the post-independence modern India, the relief from the strains of the insurgent materialistic civilization is sought for in the return to the care and comfort of the family based on freedom and understanding.

With this strong bond amidst the intricacies of a complex and challenging external reality, the Hindu family is in search of its own identity—a projection of its modified traditional base which will fit the changed context, and upon which it can draw in order to redefine itself. It is trying to come out of the shell of insularity and accommodate itself to the dominant values of the larger human society by trying to get rid of some of its evil institutions such as the dowry system, child marriage and *satī*.

What the Hindu family needs is the dismantling of the ideological presuppositions relating to the gender-biased relationships and the reconstruction of a family model with a view to the revision of sex-based roles in the socialization and education of the young.

It has to inculcate a sense of social responsibility among the young in the exercise of individual freedom, learn to relate itself to the new work culture, and the changed ways of thinking inherent in the fast-changing external reality.

*I would like to thank Kavita Panjabi for her valuable suggestions that went into the making of this chapter.

References

B.Kuppuswamy. *Social Change in India*. N.Delhi: Vikas Publishing House, 1982.

Bagchi, Jashodhara. "Representing Nationalism: Ideology of Mother-hood in Colonial Bengal." *Economic and Political Weekly*, Review of Women's Studies, October 20-27, 1990.

Chakravarty, Uma. "Whatever Happened to the Yedic Dasi?" in eds Kumkum Sangari and Sudesh Vaid, *Recasting Women: Essays in Colonial History*. N.Delhi: Kali for Women, 1989.

Creel, Austin B. *Dharma in Hindu Ethics*. Calcutta: Firma ELM Pvt. Ltd., 1977.

Dasgupta, Surama. *Development of Moral Philosophy in India*. Bombay: Orient Longman, 1961.

Dasgupta, Surendranath and S.K. Dc. *A History of Sanskrit Literature*, vol. 1. Calcutta: University of Calcutta, 1947.

Dube, Leela. "Socialization of Hindu Girls in Patrilineal India," in ed. Karuna Chanana, *Socialization. Education and Women*. N. Delhi: Orient Longman, 1988.

Lerner, Gerda. *The Creation of Patriarchy*. University Press, 1986. New York: Oxford

Lipner, Julius J. "The Classical Hindu View on Abortion and the Moral Status of the Unborn," in eds. Harold G. Coward, Julius J. Lipner, and Katherine K.Young, *Hindu Ethics: Purity, Abortion and Euthanasia*. Delhi: Sri Satguru Publications, Indian Books Centre, 1991.

Manu Samhita. Calcutta: Deepali Book House, 1985.

Radhakrishnan, Sarvepalli. *The Hindu View of Life*. New York: George Allen and Unwin Ltd. Macmillan, 1957.

Raju, Poola Tirupati. *Idealistic Thought of India*. Cambridge: Harvard University Press, 1953.

Sangari, Kumkum. "There is No Such Thing as Voluntary Sati." *The Times of India*. Sunday Review, 25th October, 1987.

Sangari, Kumkum, and Sudesh Vaid. *Recasting Women: Essays in Colonial History*. N. Delhi: Kali for Women, 1989.

Sarkar, Susobhan. *On the Bengal Renaissance*. Calcutta: Papyrus, 1979.

Sunder Rajan, Rajeswari. "The Subject of Sati: Pain and Death in the Contemporary Discourse on Sati." *Yale Journal of Criticism*, vol.3, no.2, 1990.

Chapter 9

THE FAMILY IN THE JEWISH TRADITION*

Richard L. Rubenstein

Few subjects have been the object of as much reflection by Jewish religious teachers over millennia as marriage and the family, the fundamental unit of society in Judaism. In spite of the transformations experienced by the Jewish people since biblical times, there have been important elements of religio-social continuity, especially in the traditional attitudes towards the marital relationship.[1] Paradoxically, we can best understand these views if we first consider the differences between Jewish and Christian attitudes as the latter were formulated by Paul of Tarsus.

Paul's views are useful because he began his adult career within the movement in Judaism out of which normative rabbinic Judaism arose and became dominant, namely, the Pharisees. Moreover, it is evident from Paul's writings that he was learned in the traditions of the Pharisees.[2] After conversion, Paul was distinguished from the Pharisees by the conviction that Jesus of Nazareth was the Christ, the Messiah, and that by his conversion he had partaken of both Christ's crucifixion and his resurrection. Paul tells us, "I have been crucified with Christ, and I live now not with my own life but with the life of Christ who lives within me" (*Galatians* 2:19).

Paul believed that Christ lived in him and every Christian, because in baptism Christians had died to their old selves in a real rather than a metaphorical way. In his letter to the Christians at Rome, Paul asks rhetorically: "Are you ignorant that when we were baptized in Christ Jesus we were baptized in his death? In other words, when we were baptized we went into the tomb with him and joined him in death, so that as Christ was raised from the dead by the Father's glory, we too might live a new life" (*Romans* 6:3,4).[3] It was, however, obvious to Paul that neither he nor his fellow Christians had yet experienced the final resurrection of the dead as had Christ. For Paul resurrection steins at baptism with the bestowal of the Holy Spirit, but this bestowal is merely the "earnest money" or "pledge" (*II Cor.* 1:22; 5:5) of the final transformation of humanity which will take place at the Last Day when the elect will put off their corruptible bodies and be "raised incorruptible" (*I Cor.* 15:32).

Paul did not believe that that great day was far off. On the contrary, he believed that the entrance of baptized Christians into the World to Come was imminent. *In accordance with the view shared by both Jesus and the rabbis, Paul also believed that in the World to Come, "men and women do not marry"* (*Matt.* 22:30).

Paul's views on the imminence of Christ's final redemptive triumph strongly influenced his views on marriage. Wherever possible, Paul counseled, Christians ought to remain in the same state (*klesis*) as that in which they were baptized (*I Cor.* 7:20). Those who were married were not to "look for freedom" (7:27). Those who were "free of a wife" were not to "look for one" (7:27). Marriage was to be preferred to fornication (6:12-18; 7:5,9) or resort to a prostitute (6:15-16), which at the time was often a ritual act involving communion with a sacred prostitute.[4] Nevertheless, even when Paul counseled those who were married to remain so, he stressed his conviction that his own celibate state was preferable to marriage in the interim period (7:8, 28). Paul wrote to the Corinthians:

> I want you to be free from anxious care. The unmarried man cares for the Lord's business; his aim is to please the Lord. But the married man cares for worldly things; his aim is to please his wife; and he has a divided mind... (7:32-34).

Paul's preference for celibacy was consistent with his beliefs concerning the timetable of redemption. The sexual act is fundamentally nature's way of assuring the generational continuity of her mortal offspring. As noted, Paul confidently believed that the End was near and that the redeemed cosmos would no longer be subject to the hazards of mortality. (See *I Cor.* 7:31; 15:24-28; *I Thes.* 4:13-17; 5:2-9; *Phil.* 3:20-21). Hence, the reproductive act ceased to have any relevance for him.

Unlike baptism, Jewish circumcision is not a ritual of death and resurrection. Circumcision is a premessianic ritual that ties the sons to the fathers and to their world, the world of the patriarchal family. Circumcision roots the young Jew in his place in the order of earthly generations. It marks the young Jew's entrance into his biological family and is his initial preparation for his masculine sexual role as *paterfamilias*. Heterosexual relations can logically be seen as spiritually subordinate to celibacy by those who, like Paul, are convinced of the world's imminent entrance into deathless immortality. Under such circumstances, nature's method of assuring the generational continuity of mortal individuals becomes irrelevant. Because Judaism is premessianic and is normally, though not always, suspicious of messianic movements, generational continuity and the institutions and traditions that fostered it, such as marriage and the family, have always been indispensable.[5]

The normative Jewish view concerning the primacy of marriage is expressed in a Midrash on the death of Nadab and Abihu, the two sons of Aaron.[6] Scripture depicts Nadab and Abihu as dying as a result of "a fire from the Lord" (*Lev.* 10:2). Although Scripture states that the two had offended by presenting before the Lord "illicit fire which He had not commanded" (*Lev.* 10:1), many of the rabbis were not satisfied that this offense was the sole cause of their demise. According to R. Levi, they were punished for a graver offense, their refusal to marry, in accordance with the biblical tradition that they had no children.[7] R. Levi's interpretation is consistent with the tradition that both ordinary Jews and scholars are religiously obligated to marry.[8]

In the Bible and the Talmud the basic family unit was patriarchal and both polygamy and concubinage were theoretically permitted.[9] Nevertheless, the monogamous family came to be regarded as the ideal. This ideal is expressed in *Proverbs* 31:10-31, the praise of the Woman of Valour which is traditionally recited at the Sabbath evening meal by the husband:

> A woman of valour who can find? for her price is far above rubies. The heart of her husband cloth safely trust in her, so that he bath no need of gain. She doeth him good and not evil all the days of her life (31:10-13)... She looketh well to the ways of her household, and eateth not the bread of idleness. Her children rise up and call her blessed; her husband also, and he praiseth her (31:28-29).

This is obviously an idealized image. Nevertheless, it shows that the monogamous ideal was rooted in Judaism by the time the Wisdom literature was composed. According to George Foote Moore, no instance of plural marriage is recorded among the more than two thousand Sages mentioned in the Talmud.[10] By the tenth century, Jews who had been domiciled in lands under Muslim control, where it was possible to take a second wife, began to join their co-religionists in European Christian lands where the Western Church had issued decrees against polygamy as early as the fifth century.[11] The practice of polygamy was officially forbidden by the *takkanah* or Ban of Rabbenu Gershom b. Judah of Mayence (d. 1028). The *takkanah* prohibited a man from marrying a second wife unless permitted to do so by 100 rabbis from three different "countries," a practical impossibility. The *takkanah* also prohibited a man from divorcing his wife against her will, an action which might otherwise have been taken to evade the *takkanah*.[12] However, the prohibition was only binding among Ashkenazic communities, that is, the predominant communities of northern and Eastern Europe and later North and South America and Australia. It was never binding among Sephardic communities which included Spanish Jews before 1492 and their descendants thereafter, as well as Jews in the Islamic world.

A release from the ban might be obtained under exceptional circumstances. For example, if a wife becomes mentally incapacitated and cannot maintain a normal married life, the husband would normally be entitled to a divorce. Since the wife is not legally capable of consenting, divorce is impossible. A rabbinical court may permit a second marriage provided the husband continues to assume all of the expenses, including medical, of the first wife. Should the first wife recover, she cannot demand that the husband divorce the second wife and the husband is legally obliged to divorce the first wife. Should the latter refuse, the husband is free of all obligations toward her save the payment stipulated in her *ketubah* or marriage contract.[13] Release from the ban is also possible in the case of an adulterous wife who rejects the rabbinical court's order to consent to her husband's request for a divorce.[14]

In the State of Israel, where traditional Jewish law concerning marriage and divorce is legally binding on all Jews, a national rabbinical conference called by the Chief Rabbis of both the Ashkenazic and Sephardic communities ruled that monogamy was legally obligatory. In addition, the state enacted laws making bigamy a criminal offense save when a rabbinical court permits a second marriage and this permission is ratified by the chief rabbis of both communities.[15]

In Judaism the fundamental purpose of the family is generational continuity in both the biological and the religio-cultural sense. From biblical times onward, the cognitive universe of the Israelites was very different from that of their neighbors which often proved highly seductive to the Israelites. It was the family's responsibility to inculcate those values in the young which would be most likely to assure religio-cultural continuity. This responsibility was intensified by the defeat of the Jews by the Romans in 70 and 135 C. E. and the triumph of Christianity as the official religion of the Roman Empire.

The Jews had experienced defeat by their most important political and religious rivals. Of especial importance is the fact that Christian supersessionary claims were combined with the political power which derived from that faith's effective cognitive monopoly throughout the European world. As a result, the family assumed a heightened importance to compensate for the absence of autonomous Jewish political institutions and the numerical weakness of Judaism in the Diaspora.

An important consequence of the defeat of the Jews by Rome and Christianity was that the Jews became a "pariah people." Max Weber regarded the Jews as the "most impressive historical example" of such a people.[16] Although his description of a "pariah people" could be applied to the ethnic Chinese in Southeast Asia and to the Indians and Pakistanis in Africa before World War II, it fits the pre-Enlightenment, traditional Jewish community:

> These people form communizes, acquire specific occupational traditions of handicrafts or other arts, and cultivate a

belief in their ethnic community. They live in a "diaspora" strictly segregated from all personal intercourse, except that of an unavoidable sort, and their situation is legally precarious. Yet, by virtue of their economic indispensability, they are tolerated, indeed, frequently privileged, and they live in interspersed political communities.[17]

Pariah status is a function of both power relations and the social division of labor. Privileged caste and status groups inevitably regard their status honor as the highest and have traditionally regarded pariah groups with contempt. Since the privileged group has the ability to define social reality, there is always danger that the less powerful group will introject the more powerful group's disdain and fall victim to self-contempt with all of its negative psychological and social consequences. In the most extreme case, the weaker group may disintegrate into an anomie underclass.

Self-contempt was never a problem among traditionally religious Jews. The phenomenon of Jewish self-hate first became a problem among post-Enlightenment assimilated Jews, especially in Germany and Austria-Hungary, who were in far greater contact with non-Jews than their traditional ancestors had been. The assimilated Jews had lost or abandoned their traditional religio-cultural moorings but discovered that no personal achievement could remove the stigma of pariah status. In some cases such as that of Otto Weiniger, a pre- World War I Viennese assimilated Jew, the sting of self-hatred could only be undone by suicide.

Not so, traditional Jews. Their faith in the election of Israel by the sovereign Creator of Heaven and Earth and their conviction that their traditions alone were fully in accord with the Divine Will as revealed to the absolutely incomparable and authoritative religious teacher, Moses, gave them a sense of status honor no less unshakable than that of the powerful. The negative experiences which the powerless inevitably experienced only intensified their faith that in the end "the last shall be first."

Apart from any question of credibility, this system of beliefs prevented the Jews from becoming a morally anomie underclass. It did so by emphasizing the importance of discipline and self-mastery. Like any group under constant threat, Jews were trained to avoid alcoholism, licentious behavior, blood sports, gambling and aggressive provocations. I shall never forget watching a drunken peasant who could barely stand up trying to make his way through a railroad station in Lublin, Poland in 1965. Undoubtedly, liquor was a comfort which enabled him temporarily to forget the hardships life had thrust upon him. I asked my Polish hosts what would happen to the man. They told me the police would take him, keep him overnight until he sobered up, and then send him home. I thought to myself that in the many centuries of Jewish domicile in Poland no Jew ever felt secure enough to let himself go the way the peasant had. To have done so was to place oneself in a potentially life-threatening situation.

Judaism was not a religion of law and discipline because it knew nothing of God's love, as has been perennially suggested in Christian theology. There is a much simpler explanation for the importance religious law assumed in Judaism: only as a religion of law could the Jews have even a remote chance of survival in what was all too frequently an hostile environment.

With the pleasures of letting go outside of the home largely prohibited by Jewish law as well as by social reality, it was inevitable that Jews would seek to find their deepest emotional satisfactions within the home and they were encouraged to do so by their religious teachers. Homosexuality was looked upon with profound disfavor. In traditional Judaism marriage has two fundamental purposes, procreation and the satisfaction made possible by the marital relationship. This satisfaction does not derive from the sexual relationship alone; companionship and intimacy, the sharing of life together, are also a profound source of satisfaction even when the difficulties and tragedies of life are shared.

The importance of marital pleasure independent of procreation is affirmed in the Seven Blessings which are recited as part of every marriage ceremony. These blessings include the following:

> O cause these loving companions greatly to rejoice, even as of old Thou didst gladden Thy creature in the Garden of Eden. Blessed are Thou, O Lord, who causest bridegroom and bride to rejoice.
>
> Blessed art Thou, O Lord our God, King of the universe, who has created joy and gladness, bridegroom and bride, mirth and exultation, pleasure and delight, love, fellowship, peace, and companionship... Blessed art Thou, O Lord, who causest the bridegroom to rejoice with the bride.

The text of the Seven Blessings is very old. The wording currently used is already found in the Babylonian Talmud which, as noted above, was redacted toward the end of the fifth century.[18]

As important as marital pleasure and companionship may be, procreation is a fundamental religious obligation for every Jewish male. This was already prescribed by the Mishnah and commented upon in the Gemarra:

> *Mishnah:* A man may not desist from the duty of procreation unless he already has children ... *Gemarra:* If he has children he may desist from procreation but not from [further] marriage. This is in keeping with what R. Nahman said in the name of Samuel: Even if a man has many children, he is not allowed to remain unmarried, as it is written, 'It is not good for man to dwell alone' (*Gen.* 2:18).[19]

Although marriage in Judaism is in no sense a sacrament, it is *kiddushin*, the sacred relationship whereby the wife is consecrated to her husband and absolutely forbidden to all others for the duration of the marriage.[20] Nevertheless, although the husband acquires rights over his wife's ishut (wifehood), he acquires none over her person.[21]

Scripture stipulates the husband's fundamental obligations toward his wife as follows: "her food, clothing and sexual rights [*sh'er, k'sut* and *onah*] he shall not diminish" (*Exodus* 21:10). The meaning of the husband's obligation not to diminish his wife sexual rights or *onah* was widely discussed in Talmudic and post-Talmudic literature. The Talmud declares: "A man is required to give joy to his wife..."[22] Positively, this meant that the husband was expected to be considerate of his wife's sexual needs and make the act a source of joy to her; negatively, it meant that under no circumstances was a husband entitled to force himself upon his wife against her will.

R. Moses ben Nahman, known as Nahmanides (d. 1270), a kabbalist and one of the most important rabbinic authorities of the Middle Ages, offered an idealized portrait of how the husband should approach the wife:

> Therefore engage her first in conversation that puts her heart and mind at ease and gladdens her. Thus your mind and your intent will be in harmony with hers. Speak words which arouse her to passion, union, love, desire and *eros* [Hebrew, *agavim*]—and words which elicit attitudes of reverence for God, piety and modesty...
>
> *Never may you force her, for in such union the Divine Presence cannot abide.* Your intent is then different from hers, and her mood not in accord with yours. Quarrel not with her, nor strike her in connection with this act. As our Sages taught: "Just as a lion tramples and devours and has no shame, so a boorish man strikes and copulates and has no shame" (*Pesahim* 49b). Rather win her over with words of graciousness and seductiveness... Hurry not to arouse passion until her mood is ready; begin in love; let her "semination" take place first.[23] (Italics added)

Nahmanides' epistle is important because it shows that in spite of the patriarchal character of the traditional family, concern for the woman's conjugal rights was never absent from the tradition.

Nahmanides was one of the most important theological critics of the greatest philosopher and legal authority of the Middle Ages, Rabbi Moses b. Maimon or Maimonides (1135-1204). Maimonides' views on the subject of marriage were influenced by Aristotle. In his great philosophical work, *The Guide to the Perplexed*, Maimonides placed sexual pleasure on a lower level than philosophical speculation, an atypical view for a Jewish religious authority. Maimonides accepted Aristotle's opinion that sexual pleasure is dependent on the sense of touch, which is the lowest in dignity of the five senses, rather than the intellect which is highest faculty.[24]

Although Nahmanides was exceedingly respectful in his response to Maimonides' position, he was emphatic in his opposition:

> Know that sexual intercourse is holy and pure when carried on properly, in the proper time and with the proper intentions.... The matter is not as our Rabbi and Guide—of blessed memory—supposed, in his *Guide to the Perplexed*, where he endorses Aristotle's teaching that the sense of touch is unworthy. God forbid. That Greek scoundrel is wrong and his error proceeds from his view of the universe. Had he believed that one God created the world he would not have slipped into such error.... If we were to say that intercourse is repulsive then we blaspheme God who made genitals...Hands can write a Torah scroll and are then honorable and exalted; hands, too, can perform evil deeds and then they are ugly. So the genitals.... Whatever ugliness there is comes from how man uses them. All organs of the body are neutral; the use made of them determines whether they are holy or unholy.... Therefore marital intercourse, under proper circumstances, is an exalted matter.... Now you

can understand what our Rabbis meant when they declared that when a husband unites with his wife in holiness, the Divine Presence abides with them.[25]

The rabbinic stress on the sacred character and primacy of marital relations also influenced the Jewish interpretation of *Genesis* 38:7-10 dealing with Er and Onan:

> And Er,...,Judah's first-born son, was wicked in the sight of the Lord, and the Lord slew him. And Judah said unto Onan: "Go unto thy brother's wife and perform the levirate duty and raise up offspring for thy brother." Now Onan knew that the seed would not be his; and it came to pass when he went into his brother's wife that he would spill it on the ground, lest he should give his seed for his brother. And the thing that he did was evil in the sight of the Lord; and he slew him also.

According to David Feldman, a preeminent rabbinic authority on the laws of marriage in traditional Jewish law, this passage was more important for the Church than the synagogue.[26] The very term "onanism" reflects Christian interpretation. Augustine held that *Genesis* 38:7-10 refers to contraception in marriage and teaches us that it is wrong to lie with one's wife when conception is deliberately avoided.[27] The same interpretation of *Genesis* 38:7-10 is to be found in the writings of a modern authority, Leon Josef Cardinal Suenens:

> She [the church] will never say that the use of contraceptives is licit. Onanism was condemned in no uncertain terms in *Casti Connubii* which recalled all of the Church's teaching on the subject.[28]

By contrast, rabbinic tradition stresses Onan's refusal to give Tamar offspring rather than the fact that he "poured his seed upon the ground." A sister-in-law is forbidden to a deceased husband's brother except when the deceased expires without offspring. Onan's marriage to Tamar was only licit because Onan was under obligation to raise up offspring for his dead brother in a levirate marriage. By refusing to get his wife with child, Onan nullified the whole purpose of such a marriage which then became a forbidden incestuous relationship punishable by death "from Heaven." In contrast to an ordinary marriage, in a levirate marriage no purpose other than the continuation of the brother's line is legitimate.[29] Clearly, for the rabbis neither *coitus interruptus* nor contraception is the fundamental issue in Onan's offense.

Moreover, there was even a minority opinion, among the rabbis, R. Eliezer's, that in the case of a lactating mother, the husband might practice *coitus interruptus* to prevent a second pregnancy which could reduce the milk available for the nursing child.[30] The majority did not concur with R. Eliezer and forbade *coitus interruptus*. Nevertheless, the Rabbis never forbade contraception outright but sought to define the exceptional circumstances under which it might be utilized.

Even so-called "unnatural intercourse" was not unconditionally prohibited. The Talmud records an incident in which a wife told the court of R. Judah, "I prepared the table for him, but he overturned it." The court ruled that "a man can do with his wife as he wills."[31] What was permitted was, however, not encouraged and the pious were encouraged to eschew such conduct.

The basic position of traditional Judaism on the sin of Onan and inferentially on contraception was enunciated by a thirteenth century Italian rabbi, R. Isaiah da Trani:

> And if you ask how the Sages permitted [unnatural intercourse, which involved] emission of seed like the act of Er and Onan, the answer is: What is the act of Er and Onan which is forbidden by the Torah? Wherever his intent is to avoid pregnancy so he not to mar her beauty and/or so as not to fulfill the commandment of procreation. But if his intent is to spare her physical hazard, then it is permitted. So

also if he does so for his own pleasure but not to avoid pregnancy.... Er and Onan, whose intent was to avoid pregnancy, sinned; but he whose intent is for pleasure, does not sin. For "a man may do with his wife what he will" and it is not called destruction of seed. If it were, then he would not have been permitted to have relations with the minor, the pregnant, or the sterile woman.[32]

The views of this thirteenth century rabbi are not a matter of antiquarian interest. They were published in Jerusalem in 1931 and have been cited with approval by contemporary authorities. As Feldman points out, pleasure is affirmed as a legitimate objective of marital relations and contraception, which is deemed appropriate if its purpose is avoidance of injury to the woman. Moreover, within marriage a heterosexual act is deemed licit even if it is non-procreative in character. Nevertheless, the tradition remains strongly procreationist and rejects total birth control. There is a vast legal and homiletic literature in Judaism on the subject. Not all of the rabbis were as lenient as Isaiah da Trani, but the position of Judaism was never one of absolute condemnation of contraception.

Finally, although the rabbis strongly disapproved of abortion, their opposition was never unconditional. As in Christianity, a crucial question was when the fetus came to be regarded as possessing a soul and when it was regarded as a viable human being. As we shall see, these two questions did not always receive the same response. One of the earliest recorded dialogues on the question is that between the Roman Emperor Antoninus and R Judah the Prince, the compiler of the Mishnah, who was also known simply as "Rabbi" because of his preeminent authority:

> Antoninus said to Rabbi: "From when is the soul endowed in man, from the time of visitation [i.e., conception] or from the time of the [embryo's] formation?" Rabbi replied: "From the time of formation." The emperor demurred: "Can

meat remain three days without salt and not putrefy? You must concede that the soul enters at conception." Rabbi said [at a later time]: "Antoninus taught me this, and Scripture supports him, as it is written: 'And thy visitation has preserved my spirit.'"[34]

Another reason for believing in the entry of the soul at conception was the belief that the child is instructed in the Torah while in the mother's womb[35] and the depiction in the Midrash of the struggle of Jacob and Esau in Rebecca's womb as a struggle between the good and evil inclination.[36]

In spite of assigning an early moment for the entry of the soul into the body, the Talmud asked the further question of when a child can enter the World to Come (*Olam Ha-Ba*). There were a variety of answers including conception, birth, circumcision (i.e., the eighth day), and when the child is able to say "Amen."[37] According to Feldman, the further back in time the rabbis assigned the infant's eligibility for the World to Come, the less serious the offense of abortion became. While Judaism regarded the "Evil Inclination" or the *Yetzer Ha-Ra* as present from Youth," no infant was regarded as stained with Original Sin from conception and, hence, abortion was seen as terminating life in this world but not in the World to Come.[38] As we have noted, the well-being of the mother takes priority over the rights of the fetus in Judaism, as is evident in the following tradition from the Mishnah:

> If a woman has a [life-threatening] difficulty in childbirth, one dismembers the embryo within her, limb by limb, because her life takes precedence over its life. Once its head [alternate reading: "greater part"] has emerged, it may not be touched, for we do not set aside one life for another.[39]

Even after the emergence of the head, later authorities challenged the inviolability of the child, if its birth endangers the mother, on the principle that an onlooker may kill an aggressive pursuer who endangers another's life. This principle was enunciated by no less an authority than Maimonides:

> This, too, is a Commandment: Not to take pity on the life of a pursuer. Therefore the Sages ruled that when a woman has difficulty in giving birth, one may dismember the child in her womb—either with drugs or by surgery—*because he is like a pursuer seeking to kill her.* Once his head has emerged, he may not be touched.[40]

In modern times some very important rabbis, including the late Chief Rabbi of Israel's Ashkenazic community, Issar Yehudah Unterman, held that abortion is "akin to homicide." Because it was "akin" to so grave an offense, only in cases of exceeding gravity such as saving the mother's life could it be permissible.[41] Practically speaking, Unterman's opinion was not in reality very different than Maimonides'. Rape was also considered a reason for abortion but most authorities forbid abortion for eugenic reasons such as the expectation that a deformed child would otherwise be born.[42]

Rabbinic laws concerning the relations between husband and wife, contraception and abortion offer insight into the character of the family in Judaism. In spite of a pronounced patriarchal bias, Jewish religious authorities were considerate of the woman's emotional needs and marital rights. Undoubtedly, the distinctive character of the Jewish family prevented the dissolution of the Jewish community into an anomie underclass. The qualities of discipline, self-control and literacy fostered by the family contributed to both the moral and the biological survival of a continuously endangered community. The qualities of discipline and self-control were also fostered by the fact that pre-messianic Judaism was future-oriented. Delayed gratification was encouraged and immediate gratification discouraged.

As we have seen, the decisive importance of the Jewish family was intensified by religious persecution and hostility.

Not surprising, the family could not easily withstand the assaults of radical secularization especially after World War II. Although there are occasional exceptions, the stronger a Jew's commitment to tradition, the less his or her family will have members afflicted with drug addiction, alcoholism, teenage pregnancy or AIDS. Among secularized Jews in Israel and the Diaspora, teenage pregnancy is not a significant problem but the number afflicted with drug addiction and AIDS has increased. Moreover, even some non-traditional Jews committed to heterosexual marital relationships regard gay and lesbian relationships as valid alternative lifestyles. This view has been reinforced by the decision of the Central Conference of American Rabbis (Reform) to permit the ordination of men and women openly committed to those lifestyles. Neither the Conservative nor the Orthodox movements concur or are likely to concur in this decision. In addition, secularization has fostered the same growth in the proportion of single-parent families among American Jews as among other religious groups.

The situation is altogether different among Orthodox Jews, especially in Israel. After the destruction of European Jewry in World War II, the procreationist values of Jewish tradition came to be emphasized even more than before the war. Almost instinctively, by having large families, Orthodox Jews have sought to replenish the depleted stock of both biological and religious Jewry.

For more than two millennia the family has been the primary institution of Jewish life. It is no longer certain that it will continue to be so, at least among non-traditional Jews. One must, however, ask whether Judaism could survive should the family lose its primacy.

Notes

*This chapter appeared in *Dailogue and Alliance*, vol. 9, no. 1, (1995). ©International Religious Foundation, 4 West 43rd Street, New York. Reprinted by permission.

[1]The most comprehensive and authoritative study of the laws pertaining to the Jewish family in English is David M. Feldman, *Marital Relations, Birth Control and Abortion in Jewish Law* (New York: New York University Press, 1968). I have been helped immeasurably by Feldman's magisterial exposition.

[2]See Richard L. Rubenstein, *My Brother Paul* (New York: Harper and Row, 1972).

[3]See also Col. 2:12.

[4]See Jean Hering, *The First Epistle of Saint Paul to the Corinthians*, trans. A. W. Heathcote and P.J. Allcock (London: Epsworth Press, 1962), p. 45.

[5]According to Josephus, celibacy was practiced by the Essenes, but was regarded as sectarian and was emphatically rejected by the Jewish religious mainstream. Josephus, *The Jewish War*, trans. G.A. Williamson; Rev. E. Mary Smallwood (Harmondsworth, Middlesex: Penguin, 1991), 2:120-21.

[6]Midrash is both an activity, the illustrative interpretation or expansion of the biblical text, and a body of literature. There are two basic types of Midrash, *Midrash Halakhah*, which expands on the legal portions of Scripture, and *Midrash Aggadah* which comprises the legendary and homiletic hermeneutic of Scripture.

[7]*Midrash Wa-yikra Rabbah* (Vilna: Romm, 1887), 20:10

[8]For an exposition in depth of this point, see David M. Feldman, *Marital Relations*, pp. 27 ff.

[9]Traditionally, Jewish law consists of the Written Law, the Five Books of Moses or the Torah, and the Oral Law, the unwritten tradition which interpreted and supplemented the Written Law. The Mishnah was the first canonical reduction of the Oral Law to writing. It was the work of Rabbi Judah the Prince (d. 219). The Mishnah, a single volume work, forms the basis for the Talmud which retains its fundamental divisions but expands upon them in sixty-three

tractates or *massekhtot*. The Talmud was completed in two versions, the Jerusalem Talmud toward the end of the fourth century and the Babylonian Talmud before the end of the fifth. In general, the Babylonian Talmud is more authoritative as a source of Jewish law.

[10]George Foote Moore, *Judaism* (Cambridge: Harvard University Press, 1972), vol. II, p. 122.

[11]Feldman, *Marital Relations*, pp. 37-8.

[12]Article, "Bigamy and Polygamy," Encyclopaedia Judaica. Jerusalem: 1972).

[13]Joseph Karo, *Shulhan Arukh* (Volga: Romm, 1911), *Even HaEzer* 1. The *Shulhan Arukh* is the authoritative code of Jewish law.

[14]*Shulhan Arukh, Even HaEzer* 1:10.

[15]Article, "Bigamy and Polygamy," *Encyclopaedia Judaica*.

[16]Max Weber, "Class, Status, Party," in H.H. Gerth and G. Wright Mills, *From Max Weber: Essays in Sociology* (New York Oxford University Press, 1946), p. 189. This selection is taken from Max Weber, *Wirtschaft und Gesellschaft: Grundriss der Vcrstchenden Sociologie* (Tubingen: Mohr), Part 3, pp. 631-40.

[17]Weber, *loc. cit.*

[18]*Ketuboth* 8a.

[19]*Kiddushin* 29b. As noted above, the Mishnah was redacted under R Judah the Prince. The Gemarrah is the text comprising the interpretation and expansion of the *Mishnah*. Together *Mishnah* and *Gcmarrah* comprise the Talmud.

[20]*Kiddushin* 2a-b.

[21]Article, "Marriage," Enyclopaedia Judaica.

[22]*Pesahim*, 72b.

[23]Moses ben Nahman, *Iggeret HaKodesh* [Epistle of Holiness] Jerusalem: Massorah, 1955), p. 159. The translation is by Feldman, *Marital Relations*, p. 74. I am indebted to Feldman for this citation. There is a difference of opinion among modern scholars concerning whether *Iggeret HaKodrsh* was written by Nahmanides or a member of his school.

[24]Moses ben Maimon, *The Guide to the Perplexed*, Part II, Sec. 36.

[25]*Iggeret HaKodesh*, p. 175. The rabbinic statement cited at the end of the passage is from the Babylonian Talmud, *Sotah* 17a. The translation is by Feldman, *Marital Relations*, pp. 99-100.

[26]Feldman, *Marital Relations*, p. 145.

[27]John T. Noonan, Jr., *Contraception: A History of Its Treatment by the Catholic Theologians and Canonists* (Cambridge, MA Harvard University Press, 1965), p. 137.

[28]Leon Josef Cardinal Suenens, *Love and Control: The Contemporary Problem*, trans. G.J. Robinson (Baltimore: Newman Press, 1961), p. 103. For this citation I am indebted to Feldman, *op. cit.*, p. 148.

[29]Feldman, *op. cit.*, pp. 150-51.

[30]*Yebamoth,* 34b.

[31]*Nedarim,* 20b.

[32]*Tos'fot RiD* (R Isaiah di Trani) to *Yebamoth* 12b Jerusalem: Zuckerman, 1931), cited by Feldman, *op. cit.*, p. 162.

[33]Feldman, *loc. cit.*

[34]*Sanhcdrin,* 91b.

[35]*Niddah* 30b.

[36]*Genesis Rabbah* 63.6.

[37]*Sanhedrdin* 110b; see Feldman, *op. cit.*, pp. 273-74.

[38]Feldman, *op. cit.*, p. 274.

[39]*Mishnah*, Oholot, 7, 6.

[40]Moses ben Maimon, *Mishnah Torah* (Vilna: Rosencrantz, 1900). "Laws Concerning the Murderer and the Protection of Life," 1, 9; cited by Feldman, *op. cit.* p. 276.

[41]Issar Yehudah Unterman, *Shevet Miyehudah* (Jerusalem: 1955), pp. 26-30.

[42]Feldman, *op. cit*, pp. 284-94.

Chapter 10

THE MUSLIM FAMILY: IDEALISM AND REALISM

Abdelmoneim Khattab

Introduction

According to sociologists every society requires five subsystems referred to as "the prerequisite for society survival" or, "the functional systems for survival." As in a watch, each subsystem enables the society to function in a viable and meaningful way.

Briefly speaking, these subsystems are:

- The *political system* which accommodates conflicts and maintains order in the society.
- The *economic system* which produces and distributes goods and services to fulfill the needs of its members.
- The *educational system* which trains the new generations enabling them to play their roles in the society's activities.
- The *religious system* which deals with emotional crises and enables the society members to maintain a sense of purpose while facing life's hardships.
- The *family system* which is entrusted with procreation to replace the dying members of the society. It also plays the role of socializing the new generations to transmit the cultural traits and to preserve the ancestors' traditions.

The aim of this chapter is to concentrate on the family system, specifically in the context of the Islamic Faith. The writer will examine the influence of Islam on the Muslim family in the last 1500 years; its early beginnings when the faith was strong; the changes which have taken place and the factors which seem to be influencing that change. Finally, the paper will try to predict the future of the Muslim family in the light of the emergence of the new world Islamic Movement. This movement referred to as "Muslim Fundamentalism" by the West is, in fact, a return to the essentials of the faith.

Islam

Since the subject under discussion is the family in the framework of the Islamic Faith, it seems appropriate to have a word about Islam. The word Islam is an Arabic word adapted from the infinitive *"silm"* which means "peace" in English. It is the message revealed to the prophet Muhammad (peace be upon him) in the seventh century after Christ. Its aim is to establish peace between man and his Creator, between man and himself and between man and his fellow men in the society.

The most significant source of Islam is the holy Qur'an revealed to the prophet of Islam through the Angel Gabriel over a period of twenty-three years. To the followers of Islam, the Qur'an is a Constitution laying down the rules by which a Muslim should conduct life's daily affairs.

This Islamic Constitution contains a complete family code organizing all the familial relationships. It defines the rights and obligations of each family member towards the other. It also includes a set of obligations and prohibitions for individual relationships as members of the larger society. This Islamic family law was in force throughout the Muslim world from the time of the rise of Islam until the breakup of the Ottoman Empire by the west.

The Family

For the sake of this survey, the Muslim family will be dealt with as a sort of kinship carrying one last or family name. The holy Qur'an defined the family within the confines of marriage between a man and a woman whereby mankind is multiplied. It states:

"يأيها الناس اتقوا ربكم الذى خلقكم من نفس
وخلق منها زوجها وبث منهما رجالا كثيرا ونساء"

"O Mankind! fear your God who created you from a single soul created of a like nature his mate and from the two scattered (like seeds) countless men and women." Chapter 4:1

This Quranic verse describes the family in terms which sociologists today call "the nuclear family." But, before the rise of Islam, in some parts of the Arab world, the family unit was based on loyalty to different groups of kinship. These groups were organized in structured sizes as follows:

- *Qabilah* (Tribe) was the largest size of the familial groupings. It was divided into two or more sub-tribes referred to as *Ashira*.
- *Ashira* was the sub-tribe. The word "Ashirah" seems to be adapted from the Arabic word "Asharah" which means ten in English. This indicates that this group consisted of ten levels of descendants.
- *Firqah* was a sub-division of Ashirah.
- *Fakhith* was a sub-division of Firqah.
- *Hamulah* was a sub-division of Fakhith.
- *The extended family* was a sub-division of the Hamulah. Each tribe usually claims that it is made up of descendants of a single ancestor whose name they all bear (W. Goode, pp. 130,131).

255

This structural type of kinship gradually gave way to the emergence of the nuclear family. It is noteworthy that Islam did not recommend this structural type of kinship as previously stated. William Goode, in his study of the family in the Arab world remarks: "Perhaps one of the more striking aspects of these traditional larger groupings of kinship is the very small place they occupy in Muslim Law. Although the law is concerned in great detail with the family, from the formation of the marriage to its dissolution, as well as the problems of affiliation and succession, for the most part it deals almost entirely with the small family and has not typically recognized the larger kin groupings as being of legal significance."

Whether the Muslim family is viewed as a nuclear family or a larger kinship structure, it is considered to be the most fundamental unit in the socialization process of the child. It also continues to serve as a socializing agency for adults. Usually, when one seeks to explain juvenile delinquency, exceptional eminence, profound humanitarianism or deep-seated prejudice, an investigation is made into the kinds of family in which the individual was reared. For this reason, family is considered to be the first brick in the societal structure and its health or sickness reflects, in the end, upon the larger society.

Family Types

In "Handbook of Marriage and The Family," Christensen has classified the family based on:

1. *Size.*

   Nuclear: consisting of husband, wife and their immediate children.

   Extended: consisting of more than one nuclear family related to each other by blood.

2. *Formal Authority.*

   Patriarchal: in which the father is dominant.

Matriarchal: in which the mother is dominant.

Equalitarian: equal dominance of father and mother.

3. *Number of Persons United in Marriage:*

Monogamous: one man marries one woman.

Polygamous: one man marries more than one woman.

Polyandrous: one woman marries more than one man.

4. *Lineal Descent.*

Patrilineal: privileges and duties of descent follow the male line.

Matrilineal: privileges and duties of descent follow the female line.

Bilineal: privileges and duties of descent follow both lines.

5. *Place of Residence.*

Patrilocal: the couple resides with the husband's parents.

Matrilocal: the couple resides with the wife's parents.

Neolocal: the husband and wife have their own independent residence.

Formation of the Muslim Family

Upon the advent of Islam in the seventh century CE, the pagan Arabs were practicing many forms of marriage. These marriages led to a sort of sexual chaos. To organize the people's sexual life, and to clearly establish the unit which serves as a solid foundation for human society, Islam initiated its own institution of marriage, giving special attention to the family unit. Since the family is entrusted with the two most important responsibilities of replacing the old with the young, and of educating and training the new members to play their proper roles in the larger society, the Holy Qur'an and the Prophetic Traditions have laid down very specific rules for organizing and forming the family.

Mate Selection

Generally speaking, the family is formed by one of the following methods of mate selection:

- *Arranged Marriage:* where the elders select the mates for their children who normally have little or no say in the matter.
- *Romantic Love Marriage:* where the two parties select each other with little or no say by the elders.
- *Islamic Marriage:* where the two parties select each other in the framework of Islam and obtain the consent and sanction of their elders.

Islam cites four criteria on which to base the mate selection. The Prophet of Islam (peace be on him) said: "a woman is married for her wealth, her beauty, her social status or for her religiosity. However, select the religious one in order to achieve success in your marital life." Based on this saying it is understood that Islam emphasizes the selection of a religious mate to ensure a successful life (Bokhari on marriage).

However, with time these ideals of mate selection weakened. It is very rare in our era to find a person selecting a mate on the basis of religiosity. Materialism has played a great role in changing the pattern of mate selection. Religiosity has been replaced with wealth, beauty and social status as the preferred reasons for marrying somebody. The writer, being a religious leader authorized to perform marriages, has drawn this conclusion from his personal observations and experiences.

Betrothal

The second stage in the formation of the Muslim family is the betrothal. In ancient Arabia it was the duty of the father or the elder brother to find, from among the nearest male relatives, a match for a girl when she reaches puberty. The most common practice was "the cousin marriage." The betrothal was a common practice at the time of the Prophet who sanctioned it as a final step toward marriage. (Ruth Nanda Ansher, p. 209)

In modern Muslim communities, negotiation for betrothal generally starts in the family of the boy. Customarily, word is sent to the bride's family informing them that a specific young man is interested in marrying their daughter. A meeting between the two families is then arranged. In this meeting the father or another elder of the boy's family makes the formal proposal for marriage thus: "I have come to ask for the hand of your daughter whose name is...for my son (or brother) whose name is..." (Muhammad Abdul-Rauf, *Marriage in Islam* p. 35).

Having heard the expressed intention of the prospective groom, the girl's representative either declares his approval or declines. If the response is positive, the custom is to offer a gift to the bride from the groom. Currently, the gift usually consists of a gold ring with the groom's name engraved on it. He places the ring on her right hand which would indicate that the girl is engaged After the legal marriage contract is signed by the two parties, the ring is moved to the left hand of the bride as an indication that she is married. It is also a custom that the groom purchases another ring for himself with his fiancee's name engraved upon it, to be worn on his right hand during the betrothal period, then moved to the left hand after marriage. It is appropriate also to mention that the betrothal meeting is held only after the approval of the girl's family as well as the girl herself; this is a change from the old unislamic pattern in which a girl had no say and her marriage was arranged by the elders.

Dowry

Islam makes it incumbent upon a groom to pay a dowry to his wife. This is in contrast to the practice prevailing in some other societies, for example, in India, where the girl pays a dowry to the prospective husband. The dowry can be money, jewelry or any other item of value. The amount of the dowry is not limited and is mutually agreed upon by the two parties.

Some sociologists refer to the dowry as "the bride price" which, in the view of the writer, is incorrect. Customarily, the dowry is an amount of money agreed upon by the two families to be paid by the groom or his family to the bride's family. This money is utilized to help the bride's family pay the cost of a furnished apartment for the new couple. In practice, the bride's family usually matches the amount paid by the groom's family. In some instances, the dowry is divided; a part is paid before the marriage and the remainder is paid after divorce or death of the husband, whichever happens first. The late dowry also serves to deter the husband from divorcing his wife for no good reason.

Marriage Contract and Wedding

The most important step in the process of the Islamic marriage is the marriage contract. Marriage in Islam is a sort of contract. Whatever has been written in this contract will be the future rules of the marital relationship. However, the Islamic family law as stipulated in the Holy Qur'an and the Prophet's Traditions must supersede any article cited in the marriage contract.

This contract is to be signed by the groom and the bride or by their attorneys before at least two witnesses. Publicizing the marriage is preferred and more desirable. In the Muslim traditional family, the bride would authorize her father, brother or any close relative to act on her behalf while the marriage was being performed. Women would not appear in public before the men in such a ceremony. This pattern is changing. It is customary at the present time to see Muslim brides, especially in urban areas, attending their marriage, pronouncing the vows, and signing their own marital contract.

The next step is the wedding by which is meant the consummation of marriage by the groom and bride upon assuming a common residence. This residence could be part of the groom's family, the bride's family or the independent residence of the new couple.

The Muslim wedding can, and does, include some kind of entertainment. Islam prohibits the use of liquor and mixed dancing. In reality, however, some Muslim weddings of today have deviated from this rule. Dr. Mohammad Rauf states in his book *Marriage in Islam:*

> True, there is nothing wrong in adopting the western customs so long as no prohibition is violated and extravagance is avoided. I must confess, however, that I was appalled when I attended a reception of this type for the first time. I loathed the appearance of some women who had applied heavy cosmetics and were indecently clothed; and I was astonished to see liquor lavishly served. I hated the sight of women dancing with strange men, close to each other, in an ecstatic mood. This sort of experience has been repeated many times, and always I have found it dull and even painful (pp.44,45).

Like the Jews, the Muslims of North Africa ritualized the virginity test. In Islam, a virgin is defined as a person who has never been touched by a member of the opposite sex. In other words, in the case of a woman, her hymen is still intact. Though this practice has nothing to do with Islam it has been a custom in the North African countries for a long time. This ritual has been described by Patai:

> "The public ascertaining of the bride's virginity has continued to be practiced in the Middle East in tradition-bound social areas down to the present day... A woman used to be stationed in front of the wedding chamber and as soon as the bridegroom had deflowered his bride, he handed to her the bloodstained napkin which she thereupon showed to all the assembled guests, proclaiming in a loud voice that the bride was found to have been a virgin." (W. Stephan, 1963, p.225) (Patai, 1959, pp.67, 68)

This custom is becoming obsolete now and is rarely practiced in the Muslim world at the present time.

The Islamic Purpose of Forming a Family

Islam pays special attention to the family unit because of its effect on individual members and eventually on the larger society. The following role and function of the Muslim family have been clearly stated in the holy Qur'an and the prophetic tradition:

1. *Preservation of Chastity:*

Islam emphasizes morality to protect the larger society from the consequences of children born out-of-wedlock. Since the sex drive is a powerful instinct in man, the Islamic faith confined it to the institution of marriage and family. Muhammad, the prophet of Islam said "O Youth: whoever among you can afford marriage let him marry. If he cannot, let him fast, this is the best means of guarding against unchastity" (Bukhari).

2. *Procreation of Children:*

Islam recommends that children be born within the confines of the family unit. This safeguards the child's needs for both the father and mother, protects the society against social ills, and provides a suitable environment for rearing and socializing the new generation. Once, the Prophet of Islam said: "marry in order that you may multiply by generations, I shall pride myself in you among the nations on the Day of Judgment" (Bukhari).

3. *Rearing and Socializing the Newborn:*

The human infant comes to the world as a biological organism with animal needs and impulses. From the beginning, however, the organism is conditioned to respond in socially determined ways. The individual learns group-defined ways of acting and feeling, and he learns many of them so fundamentally that they become part of his personality. The process of building group values into the individual is called socialization.

From the point of view of society, socialization is the way culture is transmitted and the individual is fitted into an organized way of life. From the point of view of the individual, socialization is the fulfillment of his potential for personal growth and development. Socialization regulates behavior, but it is also the indispensable condition for individuality and self awareness. Man's biological nature makes socialization both possible and necessary. For example, socialization could not be possible if man did not have the inborn capacity to learn and use language. The long period of childhood dependence would be relatively fruitless if the child was not highly educable throughout. Also, man's ability to learn is directly related to his capacity for language. Other animals have intelligence, but because he has language, man alone has reason. The function of language is to express and arouse emotion as well as to convey values, attitude and knowledge.

Though there are other agencies of socialization, the family is considered to be the most effective one in transmitting culture to the emerging generation. The family performs the function of socialization in two ways: It develops in the young, and maintains in the adult, the social and spiritual sentiments which are indispensable to healthy societal functioning. The family also acts as a culture-transmitting agency because in its confinement the individual acquires his first experience in social participation and his first attitudes toward attainment and acceptance of social status. In the Muslim family, the essential function of transmitting the religious traditions and Islamic values to the new generations is stated in the Holy Qur'an where a father advises his son:

> Behold! Luqman said to his son by way of instruction: O my son! join not in worship (others) with God. For false

worship is indeed the highest wrong doing. (*Qur'an* XXXI:13)

O my son! (said Luqman) establish regular prayer, enjoin what is just, and forbid what is wrong: and bear with patient constancy whatever betide you, for this is firmness (of purpose) in (the conduct of) affairs. And swell not your cheek (for pride) at men nor walk in insolence through the earth; for God loves not any arrogant boaster. And be moderate in your pace, and lower your voice, for the harshest of sounds without doubt is the braying of the ass." (*Qur'an* XXI: 16-19)

Since prayer is fundamental to the Islamic faith and because it is the only pillar that must be performed five times every day, Islam recommends parents to teach their children how to pray at seven years of age. If children do not perform their prayers regularly by ten years of age, parents are instructed to discipline them so that on reaching adulthood, they will feel fully responsible for performing this ritual and consequently become accountable before God for their deeds.

Transmitting religious traditions to the new members is not the only role performed by the family in the area of socialization. The family also attempts to encourage children to build up their strength and physical health after the prophet, advised the Muslims: "Teach your children how to swim, how to throw arrows and how to be good horse riders."

As the family is not the sole agency of socialization, and because the child's peers can play a vital role in shaping his/her behavior, Muslim parents mediate or "stand between" the child and other groups by attempting to control the child's spontaneous associations by placing the child in formal groups, by motivating his participation in various associations and by helping him to interpret his learning experiences from groups outside the family according to the tenets of Islam. In this respect, broken homes are often unable to perform this function adequately.

Through socialization the family teaches the child to integrate into the community, to develop his potentials, and to form stable and meaningful relationships. The individual is not born with the ability to participate in group activities but must learn to take account of others, to share and to cooperate. In short, socialization is a kind of social control exercised both to strengthen group life and to foster the development of the individual.

The family role as a socializing agency does not stop with the child but expands to include the adult. Adults learn their parental role from their family of orientation. In the Muslim world where the nuclear family unit is dominant, the extended family continues to have its influence upon its nuclear branches. Together, the two form a very close net of relationships in spite of their independent nuclear status. A very important Islamic tradition is that the young must respect their elders and have due regard for their decisions. The social role played by the elders within the context of the family will be better understood by examining the part they play in solving the problems of the nuclear units in a crisis situation.

Unlike the family of the modern time, the Muslim family abhors divorce. Islam designates divorce as the most hateful legitimate act in the eyes of God. Consequently, it recommends that several steps be taken before resorting to divorce as a final remedy. In case of such a crisis, Islam advises family members first to communicate with each other and attempt to solve their own problems without any outside interference. If this step does not achieve the desired goal of reconciliation, a trial separation between the couple is to take place for a period of less than four months. This period of separation may soften the feelings of both parties towards each other and consequently may solve their conflict. If this step fails, a sort of a family court is to be formed with one arbiter selected by each party. The role of the arbiters is to listen to each of the contending parties, evaluate the situation, then issue their judgment. If this step also fails, then divorce will be the final remedy for this dispute. The enactment of these recommendations made by Islam emphasizes the role played by elders in the life of the adult members of their extended families. This Islamic pattern is mostly limited to the non-urban areas in the Muslim world at the present time and rarely found in urban settings.

Topics Related to Marriage and Family

In the light of this information pertaining to marriage and family formation, it appears appropriate here to say a word about some topics closely related to the Muslim family. Islam holds special views on premarital activities, homosexuality, polygamy, birth control, abortion, artificial insemination and surrogate motherhood.

Pre-Marital Activities

Sociologists have written pages indicating the value of "dating" and even about "premarital intercourse." Some writers have exaggerated the estimation of these practices in "building up a meaningful relationship" between the would-be spouses. Islam does not approve of such a relationship. Dating, most of the time, leads to a greater sin known in Islam as "fornication." There is hardly need to prove the harm resulting from this illicit relationship and the ensuing injustices: the millions of children born out-of-wedlock in the United States, the social welfare agency administration costs, the social tyranny of taxes paid by morally responsible people to support the consequences of this behavior are clear evidence supporting the Islamic point of view. This view is further strengthened by social research that cast doubts on the relationship between premarital intercourse and the rate of sexual adjustment in marriage. It has also been found that couples who have not had premarital intercourse have a better chance to attain overall marital success than do those couples who have had premarital relations. (See Robert Hamblin and Robert Blood, "Pre-Marital Experience And The Wife's Sexual Adjustment" *Social Problems* 4, October 1956, pp. 122-130).

Homosexuality

In most of the Western societies, homosexuality has been legalized. It is customary now to see groups of homosexuals demonstrating and demanding recognition of their status. A considerable portion of the public has come to accept and support the idea that people should be free to select the type of life they want for themselves. This change in the Western cultural pattern is not acceptable in Islam.

Islam considers homosexuality to be a crime and a disease. To protect the larger society from this disease, homosexuality is punishable by what Islam calls "Ta'zi." According to this penalty, Muslim judges sentence the criminal to isolation in a camp where he cannot be in contact with other members of the society. It is interesting to note that Fidel Castro of Cuba has enacted this rule in his country, thereby successfully reducing the incidence of Aids. American journalists who visited this camp found it to be remedial and humanitarian at the same time. This Islamic injunction pertaining to homosexuality is not subject to change.

Polygamy

Social scientists apply the term "polygamy" both to the practice in which a woman is married to more than one husband, precisely called "polyandry," and to the more frequent practice in which a man is married to more than one wife, which they call "polygyny." The term polygamy is used in this paper in the latter sense.

Polygamy has been widely publicized in the Western world as a practice limited only to the Muslims. Some have even exaggerated it to be a distinguishing mark for the followers of this faith. This wrong notion continues to be disseminated even in our present time. In reality, however statistics reveal a staggering rate of extra-marital sex practiced in western societies. This practice can be considered as a sort of hidden polygamy where the parties do not bear responsibility for their action. In the Muslim world, the polygamy rate is negligible and its practice is discouraged by making the parties fully responsible for the consequences of their action. While it is true that Islam permits a restricted type of polygamy, monogamous marriage is the rule. Islam should not be judged by the behavior of some Muslims who abuse this rule. The Islamic faith permits polygamy only under compelling circumstances such as terminal illness, infertility, or in times of war where the number of women may exceed that of men. Even under these compelling circumstances, polygamous marriage is conditional upon the ability of the husband to establish justice between his wives. The Holy Qur'an warns the husband who is contemplating another marriage in the following terms:

$$\text{"فإن خفتم ألا تعدلوا فواحدة"}$$

But if you should fear that you will not do justice, then confine yourself to one wife (*Qur'an* IV:3).

To limit the practice of polygamy to the minimum and to guard against the abuse of this exceptional rule, the Qur'an warns:

$$\text{"ولن تستطيعوا أن تعدلوا بين النساء ولو حرصتم"}$$

And indeed you cannot do justice between women, even when you are eager to be completely just (*Qur'an* IV: 129).

Polygamy has prevailed in some areas of the Muslim world despite these clear injunctions. But this pattern is changing due to the spread of education and the financial burden of maintaining more than one family.

Birth Control

Before the development of modern science, birth control was practiced by natural means to regulate the frequency and number of desired births. Upon the advent of Islam, people were practicing "AZL" which is the prevention of the male sperm from being deposited in the female womb. This was accomplished by withdrawal at the moment of orgasm.

The idea and controversy of birth control has occupied many political and religious authorities all over the world. The United Nations propounds the idea in the interest of protecting the world from "the population explosion." The Catholic Church under the influence of the Pope prohibits this practice. Other Christian denominations either support or reject the idea. Since Islam has no clear-cut rule prohibiting birth control, Muslim schools of thought have no consensus. Those who support it advance the idea for its benefits for the family in regulating its numbers. Those who oppose it, base their opinion on the purpose for which the family was formed, namely, to multiply by generations. There is still a third opinion which supports birth control based on the approval of both husband and wife. It may be concluded then that the practice of AZL or any other natural methods of birth control, though not encouraged, are not prohibited as long as agreed upon by both husband and wife. The practice of birth control by the Muslim family is more prevalent today than in the past.

Abortion

Abortion is the total elimination of an already fertilized living human fetus. Unlike birth control, it is considered by Islam to be a serious offense against an existing life. Abortion is the most controversial topic of our time. Its practice has divided society into two camps: pro-life and pro-choice. Islam rules that deliberate abortion with no justifiable grounds is a murderous crime. Only when the continuation of pregnancy constitutes a real threat to the life of the expectant mother is abortion permitted. Few Muslim jurists legitimize abortion before four months expectancy and prohibit it after this period. This opinion is based upon the literal rendering of a *hadith* (prophetic saying) which stipulates that the soul enters the body after this period. In the view of the majority of Muslim jurists, however, Hadith should not be taken literally and abortion is thus a strictly forbidden practice at any stage unless the survival of the mother is threatened.

Artificial Insemination

This is a form of forced fertility in common use today. For this reason, anonymous sperm donors are urged to donate and sperm banks are established. Islam equates this practice with adultery unless the sperm donor is the husband and the fertilized egg is that of the wife. Only in this situation does Islam approve artificial insemination.

Surrogate Motherhood

Surrogate motherhood is the hiring of a woman to bear and deliver a child for another party. The sperm used could be that of the prospective father or obtained from the sperm bank. In either situation, Islam fully disapproves of this practice. Instead, Islam allows a Muslim man under similar circumstances to marry a second wife who can satisfy his need for having children. In the opposite situation where a man has no capacity to produce children, Islam allows a woman a final divorce so that she will be able to remarry a man who may satisfy her need for having children. In conclusion, surrogate motherhood is against Islamic ethics and consequently is forbidden by Islam.

Family Relationships

The Qur'an defines the type of relationships that must prevail between husband and wife:

"ومن آياته أن خلق لكم من انفسكم أزواجا لتسكنوا
إليها وجعل بينكم مودة ورحمة "

And of His signs is this: He created for you mates from among yourselves that you might dwell in peace together, and He ordained between you love and mercy (*Qur'an*: XXX, 21).

It is noteworthy that the above cited verse is directed to both male and female and is indicative of sex equality in marital relationship. It also lays emphasis on tranquillity as a chief characteristic of the relationship.

The relationships between parents and their children are spelled out in the Holy Qur'an as a form of pay and repay. As the parents take care of their children when they are helpless infants, so it is the duty of the children to care for their parents when they are helpless old people. These relationships are not limited to the life of the parents as Islam recommends that children remember their parents in their prayers even after their death. The Qur'an clearly states this relationship saying:

"وقضى ربك الا تعبدوا إلا إياه وبالوالدين إحسانا ،
إما يبلغن عندك الكبر أحدهما أو كلاهما فلا تقل لهما
أف ولا تنهرهما وقل لهما قولا كريما ، واخفض لهما
جناح الذل من الرحمة وقل رب ارحمهما كما ربياني
صغيرا"

Your God has decreed that you worship none but Him, and that you be kind to parents. Whether one or both of them attain old age in your life, say to them no word of contempt, nor repel them but address them in terms of honor. And out of kindness, lower to them the wing of humility, and say: My Lord! bestow on them your mercy even as they cherished me in childhood (*Qur'an:* 17: 23-24).

271

This is the ideal relationship as stated in the scripture of Islam. In reality, however, some changes have taken place. Children have become independent. They no longer reside in the extended family household and consequently, mobility and modern life have played a dysfunctional role in achieving ideal familial relationships.

Termination of Marriage

In Islam marriage is terminated either by death or divorce. The Islamic concept of divorce is fully misunderstood in the West. The ignorance as well as the malicious intent of some writers and the western mass media have led the public to believe that a Muslim can terminate his marital life by pronouncing "you are divorced" three times before his wife. This is not the case. When all other means of reconciliation fail, divorce is the final remedy for a marital dispute. However, Islamic divorce is not simple due to the financial burden it lays on the husband. Also, to be final, divorce must go through the following three phases:

1. When divorce takes place for the first time, it does not become absolutely final until the expiration of a waiting period (three months). During the waiting period, the couple can resume their marital relationship.

2. If the divorce occurs a second time, it is also revocable during the waiting period. If the waiting period expires and the couple would like to rejoin each other, a new contract ceremony has to be performed.

3. Should divorce occur for the third time, it becomes absolutely irrevocable. The divorcees may not remarry unless the wife marries someone else after the expiration of the waiting period and, is then separated from the other marriage by death or divorce. In this case, they can remarry each other after the expiration of the waiting period of the second marriage.

It is worthy of note at this point that the man is the one who initiates the divorce unless it was stipulated to the contrary in the marriage contract. Also, the woman has the right to file for divorce before the Islamic court if there is sufficient ground for her claims. This type of divorce is referred to in Islam as "Khul'a."

Changing Patterns of the Muslim Family

The patterns ruled by Islam for the Muslim family were put into practice during the golden era of Islam. These rules continued to function through several centuries. The Islamic rules, in fact, have formed what is known as the Islamic culture. This culture is believed by the Muslims to be a revelation of God rather than an invention of man. It is meant to shape the Muslims' behavior in a way that may lead them to happiness in this life as well as in the world to come.

With the fall of the Islamic Empire and the occupation of the Muslim world by Western imperialism, several factors played a role in changing Muslim family patterns. For example, the Middle Eastern Muslim society was influenced by the British or French colonialist powers. One of the most important aims of the imperialists was to keep the Muslim population subdued and thus to preserve their power . To achieve this end, they kept the colonized people in a state of ignorance, sickness and poverty. Another tactic was to divide and rule so that the Muslim population was split up into groups based on self-interest rather than being a unified community based on the brotherhood of Islam. This enabled the colonizers to play their disruptive role in changing the Muslims' way of life. Other factors underlying the change in Muslim family patterns are:

- Industrialization
- Increased mobility through new means of transportation
- Mass media of information

Industrialization

Industrialization changed the quality and the quantity of produced goods. Handicrafts were replaced by machine-made products. Workmanship, long utilized as unit production, was turned into mass production. This change had a great effect upon family patterns. The family, formerly a self-sufficient unit producing the goods needed for the family consumption, became partially or fully dependent upon the goods produced by the larger society. This, in turn, led family members to seek employment outside of the family unit. Earning a living this way resulted in greater geographical spread and less dependency upon other family members. Finally, it resulted in the breakdown of the extended family into fully independent nuclear units.

Industrialization is not limited to the machine only. It includes the science and engineering that produced those machines, the secular attitude of the modern era, the anti-traditionalism prevailing in certain areas, and the practice of job placement based on competence. Industrialization also promotes an open class system and greater geographic mobility. Industrialization, in that vague but enveloping sense, has its great influence on the change of family patterns and modes of life.

Mobility, Means of Transportation

Before the invention of the wheel, man lived in isolation. He was not aware of what was going on in the world outside of his own tribe, clan or community. The development of new methods of transportation enabled man to be more mobile and to communicate with other people. This exposed him to different cultures and modes of life. The boundaries between different countries became semi-artificial and unreal. Now man is able to have his breakfast in the Middle East, his lunch in Europe and his dinner in the United States. The transportation revolution served as a medium of socialization. The underdeveloped nations learned from the more developed nations. More and more, the people looked to the industrialized world as their role model. Consequently, family patterns and ways of life were influenced by this change in focus and have moved on the continuum from the traditional to the secular or "modern." However, such changes do not occur abruptly, but are a slow process spanning many generations and facing resistance along the way. Whenever this resistance to change is seen, the family is referred to as being in transition.

Mass Media

Human beings have a natural desire to learn and discover new ways of life. The advent of mass media has brought every aspect of knowledge of the outside world into our living rooms and socialized us, willingly or unwillingly. While the power of the written word to socialize is limited only to the literate person, the invention of the radio, television, and the VCR have made it possible to disseminate ideas among uneducated masses in the remotest corners of the Earth. In fact, television has played and is playing a greater role in the socialization process and, consequently, is influencing a change in family patterns on all levels, young and old alike. In this respect, one may say, with no exaggeration, that television alone has played a singular role in shaping the behavior of the public in one way or another.

Since industrialization, mobility and mass media play such a significant role in changing family patterns in general, their effects on the Muslim family patterns are also evident, as noted above in the section "Formation of the Muslim Family."

The Predicted Future of the Muslim Family

One would have anticipated that the change of patterns in the Muslim family would continue in the same direction as long as the factors of change continued to exist, but the contrary seems to be true. Muslims observed the adverse effects on societies which had abandoned their original traditions. They noted the permissiveness in the western societies and the mixing between the opposite sexes which alienated couples from one another and provoked jealousies and bitterness. They realized that national affluence and the availability of gainful jobs weakened the feeling of interdependence between members of a household. They found that the total independence of the young in selecting their mates without consultation with their experienced elders resulted in unsuccessful marriages. They recognized that the lack of deep religious conviction and the turning away from religious values led to a religious vacuum and family instability. They discovered that the loyalty to the machine as well as the faith in science and technology weakened religious ties. This, in turn, loosened inhibitions and gave way to irresponsible liberty that led to objectionable new "life styles" such as "group marriages" and the ensuing alarming increases in the number of illegitimate births. Learning a lesson from the above-cited social ills, the Muslim public was put on alert. They are now struggling to save the family from sliding into the evils of modernism. This attitude is not only notable in the Muslim world, but also very obvious among the Muslim minorities in the predominantly Christian world. It is brought into sharp relief by the French Ministry of Education which recently issued a law forbidding Muslim female students from attending school in their Islamic attire. (*Al-Dawa*, Weekly, 1466, November 1994, Saudi Arabia, p.13.)

No doubt, some detrimental changes have also taken place in the Muslim family, especially in the Middle East. These changes are creating a wide gap between the old and the new generations. They are resulting in the disintegration of the family and this, in turn, is effecting the society at large. The respect for elders which tied the family branches together is disappearing, as are the ethical and moral values. The practice of "enjoining the right and forbidding the wrong" which was a prominent familial characteristic hardly exists. When a society forsakes its heritage and ignores its past,. it is in danger of eclipse. To prevent the family from further deterioration, to restore its glorious past that was characterized by love, strong ties and respect, the Muslim family seems to be returning to and functioning according to the rules of God as stipulated in the Islamic revelation. The manifestation of this new trend is easily observed in the streets of large cities of the Muslim world. It is common to hear Muslim preachers, nowadays, emphasizing the Islamic faith as a complete way of life, rather than as a set of rituals practiced in the houses of worship. They urge Muslims to view family as the role model that must be emulated by the new generations. They advise the people to train their children from early childhood to distinguish between right and wrong and to apply the Islamic value system in their own practical life.

Towards this end, the long range plans of some countries of the Muslim world are worthy of note, where the people struggle to improve their economic systems without jeopardizing their traditional and religious values. For example, a visitor familiar with the Middle Eastern traditions of the twentieth century can observe a change in the family patterns as people are shifting back towards traditionalism and away from secularism. This change may be the result of several Islamic movements taking place at the present time calling upon Muslims to solve their problems through their faith rather than through foreign ideologies. It is hoped that this trend will continue through the next several decades in order for it to have a positive effect on the direction and magnitude of this transition of the Muslim family back to its roots in Islam.

References

1. Harold T. Christensen, *The Handbook of Marriage and the Family,* Rand McNally and Co. Chicago, 1964.
2. Parsons and Bales, *Family: Socialization and Interaction Process,* The Free Press of Glenco, 1959.
3. Ruth Nanda Anshen, *The Family: Its Function and Destiny.* Harper and Brothers, New York, 1959.
4. Elizabeth Bott, *Family and Social Network.* Tavistock Publication Ltd., 1964.
5. F. Ivan Nye and Felix M. Berardo, *Emerging Conceptual Frameworks in Family Analysis,* The McMillan Co., New York, 1963.
6. Dorothy R. Blitsten, *The World of the Family.* Random House, New York, 1963.
7. William N. Stephens, *Reflection on Marriage,* Thomas Y. Crowell Co., New York, 1968.
8. Muhammad Abdul Rauf, *The Islamic View of Women and the Family.* Robert Speller and Sons Inc., New York, 1977.
9. Robert F. Winch et. al., *Selected Studies in Marriage and the Family,* Holt, Rinehart and Winston, New York, 1963.
10. William J. Goode, *Readings on the Family and Society,* Prentice-Hall Inc., New Jersey, 1964.
11. Robert R. Bell, *Studies in Marriage and the Family,* Thomas Y. Crowell Co., New York, 1968.
12. Stuart A. Queen and Robert Habenstein, *The Family in Various Cultures,* J.B. Lippincot Co., New York, 1967.
13. Hyman Rodman, *Marriage, Family and Society.* Random House, New York, 1967.
14. Muhammad Abdul Rauf, *Marriage in Islam.* Exposition Press, New York, 1972.
15. Bernard Farber, *Comparative Kinship System.* John Wiley and Sons Inc., New York, 1968.
16. William N. Stephens, *The Family in Cross Cultural Perspective,* Holt, Rinehart and Winston, New York, 1963.
17. Robert F. Winch, *The Modern Family,* Holt, Rinehart and Winston, New York, 1964.

18. William J. Goode, *World Revolution and Family Patterns.* The Free Press of Glenco, New York, 1963.
19. Mohammad Hosayni Behishti and Javad Bahonar, *Philosophy of Islam,* Islamic Publication, Salt Lake City, UT.
20. Mohammad Mazheruddin Siddiqi, *Women In Islam,* Institute of Islamic Culture, Lahore, 1966.
21. Hammudah Abdalati, *Islam In Focus,* American Trust Publication, Indianapolis, 1975.
22. Hammudah Abdalati, *The Family Structure In Islam,* American Trust Publication, 1977.
23. "Commandments By God In The Qur'an." *The Message* Publication New York 1991.
24. Ahmad Ghalwash, *The Religion Of Islam.* Religious Affairs Administration, Qatar, 1973.

Arabic References

1. Muhammad M. Pickthiall, *The Meaning of the Glorious Qur'an,* Islamic Call Society, Tripoli, Libya, Published by Lebanese Book House, Beirut, P.O. Box 3176.
2. Muhammad Al-Hasany, *Islamic Rules and Family System.* Sahar Press, Jeddah, 1398 A H.
3. Salem Albahnasawi, *The Family Laws Between the Failure of Women and the Weakness of the Scholars,* Afaq Laghad House, Cairo, 1980.
4. Ali Abdallah Tantawi, *Ahkamu-lusrah bayna -shar'a wa-qanoon.* Al-Ansar Publishing, Cairo, Egypt.
5. Fathy Yakan, *Al-islam wal Jins.* Al-Resalah Foundation, Beirut.
6. Abbas Mahmoud Al-Aqqad, *Al-Marato Fi-l-Qur'an,* Dar Al-Hilal Publishing, Cairo.
7. Abdallah Olwan, *Tarbiatul-Awlad Fi-l-Islam,* Dar Assalam Publishing Beirut.

Chapter 11

SOME THOUGHTS ON THE FAMILY IN LATIN AMERICA

Armando de la Torre

Right from the start, I would like to state that the term "family" is too ambiguous for Latin Americans as to warrant an "univocal" discussion on the institution of the family without first determining what constitutes the "family" at issue: the nuclear family.

"Family" can be understood as a coresidential group consisting of a human couple and their children in the accepted "nuclear" meaning of the word (and that in contemporary Western life increasingly includes living apart from other kin).

As a legal term, a childless couple is family too, once they have established a stable intimate relationship according to a legal public procedure which specifies mutual rights and duties. In some countries, "common" living between two consenting adults of opposite sex is accorded the status and legal recognition of "family."

But it may refer also to a polygynous household of one man, several wives and their respective children (the so-called "compound family" legally impossible in Latin American or to a household formed through remarriage by those who have been widowed or divorced, each with children from previous marriages. This latter "joint" family type might be coresidential or not as long as budgetary decisions are in the main non-split within the couples and they continue to interact according to "family" roles.

Or again, "family" could refer to that dispersed version of a joint family where a single homestead is occupied by several lineally related kinsfolk under a single head. In this case—the "extended" one—members are not supposed to be cores-idential, though they keep on living close and engage in common activities.

Birth (either natural or by legal adoption) seems to be the decisive criterion for inclusion into the "family" in all mentioned above and from this other family functions derive, like socialization (training skills' scale of values), plus inheritance rights, solidarity duties, expected loyalties, material support, and so on.

But "family" has been sometimes taken also as referring to that web of correlated roles (mainly sexual roles) between consenting adults, which facilitates its extension to cover "marriages" between homosexuals, who might even be accorded the right to legally adopt children, which fulfills, as a by-product, their emotional human parenting needs.

I might further comment. Every family, as such, results from a previous choice either of those directly involved or of someone else in a position of authority to be able to choose for them. And choice entails responsibility, that is to be accountable to others for the consequences of that choice insofar as they touch other people.

Economists speak in this sense of "externalities," good or bad (usually bad), which follow from our free actions or from our free omissions. The law in general is concerned with this dimension of our free individuality, but moral prudential considerations are also called for here.

I want to concentrate on the assumption of the meaning of the term "family" as designated through its modifier "nuclear", because this is its standard primary understanding throughout most of Latin America. But I want additionally to stress the "externalities" that parents may bring to bear upon their children, who certainly do not choose the particular arrangement within which they are born.

For the first time, a large number of college level women (one-third) state their determination not to have children. If one-third of female college students have declared that they do not plan to have any children during their future married lives, they are freeing themselves from that responsibility to the extent that they behaved according to their stated intentions. However, if many will go on later to reverse this decision and have children, they will be successful only insofar as they take into account the contemporary difficulties in raising children. Parental responsibilities become unavoidable for them and will remain so until their offspring turns legally mature enough to be able to make similar decisions with the same sense of responsibility.

In Latin America, awareness of this responsibility appears to be confirmed by two parallel trends: 1) The more years of schooling a woman has, the fewer children she tends to give birth to. 2) First time pregnancies after the age of 35 are on the rise.

But there are signs too of an opposite trend: a rise in the number of abortions (performed within or without the legal framework) and the growth of the young population abandoned by one or both parents.

I mention this because my main concern in dealing with the family topic has turned nowadays to those members of the family who are natural products of choices, not their agents: young unwanted children and, in some circumstances the still unborn. Instilling that sense of responsibility should preclude unthinking behavior on the part of possible future parents; this, in my view, morally justifies family planning, provided this is done on a voluntary basis.

In order to discuss the future of the family I will proceed based solely on the assumption of a starting hypothesis or conjecture as Karl Raymond Popper visualized it:[1] a statement or a chain of statements from which we might arrive deductively at another statement relating to matters of fact that can be observed or experienced, and which can be taken as contradicting (falsifying) or not contradicting the initial hypothesis.

From this perspective, I dare to advance my "educated guess" concerning the future of the family in Latin America! especially the so-called modern nuclear family—based on long-term sexual bonding, horizontal mobility, one to five children, and female domesticity—a product of culture as well as of nature.

I think the family as such will survive in this part of the planet probably, as well as in the rest of the "Atlantic" world, for many years to come, by successfully adapting itself to the combined challenges of overpopulation, individual hedonism! and the changes in sexual roles sweeping the world over. This "adaptation" may hark back to religious, economic or even simply erotic motivations. However, it will always be geared towards assuring mutual assistance in addition to the naked survival of the human species through reproduction, only this time in a more deliberated manner (mainly through education and law) than in any other previous period of history.

The future of the family hinges on a single value judgment: whether it is worth it to pay the price for responsible parenthood. Whoever deems himself or herself not fit to face that life-long commitment (because of career ambitions, emotional unbalance, or economic constraints), should not indulge in behavior which possible outcome might be a new life. This should not be construed as an invitation to continence but rather to accountability.

That the latest biotechnological breakthroughs will also add to that survival dimension unprecedented genetic options does not necessarily entail further changes in the basic family structure: parents caring for their offspring (in or out of wedlock); a structure that remains the same even within the frame of the modern welfare state, which has shown abundantly its effect of weakening that traditional structure.

I refer to "parents" and not a single parent as head of a household because I consider this sorry trend in Latin America (as well as in the Black community of the United States) of growing parental desertions (up to a third of all children under the age of eighteen suffer from this parental dereliction of duty) as abnormally high and socially unsustainable in the long run.[2]

Nor do I foresee a substitution by "communes" for the nuclear families after so many failed attempts have been tried for the last century and a half in Europe and in America. Taking into account what we believe to have already learned about human propensities, both cerebrally and hormonally anchored, no culture can be built in the future without the firm foundation of the family unit. To those premises I may add the ingrained Roman Catholic family traditions still alive throughout most of Latin America.

Assuming all these propositions to be true, we could develop a prognosis as good as any by remembering our humanity forms only insofar as we learn to postpone certain gratifications, such as those resulting from the fulfillment of urges like the one to dominate and the one to mate.[3]

In other words: by developing his capacity for further deferment of pleasure, the human being is distanced from the pecking order of closer related primates (the large apes). In so doing, the human child enjoyed the undivided attention of a steady couple of parents, and was endowed therefore with that crucially important long span of time needed for maturing by imitation through young adulthood.

It follows that we can expect the family cell of the future to survive only if there is no less a capacity for renunciation, that is, for longer and longer term postponement of gratifications on the part of parents than that which made the human family possible.

Given also the apparent master trend in the Western world, time and again underscored by Max Weber,[4] towards social networks of increasing "rationality" (both in its psychological and technological dimensions), it is to be expected that the family of the future may evolve in the direction of a more calculating, cost-benefit conscious, and less emotional endeavor than has been the case in Latin America; something that some of us might deeply regret.

However, any increased rationality will take place up to a point. Some sociologists accurately have traced the popularity of remarriages (at least fifty percent of all divorced Latin Americans try marrying again, in some cases more than once in spite of Church opposition) to the emotional strains of people who feel lonely in the big urban sprawls where most Latin Americans presently live.

This has the ring of being particularly true for service societies (like Uruguay) where—following David Riesman's analysis[5]—the fear of solitude is strongest and the character of the people tends to gravitate toward the "others oriented" kind. A marginal utility, only barely calculated, pushes men and women to choose intimate companionship with someone else (be it of the opposite or of the same sex) in order to be able to cope with life-cycles and social crises, and this, I think, will hold true for the foreseeable future. But children also may fit into this calculus. Men and women realize their humanity through caring for the defenseless young too.

Another variable to be considered is the nature of society as a whole. Although Latin America remains a vibrant young population of which less than four percent is above the age of 65 and the median hovers around 23,[6] whose per capita income is low (around $2,800 continent wide)[7] and whose social security systems are inefficient (the exception being Chile). All this means a heavy burden on the productive young men and women who must try to make ends meet while caring for the old and the very young. This is hoped to get better as social security moves into the private sector, but at the moment this is moving at slow motion; in some countries, like Guatemala, at a crawl.

Latin American families have been traditionally closely knit; however, this appears to be less and less the case today; particularly among the millions of young rural migrants who move each year into the bustling cities.[8] Meanwhile, the old are left behind very often to fend for themselves while the young, mostly males, get lost in the transitional zones of big urban centers.

This new phenomenon deprives young and old alike of the mutually beneficial close rapport that once blossomed between generations. Moreover, it poses a growing threat to family integrity (males forsaking wives), with all its attendant social evils for their common offspring.

Among young Latins drug abuse has not reached the levels of more affluent societies like the United States or some European countries. However, it is rapidly catching up. The same holds for violent crime which, at present, seems to have surpassed even the rates of American inner cities. As in the US, the number one cause of death for young males aged sixteen to twenty-four has become violence.[9]

Since 1991, Latin America has experienced a marked economic recovery from the "lost decade" of the eighties. However, the rate of investment, especially after the recent Mexican crisis, still does not match the burgeoning population growth of an average above two percentage points a year.[10] As a consequence, unemployment remains high throughout most of the region, even in prosperous industrialized Argentina, where the latest statistics push the figure close to the 19 percent mark. This fact, particularly in the case of Mexico, explains the demographic pressure of illegal immigrants into the US and Canada, which is perceived there a serious danger to the social fabric of those unwilling hosts. Meanwhile, in the countries from which they migrate, are seen as another occasion for brain and energy drain and for family breakups.

Last but not least, the sexual mores of young females have become freer to the extent that in some countries (for instance, Venezuela) slightly over one in every two children reach the age of eighteen not having lived with the same parents for all those years.

Not everybody agrees with my view which assigns such weighted relevance to irresponsible parenthood as the number one social evil. But most concur that it deserves to be turned into a major public issue. A case at hand is Bogata, capital city of Colombia, where more than 150,000 unsupervised minors roam the streets with devastating results for themselves and the quality of life of all citizens. Any political platform that does not address this issue head-on does not bode well for whatever may be left of the once proud and healthy Latin American family institution.

F.A. van Hayek, in several of his works,[11] has stressed the point that no culture which shows itself hostile to the institutions of private property and the family can survive for long; in his view, it will last less than a century. Stretching this view a little further, I may add that any society that shows itself indifferent to caring for the young and the aged for a prolonged period of time will eventually dissolve into murderous chaos.

Families, as the cradle of the deepest-felt values internalized by an individual must be nurtured and strengthened in Latin America against some additional pervasive influences coming from the US via Hollywood and cable television.

The atomistic individualization of what is perceived by some Latin Americans to be the main trait of a secularized Calvinist American outlook threatens to weaken the stimulating pride in family name and lineage. The rat race in which we get more involved with each passing day robs us of that precious scarce time we could devote listening to our children.

The ideological fury of certain intellectual trendsetters (mainly of Marxist or anarchist persuasion) against any "old fashion" reversion, well and above the generational gap, to blood solidarity is another menace.

The superficiality of some when dealing with the delicate and highly complex issue of abortion on demand, particularly in the case of teenage pregnancy, discourages responsibility.

The boundless "pursuit of happiness" at all costs, whereby the children are its foremost casualties, hurts the family unnecessarily.

Ecological concerns which seem to blur the differences between the survival of animal and plant species and the legitimate needs and rights of people debase us all.

The globalization of taste, with its monotonous uniformity inimical of the mysterious and original in individuals tends to depersonalize society.

The tenet held by many so-called "liberals'" who trace poverty singly to overpopulation, when it could be argued reasonably well against it that wealth is mainly created by the young and the free, and that it is not certainly an exclusive advantage of the old and the few, disparages the roots of true progress through a healthy family life.

These and other contemporary "idols of the cave" leave us increasingly bereft of the warm intimacy of home and family, while we are dragged along the information super highway into a world of numberless facts and very few values by which to make choices.

If families, as we have know them, are going to have any

future at all, we must reinforce in Latin America the attitude of unwavering support for the care of the very young and the unborn. This concern has been part and parcel of our genetic code and culturally we cannot escape it unless we give ourselves over to the suicidal wish supposedly inherent to our civilization.

Three main aspects of family life—its biological foundation (the bonding urge), its legal framework (the contractual duties), and its cultural content (our goals in childrearing, in mutual help, and in our "rites de passage")—can be deliberately bent by us to a certain extent and at our own risk, but not entirely shaped by force of will and statutory legislation; that stays beyond our reach.

I cannot discern what definite shape the Latin American family of the near future might adopt. But on the premise—acknowledgedly optimistic—of a steady expansion of the middle classes, it seems reasonable to foresee these possible minimum outcomes:

- The family nucleus will continue to get smaller, perhaps falling below the replacement figure of 2.2 children per couple.
- Correspondingly, family outlays per child for health and schooling at the expense of parental leisure and entertainment will increase.
- A more inward looking religious life will take deeper roots, given the official widening cleavage between church and state and the widespread agnosticism for which Europe has set the example (and Europe counts obviously for Latin Americans far more than for their counterparts in the North).
- The lessening of ideological passions will become general following the retreat of Marxism, coupled with a more pragmatic approach to social and economic success.
- Less authoritarian ("macho" family style) should become

a common feature, although not completely assimilating the American pattern.

- Enormous geographical mobility will continue, resulting in a more tolerant cosmopolitan outlook.
- The trend is that people who marry young will divorce and remarry more often than in the past. This is reinforced by the other trend of lengthened lifespans.[12]

All these might come to pass but with a big "caveat." The world could witness, once more, the sudden emergence of charismatic leaders—always by definition unpredictable—who might start wholly new trends with regard to the overall human condition and particularly with regard to family life.

That was the message of Stefan Zweig's "The World of Yesterday"[13]: a European civilization, like the one of the *Belle Epoque* which believed to have finally overcome the barbarian impulses of darker ages and which hoped for a permanent peace grounded on rational practices and institutions, was instantly blown to pieces by the huge chain reaction of ideological passions triggered by two fateful shots in that early summer of 1914, in Sarajevo. Is not what happened there recently an unnecessary reminder?...

Charismatic leadership delivered large tracts of mankind to the brutal attempts by Lenin to undermine the traditional way of family life in Imperial Russia. The horrors under Hitler of experimentations on human individuals and of bureaucratically, superbly organized mass extermination of whole human ethnic blocks, and the totalitarian regimentation of human reproduction in China since Mao, are very serious warning signals that nothing recorded in the past history is an insurance against its repetition in the future.

Even the renewed strictures on women since the Khomeini revolution by certain groups of Muslim "fundamentalists" (whatever the propriety of the term), caught us all by surprise and make us wonder. Pope John Paul II has warned repeatedly about the "culture of death" to which we have become inured in our own century. Snuffing out life by the millions can be envisioned today as having been the end result of a century and a half of constant preaching and arguing against individual freedom and individual responsibility.

Hegel, Freud, Marx, Gobineau, the Fabians, and all those other "historicists" whose poverty K. R. Popper has so well unmasked, have brought us down to the level of mere cogs in the giant impersonal machines of the laws of dialectics in history or of the welfare state. The individual sense of being personally called to tend to his own family welfare and to mind his own family business has little by little evaporated. This takes me back to something attributed to Thomas Jefferson two centuries ago: "The price of liberty is an eternal vigilance."

But not all charismatic leadership has been for the worse. The slow and tortuous progress of the human race towards freer markets under the rule of law is a glorious monument, among others, to the human spirit as personified by the charismatic leadership associated with the persons of Jesus, Socrates, Moses, Mohammed, Bhudda, and countless more. To the ultimate efficacy of that spirit in men I toast, so that a healthier and richer life, above all a child centered family life, might beckon us into a future of better shared responsibilities for the most downtrodden of this Earth: the unwanted children.

Notes

[1]K.R. Popper, *Conjectures and Refutations: the Growth of Scientific Knowledge*, London, 1963. From the same author: *Logik der Forschung*, Vienna, 1935.

[2]Edward O. Wilson, *On Human Nature*, Cambridge, Massachusetts: Harvard University Press, 1978, Chapters two and six. From the same author, *Sociobiology: The New Synthesis*, Cambridge, MA: Harvard University Press, 1975.

[3]Marshall D. Sahlins, "The Orioin of Society," *Scientific American*, September 1960, vol. 203, no. 5, pages 76-87.

[4]Max Weber: "Wirtschaft und Gesellechaft," Tubingen, 1922, 2nd ed.

[5]David Riesman, in collaboration with Revel Denney and Nathan Glazer, *The Lonely Crowd*, New Haven, Yale University Press, 1950.

[6]Population Reference Bureau, Inc., World Population, 1994.

[7]*Ibid*.

[8]*Ibid*.

[9]*The Economist,* August, 1995.

[10]Population Reference Bureau, Inc.

[11]F.A. van Hayek, "Law, Legislation, and Liberty," Epilogue to the third volume, University of Chicago Press' 1979. From the same author, *The Fatal Conceit*, edited by W.W. Bartley III, University of Chicago Press, 1988.

[12]See Eric Ericson, *Identity, Youth, and Crisis*, W.W. Norton and Co., Inc., New York, 1968, chap. 3. From the same author: *Childhood and Society*, 2nd. ed. W.W. Norton Inc., New York, 1963.

[13]Stefan Zweig, *Die Welt van Western*, S. Fischer-verlag, 1955, pp. 13-16.

Chapter 12

THE FORMER EAST-BLOC FAMILY IN THE MODERN WORLD

Jaroslav Macháček

Introduction

This subject can be approached in many ways. The definition of its constituent concepts is essential whatever the chosen approach might be.

The Former East-Bloc (FEB) means a region well marked off geographically. It is generally viewed as a group of European countries which had been forming, both in formal and informal manner, the Soviet Union's "Empire."[1]

The second term, "modern world," has difficulties. The image of what the modern world implies and how it should work may differ in geographical, philosophical, political and other ways. Argumentation in favor of different alternatives and comparison of them would itself pose an uneasy and extensive task. Therefore a "conventional" understanding has been chosen: "Modern" stands for contemporary, this adjective representing development in spiritual, cultural, social and economic terms.

Despite the above simplification of conceptual framework, the object examined—the family in the above territorial location—remains marked with substantial diversity, not only in ethnicity, but also in social, economic and demographic terms.

We could concentrate on individual countries, describe and analyze their conditions, sort out the data and arrive at a kind of typology making possible generalizations. On the other hand, we could aim at what the countries observed have in common. The findings should characterize the past and enable deriving the features of the future. The latter approach appears much more preferable, given the limited availability of information and data.

Demographic Features

Focusing our attention first on demographic variables, giving account of relevant features in the domain of family,[2] we have chosen the indicators of marriage, divorce and birth rate.

Marriage

By marriage we mean forming families through formally recognized marriages. The crude marriage rate, in other words, the number of legal marriages performed and registered per 1000 mid-year population, conveys the information on this process.[3] The respective data have been gathered in Table 1.

Whereas most of thirteen countries making up FEB (former Yugoslavia and Austria have been selected as reference comparative units, since once parts of Austro-Hungarian Empire) experienced slight rising of the crude marriage rate in the course of the 1950s, the 1970s and particularly the 1980s saw more or less lowering this variable's level. We draw attention to the evident drop of this parameter within the final period 1990-1992 in all countries included into the observed group. (In some of these countries, this decrease in merely two years was remarkably dramatic.) This finding suggests a hypothesis of special factors—both objective and subjective ones in character—at work, when it comes to entering into marriage. Some other demographic phenomena related to

Table 1
Crude Marriage Rates - FEB Countries (x)

Year	1963	1970	1980	1988	1990	1992
Belarus	.	.	.	9.4	.	.
Bulgaria	8.2	8.6	7.9	7.0	6.7	5.0
Czechoslova-kia	7.9	8.8	7.7	7.6	8.4	-
Czech Re-public	.	.	.	7.9	8.8	7.2
Estonia	.	.	.	6.3	6.1	.
German D.R.	8.6	7.7	8.0	8.2	.	.
Hungary	8.4	9.3	7.5	6.3	6.4	5.4
Latvia	.	.	.	9.5	8.8	7.2
Lithuania	.	.	.	9.6	9.8	.
Poland	7.2	8.6	8.6	6.5	6.7	5.7
Romania	9.3	7.2	8.2	7.5	8.3	7.5
Russia(1)	9.1	9.7	10.3	9.5	8.9	.
Slovakia	.	.	.	7.1	7.6	.
Ukraine	9.2	9.8	9.3	8.9	9.3	6.6
F. Yugoslavia	8.3	9.0	7.7	6.8	6.2	6.0
Austria	8.1	7.1	6.7	4.7	5.9	5.7

1) USSR until 1992.
x) Number of legal marriages performed and registered per 1000 mid-year population.

Source: *Demographic Yearbook*, United Nations, New York, 1994, 1988, 1982, *Historical Supplement*, 1979; *Demografie*, XXXVI, 1994, no. 1, 4.

this process, which might have been brought about by the changes of political and economic systems, should also be studied.

The overall shifts can be highlighted by the comparison of values for the year 1970 (base 100.0) and the year 1992 for the marriage rate in the selected countries: Bulgaria 58, Czechoslovakia (Czech Republic) 81, Hungary 58, Poland 66, Ukraine 67, Yugoslavia 66, Austria 80. An increase has been found only for Romania: 104.

On the basis of this simple comparison of changes in the indicator's values in time, we can conclude that the tendency to become married and thus establish formal families has been reduced in the examined supranational region, especially since the beginning of the 1980s.

When these values are assessed by comparison among FEB countries in the given period, relative homogeneity can be found for years 1963 and 1970, with a maximum variation of 23 and 28 percent. This homogeneity has dwindled away, as this variation increased to 35 percent in 1980 and to 37 percent in 1990. It dropped slightly to 33 percent in 1992. A substantial decrease in marriage has come about in the 1990s, even in those countries where the levels of marriage had been comparatively high: Hungary, Poland, Bulgaria, Ukraine.

Divorce Rate

The ability to sustain marriage and family is inverse to the divorce rate. One has to emphasize, however, that the stability of family stands for a concept far broader than is generally assumed. In this context, as well as in many other relations, we have to keep in mind the type and structure of family: Nuclear, composed of more generations, extended by a wider group of relatives and so forth. In the broadest sense, the stability of family can be seen in satisfactory relations among individuals and groups of people who come together as relatives.

The claims to view stability of family this way should be fully appreciated. However, when analyzed in demographic terms, this concept usually is confined to the unity of the elementary family (not household). That means stability of marriage, whose basic characteristic in the negative sense is occurrence of divorce.

The crude divorce rate—the number of final divorce decrees granted under civil law per 1000 mid-year population[4] —has been set as key indicator for the sake of fair comparison. Table 2 contains respective data for this variable. These data show evidence of a relatively fast rising divorce rate between the 1960s and 1980s. The level of the indicator slightly increased even in the course of 1980s. At the beginning of 1990s, the changes occurred in both ways: about half the set shows a decline and nearly the same proportion is marked by an increase.

As in the previous case, when setting about comparison we choose as the base level year 1970 (100). The changes in 1990 are spelled out in the magnitude order by the following indices: Romania 364 (major alterations in legislation practice assumed), German-Democratic Republic (GDR) 184 (1988), Belarus 179, Austria 152, Czechoslovakia 150, Russia (USSR) 144 Ukraine 130, Bulgaria 109, Hungary 109, Poland 105, Yugoslavia 86.

The difference between the development in former GDR, former Czechoslovakia and former USSR, on the one hand, and the rest of the FEB countries— Hungary, Poland, Bulgaria and former Yugoslavia (if included)—on the other, is apparent. Whereas conspicuous in the first group, the increase in the latter has been very small, nearly negligible.

Particularly in the countries of the former USSR, the indicator rose to practically formidable levels and suggests that the stability of the families must have been poor.

Examining the homogeneity of the whole FEB group, again, it was higher in 1963, with a maximum variation of 67 percent, and in 1970 with 59 percent (with exclusion of Romania having extremely low value due to exceptional conditions), compared with 1980 (72 percent) and 1990 (77 percent).

Table 2
Crude Divorce Rates - FEB Countries(x)

Year	1963	1970	1980	1988	1990	1992
Belarus	.	1.89	3.24	3.16	3.38	.
Bulgaria	1.02	1.16	1.48	1.38	1.26	.
Czechoslovakia	1.22	1.74	2.21	2.49	2.61	-
Czech Republic	.	.	.	2.96	3.09	2.77
Estonia	.	.	.	3.80	3.68	.
German D.R.	1.44	1.61	2.68	2.96	.	.
Hungary	1.82	2.21	2.59	2.28	2.40	.
Latvia	.	.	.	4.10	4.04	.
Lithuania	.	.	.	3.20	3.42	.
Poland	0.64	1.06	1.12	1.27	1.11	0.75
Romania	1.92	0.39	1.54	1.59	1.42	1.29
Russia(1)	1.29	2.62	3.50	3.90	3.78	.
Slovakia	.	.	.	1.57	1.67	.
Ukraine	1.31	2.86	3.63	3.60	3.72	.
Yugoslavia	1.12	1.00	1.00	0.98	0.86	0.60
Austria	1.14	1.39	1.47	1.96	2.11	.

1) USSR until 1992.
x) Number of final divorce decrees granted under civil law per 1000 mid-year population.

Source: *Demographic Yearbook*, United Nations, New York, 1994, 1988, 1982, *Historical Supplement*, 1979; *Demografie*, XXXVI, no. 1, 4.

Most of the FEB countries have been experiencing unfavorable changes in the divorce rate. Unlike marriage with its rather small interregional differences inside the countries, variance for the divorce rate is quite significant. The data referring to some countries of the FEB group (Czechoslovakia, Poland, Hungary) provide a basis to infer substantial dissimilarities when rural areas and major urban agglomerations are compared. The respective differences may stretch to more than 100 percent.[5]

Some of analysis conducted in the Czech Republic indicate that the divorce rate is higher in the regions with a "progressive" type of population development, where a comparatively higher proportion of lower age groups is typical. Altogether, the assumption of the adverse impact, which the current process of urbanization brings about, is being verified.

Birth Rate

Giving birth to children, the reproductive function of the family, is a necessary precondition for human continuation. The birth rate represents, beside the establishment and sustainability of the family, a third crucial demographic feature pertinent to the analysis of family's current situation.

Trends inferable from the data arranged in Table 3 do not reveal any bright prospects in this respect.[6] This is true for all countries included in the FEB group. While in the 1970s and at the beginning of the 1980s the crude birth rates were keeping—over the whole set of countries—stabilized at a satisfactory level, the end of 1980s and particularly the beginning of the 1990s saw explicit and universal decline in the birth rate. All countries observed, except Poland, became threatened in the natural increase of their population. These tendencies are likely to continue in the future and deepen the burdens brought about by the aging of the population, which will also affect the situation of families in the FEB.

Using the elementary procedure of time comparison as before, the year 1970 being the base level (100), the following indices have been recorded for the year 1990: Poland 85, Czechoslovakia 84, German Democratic Republic 83, Hungary 82, Yugoslavia 79, Austria 78, Russia (USSR) 77, Bulgaria 72, Romania 64. Understandably enough, the overall decrease has been determined by the level of the base year. The changes reflect a closer clustering of values within the group.

The decline of birth rate can be estimated to approximate 20 percent for all the FEB group. Leaving aside the reference countries (Austria, Yugoslavia), the FEB countries can be divided, according to the indicator applied, into two categories. The first is made up by former Czechoslovakia, former German Democratic Republic, Hungary and Poland. The downward movement of level as well as the level itself is very similar therein. The second category can be formed by Bulgaria, Romania and Russia (USSR). The drop of level has been relatively much deeper and has brought these countries close to the bottom of ranking. The factors affecting the birth rate in a negative way are likely to be much heavier in these countries, which can also be assumed to be more sensitive in terms of a demographic response to economic and social changes, to the alterations in the way of life and also to the limitations in the sphere of population policy formerly implemented in FEB countries.

Our estimate of the degree of homogeneity in the FEB countries, this time with respect to crude birth rate, is based again on the characteristic used in the two previous cases. The data imply that birth rate variables behave differently from marriage and divorce variables in the FEB countries. The range in maximum variation was 34 percent in 1970, 28 percent in 1980, and 18 percent in 1990. It rose to 28 percent in 1992.

The remarkable reduction of birth rates at the beginning of 1990s seems to indicate a turn in the demographic development of FEB countries, and is most likely to have major impacts on processes in the sectors linked with population development.

T a b l e 3
Crude Live - Birth Rates - FEB Countries(x)

Year	1970	1980	1988	1990	1992
Belarus	.	16.0	16.1	.	.
Bulgaria	16.3	14.5	13.1	11.7	9.9
Czechoslovakia	15.9	16.3	13.8	13.4	-
Czech Republic	.	.	.	12.7	11.8
Estonia	.	.	16.1	14.2	11.8
Germany-Dem. R.	13.9	14.6	11.0	11.5	11.1
Hungary	14.7	13.9	11.9	12.1	11.9
Latvia	.	.	15.6	14.2	12.0
Lithuania	.	.	14.9	.	.
Poland	16.8	19.5	15.5	14.3	13.4
Romania	21.1	18.0	16.5	13.6	11.4
Russia(1)	17.4	18.3	16.0	13.4	.
Slovakia	.	.	.	.	.
Ukraine	.	14.8	14.5	12.7	9.6
Yugoslavia	17.8	17.1	15.1	14.1	13.5
Austria	15.2	12.1	11.6	11.7	12.0

1) USSR until 1992.
x) Number of live births per 1000 mid-year population.

Source: *Demographic Yearbook*, United Nations, New York, 1994, 1988, 1982, *Historical Supplement*, 1979; *Demografie*, XXXVI, no. 1, 4.

Beside the above demographic variables, others could be examined to characterize the trends both affecting and reflecting the development in the domain of family. However, the study of the above data gives us a basis to claim that extending the scope of demographic examination would not present findings much different from those arrived at in the previous section. The conclusion is that the FEB countries have been passing through, and are likely to experience further, dis-stimulation as for the formation of the family in quantitative terms.

Stability of the Family

Coming to qualitative aspects of the family's position in FEB countries, one is faced with the lack of analysis and investigations similar to those made in developed Western countries, which would cover, at least in some respects, the whole FEB superregion. The results of research as well as theoretical studies published by Louis Roussel[7] Fernand Mount[8] and Dirk van der Kaa,[9] among others, are not available for the FEB. It can be argued that this research and theoretical work done in the Western countries can be to some extent exploited also with regard to the development in FEB. This may be true with the strong reservation concerning the involvement of quite a number of specific factors of political, social, psychological and even environmental nature, demanding viewing different from what is typical for traditional analysis.

The stability of the family represents a factor and a value that can hardly be overemphasized. Apart from the obvious quantitative demographic impact in terms of reproduction, it has many irreplaceable positive effects on the quality of human life in general, including the very substance of the social arrangement and human mental development. Attention should be drawn to the processes having brought about substantial changes in the stability of family.

Some of these processes are at work in a worldwide scope: The changes of cultural patterns, the rise of relative economic independence and self- sufficiency on the part of both partners, general increase in share of employed married women, the consequences of detrimental forms of consumer behavior, superfluous urbanization and quite a few other phenomena.

When attempting to identify factors specific to FEB, we should not omit the impact of past and present population policies in these countries. Although primarily conceived to stimulate fertility and the birth rate, they have been also influencing unity of the family. Measures intended to prevent divorce in a direct way, which were mostly legislative ones, did occur in the more distant past. However, they did not work well, and were practiced only in short periods and in limited scope.

More significant were the indirect impacts induced by economic and social advantages built into population policy, which may in part prevent possible disintegration in some types of family. Looked at from the perspective of inception of marriage, the comparatively lower marriage age in FEB countries (19-22 years as an average for brides) has been stressed as one of the most distinct features in demographic development in FEB in comparison with advanced non-FEB regions. This has also been attributed to population policy measures.

As there was a strong involvement in the procedures and principles in population policy typical of FEB totalitarian practice or even ideology, some argue that the very existence of population policy in the sense of regulation of population development should be questioned or put under doubt.

The disputes centered around population policy notwith-standing, we cannot escape admitting that this policy, to some extent, affects the position and inner structure of family. In this context, the term "family policy" used to be a common item in the basic "vocabulary" of social strategy in several countries (e.g., Czechoslovakia, Poland, Hungary).

Demands and expectations related to married life have generally grown on the part of both sexes. This process is nevertheless more significant with women, whose lower dependency on their husbands, in economic, psychical and other terms, has brought into the family more potential factors of instability than with men.

Considering the changes in basic functions of the family—reproduction, economic functions, upbringing, cultural functions (e.g., Pisca, 1978)—we can claim that it is just the economic function that has undergone major mutations in modern times. Not only do we have the above-mentioned increasing independence of women, but women and children have ceased to practice production activities in the family sphere. Generally, the family does not function as an economic production unit any more. This applies at large as it were to all FEB countries, some minor exceptions of limited significance notwithstanding.

This reasoning refers to explicit production related to both inner consumption and external sale. What remained to an unnegligible extent, however, is the productive work of women in the household: cooking, washing, mending, cleaning and the like. This burden metaphorized as "second shift," and has been aggravated by insufficient availability of services and appliances in the FEB countries in general, and has become a common source of conflict, thus posing a threat to the stability of family. Presumably, the economic transition in FEB countries is going to entail substantial relief in terms of the supply of the services that are most required for everyday family life.

The level of education and qualification is rising faster on the part of women, partly due to the lower base earlier. This professional and intellectual advancement induces, beside others things, the effects that could work against the stability of the family. Heavy professional involvement, incentives to extend one's knowledge, and the necessity to invest time into activities connected with employment often result in severe limitation of time and energy that can be devoted to the family, especially to children. Professional promotion of both partners in marriage could sometimes issue in a strain much like that arising from competitive relations. This is typical for so called two-career marriages where a significant portion of family functions may be sacrificed to professional or scientific devotion. The question is whether the external assistance in the shape of improved and extensively offered services and welfare goods could have a compensating effect in this domain. We must admit that the changes in the mental and psychic response to this new situation is called for.

Employment of married women, especially those with little children, deemed far excessive in many FEB countries,[10] presents many problems: Psychical stress ensuing from excessive work, lack of time in general, entailing reduction of family care, controversial relations, coming about through inconsistent roles women had to assume, disparity of working and maternity duties and many other ones. Primarily, the extent of women's employment had been chosen for economic reasons. In some groups of families it represents a necessity, in other ones a striving for improvement of standard of living or effort to keep the attained consumption. It should be noted that part of the responsibility can be attached to sheer habitude to maintain the experienced way of life involving regular working activities outside the household. Indisputably, the extensive rate of women's employment has contributed in a substantial way to the trends not favorable to the stability of family.

Orientation toward attaining maximum possible incomes and standards of living, particularly in regard to material goods, has led some groups of families, fairly extensive ones, in most FEB countries to the conflict, hidden or open, with their reproduction and educational functions. This tendency signified and exemplified profound confusion as to the priorities and relevance in the area of values. Needless to point out, the unity of the family has been put at risk as a result of such attitudes.

Another factor ranking high in terms of threatening families' stability is the social and sexual behavior of the groups of adolescent age, the consequence of which is the emergence of immature marriages, combined with an irresponsible choice of partner and insufficient knowledge of the requirements and preconditions that marriage presents. At its very inception, strong factors of instability are brought in the relations of a young couple, which are evident in demographic data. They lead to an unwanted impact on the quality of married life.

Young Couples

Regarding instability, special attention deserves to be given to the position and behavior of young couples. In first few years of marriage, young partners start to act in three, often difficult, roles: as a spouse, as a parent, and as a worker or employee. To cope with all these challenges at one time, to make correct decisions, and to respond to complex situations in all three areas demands mutual support, understanding, affection, and empathy. If these elements are lacking, the integrity of family is usually exposed to erosion that may result in its discontinuation. (For more details see, e.g., Haberlová, 1987.)

The importance of young couples' marriages represents the degree and nature of dependency on parents and foregoing generations in general. A weak economic position of young marriages may induce the parents' effort to make up the economic difference for them. The nature of the inter-generational link is thus formed on the basis of disemancipation of the young couple. The tendency of parents or other members of the older generation to intervene and control does not promote sound development of relations within family. This is often particularly true in the case of sharing one apartment and household. The relations within the young family as well as between the generations involved may become even more complex and difficult by the transfer of the child-raising function to older generations.

The above-mentioned features of intergenerational links have been typical for the situation of families in the FEB countries and have proved to be factors that usually do not contribute to the stability of young families. It has to be emphasized that the basis for stability or instability are formed in the early years of married life. If the marriage tends to fail in these years, it is much less likely to continue or be a quality marriage later.

The fact that many (about nearly one-half in Czech Republic) of the first children are born less than nine months after formal marriage is an indication of the situation of young families in the FEB. This is merely an economic problem that needs attention. Premarital conception indicates a conflict between biological maturity, which occurs at a lower age, and social maturity, which seems to be occurring at a higher age.

Disintegration of families, and divorce as its final result, comes about often due to this controversial disparity in human development. Out of the total number, a great majority of divorces occur in the first five years after marriage. About two-thirds of these cases (findings for Czech practice) involve dependent children who are to a maximum extent entrusted to mothers' care. Extending reproduction of incomplete families, lacking a male figure in upbringing, also means poorer economic provision and other undesirable consequences for the children.

Despite a differentiation in terms of financial and material backgrounds of individual families, most of young couples still have to face a relative deficiency of financial means needed to set up a household. Their incomes are usually substantially lower than those of older marriages.[11] This fact can be interpreted with regard to lessening fertility of lower age cohorts of women, which have been witnessed in FEB countries. Systems of social allowances and benefits for maternity partly compensate for usual difference in available means compared with earning position; but on the whole, this situation is still disadvantageous from an economic standpoint, unless substantial contributions come from parents or relatives.

Specific elements in the support of young families comes from various kinds of loans. In the past, they were an important source of funds needed to get housing, furniture and other equipment in a number of the FEB countries. In most of them today, however, access to such loans is ceasing to correspond to their original purpose. Be it social, population or family policy, in most cases it seems to lack appropriate measures in the domain of loans as tools of family development. Potential benefits of loan policies should be reconsidered in FEB countries.

Housing

Housing has been the most difficult to obtain material condition, and much determines the way of life of young couples. It has always been one of the major issues coped with under the former regimes in FEB countries. This heritage has been transferred to the new era. It would be difficult to find a single country in the regions examined where the housing problem is being successfully resolved. Obviously, five years' period is too short for one to demand that all the accumulated problems in the housing sector are put right. Nevertheless, distinct and lucid housing policy involving the needs of young marriages should be conceived and implemented with urgency.

Former development, as well as the current state in the area of housing, has been marked with differences among the FEB countries as to accepted standards, size of the deficiency and ability to cope with the problem on the part of the state. Nonetheless, the essence of the issue and main trend in this sphere have been shared virtually by all the FEB countries. New construction had to cover the continuous reduction of housing stock brought about by regular annual disappearance of available dwelling units and had to respond to a relatively lower or higher rate of increase of national and possibly regional population. Setting up barracks-like prefabricated housing estates had been a very common way of reaction to these needs in the FEB. Location of the young couples and families in general in the districts of this kind represents, in our context, a separate subject that should be tackled especially from sociological and psychological aspects. However, the most important factor has been, and unfortunately continues to be, obtaining a separate dwelling for young couples. As pointed out elsewhere in this text, arriving at any single characteristic representing the whole FEB region in the way of synthesization would be conditioned by great simplification or even deformation of data.

However cautious we have to be about conclusions involving this kind of risk, we can claim that most of newly married couples did not possess a dwelling of their own in the first year of married life in seventies and eighties and hardly half or two-thirds (which was the case, e.g., in former Czechoslovakia) of these couples gained a dwelling till the fifth year following their marriage. A clear correlation existed between the chance of getting housing and the length of duration of marriage, number of children in the family and also income level in the household.

Incomes and Labor

The dependency of families' income on the existence of two salaries continues in the case of the majority of couples even today. An important fact is that the incomes of young families usually come from working activities. On the other hand, the more children, the less room for parents to get committed in the professional area, which impacts on the level of salaries. The families without children assume a more advantageous position in this respect, the absence of social allowances notwithstanding. These allowances and contributions, however, have to substitute the above-explained difference, which puts families with more children at a disadvantage. Regarding income of families, we cannot omit the situation of incomplete families, mostly with the mother until the age of thirty. They represent a very distinct group with specific socially-demographic features and economic conditions. Such characteristics as a lower level of education, lower marriage age, higher unemployment and other similar factors are common.

The social-economic position of families may be to a substantial degree derived from the behavior of their members in the labor market. There are groups of young people in FEB countries availing themselves with new opportunities offered by this market. In this sense they apply their education and qualification, active approach to the work, working performance and in quite a number of cases also entrepreneurial spirit. They also tend to take a second job, mostly for the sake of sufficient income for the household.

What are the attitudes and expectations of young families in the labor area? Drawing upon the results of investigations carried out in Czech Republic (Kuchařová, Lhotská, 1994) and assuming that similar inclinations can be found in other FEB countries, we can summarize the knowledge in the following points:

- Prevention of unemployment; a great deal involved with socioeconomic strategy of the state.
- Realistic outlook as to the perspectives of their professions.
- Rising capacity for mobility induced by work opportunities.
- Growing interest in work abroad.

- Tendency to make the household more economical.
- Ability to do as much as possible themselves in the maintenance work of the household.
- Seeking after better paid jobs.
- Taking second employment and/or occasional jobs.

The results of investigations suggest that higher degrees of activity in the economic sphere, in other words progress of "economization" can be observed. Apparently, standing in terms of labor and economic benefits gained through personal activity are being attached still more importance.

Relation of Generations

From demographic, social and other points of view, it is natural that attention has been focused, above all, on young families and those with children living in the original household, without means of subsistence of their own. Besides other reasons, the relatively low age of entering marriage calls for the concern about those families, living as a couple without dependent children, either in common households with adult children or separately. Be it in the age of economic activity or retirement, the ties between generations and relations within broader family are of utmost importance, especially from a psychological viewpoint.

More than one-quarter, and in some FEB countries more than one-third, of families belong to the above-mentioned category. The main distinguishing feature of intergeneration relations in physical terms is whether they live together in one household. Given the continuous shortage in housing virtually in all of FEB countries, two families—parents and their children as a married couple—living together has been, and continues to be, the case much more frequently than the involved people prefer. Obviously, there are differences among the FEB countries with respect to the capability, willingness or inclination to go through this type of common life and the effects it brings about. Living together may be perceived in many cases as a benefit and accepted with satisfaction, despite possible limitation of available space for individual members of shared households and density of contacts.

On the other hand, there are quite a number of families where this coexistence is felt as a strong detriment, on the part of one or both families involved. This factor can often threaten the stability of the younger family. Considering this, and other important facts of similar kind, a distinct long-term housing policy is something that is very urgently called for. Regarding the importance of the issue, the relatively little attention paid to it by politicians in most of the FEB countries is hardly understandable.

In the common household, the contacts that the older ones can enjoy are secured by physical proximity and may be felt, as mentioned, overabundant. It is a different situation where "older parent" families live separately. Unless the psychical ties have been broken, these families usually strive for good relations and a sufficient frequency of contact. Logically enough, the possibility of these contacts is to a great extent dependent on the distance between places where the two families live. The location can be influenced by many factors, employment or availability of housing among them. But again, the current supply of housing in the FEB countries is so scarce that it is usually impossible to find a choice of residence with regard to family relations. The low supply of inexpensive, relatively smaller but well-furnished flats for the older families, given rising level of housing cost in many FEB countries, represents a subject of its own which deserves attention.

When considering the importance of contacts between generations forming family relations, those families which for various reasons cannot enjoy these contacts with satisfactory frequency or even at all should be taken into account. Social policy as well as the structures of nongovernmental and voluntary activities should develop themselves into such a shape as to be able to respond to these challenges which face many families.

Impact of Urbanization

Another factor which has an impact on the family is urbanization. The process of urbanization in most of the FEB countries has been marked by very high rates. Table 4 presents the data documenting the rise of the urban population in the FEB countries in the last two decades. It indicates substantial changes in the way of living, social demographic and economic behavior of families.

Social changes brought about by urbanization have been studied profoundly since the time of the Industrial Revolution. Remembering impressive contributions of social philosophers, for example, Emile Durkheim, Georg Simmel and Ferdinand Tönnies, to name a few, we can realize that full discussion of the position of the family in urbanization would require far more space than is available. Nevertheless, we must point out the main specific results of fast urbanization in the FEB countries.

The increased immigration into cities has not been matched by an appropriate housing and living environment, with elements that would facilitate and enrich the lives of families, especially in the newly built housing estates. This may, in many cases, have caused strain and adversely influenced the quality of family life and work performance. It helps to undermine the stability of the family. Lack of a sense of community distracts from families' ability to establish appropriate relations among themselves and enjoy the benefits of such relations. Characteristic spatial separation of home, work place and space for leisure activities has led families to become more isolated. Formerly there were more extended family systems which have given way to nuclear families. Support and control of primary groups, among which family has key position, has been weakened.[12]

Table 4
Percentage of Urban Population in FEB Countries,
Two Time Sections

	Year	Urban percent	Year	Urban percent
Belarus	1968	40, 8	1989	65, 4
Bulgaria	1968	49, 0	1991	68, 1
Czechoslovakia	1968	62, 2	1990	65, 9
Estonia	.	.	1990	71, 4
German Dem. R.	1968	73, 3	1990	76, 3
Hungary	1968	47, 0	1992	63, 1
Latvia	.	.	1990	70.8
Lithuania	.	.	1992	68, 4
Poland	1970	52, 3	1991	61.9
Romania	1968	40, 1	1991	54, 1
Russia (1)	1968	55, 1	1989	73, 4
Ukraine	1968	53, 3	1992	67, 8
Austria	1971	51, 9	1981	55, 1
Yugoslavia	1971	38, 6	1981	46, 1

1) USSR until 1992.
Note: Different availability of data for years in the observed period.

Source: *Demographic Yearbook*, United Nations, New York, 1994, 1972, *Historical Supplement*, 1979; *Report of the Population Reference Bureau, United Nations*, New York, 1992.

Owing to the above, and other factors, fertility and natality in many urban areas has dropped remarkably compared to former trends in the traditional settlement pattern. (The correlation between changes of these variables and the increase of the share of urban population can be seen by comparison among countries.)

The above estimate of the relevance attachable to urbanization, may involve many more or less concealed deformations. By all means, we have to take into account not only the share of urban population compared to the rural, but, above all, by the changed and changing way of life, as a factor undoubtedly very important for the development of family. Due to the excessive rate and speed of these changes, quite a number of unwelcome challenges in FEB countries have arisen.

Conclusions

In conclusion, it has to be admitted that the subject treated is so extensive that even its major elements could not be fully covered by this brief chapter. Possible predictions concerning the development of families in the FEB countries would have to assess quite a number of assumptions and hypotheses. On the basis of what has been presented above, the following items appear to be essential:

- The legal, formal family will remain the prevailing form of partnership, and will concentrate primarily on reproduction.
- Marriage rates will depend on the occurrence of informal bonds, which are likely to differ within the FEB. The rates of partnerships, whether formal or informal, will probably remain on the level similar to the present one, though the number of couples may drop, as a result of long-term demographic changes.
- The age of entering marriage may generally rise a little, due to changes in the socioeconomic environment, and to

following a pattern similar to that characteristic for Western countries.

- Should the factors of various nature which are currently responsible for the relatively high degree of instability of family—particularly that of young couples—continue to exist, the consequences of this development will affect the social structure much more severely than experienced so far. And this might prompt a strong feedback effect.
- There are no signs that the external conditions of married life will improve substantially in the near future. Housing problems stand in the foreground. Three generations living together may contribute to even better human relations in some cases, and likely become even more common than at present.
- Emotional and consequently socio-psychological consequences of massive institutional involvement (nurseries, kindergartens, etc.) into the upbringing of current young generations, which was carried out by parents in the past, will be felt a long time. The importance of how childhood is spent cannot be overestimated and the negative experiences in this respect should be compensated by appropriate attention paid to it.

Obviously, functions and mission of family with regard to children cannot be confined to quantitative reproduction. More important is the qualitative reproduction, transferring positive values to the subsequent generations. The aspect of values is unquestionably the crucial one. The family has quite a unique role in this respect, and it cannot be replaced. Values recognized and accepted by parents are likely to be shared by children, provided the family is able to create and maintain good internal relations. Values and relations being two sides of one coin, it can be argued that values contribute to the establishment of good relations in the family and are worthy of acceptance. Since we can presume that the key importance of value systems in human life will be increasingly recognized by more people, we tend to have an optimistic outlook on the future of family.

Notes

[1]Including countries from other continents, which had been more or less identified with the former Soviet Union, would substantially distract from compatibility within the group and from value of comparisons.

[2]Regarding the availability of comparable data we have reduced the selection to the three most essential variables.

[3]More specific indicators of marriage as well as a number of other demographic parameters are not available for a substantial number of countries in the FEB group. As for the crude marriage rate itself, the results received cannot be prevented from possibly suffering of different age patterns in the countries examined.

[4]The outcomes of comparison may have been loaded with the differences in affecting factors (proportion of married population in the first place).

[5]The crude divorce rate in the Czech Republic made up 2.93. Whereas in country-district Louny (e.g.) it was 1.79, it attained 4.66 in the heavily urbanized district Most and 3.19 in Prague.

[6]See Macháček, J., Type of Population Development and Stability of the Family, in *Family and Society: Values for 21st Century*, Prague: Professors World Peace Academy, 1994.

[7]Roussel, L., *La famille incertaine*, Paris: Odile Jacob, 1989.

[8]Mount, F., *The Subversive Family*, London: Jonathan Cape, 1992.

[9] van der Kaa, D., *Europe's Second Demographic Transition*, Washington: Population Reference Bureau, 1987.

[10]The share of women in the active population in economic terms reached 40-47 percent in FEB countries in the eighties (former Czechoslovakia and former German Democratic Republic, 47 percent), the share of active women in the labor force of the number of women in production age was 80-90 percent in the same period (USSR, German Dem. Republic, Czechoslovakia and Bulgaria more than 90 percent), the percent of active women in the labor force in the complete families with children up to 15 years, 75-90 percent (the highest share in Czechoslovakia, German Democratic Republic, and the USSR). It is worth mentioning that all the observed shares substantially rose (generally by 20-25 percent) when the years 1970 and 1990 are compared. Fragmentary data concerning the changes of these indicators in the 1990s suggest that no significant decrease in these percentages is about to occur.

[11]Older marriages referred to are those lasting 6-15 years (according to categories as a rule used in the Census).

[12]Similar tendencies had been defined by Louis Wirth already in his study "Urbanism as a Way of Life" (*American Journal of Sociology*, 44/1938).

References

Bartko, D. *Moderní psychohygiena*, Praha: Pyramida, 1980.

Bartošová, M. Situace rodin starších osob, *Demografie*, no. 3, 1994.

Berger, J.M., Kovalskaja, G. J., Lazareva, J.M. *Evolucija sem'ji v sovremennom obščestve*, Moskva: INION AN SSSR, 1989.

Bischof, D. *Autonomie und heteronomie in Familie und Gesellschaft*, Zurich: ADAG, 1990.

Demografické ukazatele evropských a vybraných mimoevropských zemích, Praha: Federální statistický úřad, 1990.

Demographic Yearbook, New York: United Nations, 1994, 1988, 1982, 1972, Historical Supplement 1979.

Haberlová, V. *Mladá manželství po pěti letech*, Praha: VÚSRP, 1987.

Horská, P. Nejistá prognóza vývoje evropské rodiny, *Demografie*, no. 2, 1994.

Janosz, M. *Desorganizacia v rodzinie i spoleczenstwie,* Warszawa: Ekonomie, 1987.

Kuchařová, V., Lhotská, v. Ekonomická situace mladých rodin, *Demografie*, no. 3, 1994.

Kuczynska, A. (ed.). *Psychologiczne aspekty funkcionovania v rodzinie*, Wroclaw: Acta Universitatis Wratislaveinsis, 8, 1992.

Macháček, J. "Type of Population Development and Stability of Family In: Family and Society," *Values for 21st Century*, Praha: Professors World Peace Academy - CS, 1994.

Matoušek, O. *Rodina jako instituce a vztahová síť,* Praha: Sociologické nakladatelství, 1993.

Mecchan, J., A. *Family and Individual Development*, Basel: Karger, 1985.

Možný, I. *Proč tak snadno?*, Praha: Sociologické nakladatelství, 1991.

Pachl, L. "Rodina v ČSR do roku 2010," *Ústav prognozování*, Praha: ČSR, 1989.

Pavlík, Z., Rychtaříková, J., Šubrtová,A. *Základy demografie*, Praha: Academia, 1986.

Pisca, L. *Sociální politika*, Bratislava: Alfa, 1978.

Statistická ročenka České republiky, Praha: Český spisovatel, 1994.

Chapter 13

THE "DECLINE-OF-THE-WESTERN-FAMILY" THESIS: A CRITIQUE AND APPRAISAL

William R. Garrett

A vigorous debate has arisen in recent years over the status of the family in Western, industrialized societies where—since the 1960s—the divorce rate has risen dramatically, a sexual revolution has occurred, family size has sharply declined, cohabitation of unmarried adults has become more widely accepted, the number of children born out of wedlock has increased, and the family has continued to lose many of its functions to other basic institutions. Initially, sociologists and other social scientists in the late 1960s and early 1970s sounded a precipitous alarm that family life in the West had entered a period of serious decline and institutional deterioration. As the data came in for more trenchant evaluation during the late 1970s and into the 1980s, however, scholarly evaluations experienced a remarkable turnabout as more and more students of Western family life came to the conclusion that this institution was undergoing a significant transformation, but its basic health and stability was not being jeopardized. Indeed, when Brigitte and Peter Berger (1984) published their volume, *The War Over The Family* decrying the erosion of the bourgeois family, the "war" was already over for all practical purposes.

The "bourgeois family" had, to be sure, been supplanted by a variety of new family forms, but the familial institution, itself, has remained a vibrant and stable feature of advanced industrial societies.

Meanwhile, just as the social scientific community was reaching a consensus that the familial institution had weathered the storm of dramatic changes from the 1960s to the 1980s, journalists, conservative religionists, and politicians in the United States belatedly entered the controversy in the early 1990s to announce a new "war over the family." The opening round was fired by Charles Murray (1993), a fellow at the American Enterprise Institute, a conservative think-tank, in an op-ed piece printed in the Wall Street Journal. Murray targeted birth out of wedlock as the "single most important problem of our time," more devastating in its consequences than crime, drugs, poverty, illiteracy, welfare or homelessness. This remarkable judgment was predicated on the presupposition that illegitimate births were the root cause driving all these other social ills and that the upward spiral of the illegitimacy rate was primarily a function of liberal welfare benefits for unwed mothers. More remarkable still were Murray's policy recommendations, however, for they entailed (1) the elimination of welfare payments to mothers who had children out of wedlock and (2) the creation of orphanages as well as more effective adoption procedures for those who continue to have children without the support of welfare funds.

Whether or not Murray actually intended for his draconian proposals to be taken seriously, the themes which he articulated swiftly garnered an extraordinary amount of attention from both Democrats and Republicans in Washington. A Deputy Assistant to the President on the White House Domestic Policy Council, William Galston (1993:4), declared that President Clinton had read Murray's article with great interest and substantially agreed with much of the analysis, although

President Clinton could not, Galston assured his audience, concur on several of Murray's policy recommendations. More serious disagreement was registered by the democratic Senator from New York, Daniel Patrick Moynihan, who commented that the drive to cut off government welfare aid could provoke "...scenes of social trauma such as we haven't known since the cholera epidemics" (DeParle, 1994:A10).

The Republican leadership in Congress proved much more receptive to Murray's proposals, however, than Democrats had been. Jack Kemp swiftly endorsed a plan that would cut off any welfare payments to unwed mothers under the age of twenty-one and Representative Newt Gingrich of Georgia incorporated similar notions into the master plan—known popularly as the "Contract with America"—for Republican legislative action after the Republican take-over of the majority of the House and Senate (DeParle, 1993). Intoning an ideological commitment to "family values" (a vague notion never defined by its supporters in the Republican majority), the tide in Congress has clearly turned toward an anti-welfare mood, with unwed mothers now defined as the enemy who must be contained. And the religious right, led by Ralph Reed of the Christian Coalition, recently issued a "Contract with the American Family" which went beyond the plans of Gingrich to oppose abortion, sex education in schools, homosexual rights, and the like (Birnbaum, 1995).

This political context provides the background against which the current debate over family matters is now being conducted in the United States. Although other advanced industrial societies have not yet erupted into the kind of debate over welfare and family issues currently underway in the United States, the large deficit budgets of almost all of the European states suggests that it may well only be a matter of time before other nations enter into a similar sort of discussion. Thus, we are confronted with this peculiar irony: at precisely the time when many social scientists have reached the conclusion that family matters have arrived at a plateau of stabilization, journalists, conservative religionists, and especially politicians have proclaimed a state of crisis relative to contemporary family matters, a crisis which demands, in their view, drastic remedial action to avert the deterioration of social life generally.

The purpose of this essay is to review the social scientific evidence in support of the thesis that the Western family is currently in a state of serious decline. What we intend to show in this critical examination is that, while the Western family has undergone significant changes over the last-quarter century, the institution remains relatively stable and functional with respect to the various activities allocated to it by the larger society. This is not to say, of course, that the familial institution is wholly without difficulties; the claim being registered here is considerably more modest, namely, that the family in Western societies is not in crisis nor does it appear to be headed for a precipitous decline anytime soon. Defending that proposition on the basis of the available sociological evidence will be the central undertaking of this evaluative exercise.

A final preliminary comment is in order before reviewing the evidence relative to the current status of the Western family. Although a concerted effort has been made throughout to focus on the Western family, much of the data are drawn from the social experience of the United States. There are two compelling reasons for this concentration: the first is that considerably more sociological research has been undertaken on family patterns in North America than other regions of the world. The second reason for fixation on American data is that the United States has often served as a kind of bellwether, so that trends observed in the United States are frequently discerned in relatively short order as well among other advanced industrial societies of the West. Comparative data will be utilized whenever possible, however, in this effort to demonstrate that the decline of the family in the West is more social myth than empirical fact.

The Decline-of-the-Western Family:
A Review of the Evidence

Several majors items comprise the catalogue of problem areas wherein family life is allegedly failing nowadays. Among the central issues may be enumerated the following: (1) the rising divorce rate; (2) the sexual revolution and increase in illegitimacy; (3) the decline of family size; (4) the loss of family functions; (5) the generation gap; and (6) the growth in the number of women working outside the home. We shall attend to each of these putative problem areas *seriatim*.

Divorce

Clearly no issue has troubled defenders of the family more vigorously than the rising divorce rate in Western societies, especially since the mid-1960s. The knee-jerk reaction to this phenomenon normally entails the conclusion that if the divorce rate is going up, then the quality of family life must be declining proportionately. This is one of those occasions, however, when sociologists like to point out that empirical data are not self-interpreting. One simply cannot read the health of the marital/familial institutions off of the "raw" divorce rate. Traditional, patriarchal societies typically exhibited a very low divorce rate, but this was not necessarily because a harmonious relationship prevailed between husband and wife. Rather, in traditional family contexts where marriages were arranged, a woman's family was paid a "bride-price," and divorce constituted a considerable financial loss to the groom's family. Indeed, C. K. Yang (1965:81) reminds us that in classical China there was an old adage which advised wives that when marital life became intolerable "Good women should hang themselves, only bad women seek divorce." Surely most modern folk would agree that divorce is preferable to suicide as a means of exiting unhappy marriages. And it should be equally clear that a low divorce rate does not necessarily mean that wholesome marriages prevail in a given social order (Goode, 1993:319-320). Accordingly, the *meaning* of the divorce rate must be extrapolated from the raw figures which only indicate what percentage of marriages are likely to end in dissolution.

There is widespread agreement among social scientific students of the family that for marriages contracted in the 1980s and thereafter in the United States the divorce rate will be approximately fifty percent (Ihinger-Tallman and Pasley, 1987:36). This figure is up from roughly twenty-five percent at the end of the decade of the 1950s (Mintz and Kellogg, 1988:178; National Center for Health Statistics, 1990:4). Although the United States continues to manifest the highest official divorce rate among the industrialized nations, other first world countries have experienced a spiraling divorce rate over the last-quarter century as well—with some evidencing a faster rate of growth than in the United States. A few modern-ized societies, however, have gone against the trend to retain relatively low divorce rates, notably Japan, Italy, and Israel (White, 1990:904). Moreover, the United States has histori-cally had a higher rate of divorce than other Euro-American societies (Riley, 1991), with the possible exception of Sweden which has sustained liberal sexual/marital patterns for centuries. Indeed, David Popenoe (1987) has argued that if one calcu-lates the divorce rate for Sweden using not only the figures for those who legally divorce but also the number of cohabiting couples who have been together long enough to procreate at least one child—45 percent of all births in Sweden in 1984 were born out of wedlock—then Sweden would have a dissolution rate of approximately 75 percent, considerably higher than in the United States. Curiously, however, there appears to be no concern in Sweden that family life is falling apart, due in large part to the fact that Nordic nations— Denmark, Norway, Sweden and Finland—have devised social policies, replete with adequate monetary support, to care collectively with the ensuing social problems deriving from divorce (Goode, 1993:327-328).

The contrast between Sweden and the United States throws into sharp relief an important question, namely, at what point does the divorce rate become so high that the very existence of the familial institution is placed in jeopardy? The truth of the matter is that social scientists simply do not know the answer to that question or even whether there is such a point. For this reason, it is better to pursue an interpretive assessment of what divorce means to couples within contemporary industrialized societies rather than engage in moral handwringing. To get at these issues we must examine more critically who divorces, why they divorce, and the rates of remarriage.

A number of social background factors correlate strongly with the tendency to divorce, apart from the more obvious causes such as infidelity, drug or alcohol abuse, physical/mental violence directed against either a spouse or children (Gelles and Cornell, 1985), and sexual abuse of children (Crewdson, 1988). Age at first marriage is one of the more important factors, especially for couples who marry before they enter their twenties. Teenage marriages are disproportionately likely to end in divorce because they frequently involve premarital pregnancies, immediate financial problems since schooling for a well-paying job has not been completed, and psychological immaturity (Bane, 1976:32).

The most significant factor correlated with the tendency to divorce is a difference between spouses relative to their racial and ethnic backgrounds (Tucker and Mitchell-Kernan, 1990). Black/White married couples have considerably higher rates of divorce than Asian/White or Native American/White marriages (Glick, 1990:123-124). The high dissolution rates of interracial—and especially Black/White—couples clearly reflect the lingering effects of racial prejudice which makes marital adjustments all that much more difficult.

Other factors include the presence of children—childless couples proportionately divorce more frequently than couples with children. This does not mean that children hold marriages together, but that couples typically do not begin the procreation process until they are reasonably sure that their marriage will endure. Religious affiliation also tends to reduce the tendency to divorce—no doubt because believers tend to take seriously the teachings of their religious communities pertaining to the importance of fidelity to marital vows (Larson and Goltz, 1989). Social class standing also influences the tendency to dissolve a marriage, with lower class members exhibiting higher divorce rates than those in the higher classes (Martin and Bumpass, 1989). This is due, in large part, to the fact that lower status persons experience more social problems and have fewer social skills to deal with them effectively.

And finally, marriage disruption is also correlated with the employment of wives. Women who work outside the home have higher divorce rates than those who are fulltime homemakers. The relationship between these two variables is somewhat more complex than it first appears, however, and causality is difficult to establish. Some students of the family suggest that women with their own source of income attain more independence and do not have to remain in an unhappy marriage. It may also be the case that the likelihood of divorce represents a major impetus impelling women into the labor force—since when divorce occurs the first thing a woman needs is a source of income. Also, as the income potential of women increases, the probability of divorce decreases (Greenstein, 1990), a fact which some interpret as signifying that when women contribute very significantly to the total family income, then husbands are more reluctant to engage in behaviors that would alienate the affections of their working wives.

The composite of these several background factors which contribute to the likelihood of marital dissolution suggests this axiomatic conclusion, namely, that the more the backgrounds of a husband and wife diverge, then the more difficult it will be for the marriage to be sustained intact. With this insight, we are in a position to dispel at least a portion of that interpretive mystery which surrounds the whole matter of divorce. To achieve this end, we need to begin with the what has emerged in recent decades as the most highly valued feature of marriage by spouses, namely, the development of a companionate relationship in marriage (Skolnick, 1991:146).

The importance of companionship was first demonstrated in research undertaken by Blood and Wolfe (1965) who discovered that spouses ranked companionship more important than love, sex, children, or even money as the most valued aspect of marriage. Companionship embraced such elements as emotional support, intimacy, the development of a common biography, and self-fulfillment. Marriage became after the 1960s that place where one cultivated the most important relationship one expected to experience in life. In the intimate relationship with one's spouse, a person finds a haven from the tensions and pressures of normal social interaction. The security of the companionate relationship allows a spouse the freedom to express one's feelings, dreams, fears, and hopes without fear of being penalized and in full knowledge that one's spouse will lend a sympathetic ear and be an understanding friend (Garrett, 1982:302-303).

The nurturing of a companionate relationship takes a number of years to bring to fruition, of course, and couples are not always successful in achieving this ideal in marriage. What now appears to be occurring is that couples who do not develop a companionate relationship are more and more willing to seek a divorce, reenter the marriage market and try to find someone with whom they can develop a companionate marriage. Not only does this serve as an index of how important companionship is to contemporary marriage partners, but it also signifies a deep-rooted commitment to a high quality marriage. If spouses cared less about marriage as an institution, therefore, they would be more willing to remain within unhappy unions. Ironically, then, the conclusion appears intractable that the relatively high divorce rate in Western societies is sustained in no small part by a commitment to a fully satisfying, companionate marriage. And another conclusion also follows indisputably, namely, that if the divorce rate could be lowered, then it would almost certainly be occasioned by a significant rise in the rate of marital dissatisfaction. One can question whether it makes good policy sense to attempt to lower the divorce rate at the cost of increasing marital unhappiness.

Corroborating evidence for the cogency of the interpretation of divorce being developed here derives in part from the remarriage rate. While the divorce rate was doubling during the period from 1960 to 1980, the remarriage rate after divorce increased at almost the same ratio. As Cherlin (1981: 28) has pointed out, almost five out of six men and three out of four women remarry after divorce. These data indicate that persons who divorce have not given up on marriage; they have simply given up on the particular partner to whom they were married. Or, as Spanier and Thompson (1987:17) have observed: "Divorce is a response to a failing marriage, not a failing institution. The family system can remain strong while divorce rates remain high."

Similar patterns of remarriage are also in evidence among the industrialized nations of Europe—with only slightly depressed rates for the more Catholic nations of the European community (Goode, 1993:36-40). Likewise, the probability of remarriage is related to the age of those who divorce. Persons who marry early and then divorce early have a much higher change of remarriage than those who divorce, say, in their fifties or sixties. Nonetheless, the relatively high remarriage rates indicate that the commitment to marriage persists in Western social systems.

Two additional issues are related to the broader concern over divorce. These pertain to questions of whether the liberalization of divorce laws facilitates a more casual attitude toward both marriage and divorce and whether divorce has an especially harmful effect on children. Both of these concerns are sufficiently serious to warrant at least brief consideration.

The United States adopted no-fault divorce proceedings, beginning in 1970 with California, and its principles swiftly spread across the country to inform virtually all divorce actions (Weitzman, 1985). No-fault divorce established the principle that either partner could sue for divorce on the grounds of incompatibility, so that neither partner was held to be "at fault" in violating the marriage contract. The justification for this major change in divorce law was to bring legal proceedings into line with empirical reality, since many couples who had reached a state of incompatibility were admitting in court to "faults" they had not committed simply to terminate a marriage that no longer met the needs of the spouses.

The claim that a liberalization of the divorce laws by going to the no-fault system led to a more casual tendency to divorce, however, does not appear to be borne out by the data. Wright and Stetson (1978), who conducted some of the most convincing research on the impact of the no-fault system on the divorce rate, concluded that the increasing divorce rate through the 1970s after no-fault was introduced had less to do with the liberalization of the law than with the rising demand for

THE FAMILY IN GLOBAL TRANSITION

divorce. Moreover, demand is a variable which is relatively independent of the strictness or permissiveness of divorce law. The divorce rate in the United States would probably have been almost identical to what it is now had the old adversarial system been retained.

One unintended—and until recently unnoticed—consequence of embracing the no-fault divorce system has been the "feminization of poverty." Leonore Weitzman (1985:323), for example, found that in the first year after divorce, men in the United States experienced a 42 percent increase in their standard of living, while women experienced a 73 percent decline in their standard of living. Although other studies have not shown so dramatic a change after divorce, the data do clearly indicate that many women are forced into poverty and onto welfare roles after divorce and almost all experience at least some significant decline in their standard of living (Arendell, 1986). Stephanie Coontz (1992:206) concludes that what these data signify is not that we should force bad marriages to continue, but that we should devise more equitable "exit rules" from marriage so that women and children are not so frequently thrust into poverty.

Indeed, economic deprivation appears to be the most significant impact which divorce has on children. Numerous studies have been conducted by various social scientists to determine whether the children of divorce are more likely to experience mental illness, become delinquent, achieve at lower rates in school, or manifest other signs of maladjustment after their parents divorce. These studies have generally produced mixed findings, since remaining in a two-parent household filled with hostility and conflict is also traumatic (Cherlin, 1981:89-92; Furstenberg and Cherlin, 1991). Moreover, most research has shown that, while children experience distress when parents first separate and then divorce, they regain their stability within a few short years. We still have no decisive evidence on what are the long-term, behavioral effects of divorce on children, although the data are clear that when economic deprivation ensues after divorce children are often deeply troubled by the disorganization which poverty precipitates (Arendell, 1986).

On balance, then, the conclusion is warranted that divorce represents something of an internal adjustment mechanism within the institution of marriage. Wherever free mate selection is the norm and in societies that place a strong emphasis on marital quality, self-fulfillment, and companionship between marriage partners, then it is unavoidable that some mistakes will be made in the mating process or that spouses will become different persons over the course of the life of the marriage. Thus, Western societies have already become and will likely remain for the foreseeable future high-divorce-rate societies (Goode, 1993:336-337). Neither stricter laws governing marital dissolution nor more preachments urging a sudden change in our norms or practices are very likely to return us to that nostalgic time when family life was putatively more stable.

The larger question that needs to be addressed, however, is how should societal members deal with the consequences of marital disruption? So far, policy makers and citizens of Western societies have not directed very much attention toward dealing with the aftermath of the divorce process—although the Nordic nations have made considerably more headway in devising workable policies than other industrialized nations. Indeed, in most Western societies such matters after divorce as the division of assets, who will support the children and mother, what are the rights of grandparents who are now ex-inlaws, when should dating and remarriage occur, and the like are all decided anew and often in an ad hoc fashion in each case. The failure to articulate or develop established customs, norms and expectations relative to divorce patterns is indicative of the fact that divorce remains *uninstitutionalized* in Western societies. This may be due, in part, to the fact that the upsurge in divorce rates has occurred very recently in Western social experience, and, in part, because there is still a very ambiguous attitude as to whether marital disruption is to be accorded some measure of social respectability. With institutionalization, however, divorce can be integrated into the marriage system and help resolve many of the dilemmas which currently confound the process (Goode, 1993:344-345). Institutionalization will not "solve" the problem of divorce, of course, but it will aid couples as well as children cope with the social disorganization which now accompanies the processes of marriage dissolution.

The Sexual Revolution and the Increase in Illegitimacy

In the mid-1960s, the industrial nations of the West experienced a sexual revolution, evidenced by a sudden escalation in the rates of premarital sexual activity and a corresponding upsurge in the illegitimacy rate (Shorter, 1977). This was not the first sexual revolution in America—the first occurred during the "roaring twenties"—but through the depression, World War II, and the 1950s the rate of premarital sexual activity increased only gradually (Coontz, 1992:193-196). Not only did premarital sexual activity dramatically increase with the emergence of the counterculture in the sixties, but other features related to sexuality also emerged with rising rates of cohabitation, gay liberation, and more explicit sexual themes openly presented in movies, novels, magazines, television, and advertising.

Several facets of the sexual revolution are worthy of brief attention. The first is that, although premarital sexual activity increased, the *real* sexual revolution occurred within the staid ranks of legal marriage where rates of sexual activity increased more dramatically than among the unmarried (Hunt, 1974). Second, insofar as premarital sexual relations were concerned, the major change was in the behavior of women. Premarital sexual experience increased only slightly for males, but it increased markedly for females—suggesting that prior to the sexual revolution, young men had tried to have premarital sex, but women had typically said no. After the sexual revolution, women stopped saying no (King, Balswick, and Robinson, 1977). And finally, cohabitation—which initially shocked middle-class sensibilities, since it had previously only been a lower class phenomenon and, hence, was called "shacking up"—proved not to be a challenge to or alternative for legal marriage, but a new stage in the courtship process for many couples. Nowadays, the rate of cohabitation in the United States has risen to between four and five percent of all household units, with many cohabitors found among the ranks of the previously divorced (Murstein, 1986:89-93). The pattern has also appeared in other Western societies, most notably in Sweden where cohabitation before marriage is almost universal (Popenoe, 1987).

The increase in illegitimate births has occasioned more outbursts of alarm than virtually any other by-product of the sexual revolution. Much of this discussion, especially in the op-ed pages of the newspaper, has not evidenced a very penetrating understanding of the phenomenon. The usual assumption is that the sexual revolution, along with the ready availability of the pill and other modern forms of contraception, largely produced this rise in illegitimacy. The evidence does not neatly support this interpretation. For example, Sweden has the highest rates of adolescent sexual activity in the industrialized world—while adolescents in the United States, England, France and the Netherlands are comparable in their lower rates of sexual activity. However, the rates of teenage pregnancy are considerably higher for adolescents in the United States than in European nations (Voydanoff and Donnelly, 1990:11-14). Moreover, most sexually active young teens are startlingly unaware of their own biological processes, sexual drives, and the means to prevent conception—a fact that should alert conservative religionists that eliminating sex education courses is almost certainly to be profoundly counterproductive (Coontz, 1992:203). And since the growth among adolescent pregnancies has occurred among women of lower socio-economic status with relatively poor life prospects, they are not women whose behavior has been influenced by feminist ideology. Furthermore, the rate of illegitimate births is considerably higher in the United States for Black women than Hispanics or Whites—in 1985, 60 percent of all Black births, 28 percent of Hispanic births, and 14.5 percent of White births were to unmarried mothers (Zill and Rogers, 1988:39).

Several features stand out prominently in these data. The first is that the rise of illegitimate births has occurred dispro-portionately among members of the underclass, and especially the Black underclass. Moreover, while teenage out of wedlock births have stabilized since the 1980s (Voydanoff and Donnelly, 1990:15), they continue to rise in percentage terms since the overall birthrate has declined during that time. Perhaps the most serious cause for concern, however, pertains to the unraveling of the social safety net in the United States since 1980. Consequently, fewer social services—from housing to food, medical care, welfare supplements, and educational opportunities—are available to an increasing segment of the population. Other European nations continue to provide a much more viable safety net than is available in the United States (Kahn and Kamerman, 1977), and the gap between need and availability of resources will almost certainly widen in America if the proposed changes of the current Republican majority are enacted. For the tangle of pathology which poverty imposes on those trapped within it will simply foster greater impoverishment for a larger segment of the lower class population should social services be reduced even further.

The Decline in the Birth Rate

Modernization has everywhere been accompanied by a substantial decline in the fertility rate of industrializing societies. Commentators worried about the decline of the family cite this fact as evidence for the disenchantment of modern couples with family life, for if family life were still held in high esteem—so this litany runs—then spouses would also want to bring children into the union. Both survey data and actual behavior points to a quite different interpretation than that propounded by observers pessimistic about the family's prospects.

The rate of childlessness has not substantially increased over the last quarter century, although the ideology in support of childlessness has become more popular (LaRossa, 1986:13). For example, only about 2 percent of ever-married women aged 15 to 44 are childless by choice (LaRossa, 1986:36). Those who do opt for voluntary childlessness cite not only the desire to pursue a career as a reason, but also—and more commonly—so that they can spend more time with their spouse (Houseknecht, 1987). Moreover, the steady demand for children in the adoption market as well as the heroic big-technological efforts currently underway to increase fertility reflect a persistent and pressing desire for children among those who are involuntarily childless.

While the commitment to procreation has not declined substantially over recent decades, the desired number of children has fallen quite significantly. A variety of reasons account for the declining birth rate in all Western societies. Certainly, one of the most compelling reasons is the sheer economic cost of children. Whereas during the nineteenth century, children were an economic asset—as they still are in many developing countries—by the mid-twentieth century children were becoming more economically costly and emotionally valuable (Zelizer, 1985). The financial burden of raising a child from birth through four years of public higher education now runs around $175,000—and this only includes direct and indirect maintenance costs; it does not include lost income if one parent leaves the labor force to provide in-home childcare. In light of these figures, it is not surprising that fertility rates have fallen to or below zero population growth (which is 2.2 children per husband-wife unit) in most Western societies (Goode, 1993:34).

The accelerating cost of having children is only one explanation for why the fertility rate is dropping so sharply in industrialized societies, however, and it is apparently not even the most significant reason. Numerous studies have also revealed that parents more and more regard children as emotionally valuable and that, as a consequence, they are willing to invest considerably more time and psychological energy in nurturing their offspring (Zelizer, 1985). With large families of five, six or more children, it would simply be impossible to allocate both emotional and time resources on a scale parents now regard as appropriate. Thus, we are currently witnessing the continuation of what Blood and Wolfe (1965: 121) described some time ago as a shift "...from quantity to quality with respect to children."

In sum, then, the decline of family size reflects neither a disenchantment with family life nor a preference for childless marriages, but a practical adjustment to the inevitable limits of time, money, and emotional resources insofar as childrearing is concerned. (Curiously, world population pressures do not seem to have played a very significant role in fertility decisions among members of Western nations, since they are already near or below zero population growth.) Moreover, just as Western societies manifested the trend toward smaller family size, there emerged a countervailing trend toward valuing children as emotionally "priceless." Unfortunately, the heightened valuation of children in private families has not carried over into the collective realm to counteract indifference to children's needs and more effective child welfare policies, especially in the United States (Sidel, 1992).

The Loss of Family Functions

There once was a time when the family was, in the words of John Demos (1971), "a little commonwealth," by which he meant that the family performed a whole variety of functions of an economic, governmental, welfare, educational, social control, and religious character. Prior to the modern age, the family was, in effect, a miniature society. Nowadays many of these functions have been transferred to other social institutions. For example, industrialization occasioned the separation of the domicile from the workplace; monetary loans more often come now from banks or other lending institutions rather than family members; the care of the elderly has shifted to a very great extent to governmental agencies; most education—even in practical skills such as driving a car, home economics skills, and manual skills in home maintenance and repair, and even the transmission of knowledge relative to sexual matters—now takes place outside the home, and frequently in the schools; social control over the behavior of offspring is now a largely shared function with school officials and local police forces; and religious institutions have assumed major responsibility for training young persons in the basic tenets of the faith.

The wholesale transfer of functions from the family to other institutions has prompted some commentators to conclude that the family has, perforce, become less important as a consequence of its reduced social responsibilities. Talcott Parsons (1955:9-10) cogently argued some time ago, however, that the loss of family functions does not represent a decline of the family in a general sense, but rather it has facilitated the emergence of a new family form wherein this institution has now become, at once, more specialized and more proficient.

Specialization has taken place in two discrete but crucial areas, namely, the socialization of children and the stabilization of adult personalities through the cultivation of a companionate relationship between spouses. While socialization has long been a function of the family, there is a mounting body of data suggesting that parents are intensifying their efforts and consciously honing their skills in this area (Johnson, 1988: 261-265). Indeed, one notable sphere of change has surrounded the role of fatherhood. Male parenting has taken on renewed significance of late, perhaps in response to feminist critiques of the manner in which fathers typically were performing. Most fathers regarded their breadwinning function as their most important contribution to their children, but today for more and more fathers the emphasis is shifting toward nurturing as an equally important function (Griswold, 1993: 249-250).

A renewal of commitment to the companionate ideal has also figured prominently in the expectations of spouses in recent years (Skolnick, 1991:191-196). Some students of family life have, in fact, posed the question of whether expectations have been ratcheted so high that few men, in particular, are now able to meet them, given the historic difficulty of men to engage in expressive behaviors. Nevertheless, it is clear that the companionate ideal has enlarged its sphere of influence by spreading from the white collar into the working class in recent decades. The experience of many working class women is expressed in this statement given to Lillian Rubin (1976:93) when one informant declared relative to her husband, "I guess I can't complain. He's a steady worker; he doesn't drink; he doesn't hit me." But subsequent interviews revealed that this woman was not satisfied with having met these minimal conditions in marriage based on expectations from her former lower class background; she wanted in addition what many middle class women typically experienced, namely, a relationship of sharing, companionship, and emotional intimacy.

The salience of the Western family has not been reduced by the loss of many ancillary functions to other social institutions, but rather this has freed up the family to concentrate more of its energies on the functions remaining under its auspices —especially those relating to socialization and the stabilization of adult personalities. Accordingly, as the family has acquired greater proficiency, other institutions have experienced something of an unexpected and unanticipated overload—most notably the educational and governmental institutions. It does not overstate the case, in fact, to suggest that we have gained a more effective family institution at the social cost of inundating the resources of our schools and political organizations.

The Generation Gap

When Christopher Lasch (1979b:xx) observed that "...the family has been slowly coming apart for more than a hundred years. The divorce crisis, feminism, and the revolt of youth originated in the nineteenth century, and they have been the subject of controversy ever since," it is interesting to note that conflict between the generations figured prominently in what he perceived as one of the crucial ills of modern family life. The generation gap, as such, however, was not usually singled out for special attention until after the counterculture revolution in the mid-1960s. Unfortunately, the precise nomenclature, generation gap, was popularized by journalists before it was empirically tested by social scientists. The concept pointed to a putative widening gap between parents and their children on such matters as basic values, political attitudes, sexual norms, and aesthetic tastes. When the data were finally in, what they revealed was that a gap existed, but it was less often between generations than between social classes and liberal/conservative constituencies.

For example, many of the young leaders in the 1960s of the SDS, the political wing of the counterculture, were "red diaper babies," that is to say, the offspring of parents committed to pro-communist and other left-wing ideologies during the 1930s (Gitlin, 1989:65- 77). Moreover, the liberal values and lifestyle variations introduced by the youth spearheading the introduction of the counterculture—such as liberalized sexual norms, drug experimentation, a greater emphasis on pleasure-seeking, a distrust of authority, an acceptance of cohabitation and abortion as a personal choice, a sympathy for feminist ideology, a commitment to self-fulfillment, and so forth—were all more readily accepted by liberal parents of youth in the counterculture than they were by parents and youth in the working class. By 1974, however, an important seachange had occurred, whereby working class youth embraced almost fully the "new morality" and its associated life style changes introduced by the college youth of the counterculture (Yankelovich, 1974). Since that time, the cleavage in most Western societies has not so much been between generations as between political blocs of the left and right—a notion popularized by Hunter (1991) in his study of Culture Wars.

Certainly, it can be said that the liberalized viewpoint supported by the counterculture has afforded the opportunity for many people to escape from their previously ascribed statuses which harshly limited their life chances—one can mention here ethnic/racial minorities, women, gay persons, immigrants, and the poor generally. Whether the liberal agenda of the counterculture was an egalitarian celebration of self-fulfillment or a degenerative slide into hedonism depends, to a large extent, on one's ideological perspective. And surely, there was much in the lifestyle endorsements of the counterculture which exacted a high personal cost, such as drug experimentation, sexual libertinism, and a reduced level of academic and/or work-related achievement. Indeed, participants in the

344

new lifestyle experimentation fostered by the counterculture in the sixties are now reporting some reservations. According to pollster Peter Hart, "...these people did a lot, regret very little, and don't want their kids to do any of it" (quoted in Skolnick, 1991:190).

What all of this suggests is that the generation gap is really a term which designates an ongoing debate over lifestyle choices between liberals and conservatives, a debate that now has—and perhaps never had—much to do with generations. The acrimonious character of this current dispute may have this unfortunate consequence: the legitimate gains in personal freedom and self-determination achieved by the counterculture may be obscured, even as the valid concerns for moral rectitude by conservatives may be ignored. And for families in Western societies, meanwhile, wrenching conflicts will continue to plague domestic harmony and, to some extent, parent-child relationships. For the youth peer group—operating still on norms largely established by the 1960s counterculture—provides in all Western societies a reference group that informs the attitudes and conduct of youth from early adolescence through their young adult years (Shorter, 1977). And in selective areas—having to do with drug use, sexual experimentation, obscenity and profanity, and work habits—the peer group perspective is frequently at odds with parental norms and expectations. Resolving these disparities has become and probably will remain one of the most distressing features of parenting.

On issues pertaining to equality for racial, ethnic, class and gender groups; the search for self-fulfillment; and the expansion of the scope of discretionary individual behaviors, the counterculture challenged the staid conservative culture of the 1950s, while it also ushered in a more liberal perspective which many parents and societal authorities in Western nations could heartily embrace. Thus, the youth peer culture has enjoyed a variegated relationship with members of the adult world—with some aspects of the peer culture eliciting adult approval and other features triggering harsh condemnation (Yinger, 1982: 285-288).

Clearly, not all the issues bound up in the larger counterculture revolution have yet been resolved. For example, Christopher Lasch (1979a) soundly condemned the search for self-fulfillment promoted by counterculture participants as an exercise in banal narcissism, self-indulgence, materialism, and intellectual erosion, while, several years later, Robert Wuthnow (1991) gathered data which showed that members of the "me generation" in pursuit of self-fulfillment actually found it through vigorous and widespread participation in altruistic activities, volunteer and charity work. The discovery that the search for self-fulfillment had in fact manifested itself in altruistic behavior to the extent that some 45 percent of adult Americans contributed over twenty billion hours of service to their communities per year suggests at the very least that some values carried by the counterculture have managed to produce profoundly constructive consequences. To be sure, this high rate of altruism cannot be wholly attributed to countercultural influences, but a significant portion of compassionate Americans were products of counterculture social movements and deeply influenced by its value perspectives.

Women in the Labor Force

Since at least the 1950s, scholars have expressed concern over women's labor force participation, fearing that women employed outside the home would (1) leave the family nest unattended and (2) encounter more opportunities for entering into romantic relationships that could jeopardize marriage (Parsons, 1955; Shorter, 1977). Moreover, we have known for some time that trends in the rates of marital disruption and women's labor force participation have generally moved upward in unison during the post-World War II era (South and Lloyd, 1995:33). What has not been clear, however, is how these two variables are interrelated. An attempt to weave together a coherent interpretation of the interaction of the two variables will be undertaken after baseline data on female employment is reviewed.

By 1985, 61 percent of all married women with a husband present in the household worked outside the home. Women with children under age six were slightly less likely to be employed (53.7 percent) than women with children between the ages of 6 to 17 (68.1 percent) (Voydanoff, 1987:24). These rates are somewhat higher than those for other European nations, with the exception of Sweden. For example, from 1966 to 1986, the percentage of women aged 15 to 64 who were employed increased by 20 percent in the United States, compared to roughly 11 percent in Britain, only 2 percent in West Germany, and 3 percent in Austria (from 1970 to 1986) (Davis and Robinson, 1991:82-83). In Sweden, the number of women in the labor force is only 4 percent less than that of men— giving Sweden by far the highest rate of female labor force participation of any Western society (Casper, McLanahan, and Garfinkel, 1994:600).

Assessing the meaning of these data in relation to the rising divorce rate since the 1960s is considerably more complex a task than simply reporting them. Patricia Voydanoff (1987:46) flatly declares that "(t)here is no consistent body of evidence indicating that wife employment is associated with divorce." This, she continues, is due to the operation of two counteracting processes, variously labeled the "independence effect" and the "income effect."

The "independence effect" entails the following argument: for members of a dual-earner family, divorce is less difficult. Historically, many men have been held in their marriages by the responsibility to provide for their wives' financial dependence. When a wife works, this responsibility is no longer felt as keenly and men in unhappy marriages are much more likely to seek divorce. Similarly, women who are financially independent are more likely to terminate an unhappy union. Thus, we have a situation in which "...people are dissatisfied with their particular marriage partners, unafraid of leaving them, and willing to try again (Matthaei, 1982:311).

Andrew Cherlin (1981:53-54) describes an alternative scenario that has come to be known as the "income effect." In this instance, the earnings a wife brings home could ease the financial tension experienced by a family unit and thereby reduce the likelihood of marital dissolution. Moreover, a wife's earnings may well make her more desirable as a marriage partner and a husband less willing to consider divorce, since this action would result in a substantial decline in the family's income (Voydanoff, 1987:46). Employed wives with high levels of education who are working out of choice and who receive both support and approval from their husbands have notably higher levels of marital satisfaction than women who are homemakers (Voydanoff, 1987:47). And higher marital satisfaction translates into a lower likelihood of marriage dissolution.

A more disconcerting argument has recently been developed which suggests another interpretation to the conundrum of the relationship between working women and the probability of divorce. The first stage of this alternative account was developed by Norval Glenn (1991) who proposed that something new may have entered into the outlook of couples nowadays, namely, that the commitment to marital permanence has declined rather substantially. The upshot is that, while partners are still marrying, they are not leaving the marriage market. Accordingly, if they find a more attractive marriage prospect, then they are less hesitant nowadays to divorce their present spouse and remarry the more desirable person.

Evidence partially in support of this interpretation has recently been provided by South and Lloyd (1995) who found a positive association between an area's unmarried female labor force participation rate and martial dissolution. Specifically, they discovered that when there was a large pool of young women in the labor force in a particular region, then there was an increased probability that men will find a more attractive alternative to their current wife. Moreover, this is especially the case where the marriage market is set within a social climate that is increasingly tolerant of divorce, where skepticism abounds about the permanence of marriage, when even married persons tentatively remain within the marriage market, and when there is the opportunity afforded at work for men and women to encounter a more attractive mate than their present spouse (South and Lloyd, 1995:33).

The ambiguity of these various research findings makes it impossible to render a definitive account of the relationship between working women and the divorce rate. The best that can be said, perhaps, is that working women may well increase the probability of subsequent marital instability, but there are also other benefits to family living derived from women's increasing participation in the labor force which may outweigh the putative risks. This appears to be the case, primarily, in those instances where women work by choice, enjoy interesting jobs, are well-paid, and have the support of their husbands. On this issue, however, considerably more research will have to be undertaken before we can rise above the level of conjecture and hypothesis and propound a more definitive account of the relationship between working women and family stability.

Conclusion: The Status of the Western Family

Several observations are warranted in light of this relatively swift review of the evidence in support of the decline-of-the-Western-family thesis. Perhaps the most obvious is that the marriage and family systems in the West have experienced considerable social change and transformation over the last four decades or so. Family forms are much more pluralistic today than ever before in Western history. Change does not automatically mean the decline of the family system, however, since what we may be witnessing is what Talcott Parsons (1955:4) long ago termed the "disorganization of transition." Indeed, one subplot to this survey has been to demonstrate that assessing the meaning of trends relative to family matters is a complicated process which entails teasing out the implications of various forms of data rather than simply jumping to hasty conclusions.

What, then, shall we say about the status of the contemporary Western family? At the risk of appearing naively optimistic, the sociological data facilitate the interpretation that the Western family is remarkably stable, given the sorts of changes with which it has had to cope over the last forty years or so. This judgment is based on the fact that none of the alleged problems confronting the family appear to have undermined its essential stability and proficiency. The rising divorce rate is not *ipso facto* an indication of familial decline. Indeed, as we suggested above, to a large extent, the high divorce rate is a function of the Western commitment to high quality marriages. Similarly, the sexual revolution, with its associated rise in the illegitimacy rate, the declining birth rate, the loss of family functions, and the generation gap are all symptoms of change, but not necessarily of decline or decay. Many of these changes have, in fact, made the family stronger and more specialized in the performance of its central functions. The increase in the number of working women poses a somewhat more complex interpretative problem. The data with respect to this issue are somewhat more mixed in comparison to other analytical areas. My own hunch is that subsequent data will reveal that working women enhance the quality of the marital experience—in part through their own increased levels of personal fulfillment and in part through the added resources which they are able to bring to family life.

The collective import of the trends surveyed in this analysis, then, tends to suggest that the Western familial institution is not in danger of social disintegration anytime soon. If this is the case, then how do we account for the numerous expressions of concern over the health and stability attending marriage and family life in the West? The answer to this question is a kind of Catch-22. That is to say, so long as societal members worry over the decline of the family, we may be fairly well assured that the family is in reasonably good shape. And conversely, when members of Western societies stop feeling concerned about the quality of their family life, then decline will probably already have begun in earnest.

References

Arendell, Terry, 1986. *Mothers And Divorce*. Berkeley, CA: University of California Press.

Bane, Mary Jo, 1976. *Here To Stay: American Families In the Twentieth Century*. New York: Basic Books.

Berger, Brigitte and Peter L. Berger, 1984. *The War Over the Family*. Garden City, NY.: Anchor Books.

Birnbaum, Jeffrey H., 1995. The Gospel According to Ralph." *Time*. 145:20:28-35.

Blood, Robert 0., Jr., and Donald M. Wolfe, 1965. *Husbands Wives: The Dynamics of Married Living*. New York: Free Press.

Casper, Lynne M., Sara S. McLanahan, and Irwin Garfinkel, 1994. "The Gender-Poverty Gap: What We Can Learn From Other Countries." *American Sociological Review*. 59:4:594-605.

Cherlin, Andrew J., 1981. *Marriage, Divorce, Remarriage*. Cambridge, MA: Harvard University Press.

Coontz, Stephanie, 1992. *The Way We Never Were: American Families and the Nostalgia Trap*. New York: Basic Books.

Crewdson, John, 1988. *By Silence Betrayed*. New York: Harper & Row, Publishers.

Davis, Nancy J., and Robert V. Robinson, 1991. "Men's and Women's Consciousness of Gender Inequality in Austria, West Germany, Great Britain, and the United States." *American Sociological Review*. 56:1:72-84.

Demos, John, 1971. *The Little Commonwealth: Family Life in Plymouth Colony*. New York: Oxford University Press.

DeParle, Jason. 1994. "Scrap Welfare? Surprisingly, The Notion is Now a Cause." *New York Times*. April 22:A1.

Furstenberg, Frank, and Andrew Cherlin, 1991. *Divided Families*. Cambridge, MA: Harvard University Press.

Galston, William A., 1993. "Beyond the Murphy Brown Debate: Ideas for Family Policy." Paper presented at the Institute for American Values Family Policy Symposium. New York City, December 10.

Garrett, William R., 1982. *Seasons of Marriage and Family Life*. New York: Holt, Rinehart, and Winston.

Gelles, Richard J., and Claire P. Cornell, 1985. *Intimate Violence In Families*. Newbury Park, CA: Sage Publications.

Gitlin, Todd, 1989. *The Sixties: Years of Hope, Days of Rage*. New York: Bantam Books.

Glenn, Norval D., 1991. "The Recent Trend in Marital Success in the United States. *Journal of Marriage and the Family*. 53:261-270.

Glick, Paul C., 1990. "Demographic Pictures of Black Families." pp. 111-132 in Harriette Pipes McAdoo, ed., *Black Families*. 2nd ed., Newbury Park: Sage Publications.

Goode, William J., 1993. *World Changes in Divorce Patterns*. New Haven, CT: Yale University Press.

Greenstein, Theodore N., 1990. "Marital Disruption and the Employment of Women." *Journal of Marriage and the Family*. 52:3:657-676.

Griswold, Robert L., 1993. *Fatherhood in America: A History*. New York: Basic Books.

Houseknecht, Sharon K., 1987. "Voluntary Childlessness." In Marvin B. Sussman and Suzanne K. Steinmetz, eds., *Handbook of Marriage and the Family*. New York: Plenum Press.

Hunt, Morton, 1974. *Sexual Behavior in the Seventies*. Chicago: Playboy Press.

Hunter, James Davidson, 1991. *Culture Wars*. New York: Basic Books.

Johnson, Miriam M., 1988. *Strong Mothers. Weak Wives*. Berkeley, CA: University of California Press.

King, Karl, Jack O. Balswick, and Ira E. Robinson, 1977. "The Continuing Premarital Sexual Revolution Among College Females." *Journal of Marriage And the Family*. 39:455-459.

Ihinger-Tallman, Marilyn, and Kay Pasley, 1987. *Remarriage*. Newbury Park, CA: Sage Publications.

Kahn, Alfred J., and Sheilia B. Kamerman, 1977. *Not For the Poor Alone: European Social Services*. New York: Harper.

Larson, Lyle E., and Walter Goltz, 1989. "Religious Participation and Marital Commitment." *Review of Religious Research*. 30:4: 387-400.

LaRossa, Ralph, 1986. *Becoming a Parent*. Newbury Park, CA: Sage Publications.

Lasch, Christopher, 1979a. *The Culture of Narcissism*. New York: Warner Books.

Lasch, Christopher, 1979b. *Haven in a Heartless World: The Family Besieged*. New York: Basic Books.

Martin, Teresa Castro, and Larry Bumpass, 1989. "Recent Trends in Marital Disruption." *Demography*. 26:37-51.

Matthaei, Julie A., 1982. *An Economic History of Women in America*. New York: Schocken Books.

Mintz, Steven, and Susan Kellogg, 1988. *Domestic Revolutions: A Social History of American Family Life*. New York: Free Press.

Murray, Charles, 1993. "The Coming White Underclass." *The Wall Street Journal*. October 29.

Murstein, Bernard I., 1986. *Paths to Marriage*. Newbury Park, CA: Sage Publications.

National Center for Health Statistics, 1990. "Births, Marriages, Divorces, and Deaths for June 1990." Monthly Vital Statistics Report. Hyattsville, MD: Public Health Service.

Parsons, Talcott, 1955. *Family, Socialization and Interaction Process.* New York: Free Press.

Popenoe, David, 1987. "Beyond the Nuclear Family: A Statistical Portrait of the Changing Family in Sweden." *Journal of Marriage and the Family.* 49:1:173-183.

Riley, Glenda, 1991. *Divorce: An American Tradition.* New York: Oxford University Press.

Shorter, Edward, 1977. *The Making of the Modern Family.* New York: Basic Books.

Sidel, Ruth, 1992. *Women and Children Last: The Plight of Poor Women in Affluent America.* New York: Penguin Books.

Skolnick, Arlene, 1991. *Embattled Paradise: The American Family in Age of Uncertainty.* New York: Basic Books.

South, Scott J., and Kim M. Lloyd, 1995. "Spousal Alternatives and Marital Dissolution." *American Sociological Review.* 60:1:21-35.

Spanier, Graham B., and Linda Thompson, 1987. *Parting: The Aftermath of Separation and Divorce.* Updated Edition. Newbury Park, CA: Sage Publications.

Tucker, M. Belinda, and Claudia Mitchell-Kernan, 1990. "New Trends in Black American Interracial Marriages: The Social Structural Context." *Journal of Marriage and the Family.* 52:1: 209-218.

Voydanoff, Patricia, 1987. *Work and Family Life.* Newbury Park, CA: Sage Publications.

Voydanoff, Patricia, and Brenda W. Donnellly, 1990. *Adolescent Sexuality and Pregnancy.* Newbury Park, CA: Sage Publications.

Weitzman, Lenore J., 1985. *The Divorce Revolution.* New York: Free Press.

White, Lynn K., 1990. "Determinants of Divorce: A Review of Research in the Eighties." *Journal of Marriage and the Family.* 52:4:904-912.

Wright, Gerald C., and Dorothy M. Stetson, 1978. "The Impact of No-Fault Divorce Law Reform on Divorce in American States." *Journal of Marriage and the Family.* 40:575-580.

Wuthnow, Robert, 1991. *Acts of Compassion: Caring for Others and Helping Ourselves*. Princeton, NJ.: Princeton University Press.

Yankelovich, Daniel, 1974. *The New Morality: A Profile of American Youth in the 70s*. New York: McGraw-Hill.

Yinger, J. Milton, 1982. *Countercultures*. New York: Free Press.

Zelizer, Viviana A., 1985. *Pricing the Priceless Child*. New York: Basic Books.

Zill, Nicholas, and Carolyn C. Rogers, 1988. "Recent Trends in the Well-Being of Children in the United States and Their Implications for Public Policy." pp. 31-115 in Andrew J. Cherlin, ed., *The Changing American Family and Public Policy*. Washington, DC.: The Urban Institute Press.

Part Three

Family Change, Family Stability
and Public Policy

Chapter 14

PHILOSOPHIC REFLECTIONS ON THE FAMILY AT CENTURY'S END

Jean Bethke Elshtain

By education and training, I am a political and civil philosopher. This means that I tend to what is happening to the social and political fabric of my own society in particular, and other societies more generally. Although my focus for this paper, as far as the data is concerned, will be on trends manifest in the United States, I will move back and forth between contemporary concerns and historical and philosophical claims in order to make my case.

The evidence from the streets, the neighborhoods, the schools. the churches. and our homes: the eloquent and often terrifying testimony of events-violence suffered and perpetrated; children unhappy, ignored, home alone; teen mothers, isolated and hovering in drug-ridden dangerous places; teachers afraid of their students; students afraid of other students; civic leaders gazing at a precipitous decline in involvement and participation in all community activities at all levels: this is one face of America today. The evidence is overwhelming, based on hundreds of studies by reputable scholars from dozens of disciplines: indeed. none but the individual committed to the status quo can cast his or her eyes over this encroaching wasteland and say, "This is good. Let's have more of it." It is, of course, all too easy to work oneself up into a lather about teen pregnancies, deadbeat dads, violent youth, and children in poverty. We do that in North America all the time. But we tend to overlook a common denominator that lies beneath or behind so many of these phenomena—the spreading collapse of marriage. With each passing year, an ever smaller percentage of citizens in the United States is married. An even larger percentage of the nation's children live in households absent a parent—most often the father: this figure now stands at about one-third of American children overall. Mind you, I, for one, have no desire to "marry everyone off." I recognize that many people choose not to marry and that they live rich and interesting lives and contribute to their communities in a variety of ways. No, my concern is with how difficult it is to grow up in America. Because, where children are concerned, regularity in human relationships is vital and such relations go by the names "marriage" and "family."

What do we see when we look around? We see that more and more children are growing up with little or no experience of married life, hence no living examples of what it means for two people to commit themselves to one another over time. More American children everyday are growing up with little or no confidence that they could be, or even want to be, in an enduring marital relationship, as the *Marriage Report of the Council on Families in America* argues. (New York: Institute for American Values, March, 1995.) Over the past three or four decades, the message American children receive from the wider culture is one that is high on romance and sex but hostile or, at best, indifferent to marriage. It does not seem at all far-fetched to say that we, as a society, are failing in the task of social reproduction or, in more econometric terms, there is a strong failure in social capital formation. All this means, in laymen and women's terms, is that we are not imparting to the next generation a set of fundamental norms and beliefs about the meaning and purposes, responsibilities and freedom, of marriage and family life. This, in turn, has a debilitating effect on civic life overall. Democratic civic life relies on persons who have been formed in such a way that they are capable of commitment; understand and accept responsibility; share a sense of stewardship about their communities; appreciate the fact that the creation of decent and relatively stable relationships and societies is a complex and fragile task, not an automatic outcome when human beings share a territorial space or even a bedroom. Perhaps a few bits of dismal data are in order. In the decades 1960-1990, the percentage of out-of-wedlock births skyrocketed from 5.3 percent to 30 percent. If the children from such single-parent units were doing just fine, perhaps there would be no problem. But they are not: they are at far greater risk than children from two-parent households. As well, in those same decades, the divorce rate doubled or tripled, depending upon how it is calculated. As a result, the percentage of children living apart from their biological fathers rose from 17 percent to 36 percent and rising. Juvenile violent crime has also increased in the past three decades. Reports of child neglect and abuse have quintupled since 1976. The teen suicide rate has tripled. As reported recently in the *New York Times,* children from broken homes have two to three times more behavioral and psychological problems than do children from intact homes. (Susan Chira, "Struggling to Find Stability When Divorce is a Pattern." The *New York Times,* March 19, 1995, pp. 1, 17.) Finally, the poverty rate of young children stands at 25 percent, the highest since 1969, and family formation, or the failure to form families, has been indicted as a central causal factor in the growth in childhood poverty. (The *Marriage Report* summarizes this data.)

Because all societies have a stake in the creation and sustaining of norms surrounding sexuality, child-rearing, and other vital human activities tied to our complex social and embodied identities, all societies have attempted to regularize these activities in some way. No society has ever declared any of this to be a matter of indifference. There are many possible arrangements, of course, some more restrictive; some less. But sometimes, it seems, "less" can become "more." That is, as a general laissez-faire attitude toward social arrangements spread, it fuels many different varieties of social troubles. Or so our recent history suggests. Ironically, the growth in "self-expression" and "individualism" appears to go hand-in-hand with a growth in fearfulness, destructive forms of dependency, and even greater social conformism as the primary reference group for the young becomes an age-specific cohort, with adults scarcely in the picture.

There are big conceptual and historical issues here. There are also simple, humble truths. The humble truth is that every child needs and deserves the love and provision of caring adults in a relationship that perdures. The committed, two-married-parent family is the best environment we know anything about in which to rear children. Because it is the main teacher of the next generation, and a protector and defender of our love of, and commitment to, pluralism, it is also an irreplaceable foundation for long-term civic vitality, endurance, and flexibility. A British observer, summarizing the data for his own society, reports that: "...every form of psychosocial disorder among young people—crime, suicide, depression, eating problems, vandalism, alcohol and drug abuse—can be linked to the modern-day cult of juvenile freedom, to their spending power, their moral and social independence from their parents, and their entire lifestyle of music, clothes, sex and whatever. In short, the problem is a colossal and chronic breakdown in parenting. By no means does this only apply to Britain." (Clifford Longley, "Valuing the Family," *The Tablet*, 10 June, 1995, p. 735.)

What we seem to have lost along the way is an earlier conceptual richness that recognized, as *The Marriage in America Report* argues, that marriage contained, or encompassed, at least five basic dimensions. It was viewed as, in some sense, a natural institution, flowing from basic bodily imperatives. It was a sacramental institution, surrounded by rituals and sacral norms. It was an economic institution. an arena of both production and consumption; of human fabrication and laboring. It was a social institution, helping to create cultural forms that encouraged certain kinds of behavior and discouraged others. It was a legal entity, protected and regulated by a complex body of public and private law. In each of these arenas, the family has sustained a series of body blows that have had the effect, over time, not so much of transforming the family with each of these five interlocked imperatives in mind—but deinstitutionalizing the family by removing many previous imperatives and norms and putting nothing in their place. Let me reiterate: *If* what we were currently seeing was a growth in child well-being, there would be little reason to raise the alarm. But that is not what we see. It is arguably also the case that seductive but elusive chimera, "adult happiness," has not been well served either, but that is not my primary concern.

Let's take a brief look, in the form of a review and overview, of how scholars of the family themselves have played a role, for some unwitting, for others quite knowing, in these developments. The dominant conceptual framework within which the family was studied in the American academy, at least from mid-century on, was a school of sociology called functionalism. For the functionalist, the family is a structure that performs certain functions. To be sure, the family is a universal institution. No society has yet been discovered in which an entity which could be either identified or labeled 'family' did not exist. For the functionalist, the important question is what functions the family performs for the wider society. But there were serious drawbacks to this approach. For one thing, it tended to promote an ahistorical approach to the family. For another, functionalists were (and are!) rather flatfooted when it comes to consideration of the sacramental and the biological, or embodied, dimensions of human life, focusing almost exclusively on "socialization" and on "systems maintenance." This meant, as well, that the family's role in civic life-in the creation of citizens was also ignored, as functionalists viewed men and women in and through the language of roles almost exclusively.

The central claim of functionalists was that: "Whenever a country becomes modern, industrial, urban, family organiza-tion shifts from large kinship groups to a more isolated nuclear or conjugal pattern." (Arlene Skolnick, "Families Can Be Unhealthy for Children and Other Living Things," *Psychology Today*, vol. 5, no. 3, August, 1971, p. 20.) This assumption received its most elaboration theoretical formulation in the works of Talcott Parsons. Parsons claimed that the nuclear family was a product of the economic and social forces of the past several hundred years. He posited an alteration in family structure along with changes in family function and viewed this alteration as the ineluctable result of forces impinging on the family from the outside. The assumption was that the basic nuclear family configuration (mother, father, children) did not exist before the forces of modernization brought it into being. (See Talcott Parsons, "The Family in Urban industrial America," in *Sociology of the Family*, ed. Michael Anderson. Baltimore, Maryland: Penguin Books, 1971, pp. 43-62.)

The functionalist model held that the extended family was the ideal typical family prior to industrialization. In this schema, the extended family placed undue restraint on many things, including the creation of a mobile labor force. Because a mobile labor force is necessary to the maintenance and stability of modern society, family structure altered to meet the new demands of the "macro-order." The picture of a tidy fit between industrialization and the nuclear family became nigh irresistible. Notice that there is no room in this model for families to resist change, or to serve as catalysts for change. Families were seen as entities shedding one "function" after another as the macro-order mutated. The family, having lost many functions, was then forced to become "a more specialized agency." in Parsons' terms: indeed, he claimed that it was "important that socializing agents should not themselves be too completely immersed in family ties," as a too strong commitment to the family would handicap such persons in their ability to "fit" with the needs and demands of a mobile, opportunistic society. (Parsons, p. 59) Women got assigned an "expressive" role; men, an "instrumental-adaptive role."

Having construed the family within functionalist terms, scholars deprived themselves of any normative stance from which to evaluate what was, in fact, happening to and with families. So long as the abstract "needs" of the overall social order were served, then all must be well (more or less) with families. The importance of parenting to the well-being of real flesh and blood children—rather than the abstract needs of an abstractly construed "social order"—was slighted or ignored altogether. It was easy to accept any changes that appeared in family norms, including the rise in divorce, as just the latest variation in the family's endless mutability given the demands of social life. Mothers and fathers fell out of the picture as role players came to dominate. This led, in turn, to the notion that so long as a "role" was being served, it scarcely mattered who occupied the role. Indeed, I heard one family sociologist (at a feminist conference in mid-1970s), argue that "antibiotics and birth control made mothering unnecessary." She advocated the total replacement of mothers by professional childrearers in order that women, too, could be part of the mobile labor force required by industrial capitalism.

Because the functionalist schema extended to internal family relations as well, and because it tended to celebrate greater "role differentiation" as an inevitable thing (and inevitability within functionalism tends, implicitly, to be equated with "what is good"), academic scholars tended to be unabashed celebrants of the "role divergence" that comes with a rapidly changing social order. The story went like this: The family performs pared down functions. It turns out that many other institutions could perform these functions as well. It further happens that we don't really need "mothers" and "fathers" so long as various persons or institutions are assigned "nurturant" and "socialization" tasks. This no doubt overstates, but not by much.

To be sure, there were critics, including the so-called Cambridge School of historic demographers, who challenged the abstractedness of the functionalist formula. They argued that, in fact, the basic mother-father-children configuration had always been the pattern, certainly in Western societies, with variations on that mode. The so-called "nuclear family" was not a recent invention, coming into being only with industrialization. (Peter Laslett, "The Comparative History of Household and Family," *Journal of Social History*, vol 4, no. 1, Fall, 1970, pp. 74-87.) The demographic evidence indicated that a basic nuclear or conjugal household had long pertained and that, even in pre-industrial epochs, marriage meant the formation of a new household, often with members of the couple's households of origin figuring as central or adjunct members, so to speak.

Of course, calling into question the dominant functionalist model means one is obliged to offer another set of categories and explanatory features, especially if one hopes to make the case that the family is in trouble; that what we are witnessing is, in fact, family decline. How do we know? Here the focus must shift to the well-being of children and on that score, as I have already indicated, things do not look good. There are ways in which a wider order may be served, particularly in its current consumption-driven, expressivist forms in the United States, even as individuals are ill served and the overall society itself, over time, reels from the changes that are taking place, although it may come to realize that too late. My claim is that our societal experiment in loosening the ties that bind has failed: that it has failed our children, first and foremost, but that also, in ways we are only just beginning to recognize, it has failed adults understood as moral agents and responsible citizens, not just as a "mobile labor force."

This is the harsh truth of the matter: Americans, at the end of the twentieth century, suffer from the effects of a dramatic decline in the formation of social bonds, networks, and trust coupled with a diminution in investment in children. Children have borne the brunt of decades of negative social trends whose results are just now coming into clear focus; standing out in harsh relief. Family breakdown, in turn, generates unparented children who attend schools that increasingly resemble detention homes rather than centers of enduring training, discipline, and education and contributes to out-of-wedlock births and adolescent violence that, so far as we know. is now at unprecedented levels.

Here a reminder from the perspective of political and civil philosophy is in order as a way to reaffirm the *civic dimensions* of this question. Democratic theorists historically have either taken for granted a backdrop of vibrant, informal and formal civic associations, or they have articulated explicitly the relationship between democracy and the everyday actions and spirit of a people, most famously de Tocqueville in *Democracy in America*. Democracy requires laws, constitutions, and authoritative institutions, as I argue in my book, *Democracy on*

Trial (Basic Books, 1995), but it also requires what might be called democratic dispositions. These include a preparedness to work with others for shared ends; a combination of often strong convictions coupled with a readiness to compromise in the recognition that one can't always get everything one wants; a sense of individuality and a commitment to civic goods that are not the possession of one person or of one small group alone. The world that nourished and sustained such democratic dispositions was a thickly interwoven social fabric—a web of mediating institutions, of which the family was one. (Note the very different model implied here: rather than the family as a sub-system playing functions for a wider system—a series of boxes with connecting lines, with some dominating over others—the implied picture is one of a web of interlaced institutions, a social ecology.)

Now, in his great book, Tocqueville warned of a world different from the democracy he surveyed. He urged Americans to take to heart a possible corruption of their way of life. In his worst fears, narrowly self involved individualists, disarticulated from the saving constraints and nurture of the overlapping associations of social life, would require, even come to demand, more control from above to muffle at least somewhat the disintegrative effects of what he called a bad form of "egoism." Only small scale civic bodies enabled citizens to cultivate the democratic virtues and to play an active role in the democratic community.

But the tale I am telling argues that the deinstitutionalization of the family is part and parcel of a wider unraveling of the institutions of civil society tied, in turn, to a dramatic upsurge in all forms of social mistrust, generalized fearfulness, and cynicism. Recent studies show that Americans, without regard for race, cite very similar social problems: fear of crime, concern about poor education, the decline of home and family.

Indeed, if anything, African-Americans are more insistent that their society faces a crisis in values, beginning with the family.

What, then, is to be done? The sociologist, Robert Bellah, reports that Americans today brighten to tales of community, especially if the talk is soothing and doesn't appear to demand very much. Yet when discussion turns to institutions, and the need to sustain and to support authoritative civic institutions, attention withers and a certain sourness arises. This bodes ill for liberal democratic society, a political regime that requires robust yet resilient institutions that embody and reflect, the urgencies of democratic passions and interests. As our mediating institutions, from the Parent Teachers Association to political parties, disappear or are stripped of legitimacy, a political wilderness spreads. People roam the prairie fixing on objects or policies or persons to excoriate or to celebrate, at least for a time, until some other enthusiasm or scandal sweeps over them. If we have loss of the sturdiness and patience necessary to sustain civil society over the long haul, liberal democracy is in trouble.

This is why the family matters. This is why conformist insouciance concerning what is happening to the family rings increasingly hollow. This is why the functionalist perspective is not up to the conceptual task, given its inability to account for change as anything other than a kind of lock-step transmutation of certain structures to keep up with functions they are either deprived of, or new job descriptions they are assigned, by the "macro-order." What we require here at century's end is a way to reweave the threads of community; to restore our faltering faith in cultural forms themselves. The speed and glitz of late modernity—at least in the consumerist West— helps to stoke the fires of great impatience. Americans are especially known for being an impatient people. We want things to happen right away. We want problems to be solved overnight. But that isn't going to happen, not when we are faced with problems of such social, economic, sacramental, legal, political and, yes, embodied power and force. Late twentieth century moderns are dealing with the wreckage that mounted because, in the words of Vaclav Havel of the Czech Republic, we have forgotten that we are not God.

Although the family is the locus of private life, it is also critical to public life, to the life of the community and to civic associations. Here the testimony of parents and experts converges. When parents are asked to tell their own version of our current discontents, they lament the fact that it is harder to do a decent job raising children in a culture that is unfriendly to families and family attachments. The overwhelming majority of Americans, between 80-85 percent, believe that being a parent is much more difficult than it used to be. Pessimism about the decline of family norms is on the rise among all groups, especially among women and African-American and Hispanic citizens.

The family of which I speak is not an isolated unit but very much a social institution, nested in a wider surround, that either helps to sustain parental commitment and accomplishment or puts negative pressure on mothers and fathers. That pressure obviously takes many forms. I have articulated just a few. Being a parent is more than playing a role. Being a parent is more than a "life-style choice." It is an ethical vocation. We, as a society, and this I would urge on all societies more generally, should, insofar as this is possible, lighten the burdens and smooth the paths for parents in order that the complex joys of family life might rise to the surface and in order that the undeniable burdens of family responsibility might be more openheartedly borne.

Children lost to society in increasing numbers may be a growing phenomenon, but it is one we must name for what it is: a loss, a crying shame. Protecting, preserving, and strengthening family autonomy and the well-being of mothers and fathers is a way of affirming our commitment to the individual and to democratic social life. We have, it appears, lost the recognition that the rights of persons are fundamentally social. What is at stake in the family debate, and in our response to it as we near century's end, is nothing less than our capacity for human sociality and community.

Here are a few concluding questions for further consideration; indeed, they are inexorable questions given my analysis:

- What are the root causes of family disintegration? What are the effects of this deinstitutionalization?
- Why is concern with the family a civic and ethical issue?
- What does the family (mothers and fathers; brothers and sisters; grandparents; uncles, aunts, cousins; etc.) do that no other human institution can?
- What is the role or responsibility of individuals, communities, business, and government in dealing with family issues?
- How can we move to stem the tide of out of wedlock births, teenage violence, family breakdown without enhancing the avowedly coercive apparatuses of states?

This is a tall order. If we are not up to the task, the twenty-first century will be a tale of further coarsening of social life and deepening pressure on democratic society to enhance its coercive powers in order to save us from ourselves. If we hope to forestall this unhappy prospect. we must tend to our social ecology before it is too late. The family belongs on the list of endangered species.

Chapter 15

FEMINISM AND THE FAMILY

Patricia Lança

> The overthrow of mother-right was the defeat of the female
> sex, an event affecting the history of the world. The man
> seized the reins in the house also, the woman was degraded,
> enslaved, the slave of the man's lust, a mere instrument for
> breeding children.... The first division of labour is that
> between man and woman for child-breeding...the first class
> antagonism which appears in history coincides with the
> development of the antagonism between man and woman in
> monogamian marriage and the first class-oppression with
> that of the female sex by the male.
>
> —*Friedrich Engels*[1]

The history of "the woman question," as it used to be known
in the nineteenth century, is, of course, essentially the history
of the family. The quotation cited above serves to illustrate
where gender-feminism actually began. Engels' treatise *The
Origin of the Family, Private Property and the State*, was not a
history of women's place in the home but an attack on the
family. Ultimately, as Engels knew, the history of the family
involves the woman question.

It is the purpose of this paper to demonstrate the falsity of
Engels' position as well as the depths to which his views have
led in our day in radical feminist thinking. They constitute a
generalized attack not only on the family but on social stability
and a healthy relationship between the sexes. What I want to

do is to examine the basic tenets of "new wave" or "gender" feminism and their implications for the family.

It is important at the outset to distinguish between gender-feminism and equity-feminism. The latter, which I support, sees the emancipation of women as part of an ongoing process of liberation of the human spirit and gradual growth of the autonomy of the individual such as we find in many other areas of social history. Examples are the move from slavery to its abolition and full citizenship for blacks; recognition of the dignity of labor and the growth of workers' and farmers' organizations; the rise and extension of representative democracy; and movements against discrimination in favor of racial and religious equality. Thus, women's emancipation is to be seen as part of a continuing civilizing process, one that is organically connected with human growth in the following hierarchical line: knowledge, science, technology, industrialization, democracy. This knowledge-based development has proceeded in close interaction with the evolution of economic and political structures and has profound ethical and moral implications connected especially with the concepts of justice and freedom. The emancipation of women has equally deep implications for the way the family is to develop in the future.

Such an approach to feminism rejects analyses inspired by Marxist historicism and the notion that history is mainly determined by class or group conflict, though conflict there certainly is and has been. As Karl Popper taught, history— and especially social history—is to be seen as the history of the growth of human knowledge and the extraordinary consequences of this growth. In the early stages, certain social institutions appear to have been an ineluctable necessity if societies were to survive and flourish and produce the leisure necessary for the growth of knowledge to take place. Some of these institutions have disappeared; others, in particular the institution of the family, are still with us, and although family structure varies according to time and place, there is no indication of anything that could successfully replace it.

Let us consider slavery as a paradigm case. Although today slavery is considered an abomination, we must recognize that all civilizations have engaged in slavery at one time or another, and only those who nurture romantic ideas about the Third World attempt to make part of humanity feel guilty about the role its ancestors played in slavery. In Greek antiquity it was generally felt that the greatest misfortune, one that might befall anybody, was to become a slave. Slavery was one of the inevitable consequences of war: A free man might be enslaved, and a slave could become free.

Thinkers like Aristotle believed that slavery was not morally defensible but simply a necessary evil without which the civilized life of cities such as Athens was not possible. It was only when slavery no longer appeared necessary that it was possible to apply a moral standpoint and support its abolition. Moral judgments, as the relativists are so fond of telling us, must take account of the context. It makes no sense to issue a moral condemnation against the slave owner or slave trader who lives in a society where slavery is the norm. It makes a great deal of sense, however, to condemn its practice within a society or world that has rejected slavery. Such was the case with the American abolitionists in the nineteenth century. Here there had been moral progress as a spin-off from the technological progress that made slavery unnecessary and undesirable from an economic point of view.[2]

The woman question and the history of the family begin to take a clearer shape if we look at them in a similar light. Just as the ancients could not envisage a world so technologically altered as to make slavery both unnecessary and undesirable, neither until the nineteenth century could anybody envisage a world in which the survival of society did not depend upon the protection, and hence subordination, of women by men. The ancient Greeks could certainly imagine an individual's circumstances changing in such a way that he became a slave or a free man, because while they did not look upon the institution of slavery as natural but as necessary, and as far as the individual was concerned, the fruit of chance. Here resides a crucial difference with the woman question. A woman's position was regarded as not only necessarily but naturally subordinate. And if women were almost always to be encountered in subordinate positions, it followed that society (women as well as men) would take the view that women were indeed inferior in various ways: from inferior physical strength the extrapolation to inferior intellectual and creative powers was but a step. If most women's entire lives were primarily occupied in child care and their status in law and custom was not much higher than that of children, it is understandable that women would be regarded as childlike.

Today that natural state of affairs which required the subordination of women has changed out of all recognition. For good or ill, sexual intercourse is no longer inevitably tied to procreation. Labor conditions and relations make it possible for women to do most jobs that were previously restricted to men. The expansion of market economies—demand for labor and demand for consumers—has caused women to emerge from the home. Greater scientific knowledge and empirical demonstration have shown that, with similar opportunity and training, women are as capable as men in most fields that do not involve physical strength. In consequence women have claimed and won full rights of citizenship. Justice, as well as the requirements of a modern economy, demanded the change. Gender-feminists, however, usually forget that when this process became incipient in the last century, the first to support women's emancipation were men, as with slavery, whose abolition in Europe and America was first demanded by the vilified white Anglo-Saxon Protestants.

It is not my intention to suggest that the different aspects of human emancipation—that of slaves, peasants, workers, colonized peoples, or women—owe themselves to any kind of historical or economic determinism or that they may come about without a struggle. Of course there is resistance to change: knowledge and emancipation have to be fought for. It is always a minority that leads the way on the path of moral progress. And so, wherever women are now free in the world they should and do pay homage to their grandmothers and great-grandmothers and even further back to Aphra Behn, Mary Wollstonecraft, and all the other pioneers of the movement for women's emancipation.

Unfortunately for the dignity of the cause, there have arisen in recent decades aberrant schools of thought among some women intellectuals that are jeopardizing the advance of both emancipation and knowledge. They are dangerous trends that threaten both rationality and the family, and they need to be combated.

Gender Feminism and Marxism

Every living species tends to adopt strategies favorable to survival, and therefore, seen against the background of real history and not of some imagined fantasy world, the confinement of women to the home seems to have been a necessary state of affairs if the family and human culture were to flourish. Such confinement would tend to be accentuated the higher the social level. Women were indeed a "protected species," to use an ecological metaphor, and this protection was necessarily paid for in economic dependence. Apart from the lowest classes in society, the life of women has generally been immeasurably less dangerous and insecure than that of men. These were the ones who had to go to war to defend hearth and home. They were the warriors, the navigators, the adventurers, and necessarily so. The cult of honor and glory provided a stimulus to manliness, and cowardice was regarded as a womanish weakness. In these circumstances it is hardly surprising that the public life of politics or art, both requiring single-minded dedication, should have been largely monopolized by men. Nor is it surprising that the images men and women cultivated of themselves and of each other should have developed so as to reinforce functions seen as necessary for society's survival.

Gender-feminist theory is in reality a subclass of the Marxist theory of capitalism and the role of the working class; a theory that, under the influence of Maoism, was later to include the "colonial revolution" as a motor force of history. These ideas have their intellectual roots in failure to see capitalism as a process rather than as a system, a process that was in fact better described by Adam Smith than by Marx. Popper's characterization of Marxism as nonscientific and circular, a "closed system," may with equal force be applied to feminist theorizing. Like Marxism (and Freudianism too) gender-feminism states its theories in such a way that they are not susceptible of falsification. The more the adversaries of the theory criticize it, the more they are said to be demonstrating the truth of the theory they oppose: The anti-Marxist is held to be simply demonstrating his incorrigibly "bourgeois" and class-ridden view of the world; the anti-Freudian his subconsciously motivated resistance to revelation of his repressions; and the adversary of gender-feminism how deeply he or she has been conditioned by male-dominated, or "phallocentric," society into accepting his or her gender role. Hence all criticism is to be discounted as hopelessly flawed by class or self-interest and false consciousness." Indeed, adversaries of gender-feminism are frequently accused of being "women who hate women."

A related ploy used by radical feminists, like their Marxist ancestors, is first to declare war on moral discourse by an appeal to cultural relativism and then to recoup for themselves a monopoly of moral concern by finding an enemy against whom to direct moral indignation. This is an example of the well-known process described by Michael Polanyi, in reference to communism, as "dynamo-objective coupling."

> Alleged scientific assertions, which are accepted as such because they satisfy moral passions, will excite these passions further, and thus lend increased convincing power to the scientific affirmation in question—and so on, indefinitely. Any criticism of its scientific part is rebutted by the moral passions behind it, while any moral objections to it are coldly brushed aside by invoking the inexorable verdict of its scientific findings. Each of the two components, the dynamic and the objective, takes it in turn to draw attention away from the other when it is under attack.[3]

In his *Origin of the Family, Private Property and the State*, Engels expounded the Marxist theory of the family and the role of the sexes. Although the book was to become one of the great Marxist classics and compulsory reading for all new party members, wherever communists took power the implications of the theory were as easily forgotten in practice as were most other Marxist theories. Engels' views are, however, worthwhile noting, because they show unmistakably where gender-feminism has its roots. Basing himself on the discredited findings of the American anthropologist Lewis Morgan, who had studied the practices of the Iroquois, Engels believed he had discovered a great universal truth about the family.[4] It must be said that he exhibited little scientific rigor when he generalized about some universal matriarchal society in the supposed idyllic stage of "primitive communism" on the basis of contemporary: observations of nineteenth-century American Indians. From such flimsy evidence Engels extrapolated a universal move from a matriarchal to a patriarchal society, and it is a Marxist commonplace that this was recognized in classical antiquity because, it is alleged, the *Oresteia* of Aeschylus celebrates that change.

Women and History

The woman question is, in fact, deeply connected with the development of capitalism, though not in the way the gender-feminists understand. For capitalism is nothing but the process of wealth producing, which has existed, albeit in incipient form, since civilization began. Capitalism has prospered more or less according to the degree of freedom guaranteed by political structures. History confirms that the freer citizens and institutions are, the more successful is capitalism in creating wealth; and the more wealth that is created in an atmosphere of freedom, the more human well-being has tended to grow, as have knowledge, technology, and art. As we know, where human beings have no leisure there can be no culture, and until capitalism was well advanced and the living standards of most people had risen, in some places, to levels we began to experience in the last two centuries and especially since the Second World War, there could be no access to things of the mind and the spirit for the vast majority of mankind whether men or women. Where the state is weak or nonexistent and societies are anarchic and insecurity prevails, most people have no alternative but to be dependent on the strong, the warriors and the warlords, and the consequence is feudal dependency.

All these propositions would constitute a tedious relation of historical commonplaces were it not the case that gender-feminism ignores them and the application they have to the question of women's emancipation, which cannot be understood without reference to human history. So we shall take them a little further.

There was literally no possibility of women generally being other than dependent on men before three developments took place: first, knowledge of and access to birth control; second, expanding economies that took production out of the home;

and third, the technological advances that made it possible for women to perform many of the tasks in agriculture, industry, and the armed forces that had hitherto been the preserve of men. It is clear that these developments are all intimately connected with the development of capitalism. At the dawn of civilization, so that women would not be the prey of men in general, mothers and their children required the protection and maintenance guaranteed by men on whom they had some claim. This is where the family originates and not in some perverse determination by men to dominate the female sex —which is not, of course, to deny that there have always existed domineering and cruel men just as there have always existed manipulative and exploitative women.

When an entire class of human beings (in this case, the female sex) is dependent on another (the male sex) for protection and maintenance, whether members of the dependent class are well treated or not by those upon whom they depend is largely a question of the temperament and moral qualities of each party and the moral atmosphere of the culture concerned. And so, when we look at history and those traditional models of the family still in existence today, we find all kinds of epiphenomena typical of the human condition: the battered wife and the hen-pecked or financially exploited husband; the abandoned and penniless woman and the male alimony hostage; the Messalina and the Don Juan; the tyrannical father and Lear's elder daughters. And this is to name but a few.

However, we are not here concerned with the vices and virtues of the sexes, which seem to be fairly evenly distributed, but with the question of freedom and equality of rights and opportunity. Women could not become free and enjoy equal rights with men until there was the possibility of biological and economic independence. Women having achieved their new status, the question that arises today is what effect all this will have on the family? But first let us unpack the gender-feminists' arguments and deal with them in greater detail.

The militant feminist, whose attitude to the family is openly hostile, maintains, with Simone de Beauvoir, "women are not born female: it is society that makes them so." This facile playing with words, which reaches its apogee in deconstructionist theory propounded by the likes of Foucault and Derrida and their disciples, leads to such aberrations as the contention that death, too, is a social construct. In reality, these social construct arguments come from the same stable as do those that, in the nature-versus-nurture debate, deny the importance of innate qualities. In response, two things need to be proclaimed loud and clear: first, that being male or female is not a social construct but a biological fact of life that has to do with the sexual method of reproduction common to mammals, birds, reptiles, fish, and insects. De Beauvoir spoke like the ostrich with its head in the sand telling birds with functional wings that flying was only a social construct. Second, however differently various societies may see the role of women, the latter are nowhere external to society but themselves play an important, if not the most determinant, part in defining their own role as well as that of men. It is the women, after all, who are everywhere the first educators and molders of children.

The gender-feminists who complain so bitterly that women are ignored by historians, not to mention the inventors of that grotesque neologism "herstory," seem to want to get their revenge by ignoring history. So let us try to pinpoint their basic premises and then look at the arguments against them.

Gender-Feminism's Articles of Faith

First, it is held that women's age-long exclusion from public life and confinement to the domestic tasks of wife and mother constituted a deprivation of rights and were imposed by men on their unwilling female victims through a process of discrimination and violence.

Second, the subordination of women to a paterfamilias and women's secondary status before the law are said to represent juridical formalization of the male tendency to oppress and exploit.

Third, insistence on premarital virginity and marital fidelity in the female are said to have been taboos developed by and in the interest of the male sex as part of its view of women as procreative chattels whose generative capacities must remain within the strict control of the male so that men might be certain about the paternity of their heirs.

Gender-feminists add two more articles of faith whose effect is to shore up the first three.

Fourth, to ensure women's acceptance of their subordinate role, male-dominated society is said to have developed an almost infinite array of stratagems by which to indoctrinate women in their "gender role," that is, to condition them into accepting their inferior status.

Fifth, and probably most hurtful of all to the female intellectual, is the alleged exclusion of women from history.

The gender-feminists need to be reminded of a number of matters so basic as to appear obvious to all who are not blinded by prejudice. The naturalness of women's subordination was not simply apparent. It was also very real: It flowed from biological facts that, until artificial intervention was possible, have remained unchanged from time immemorial. And in many parts of the world even today such intervention is still not possible. It is probably this very naturalness that arouses such deep, almost visceral feelings on both sides of the debate, not least of which is the sense of deep injustice felt by some women at what they see as being a raw deal imposed on them by nature. Here then is a list of the matters in question.

First, some animal species are monogamous; some are promiscuous. Only the human female is sexually available at all times, while the human male is always "in season." How this came about, and what family arrangements prevailed among the various branches of the human race in the long prehistory of home sapiens up to ten thousand years ago, we do not at present know, and no theory about the family can be based on what amounts to mere conjecture.

Second, it is an immensely long infancy and childhood that has made possible the development of human language, intellect, personality, and, in the long run, society itself. Helpless young babies required their mothers' presence even more in the past than is the case now (when we know how to provide safe substitutes for breast feeding). Nursing mothers, often in charge of several children, were hardly in a position to defend themselves, let alone engage in warfare or hunting. They needed men to protect them and their young against other men and wild beasts. This "division of labor" referred to by the founding fathers of Marxism, better described as a division of social as well as biological function, is to be encountered among many animal species. The heavier, more robust build of the male animal, and his frequently protective behavior to females and young, can hardly be ascribed to some mysterious indoctrination into a gender role.

Third, in preindustrial economies with rudimentary technology, the only productive work women could engage in compatible with child bearing and rearing was, with few exceptions, in the home and the fields around the home. And it was there, in the family, that artisanal production was to remain for many millennia.

Fourth, the glory-associated activities of hunting and war were dangerous and required superior physical strength and the development of special skills and characteristics. Only a group bent on tribal suicide would send its mothers into battle or permit them to roam far afield. It was thus essential for survival not just of society but of the species itself that the male sex should be reared in the cult of valor and military prowess, qualities that women were just as anxious to cultivate in their sons as were the men themselves.

Fifth, had the premarital virginity and marital fidelity taboos not been virtually universal, females, especially the young, could not have been protected from predatory and irresponsible males.

Sixth, and a point that is frequently forgotten, it is only in the present century that the world faces the danger of overpopulation, and it was only in the beginning of the nineteenth that Malthus drew attention to that possibility. Before then the human race often faced serious threats to its very survival. Have feminists not heard of the extermination of at least a quarter of the population of Europe by the Black Death in the late Middle Ages? With manual labor the only means of production, it is hardly surprising that there should have developed taboos against not only homicide but also all forms of infanticide including abortion. Indeed, it is precisely in the Christian West that these taboos have been most highly developed. We may also mention in this connection the taboo against any sexual activity that did not involve the possibility of procreation regarded as the duty of all who did not devote their lives specifically to the service of God.

But need we really go back as far as primitive, ancient, or medieval society to find illustration of the fallacies in feminist arguments? All we need do is contemplate the lot of women in, say, Jane Austen's time, before the advent of the much-traduced Victorian age. Rubber had not yet been discovered in Brazil and, though eighteenth-century diarists speak of leather articles, condoms and other contraceptives were not generally available. A healthy, fertile, sexually active woman was likely to have a pregnancy a year—if she did not die in childbirth, of miscarriage, or of any of the other multiple ills that beset people before medicine began to make its spectacular advances.

Let us be anachronistic for a moment and imagine the lot of a girl of any class who "dropped out" of the accepted pattern. If parents accepted a pregnant, unmarried daughter, they would have extra mouths to feed instead of the prospect of a son-in-law. If they turned her out, what could she do but sell her body? It was therefore perfectly natural that families should regard an extramarital pregnancy as an unmitigated disaster and regard premarital virginity as the only safeguard available: hence the taboo inculcated into the young of both sexes, a taboo that for evident reasons was not symmetrical in its application. Dependent as they were, the immense majority of women were in no position to question the taboo. There were few employment possibilities for women outside of domestic service.

Indeed, what is strikingly absent from feminist thought is the awareness that until the advent of a modern economy, employment possibilities off the land were precious few for anybody, women or men, and hence dependence on the family as an economic unit was almost total. Work available for the male sex was rough, dirty, and often dangerous. Always it meant long hours, usually at subsistence-level pay. As Hobbes pointed out, life for most was nasty, brutish, and short. Is it surprising that chastity for an unmarried woman was regarded as a safeguard rather than a burden? Or any less surprising that life in a convent often presented itself as a haven of refuge from a hostile world and incidentally the only place where a woman could engage in intellectual activities?

Sex, Sickness, and Society

But there is yet another fact the gender-feminists ignore. When they first began to talk loudly about the rights of women over their own bodies and the right to sexual pleasure and indulged in arcane debate about the mechanics of the orgasm, and laid the blame on men for allegedly denying women these delights, it seemed as though the extremists had forgotten or had never learned why most women throughout the ages feared sex as much or more than they desired it and would consent to it only under certain very precise conditions, namely marriage and the man's assumption of responsibility for his wife and progeny.

An enormously high incidence of death and frequently of suffering was involved in childbirth, together with a host of postpuerperal diseases. Indeed, a universal dread of sickness, and a strong sense of puritanism, followed hard on the heels of syphilis in Europe. In northern Europe, let it be stressed, the manifestations of this disease were more virulent than in the south because of the general absence of malaria, resistance to which seems to attenuate the effects of syphilis. This medical fact therefore seems to provide an explanation for the geographical distribution of puritan values. Far from being the malefic invention of frustrated or perverted clerics, as fashionable orthodoxy would have it, or of possessive males as the feminists pretend, premarital chastity for both sexes and fidelity in marriage were, quite literally, the only guarantees of immunity from a disease, then untreatable, whose course was quite as horrific as that of AIDS. All these factors were sufficient to persuade most women that the most precious right a woman had over her own body was the right to say "no." (There is a curious echo of this ancestral precept in the militant feminists' most recent obsession: sexual harassment, an anachronism if ever there was one in an era when women are supposed to be in a position to defend themselves.)

If Marxism has been responsible for a generalized acceptance of a whole series of false political and economic ideas, Freudian theory, whose central concepts have today become household phrases, has caused much muddled thinking on questions related to sexual matters and family life. Uncritical acceptance of the idea that self-discipline leads to sexual repression, and this to pathological conditions, lays the ground for permissiveness, and from this to the prevalent hedonistic ethos. And yet nobody familiar with contemporary psychological miseries in societies that have never been so materially well off or liberal about sexual matters can honestly believe that hedonism and permissiveness inevitably lead to well-being. But it is the false notion that these are good in themselves that prevents so many people from even considering that there may be something to say in favor of traditional values.

Only a little reflection is required, however, to recognize that if the sex drive is one of the most potent instincts (and Freud himself based all his work on the presumption that it was the most powerful of all drives), then it is no wonder that all organized societies since the dawn of civilization have sought to contain this instinct and canalize it into channels favorable to survival. Gender-feminists, like all those who believe that the "bourgeois family" is just one more invention of "dead white European males," ignore the most basic tenet of civilized life: that organized society requires there to be rules. Without them, as every child used to be taught, life becomes intolerable. Given that nature has endowed our species with a powerful sex drive and made human beings (unlike most animal species) inclined to be sexually active in and out of season, it is evident that for society to flourish some mechanism was necessary to control sexual activity as well as to protect women and their offspring.

Everywhere, regardless of whatever formal differences of structure may exist, the mechanism that has evolved is the family. Polygynous or monogamic, the institution of the family has everywhere established clear rules regarding the behavior of its members, their rights and duties among themselves and toward other families. Anthropologists have devoted tomes to describing kinship patterns and the stratagems that have evolved in different societies to prevent incest. And yet what else is the taboo on incest but a taboo on a particular form of sexual activity that, without the taboo, would be practiced by human beings as commonly as it is by so many animal species, with disastrous effects on life within the family?

Gender-Feminism and Family Breakdown

All this is so apparent that it is difficult at first sight to understand how anyone could fall for gender-feminism. However, like other emancipatory movements, women's emancipation, too, attracts to its banner the less thoughtful and the activists whose emotional posturing distorts reality and constitutes a threat not only to women themselves but to the whole of society.

In most of the Western world women's emancipation is now virtually complete, both from a juridical point of view and also to a large extent in practice. All that remains is for women to adjust themselves to the new possibilities and to take advantage of them. Why, then, should it be at such a moment that the gender-feminists have become most strident, most complaining, and most influential? The answer lies partly in the social disruption caused by the very success of the movement for women's equality.

From a historical point of view the process has been a rapid one, as rapid as technological development itself, and has affected different sectors of society unevenly, being generally most widespread among the better educated and least significant lower down the social scale.

Whatever controversy and struggle may have occurred in the workplace or on the campus, the real battlefield has been in the home and the heart of the family. A large number if not the majority of men are still under the influence of age-old stereotypes perpetuated by their mothers as well as their fathers and reinforced by the media.

Many men come to marriage today with basically very different aspirations from those of the women they marry. When the first fine, careless rapture is over, the couple find themselves subject to all the stresses and strains of contemporary life. Both parties tend to be disappointed—and now it is not just the old disappointment of fading romance typical of earlier generations this century. It is the disappointment of finding that the spouse has become a rival, an adversary on the income-earning front and in the struggle for leisure and other benefits in the home. Or it is the blow to the husband's self-image when he finds that he is not indispensable for bringing home the bacon, a disappointment that often turns into growing irresponsibility. Marriages break up under the strain, but the battle of the sexes does not end there. It continues: over-possession of the marital home, custody of children, alimony, and so on. In a society where the mass media constantly transmit contradictory, indeed incoherent, signals, it is difficult not to become disoriented. In contrast to the publicity given to the demands of gender-feminism, we find that the media, especially the advertising industry, continue simultaneously to laud the qualities of youth, beauty, and domesticity and the traditional relation between the sexes as supremely valuable. The media continue to foster the time-honored image of women as either sex objects or mother figures. Material and sexual success is shown as everyone's aim, and failure in any sphere is the worst of sins.

All too many women whose marriages have broken down, or who have always been single mothers, find it difficult to cope with the stress of career, lone child rearing, and deprivation of masculine economic support. The lifestyle that results is often also one of enforced celibacy. Such women become embittered and easy prey for the hate-mongering of gender-feminists. In such circumstances is it any wonder that there should exist an angry, soured, and uncomprehending minority of women who find in the theories of gender-feminists a plausible explanation for the woes that beset them? Their position and reactions are similar to those of the unemployed worker or disaffected intellectual who laps up Marxist theory and, in extreme cases, becomes an adept of terrorism.

When people are unhappy and desperate, they are prone, as history has amply demonstrated, to fall for simplistic doctrines, in particular those that provide a vehicle for emotional discharge. And let us not forget that gender-feminism's claims have had their effects on men, too. Some have reacted negatively, thus reinforcing the gender-feminists' case. The "male chauvinist pig" still flourishes, as does the "gold-digging" female. But these are at the extreme ends of the spectrum.

What is more commonly the case is that because of gender-feminist success in a number of fields as well as the normal process of female emancipation, many men have become perturbed and insecure in their identity and self-image. And this is not a healthy recipe for successful marriage and fatherhood.

Thus, gender-feminism is particularly dangerous because it is yet one more factor among many that are working to undermine the family. In left-wing thought there has always existed a triad whose invocation immediately marked out the author as an incorrigible reactionary. To talk about the sanctity of God, country, and family is enough in certain circles to arouse guffaws of derision. The Jacobins of the French Revolution and just over a century later Lenin's militant atheists declared war on religion, although both were later to fabricate new gods of their own. The communists of the nineteenth and early twentieth centuries declared war not only on God but also on nationalism, and after 1917 internationalism was used as a banner with which to camouflage Soviet imperialism.

No significant movement, however, dared to declare open war on the family. The communists wherever they came to power were proud to boast of their pro-family policies, and the Soviet Union gave prizes to the champion mothers of many children. They quoted Lenin's remarks on the subject of the family, unexceptionable by conventional standards: his famous glass of water theory of sex, comparing the promiscuity of adepts of free love with drinking water from a puddle in the road; or his reprimand directed at those communist couples who refused to have children for lacking faith in the glorious socialist future.

In practice, as a matter of public policy (whatever was done by their leaders in private), communist regimes generally have adopted standards on sexual matters that Europeans and Americans would regard as puritanical: generalized persecution of homosexuals in the Soviet Union and Fidel Castro's segregation of AIDS patients are cases in point.

Gender-feminism, however, takes the bull by the horns on this question. Nevertheless, it was indeed a communist who, doctrinally at any rate, adumbrated the first attack on the family, and it was one who was to inspire gender-feminists over a century later. Were it not for the persisting pernicious influence of these ideas, we could afford to be generous with such mistaken views, as we could with Marx, knowing as we do that he was basing himself on the deficient information available in the mid-nineteenth century. But if Engels had no access to modern studies of animal behavior and Marx could not even dream of the technological marvels and wealth that capitalism was to produce, our contemporary theorists have no such excuse. And yet the basic premises of gender-feminism bear a remarkable likeness to what Engels believed he and Marx had discovered.

Can the Family Survive the Gender-Feminist Attack?

The arguments against gender-feminism need to be marshaled and reaffirmed because, although the process of female emancipation has largely been completed (at least in the much-maligned West), the present virulence of feminist militancy raises questions vital for the future of the family and of free society.

Sociologists, when discussing the family, identify a number of its functions: the sexual, the reproductive, the economic, and the socialization function as well as that of caring for the sick and aged. However, any realistic appraisal of the family in late industrial societies shows that all these functions are now freely exercised outside the family. The only economic function that continues within it is that of consumption, not production. Even socialization and education have been taken over increasingly by agencies outside the family, to an extent where, indeed, there are families that have to fight against the social services for their continued existence. And yet there are more and more serious studies available showing that many of society's current ills are directly attributable to the breakdown of the family. This on the one hand. On the other is the fact that there is also plenty of sociological and psychological material on the dysfunctional family and the dire effects it may have on its members. Indeed, familiarity with the contemporary novel and cinema, both victims of the penetration of Freudian theory in literary circles, leads to the conclusion that the family is an institution we could well do without. So the gender-feminists' diatribes converge with those of others interested in denigrating the family. And yet, if marriage and the family were to break down irremediably, what would take their place? And is the family still needed in the new society that the information revolution is bringing about?

To try to answer these questions we need to look again at the list of family functions given above to see if it is complete.

It is clear that one very important, if not the most important function, has been left out: the role of the family as repository and nurturer of affection, that most important of human emotions. It is in a healthy family that children learn to love and to develop emotionally. It is in a loving home that adults find refuge, comfort, and encouragement in a troubled world. It is inside the family unit that children learn about sharing, self-discipline, loyalty, duty, and the other old-fashioned virtues. It has long been the traditional ideal that through the emotional health of the family people learned the first lessons that would help them to develop a positive approach to society outside. We all know that ideals are often not achieved, but the ideal was there nevertheless. Before female emancipation the family was a patriarchal, often authoritarian, and sometimes cruel organism. If, however, we are to see women's emancipation as part of the civilizing process, then we should surely see it as contributing not to the break-up of the family but, on the contrary, toward its betterment.

Unlike gender-feminism, equity-feminism seeks equal responsibility of women with men for the conduct of family affairs: an equal partnership of husband and wife that should be mutually enriching and provide the best possible example for children. It used to be one of the arguments in favor of female equality, used by pioneers of women's emancipation like John Stuart Mill, that educated mothers would make for better educated children. Surely this is true and should be upheld to refute de Beauvoir, who told Betty Friedman she did not believe that women should have the choice of staying at home to raise children. Society, she thought, should not allow women this choice because, if it did, too many women would prefer the option of staying at home.[5] The staggering authoritarianism of a figure who has become a guru for radical feminism reveals a great deal about the democratic convictions of her supporters, and raises serious questions about how much less authoritarian than men women might be as single mothers or lesbian parents.

If the family were to disappear and the state to take upon itself the monopoly of what were formerly family functions—as we have seen described in Huxley's Brave New World, in Orwell, and in many a science-fiction fantasy—what place would there be for affection? Even in the Soviet Union child psychologists discovered quite early on that children brought up in institutions suffered from learning and emotional difficulties. In consequence they recommended that the anti-family tendencies of the early Bolsheviks be abandoned and the integration of children in families be sought. This is ABC for all well-trained teachers and children's welfare officers. In fact, a good case can be made for the view that precisely the lack of early experience of caring relationships, healthy emotional development, and positive male and female role models lies behind the growing numbers of violent and destructive young people. Nevertheless, there can be little doubt that bureaucracies have a fatal tendency to grow, and in the welfare states of the European Union and in North America there has been increasing encroachment of the social service machine on spheres that should properly be the province of the individual citizen.

Not to mention the positively sinister phenomena connected with the false detection of child abuse reported in several countries. At the same time as the social service bureaucracy expands, seemingly with poor results in remedying the ills it claims to deal with, government economists and experts in public finance everywhere warn loudly that Western countries can simply not continue to afford welfare provisions on the present scale. Shrinking birthrates throughout the European Union and a steadily aging population threaten the entire structure of the welfare state, and in many places measures are already being taken to reduce it. So it seems as though we are in the presence of several conflicting trends: a positive epidemic of cases of family breakdown and single mothers; rising juvenile crime, drug abuse, and civil disorder; a social service bureaucracy demanding ever-growing rights of interference; and government overspending on welfare leading to huge budget deficits and the demand for lower public spending. And finally, we are confronted with a deep crisis in values that is itself, at one and the same time, cause and consequence of our other ills.

The breakdown in the family, therefore, forms a basic part of a generalized crisis in Western society that shows little sign of abating. The resurgence of sexually transmitted disease and especially the appearance of AIDS might give us cause to reflect upon the wisdom for today of a number of traditional values. Yet we find instead that the feminist lobby is intensifying its attack on the family and precisely those values.

When feminists, instead of supporting the family and its traditional functions, campaign for their further destruction, they are helping to bring about the totalitarianism that the expansion of the various socialist subsystems in Western society threatens to bring about. Every one of the radical feminists' demands—quotas, unrealistic measures against discrimination and sexual harassment, institutionalized care of children, favoring the single parent—all these, if put into practice, could only result in an immense expansion of the "nanny state" and its stranglehold on every sphere of life. This bureaucratic nightmare looms even closer with the threats presented by European federalism and the powerful feminist lobbies that exist in Brussels and Strasbourg. Those who yearn for totalitarianism and mourn its breakdown in eastern Europe are, of course, quite right in aiming their attack in this direction. It was after all, the family that proved to be at the heart of resistance to the tyranny or "real socialism." Perhaps this was so because the Soviets and their allies failed to take up the radical feminist agenda first mooted by Engels. The liberal Left Establishment of the nineties, however, seems set on correcting this failing, and its success in doing so constitutes a very real threat to a free society.

Not that the liberal Left would subscribe to the more strident pronouncements of the gender-feminists. They do not even recognize what allies the gender-feminists have. The adherents of the "politically correct" movement do not even seem to understand who invented the expression and that, like gender-feminism, "political correctness" comes directly out of the arsenal of Marxist theory, as a brief consultation of 1950s issues of the American Marxist journal *Masses and Mainstream* would rapidly confirm. The liberals do not seem to realize that ever since communist practice in the countries of "real socialism" ceased to attract the wide numbers of Western intellectuals it once did, and particularly since in material terms capitalism has been able to deliver the goods while communism in Europe has collapsed, Western Marxists have been on the lookout for new allies susceptible of manipulation. They have, indeed, been quite open in stating that the Left should seek a coalition with "oppressed minorities" such as ethnic groups, feminists, and "gay" and lesbian organizations—what is sometimes known as the "rainbow coalition." Liberal Left intellectuals, long habituated to running down the "bourgeois" family and so-called middle-class values, behave in this respect in the tradition of the duped fellow travelers who used to come back from the USSR full of praise for its achievements.

The inherent fissionability of such a coalition and of the groups within it, as well as the incongruity of so many of its positions, would seem enough to guarantee a short lifespan and little influence. And so it would have been some years ago, when citizens, churches, governments, and courts paid at least lip service to family values. Today in the West we live in what has become known as the "condom culture," where an Anglican bishop of London can pronounce adultery to be not a sin but simply an act of unkindness; where a number of Western countries legally recognize homosexual marriages and "homosexual parenthood," where the number of childless couples and unmarried mothers is soaring. Where all this can be accepted with relatively little protest, the antics of gender-feminists and their friends are regarded with tolerant amusement and even sympathy.

But when we add to the atmosphere of moral decadence the physical degradation of our societies, evidenced by inner-city decay, unsafe streets, rising crime rates, and growing drug abuse with all the ills that come in its wake, we can scarcely be surprised at the depressing picture of the future conjured up by radical feminist philosopher Ann Ferguson's "individual meshing together of androgynous human beings."

In this bleak scenario, what grounds can we have for optimism? Is there, in fact, any hope at all for the future of the family? I believe there is—but it is one in which gender-feminism has no place. What does have a place—indeed, the factor that gives us most ground for believing in the future of the family—is the combining of the values of equity-feminism with old-fashioned family values, and these are what should be taught in schools to young people, together with a proper appreciation of human history and the long, hard struggle it has been to evolve toward the ideal of marriage as a partnership of equals, a partnership that gender-feminism seems bent on destroying.

Notes

[1]Frederick Engels, *The Origin of the Family, Private Property, and the State* (New York, Liking Penguin, 1986), 82. Omissions in the quotation refer to the author's remarks about how he and Karl Marx had previously set down some of these opinions jointly.

[2]For a discussion of moral attitudes to slavery and the woman question, see Bernard Williamns, *Shame and Necessity* (London: Sather Classical Lectures, 1993).

[3]Michael Polanyi, *Personal Knowledge* (Chicago: Univ. Chicago Press, 1974) 230 35.

[4]Lewis Morgan, *Ancient Society, or Researches in the Lines of Human Progress from Savagery through Barbarism to Civilization* (London, 1877) quoted in Engels, *Origin of the Family*.

[5]Quoted in Christina Hoff Summers, *Who Stole Feminism? How Women Have Betrayed Women* (New York: Free Press, 1994), 25-57.

Chapter 16

FATHERLESSNESS IN THE UNITED STATES

Mitchell B. Pearlstein

Introduction

This chapter is grounded in three interlocking ideas:

- The explosive and continuing increase in fatherlessness in the United States—due to both divorce and out-of-wedlock births—constitutes America's greatest social disaster.
- American elites—particularly those in politics, the media, and higher education—generally have worked feverishly over the last three decades not to publicly address this problem.
- Despite such servility to political correctness, ideological cant and wishful thinking, fatherlessness, in fact, is finally rising to political salience, as both scholarly and everyday evidence can no longer be ignored.

If just three quick sets of statistics can convey this remarkable decline in family life they are these:

- Only 35 years ago, five percent of American babies were born out of wedlock. Currently, approximately 30 percent of all American babies come into this world outside of marriage, a sixfold increase.[1]
- Nearly 40 percent of all American children reside in homes where their biological fathers do not live.[2] By some estimates, 55 to 60 percent of US youngsters born in the

1990s will spend at least a part of their childhood in such fatherless homes.[3]

- To put such trends in international perspective, the United States now leads the world in fatherless families (superseding Sweden), as nearly 30 percent of all American families have come to be headed by a single parent.[4]

Given the starkness of these numbers, not to mention the implicit human pain embedded in them, why has fatherlessness specifically, and family non-formation and breakdown more generally, not established themselves more definitively as first-tier political issues in the United States?

As suggested, to raise such issues has been to invite four charges, mostly from the political left, that most leaders (on both the left and right) have been severely reluctant to risk: That they are blaming victims (i.e., women and children —especially poor women and children). That they are insensitive. That they are sexist. And most frightening of all, that they are racist. Fear of such epithets, no matter how ridiculous on their face, has effectively intimidated all but a few leaders, in and out of politics.

Or more precisely, it has intimidated leaders as well as other citizens from speaking their minds publicly. In the very useful metaphor of historian Barbara Dafoe Whitehead (from whom we will hear later), Americans do, in fact, talk a lot about faltering families, though much more bluntly and accurately in their "kitchen table" rather than "conference table" conversations.

Kitchen table conversations, as Whitehead has written,[5] involve families and friends and their language is that of "cultural norms and values." Conference table discussions, on the other hand, include representatives of the media, the academic world, the policy community," and their language is that of the "policy sciences—politics and economics." Which is to say that conference table conversations—those led by politicians—are almost always inappositely analytic and dry.

While this combination of quivering and missing the moral point has helped keep fatherlessness from being a high-profile public issue as such, that's not to say that surrogate issues have not been central. For if American election campaigns, for instance, have not tackled father absence per se, they have been acutely shaped and contorted for the last three decades by the inescapable products of family breakdown: increased crime, increased welfare, diminished education and similar social failures. In this important sense, fatherlessness has been a clear-cut, if simultaneously shrouded political issue.

Having said this, and as suggested above, sensitive family matters have grown modestly less cloaked in more recent years, as conditions have grown sufficiently grave and glaring. Or as baseball legend and rough-hewn philosopher Yogi Berra, has said: "You can observe a lot by just looking."

For further example, while former Vice President Dan Quayle, a Republican, was broadly criticized for talking about out-of-wedlock births in his famous "Murphy Brown" speech during the 1992 campaign, President Bill Clinton, a Democrat, has made much the same general point several times since that election. We will return to the "Murphy Brown" episode below, but the point to be made here is that growing numbers of American leaders are beginning to ferret a bit of gumption (as well as coming to more realistic grip) regarding what is acknowledged on all sides to be a very sensitive issue.

Methodologically, this paper will review major studies, essays and events of the last 30 years to aid in tracing the way in which family structure and fatherlessness have been addressed in political and intellectual arenas. Such mileposts will include Daniel Patrick Moynihan's 1965 study for the Johnson Administration, "The Negro Family: The Case for National Action"; Charles Murray's 1984 book, *Losing Ground: American*

Social Policy, 1950-1980; Bill Moyers' 1986 television documentary on the breakdown of Black families; William A. Galston's 1990 essay, "A Liberal-Democratic Case for the Two-Parent Family"; the 1991 National Commission on Children, chaired by Sen. Jay D. Rockefeller IV; Dan Quayle's aforementioned "Murphy Brown" speech in 1992; Barbara Dafoe Whitehead's 1993 magazine essay, "Dan Quayle Was Right"; Charles Murray's 1993 newspaper column, "The Coming White Underclass"; and David Blankenhorn's 1995 book, *Fatherless America*.

The purposeful bias in this list, readers should know, is that each item has served to expand recognition of father absence as a severe national problem. The list, in other words, does not contain works which have argued the opposite—that such radically changing faultily forms are either inevitable, or no big problem, or really quite salutary. Arguments such as these are cited, of course, though more in terms of context than featured presentation.[6] Readers might also note that Democrats and Republicans are about evenly split among the likes of Moynihan and Murray, Moyers and Quayle, et al. For purposes of additional context, the following surplus of numbers is horrifying.

Statistical Context[7]

- The number of children living only with their mother increased from 5.1 million in 1960 to 15.6 million in 1993.[8]
- About 40 percent of children living in fatherless households have not seen their fathers in at least a year. Of the remaining 60 percent, only 20 percent sleep in their father's home even one night a month. Only one in six see their father an average of once or more a week.[9]

- The US divorce rate nearly tripled between 1960 and 1980 before leveling off and declining slightly in the 1980s. Forty percent of all first marriages now end in divorce. This compares to 16 percent of all first marriages in 1960. No other nation has a higher rate of divorce.[10]
- Compared to children in intact families, children whose parents have divorced are much more likely to drop out of school, engage in premarital sex, and to become pregnant themselves outside of marriage. These effects hold even after controlling for parental and marital characteristics before divorce.[11]
- In general, the evidence suggests that remarriage neither reproduces nor restores the intact family structure, even when it brings more income and a second adult into the household. Children living with stepparents appear to be even more disadvantaged than children living in a stable single-parent family.[12]
- Almost half of unwed teenage mothers go on welfare within one year of their baby's birth. By the time their first child is five years old, 72 percent of white teens and 84 percent of Black teens have received Aid For Families with Dependent Children (APDC), the main welfare program in the United States.[13]
- According to a study of white families, daughters of single parents are 53 percent more likely to marry while still teenagers, 111 percent more likely to have children as teenagers, 164 percent more likely to have a premarital birth, and 92 percent more likely to dissolve their own marriages.[14]
- Sixty percent of America's rapists grew up in homes without fathers.[15]
- Seventy percent of juveniles in state reform institutions grew up in single or no-parent situations.[16]

- Seventy-two percent of adolescent murderers grew up without fathers.[17]
- Eighty percent of adolescents in psychiatric hospitals come from broken homes.[18]
- Three out of four teenage suicides occur in homes where a parent has been absent.[19]
- Premarital pregnancy, out-of-wedlock childbearing, and absent fathers are the most common predictors of child abuse.[20]
- Black babies born outside of marriage are four times more likely to receive no prenatal care than Black babies born in marriage. White infants born outside of marriage are five times more likely to receive no prenatal care than white babies born in marriage.[21]
- The mortality rate of infants born to college-educated but unmarried mothers is higher than for infants born to married high-school dropouts.[22]
- Fatherless children are five times more likely to live in poverty compared to children living with both parents.[23]
- Overall, 77 percent of white children under the age of 18 in the United States lived with both their parents in 1993, down from 91 percent in 1960. For Black children, the proportions were 36 percent in 1993, compared to 67 percent in 1960.[24]

So much for statistical prologue. We will never be far from or lack for additionally depressing numbers below.

The Moynihan Report

For a variety of reasons, the so-called "Moynihan Report," written in 1965, remains the most salient document of the last three decades on family breakdown in the United States. This is so for both sound and unfair reasons; for what it actually argued, as well as for the routinely confused way in which it was received.

Daniel Patrick Moynihan, a Democrat, is now in his fourth term as a US Senator from New York. A social scientist by training, he wrote the report—officially called The Negro Family: The Case for National Action—while an Assistant Secretary of Labor in President Lyndon Baines Johnson's Administration. In truth, his less-than 50 pages of text and tables reported nothing dramatically new, as he wrote about the effects of family disintegration and its related problems in the tradition of distinguished Black scholars such as E. Franklin Frazier and Kenneth Clark. Nonetheless, the painful commotion the report generated led directly to two decades of near public silence on the subject of fatherlessness generally, and fatherlessness in the African-American community most precisely.[25]

As we will see, much important empirical research on families was, in fact, conducted during that roughly 20-year period, from the mid-1960s to mid-1980s, with important examples of those efforts cited in the "Statistical Context" just above. But these activities— essential as they have proved to be—took place largely in offices and libraries behind the scenes. Few academics, elected officials or other public figures went out of their way during this span to seek public attention on the topic, given the absurd charges of racism thrown at Moynihan, as well as the gross misreading of his argument by many civil rights activists, others on the left, plus many journalists. He also was undercut by some of his own colleagues in the Johnson Administration. What did Moynihan (who is white) write and advocate to provoke all this?[26]

What the Report Said—and What Others Claimed It Said

"At the heart of the deterioration of the fabric of Negro society," Moynihan wrote, "is the deterioration of the Negro family. It is the fundamental source of the weakness of the Negro community at the present time."[27]

According to Rainwater and Yancey, Moynihan "sought to present a sharply focused argument leading to the conclusion that the government's economic and social welfare programs, existing and prospective ones, should be systematically designed to encourage the stability of the Negro family." It was Moynihan's view, they wrote, that too many Black marriages broke up and too many Black children were born out of wedlock because of the "systematic weakening of the position of the Negro male."

> Slavery, reconstruction, urbanization, and unemployment [Rainwater and Yancey wrote in characterizing Moynihan's analysis] had produced a problem as old as America and as new as the April unemployment rate. This problem of unstable families in turn was a central feature of the tangle of pathology of the urban ghetto, involving problems of delinquency, crime, school dropouts, unemployment, and poverty.[28]

Citing US Bureau of the Census and other data, Moynihan noted that while one-tenth of all white children were then living in "broken homes," one-third of all "nonwhite" children were living in such situations in 1960.[29] Similarly, he showed how the nonwhite out-of-wedlock birthrate was almost eight times higher than the white rate in 1963: 23.6 percent compared to 3.07 percent.[30]

For all the discomfort and anger it engendered among progressives in government, universities, civil rights organizations and the media, the Moynihan Report was an exquisitely progressive document, as the very brief Rainwater and Yancey excerpts above should make clear. In no way did Moynihan lay blame on Blacks themselves; in every way he indicted the nation's history of slavery and racial sin. And by focusing on the need to achieve equality of results, not just of opportunity, the report also helped construct the very foundation for affirmative action.

Nevertheless, while some on the left did defend Moynihan—saying that it was ridiculous to think of him as a bigot, and acknowledging that he really wasn't saying anything that hadn't already honorably been said by others[31]—criticism and perplexity were often severe.

Regarding the media, Rainwater and Yancey suggest, perhaps too kindly, that, "most of the distortion that took place was the inevitable result of the way the press handles 'social problem' reporting, with its tendency to think in terms of what is wrong with individuals rather than institutions and to concentrate on personal experiences and suffering rather than on the more impersonal forces behind personal experience."[32]

Such dynamics and pressures, however, could not explain the animus toward the report by critics such as William Ryan, a Boston psychologist and civil rights activist who would soon become better known for coining the phrase "blaming the victim." He had representative things like this to say about the Moynihan Report later in 1965:

> Unemployment, the new ideologists tell us, results from the breakdown of Negro family life; poor education of Negroes results from "cultural deprivation"; the slum conditions endured by so many Negro families is the result of lack of "acculturation" of Southern rural migrants.[33]

"[W]e are in danger," Ryan concluded, "of being reduced into de-emphasizing discrimination as the overriding cause of the Negroes' current status of inequality."[34]

The very short answer to this last charge (which was consonant with other condemnations at the time) is obviously no: Moynihan had not de-emphasized discrimination at all. He had forcefully cited it as the prime reason for instability among Black families—which, in turn, contributed to various "pathologies."

Yes, by current understandings, the Moynihan Report might be considered more of a conservative than liberal statement (in part anyway), as it focused with unusual frankness on the kinds of statistical data about families that conservatives are more likely than liberals to publicize. In addition, it was unhesitant in recognizing that fathers matter; once again, more of a latter-day conservative as opposed to liberal trait.

But at the very same time, it was a very liberal document by both past and present definitions, as it spoke with not-yet-spoiled confidence about the capacity of government—particularly the federal government—to make the lives of African-Americans measurably better via programs to increase employment, improve education and the like. While it's true that many criticized the report because it dwelled more on analysis than remedies, its subtitle after all was "The Case for National Action," and Moynihan himself at the time was a key architect of President Johnson's "War on Poverty."[35]

The Moynihan Report in Perspective

In addition to what already has been suggested, many other useful things can be said about Moynihan's study (as well as his associated writing at the time), 30 years later. The first has to do with his prescience. Something he wrote then about "inviting chaos" has come to be quoted frequently. Here is the full passage:

> From the wild Irish slums of the 19th century Eastern seaboard, to the riot-torn suburbs of Los Angeles, there is one unmistakable lesson in American history; a community that allows a large number of men to grow up in broken families, dominated by women, never acquiring any stable relationship to male authority, never acquiring any set of rational expectations about the future—that community asks for and gets chaos. Crime, violence, unrest, disorder—most particularly the furious, unrestrained lashing out at the whole

social structure—that is not only to be expected; it is very near to inevitable. And it is richly deserved.[36]

As a sociologist, Moynihan, as witness the preceding quote, naturally emphasized matters of family structure. But the primary prism through which he analyzed and prescribed was an economic one. Jobs—good jobs—for Black men were critical if Black families were to have a chance. Moreover, he wrote, government ought to actively see to it, one way or the other, that more Black men indeed had such opportunities. As with other parts and aspects of the report, these themes were misread and discounted, too.

The Moynihan Report, in fact, provided early aid in understanding what was to develop into three different, albeit connected ways of thinking about fatherlessness and poverty, especially in underclass communities.

One is the economic argument Marriage has become less of a living institution mainly because fewer men are equipped to contribute financially to families, and women thereby have come to view them as less "marriageable." William Julius Wilson of the University of Chicago, also (interestingly) a sociologist, is the leading scholar associated with this view, particularly as it applies to the loss of relatively good-paying jobs for entry-level workers in inner-city neighborhoods.[37]

A second tack is rooted in public policies: Programs such as Aid to Families with Dependent Children, goes the argument, make matters worse by seducing recipients into undisciplined choices about sex, schooling, and so forth, by driving down the personal price to be paid for laxity and failure. Such programs, as compassionately intended as they may be, nonetheless subsidize the very problems they are (poorly) designed to fill. Charles Murray, a political scientist, is the most vigorous and rigorous proponent of this interpretation.[38]

The third leg is grounded in the very culture: What can anyone expect other than an increase in out-of-wedlock births and divorce, goes this argument, when the media, universities, churches and other defenders of middle-class values lose their bearings and confidence; when basic rules—particularly those regarding sex and marriage—bend and break under counter-cultural assault, as in the 1960s and afterwards? Figures best identified with this view include William Bennett, a philosopher and writer who served as Secretary of Education under President Reagan; David Blankenhorn, a former community organizer and now president of the Institute for American Values and chairman of the National Fatherhood Initiative; and economist Glenn Loury.[39]

Loury, for instance, recently wrote:

> People are not automata; their behavior in matters sexual may not be easily manipulated by changing their marginal tax rates or their recipiency status under welfare programs. It is my conviction that the problem of illegitimacy and family breakdown are, at base, cultural and moral problems, which require broad societal action in addition to legislative change.... [I]n every community there are agencies of moral and cultural development which seek to shape the ways in which individuals conceive of their duties to themselves, of their obligations to each other, and of their responsibilities before God. These mainly though not exclusively religious institutions are the natural sources of legitimate moral teaching—indeed, the only sources.[40]

Needless to say, none of these approaches stand alone, and all recognize (to one degree or another) the effects of racism, past and present. While focusing on the economic dimension, Moynihan instructively dealt with all three. As for the rest of this paper, we will return to each of them.

A final point about the landmark Moynihan Report before moving more rapidly through the 30 years which have followed.

Was it really surprising that the report caused the passionate and intimidating fight that it did? Of course not, as not only did Moynihan take on keenly sensitive questions of family life, he combined them with keenly sensitive questions of race. Yet it isn't as if the two could have been neatly separated, either then or now. For if American families in general have been flailing for decades, African-American families have been in even greater trouble over the period.

The Interregnum

I did not realize until after selecting the nine or ten main studies, television shows, and other documents and events chronicled in this paper that the gap between the first and second items stretched for almost 20 years. As noted, this is not to say that nothing of consequence happened regarding fatherlessness in the United States between the release of the Moynihan Report in 1965 and Charles Murray's *Losing Ground* in 1984; only that very little happened publicly.[41]

Or, much more precisely, that very litte happened aloud in terms of seriously questioning the wisdom and effects —especially the effects on children—of exploding out-of-wedlock and divorce rates. Not only was the spirit of the age far from conducive to such skepticism, it was decisively hostile to it, as it was during that period when radical forms of feminism and other 'liberating"[42] (and simultaneously cloistering) ideologies were remarkably successful in curtailing debate to their tastes. As Moynihan gave early evidence, to violate the rules of dogma and language of the various "progressive" movements then feverishly underway, was to invite great trouble.

Yet as also suggested above, much of the serious empirical research that is now regularly cited as demonstrating that children have been very poorly served by family deterioration took place during the 1970s and thereabouts. For instance, according to Barbara Dafoe Whitehead:

The National Survey on Children, conducted by the psychologist Nicholas Zill, had set out in 1976 to track a large sample of children aged seven to eleven. It also interviewed the children's parents and teachers. It surveyed its subjects again in 1981 and 1987. By the tune of its third round of interviews the eleven-year-olds of 1976 were the twenty-two-year-olds of 1987. The California Children of Divorce Study, directed by Judith Wallerstein, a clinical psychologist, had also been going on for a decade. E. Mavis Hetherington, of the University of Virginia, was conducting a similar study of children from both intact and divorced families. For the first time it was possible to test the optimistic view against a large and longitudinal body of evidence.[43]

The results of this collective test were commonsensical: Kids (and their moms in particular) were being hurt. Whereas children had been imagined as unrealistically "adaptable," and whereas "optimistic" writers such as Carol Stack had argued (in Whitehead's words) that "the single-mother family is an economically resourceful and socially embedded institution," it was now objectively clear that the opposite was true. Off-stage, scholars such as Zill, Wallerstein, Sara McLanahan and Irwin Garfinkel[44] had put the "interregnum" to good use, making it much more difficult down the road for Pollyannish strictures to reign and rule.[45]

Losing Ground

More potently than any other document over the 30 years under review, Losing Ground: American Social Policy, 1950-1980, argued not only that welfare-state programs—as well as consonant policies such as affirmative action and bilingual education—were ineffective in alleviating social problems, but that such ventures tended to actually make matters worse. Such "matters" include fatherlessness. "I will suggest," Murray wrote:

that changes in incentives that occurred between 1960 and 1970 may be used to explain many of the [deleterious] trends we have been discussing.... All were results that could have been predicted (indeed, in some instances were predicted) from the changes that social policy made in the rewards and penalties, carrots and sticks, that govern human behavior.[46]

Exactly what kinds of rewards and penalties, carrots and sticks did he refer to in this book, released in 1984? In addition to grounding his argument in detailed statistical analysis, Murray used two imaginary characters, "Harold" and "Phyllis," to speculate about how poor people with "few chips" might take advantage of their available options. Here's an example:

The bottom line is this [in 1970 compared to 1960, when governmental programs were less generous]: Harold can get married and work forty hours a week in a hot, tiresome job; or he can live with Phyllis and their baby without getting married, not work and have more disposable income [because of welfare]. From an economic point of view, getting married is dumb. From a noneconomic point of view, it involves him in a legal relationship that has no payoff for him. If he thinks he may sometime tire of Phyllis and fatherhood, the 1970 rules thus provide a further incentive for keeping the relationship off the books. [Emphasis supplied.]

Of Phyllis' possibilities, and those of young women in similar circumstances, Murray likewise wrote:

It is commonly written that poor teenaged girls have babies so that they will have someone to love them. This may be true for some. But one need not look for psychological explanations. Under the rules of 1970 [which likely have grown even more enabling in the 25 years since], it was rational on grounds of dollars and cents for a poor unmarried woman who found herself to be pregnant to have and keep the baby even if she did not particularly want a child....

If Phyllis and Harry marry and he is employed, she will lose her AFDC benefits. His minimum wage job at the laundry will produce no more income than she can make [through welfare], and, not incidentally, he, not she, will have control of the check. In exchange for giving up this degree of independence, she gains no real security. Harold's job is not nearly as stable as the welfare system.[47]

It goes without saying that Murray was not well-received across the spectrum. He was vigorously accused by many on the left as not only distorting the analysis and numbers, but doing so in mean-spirited and perhaps racist ways.[48] Charles Murray is as well-practiced as anyone in American intellectual life in defending himself; he needs no extra bolstering here. But the fact is, in no way was he guilty of such transgressions, and one can now detect a near-straight line between his critique of the American welfare system in the mid-1980s and near-universal recognition today of that system's perversely unintended consequences.

The fact, moreover, that elimination of virtually all welfare programs is now sometimes viewed in even polite quarters as a legitimate and ultimately benign idea is directly tied to Murray taking that position in *Losing Ground*—a recommendation, not incidentally, which provided many critics with an easy excuse at the time for dismissing everything he wrote. Similarly, the fact that the welfare-reform debate has changed fundamentally over the last two years—from emphasizing helping single mothers find jobs outside of their homes to dramatically reducing the number of children growing up in single-family homes in the first place—is once again a product of Murray's scholarship and advocacy. Though in this instance, the most important document was his 1993 newspaper essay, "The Coming White Underclass."

416

"The Vanishing Family—Crisis in Black America"

If *Losing Ground* was a breakthrough in intellectual and nearby circles, Bill Moyers' 1986 television documentary, "The Vanishing Family—Crisis in Black America," was a watershed in broader circles.[49] Prior to each, obviously, lips hadn't been zippered entirely on questions of families and fathers—including Black families and fathers. But these two "events"—one a learned book and the other a network TV show—not only increased the salience of such tough issues, but also made it more acceptable for scholars as well as other citizens to talk more freely about them out in the open. They did so a bit, anyway.

Moyers came to network television unconventionally, by way of a 1960s stint in the White House. He had been a very senior assistant in the Johnson Administration, who according to Rainwater and Yancey, had been "fascinated" back then by the Moynihan Report.[50] This is how two writers described his two-hour portrait of young Black men and women in Newark, New Jersey, first broadcast in January 1986. The first is by the sociologist and theologian Michael Novak..[51]

> According to one of the bravest TV documentaries ever made…there is a crisis in Black America…. Only a tiny fraction of Black children born in America has a father at home during all 16 years of childhood. Nearly 60 percent are born out of wedlock. Such matriarchy is proving colossally destructive.

Insofar as "mere is no basic alternative except the family for character formation," Novak argued, "the vanishing Black family raises what Harvard's Glenn C. Loury calls "The Moral Quandry of the Black Community." Dare one call attention to this sinking, Titanic-like underclass culture? Dare one not?"

THE FAMILY IN GLOBAL TRANSITION

Novak said of the "immensely attractive young women and young men" in the program: "How bright and alive they seem, yet how ineffably sad."

He quotes Timothy, then 26, who had already fathered six children by four different women. "Well," he said, "the majority of the mothers are on welfare.... What I'm not doing, the government does." This didn't seem to "bother" Timothy at all, Novak reported.[52]

Clarinda, then 15, is quoted for good measure: 'I wouldn't want no man holding me down, because I think I could make it as a single parent"—as her mother had tried, as well as her grandmother.

Newsweek magazine, for its part, called "The Vanishing Family" perhaps "the most important documentary in recent memory."[53] Among other things, the brief review noted how "Mother's Day" in one woman's Newark neighborhood (according to the program) came not only in May, but every month when welfare checks arrive.

"For all the depressing insights," the piece concludes, "the program ends with a refreshing idealism about bringing values back. 'If you say it in your corner and I say it in my corner, and everybody's saying it,' concludes Carolyn Wallace, a local activist, 'it's going to be like a drumbeat.'"

Moyers' television documentary and Moynihan's government report were separated by two decades. They were also, quite obviously, two fundamentally different enterprises. But whereas the Moynihan Report was contorted into a barrier to further public consideration, "The Vanishing Family" seemed to serve a constructively opposite end. Again, this is not to say that debate became safely and comfortably freewheeling; just better than it was. A kind of ice age had been broken. As for why the improvement, two thoughts seem soundest.

Moynihan was relatively unknown in 1965, meaning that many had not yet come to accept his good intentions as a given. Moyers, on the other hand, was a certified liberal (meaning that he was accepted on racial issues), and had been thought as such for more than 20 years. We will see immediately below how William Galston's 1990 essay about the importance of two-parent families proved unusually influential, in part, precisely because of his good progressive name.

Of probably greater consequence, however, is that by the mid-1980s, familial conditions in the United States—particularly but not solely among African-Americans—had ruptured badly enough so that evasion began to give way to modest candor. Enough people were finally afraid enough.

"A Liberal-Democratic Case for the Two-Parent Family"

An exchange of complimentary notes about what the other had written, either in late 1990 or early 1991, between a former assistant secretary of education in the Reagan Administration, Chester E. Finn, Jr., and the former issues director in Walter Mondale's 1984 presidential campaign, William A. Galston, was illustrative of a this then-emerging, very rough consensus about family failure.

Republican Finn, in an essay about endangered families and children, had written in 1990:

> We know that a well-functioning society must condemn behavior that results in people having children who are not prepared to be good parents. I find it astonishing that, in the fact of that knowledge, today we seem to attach more opprobrium to dropping out of school, experimenting on a cat, or uttering nasty remarks on campus than we do to giving birth to what, not so many years ago, were called "illegitimate" children.... Children fare better in some circumstances than others, and no decent society will remain silent when it comes to pointing out which circumstances are which.[54]

Democrat Galston wrote similarly at about the same time:

A healthy liberal democracy, I suggest, is more than an artful arrangement of institutional devices. It requires, as well, the right kinds of citizens, possessing the virtues appropriate to a liberal democratic community. A growing body of empirical evidence developed over the past generation supports the proposition that a stable, intact family makes an irreplacable contribution to the creation of such citizens, and thus to promoting both individual and social well-being. For that reason, among others, the community as a whole has a legitimate interest in promoting the formation and sustaining the stability of such families.[55]

In the exchange of letters, Finn essentially told Galston that he liked his paper, and Galston returned the salute. This was an encouraging symbolic event given the extent to which leading Democrats and others on the political left were still muffling themselves on "traditional" family questions so as not to offend feminists, civil rights leaders and other major components of the party's base.

Galston's paper was very much a breakthrough. As we will see below, a slightly different version of it[56] was key in persuading Democratic members (plus staffers) of the National Commission on Children, in 1991, to endorse unusually direct language on the importance of two-parent families. Similarly, if not the paper itself, then certainly Galston himself and his circle of colleagues, were influential in shaping candidate Bill Clinton's 1992 successful campaign rhetoric about paternal responsibility and welfare reform, among other things.[57] At root, "A Liberal-Democratic Case" gave essential and welcome cover to men and women on the left side of the continuum who had perhaps long shared its ideas, but who had been reluctant for all the aforementioned reasons to speak out. In addition to the just-cited paragraph, what else did Galston, a political theorist, say?

Of poverty, he argued that "after a decade-long economic expansion," the poverty rate for children is "nearly twice as high as it is among elderly Americans." And that "it is no exaggeration to say" that "the best anti-poverty program for children is a stable, intact family." (Emphasis in the original.)[58]

Yet if the "economic effects of breakdown are clear," he wrote, the "non-economic effects are just now coming into focus." Here, Galston noted that while "scholars over the past generation have disagreed over the consequences of divorce, work done during the 1980s has on balance reinforced the view that children of broken families labor under major non-economic disadvantages."[59] He quotes Karl Zinsmeister on this "emerging consensus":

> There is a mountain of scientific evidence showing that when families disintegrate, children often end up with intellectual, physical, and emotional scars that persist for life.... We talk about the drug crisis, the education crisis, and the problems of teen pregnancy and juvenile crime. But all these ills trace back predominantly to one source: broken families.[60]

Of the "education Crisis," more specifically, Galston contended that "recent studies confirm" what many educators have suspected for a while: "[T]he disintegrating American family is at the root of America's declining educational achievement" (Emphasis in the original.)[61]

In light of all this, Galston was nonetheless and appropriately compelled to caution that a "general preference" for two-parent families does not mean that all marriages ought to survive, or that "endorsement of the two-parent family" be confused for "nostalgia for the single-breadwinner 'traditional' family of the 1950s." His left flank thus protected (at least a little), Galston went on to say the following in perhaps the essay's most important passage:

Having entered these disclaimers, I want to stress that my approach is frankly normative. The focus is on what must be a key objective of our society: raising children who are prepared intellectually, physically, morally, and emotionally—to take their place as law-abiding and independent members of the community, able to sustain themselves and their families and to perform their duties as citizens. Available evidence supports the conclusion that on balance, the intact two-parent family is best suited to this task. We must then resist the easy relativism of the proposition that different family structures represent nothing more than "alternative lifestyles"—a belief that undermined the Carter Administration's efforts to develop a coherent family policy and that continues to cloud the debate even today. (Emphasis in the original.)[62]

Which takes us to the previously mentioned National Commission on Children, more commonly known as the "Rockefeller Commission on Children," after its chairman, Sen. Jay D. Rockefeller IV of West Virginia.

The National Commission on Children

It should not constitute anything remarkable to declare that fathers matter. But it was remarkable—which is to say it was big news on television talk shows and the like—when a federal panel, with more liberal than conservative members, unanimously endorsed language like this in 1991: "Children do best when they have the personal involvement and material support of a father and a mother and when both parents fulfill their responsibility to be loving providers."[63]

Suffice it to say that chances would have been slim for such a straight-arrow proposition to have been included in any similar federal report any time earlier in the 30 years under review. (Also suffice it to say that few report writers would have ever considered the need for such a statement anytime prior to 1965, as no one had yet seriously proposed that fathers are superfluous.) But along with a recommendation to allocate $40 billion in the first year for a refundable child tax credit, the report's most noted portion was its strong endorsement of two-parent families. "There can be little doubt," it said,

> that having both parents living and working together in a stable marriage can shield children from a variety of risks. Rising rates of divorce, out-of- wedlock childbearing, and absent parents are not just manifestations of alternative lifestyles, they are patterns of adult behavior that increase children's risks of negative consequences. Although in some cases divorce is the least harmful outcome of a troubled marriage, today's high rate of family breakdown is troubling.[64]

Naturally, the report also said that the nation "must never fail to reach out and protect single-parent families as well," and that, "Many single parents make extraordinary efforts to raise children in difficult circumstances."[65] Yet such boilerplate —necessary and gracious as it was—could not subtract from the significant step forward represented by the unambiguous, if culturally and politically pregnant passage right before it: the one about two-parent families being important. As we will quickly see, this advance did not necessarily clear the way for Vice President Dan Quayle to speak safely on the question of single parenthood during the 1992 presidential campaign, but it was, all things and history considered, real progress.[66]

"Murphy Brown"

Right before the (real) Mother's Day in May 1992, historian Barbara Dafoe Whitehead wrote a syndicated newspaper column about the impending birth of a baby to a fictional, unmarried television character, Murphy Brown, the star of a successful comedy series of the same name. Whitehead was neither amused nor impressed. "Baby Brown," she wrote, "points to our society's acceptance of out-of-wedlock child-birth. Certainly over the past several decades, the shame and blame attached to unmarried pregnancy has steadily eroded. But with Murphy Brown, unwed childbearing becomes positively appealing."[67]

Very shortly afterwards, and inspired by Whitehead's column, then-Vice President Dan Quayle delivered what came to be known as his ``Murphy Brown speech," although its specific reference to the show consisted of only one sentence—a grand total of 39 words.

> It doesn't help matters," Quayle said in a reselection speech, "when prime time TV has Murphy Brown—a character who supposedly epitomizes today's intelligent, highly paid, professional woman—mocking the importance of fathers, by bearing a child alone, and calling it just another 'lifestyle' choice."[68]

At which point a fair amount of hell—and mocking hilarity—broke loose.[69]

It is true, of course, that if someone other than the routinely and unfairly belittled Quayle had said what he had said about Murphy Brown the reaction might have been more sober. Commentators might even have paid more than passing attention to other things he said in what was a substantial speech about families, poverty, values and, most immediately, the Los Angeles riots, which had erupted just weeks earlier. "I believe," the vice president said, "the lawless social anarchy which we saw is directly related to the breakdown of family structure, personal responsibility and social order in too many areas of our society." He also said:

> Children need love and discipline. They need mothers and fathers. A welfare check is not a husband. The state is not a father. It is from parents that children learn how to behave in society; it is from parents above all that children come to

understand values and themselves as men and women, mothers and fathers. . .

Ultimately...marriage is a moral issue that requires cultural consensus, and the use of social sanctions. Bearing babies irresponsibly is, simply, wrong. Failing to support children one has fathered is wrong. We must be unequivocal about this.... Now is the time to make the discussion [about values] public.

As it happened, I was participating in a program at the Minneapolis-based *Star Tribune* on the afternoon that Quayle spoke, and I got to sit in on the daily meeting at which lead stories are chosen for the following day's newspaper. When it was time for the appropriate editor to offer his favorites, he proposed the Quayle story with no small dripping of sarcasm: "Quayle," he said, "is even criticizing Murphy Brown now." The point is not that this one editor at this one newspaper saw little more than a joke; the point, rather, is that Quayle's good speech was received by many with more silliness than seriousness.

First reactions by President Bush and his senior aides, one must note, were not much more encouraging, as they perfectly reflected the deep and continuing ambivalence and political nervousness implicit in the issue. "Quayle was not helped," a reporter wrote a few days after the speech, "by the uncertain reaction from the White House, where press secretary Marlin Fitzwater and then President Bush himself seemed hesitant to join the vice president in his assault on Hollywood. Aides traveling with Quayle said they spent much of Wednesday morning [the day after the speech] on the telephone trying to convince colleagues in the White House that Quayle had not committed a serious blunder."[70]

As for the issue of fatherlessness itself, the "Murphy Brown" episode demonstrated that while progress continued to be made in discussing it with a measure of frankness, both at the upper reaches of government and in the nation more widely, the topic remained an exceptionally tough and divisive one. It was in this context that Whitehead, in April 1993, published the most compelling popular review of the scholarly literature on absent fathers up until (and since) then. That it was titled "Dan Quayle Was Right"[71] and ran in a venerable mainline magazine—*The Atlantic Monthly*—only showcased it better.

"Dan Quayle Was Right"

Whitehead opened by offering a sampling of a "growing body of social-scientific evidence" showing that children in families disrupted by divorce and out-of-wedlock births, generally speaking, do worse than other children on various measures of well-being. For instance, 22 percent of children in one-parent families will suffer poverty during their childhoods for seven years or more versus only two percent for children in intact families; or that children in disrupted families are at much higher risk of physical and sexual abuse; etcetera. Yet despite this increasing evidence, "it is nearly impossible," Whitehead wrote, "to discuss changes in family structure without provoking angry protest."

Many people, she said, view such discussions as little more than attacks on single mothers and their children, while others believe that major changes in family structure, though "regrettable," are impossible to reverse, and hence society is obliged to adapt accordingly. Such views, Whitehead acknowledged, "are not to be dismissed," as they help to explain why family structure "is such an explosive issue for Americans."

> The debate about it is not simply about the social-scientific evidence, although that is surely an important part of the discussion. It is also a debate over deeply held and often conflicting values. How do we begin to reconcile our long-standing belief in equality and diversity with an impressive body of evidence that suggests that not all family structures produce equal outcomes for children?...How do we uphold

the freedom of adults to pursue individual happiness in their private relationships and at the same time respond to the needs of children for stability, security, and permanence in their family lives?

This is why, she wrote (referring to the Dan Quayle-Murphy Brown altercation of a year earlier), that "every time the issue of family structure has been raised, the response has been first controversy, then retreat, and finally silence."[72]

From another angle, Whitehead asked why—given the power of the evidence—had rampant family disruption not come to be viewed as a "national crisis"? Here she talked of a "shift in the social metric," from child well-being to adult well-being. However difficult divorce and out-of-wedlock births may be, "both of these behaviors can hold out the promise of greater adult choice, freedom, and happiness."[73]

Much of "Dan Quayle Was Right" is devoted to three "bold new assumptions" about family change that Whitehead argued took hold in the 1970s—but which subsequent research has refuted.

- First assumption: Women are now financially able to be mothers without being wives.
- Second assumption: Family disruption does not cause lasting harm to children—in fact, it can actually enrich their lives.
- Third assumption: Such new family forms and "diversity" will make America a better place.

Her key summarizing paragraph is worth quoting at length:

Not a single one of the assumptions underlying [the view that such family change has led to social progress] can be sustained against the empirical evidence. Single-parent families are not able to do well economically on a mother's income. In fact, most teeter on the economic brink, and many fall into poverty and welfare dependency. Growing up

in a disrupted family does not enrich a child's life or expand
the number of adults committed to the child's well-being. In
fact disrupted families threaten the psychological well-being
of children and diminish the investment of adult time and
money in them. Family diversity in the form of increasing
numbers of single- parent and stepparent families does not
strengthen the social fabric. It dramatically weakens and
undermines society, placing new burdens on schools, courts,
prisons, and the welfare system.[74]

Whitehead's frequently cited essay increased popular
understanding of father absence. It also modestly defused the
subject, making it a fitter one for public conversation in the
first place. But maybe most beneficially, "Dan Quayle Was
Right" made it more difficult for those who professionally
should know better—academics, journalists, politicians—to
plead continued ignorance about the demonstrated effects of
fatherlessness.

"The Coming White Underclass"
Yet if it was Whitehead who succeeded in further showing
that the problem posed by father absence confronting the
United States in the early 1990s was real and large, it was
Charles Murray who most dramatically encapsulated just how
immense it really was. "Every once in a while," he wrote (in
what was described as "the most faxed op-ed of the year"), the
"sky really is falling, and this seems to be the case with the
latest national figures on illegitimacy."[75]

Writing in the fall of 1993, and using data which had just
been made available, he noted that 1.2 million American
children had been born out of wedlock in 1991, which was
"within a hair" of 30 percent of all live births. Out-of-wedlock
births to Black women, he reported, had reached 68 percent in
1991, with the figure "typically" in excess of 80 percent in
inner cities.

"But the Black story, however dismaying," Murray wrote, "is old news. The trend that threatens the US is white illegitimacy. Matters have not yet gotten out of hand, but they are on the brink. If we want to act, now is the time."

More than 700,000 babies, he wrote, were born to single white women in 1991, representing 22 percent of all white births. (Recall that the out-of-wedlock birth rate reported by Moynihan for Black women less than 30 years earlier, in 1963, was just over 23 percent.) Murray argued that "elite wisdom" held that this trend in white births was cutting across social classes, "as if the increase in Murphy Browns were pushing the trendline." But such a view was inaccurate, he said. Instead, women with college degrees contributed only four percent of white nonmarital births, while women with high school educations or less contributed 82 percent. Likewise, women with family incomes of $75,000 or more contributed but one percent of out-of-wedlock births, while women with family incomes under $20,000 contributed 69 percent of them.

"White illegitimacy," Murray wrote, "is overwhelmingly a lower-class phenomenon," which "brings us to the emergence of a white underclass"—something that the United States has never had.

Why, exactly, did he see this as a huge problem?

> As the spatial concentration of illegitimacy reaches critical mass, we should expect the deterioration to be as fast among low-income whites in the 1990s as it was among low-income Blacks in the 1960s. My proposition is that illegitimacy is the single most important social problem of our time—more important than crime, drugs, poverty, illiteracy, welfare or homelessness because it drives everything else.

While acknowledging that the "steep climb" in Black non-marital births had been "calamitous" for African-Americans, he said that the "brutal truth is that American society as a whole could survive when illegitimacy became epidemic within a relatively small ethnic community."[76] The nation as a whole, he concluded, could not survive "the same epidemic among whites."

As one might expect, this warning made an impression. And as a sign that Americans were increasingly prepared to address the problem of fatherlessness, Murray subsequently reported that the piece had not led critics to vilify him in the way he thought they might—as they did, for instance, after Losing Ground, and as they would again after The Bell Curve. Instead, he was interviewed a lot and invited to speak frequently.

Also making an impression, as noted earlier, were Murray's recommendations, including his proposal to "end all [governmental] economic support for single mothers." We will turn to these recommendations in the Conclusion.

Fatherless America

If Murray's "The Coming White Underclass" was unusually pointed, David Blankenhorn's *Fatherless America Confronting Our Most Urgent Social Problem*, published earlier this year [1995], is unusually nuanced.[77] Blankenhorn does not deal with questions on out-of-wedlock births, divorce, separation, desertion and such narrowly. Instead, he discusses the ways in which the very idea of fatherhood in the United States has been reconstructed (which is to say, emasculated) as a cultural fact and principle. He writes, for example:

> Men in general, and fathers in particular, are increasingly viewed as superfluous to family life: either expendable or as part of the problem. Masculinity itself, understood as anything other than a rejection of what it has traditionally meant to be male, is typically treated with suspicion and even hostility in our cultural discourse. Consequently, our society is now manifestly unable to sustain, or even find reason to believe in, fatherhood as a distinctive domain of male activity.[78]

Does every child deserve a father?, Blankenhorn says our current answer "hovers" someplace between "no" and "not necessarily."[79] In contrast, he describes the length to which Washington tried not to draft men with children during World War II, as it was commonly understood 50 years ago that fathers were, in fact, very important in the lives of their sons and daughters.

Making a similar point statistically, Blankenhorn says that while the "principal" cause of fatherlessness is now "paternal choice," at the turn of the century, middle-aged widowed men surpassed middle-aged divorced men by more than 20 to 1.[80]

In dissecting America's new "cultural script," Blankenhorn writes of "Old Fathers," "New Fathers," "Deadbeat Dads," "Visiting Fathers," and "Nearby Guys," among other variations on a diminished theme. Or as summarized by Chester E. Finn, Jr., Blankenhorn investigates "how our contemporary obsessions with widening individual rights, pursuing pleasure, rejecting authority, defying tradition, mocking institutions, relativizing values, diminishing religion, and sloughing off responsibility have conspired to weaken the family and devalue fatherhood."[81]

In language akin to Murray's, Blankenhorn contends: 'the most urgent domestic challenge facing the United States at the close of the twentieth century, is the re-creation of fatherhood as a vital social role for men. At stake is nothing less than the success of the American experiment. For unless," he writes,

> we reverse the trend of fatherlessness, no other set of accomplishments— not economic growth or prison construction or welfare reform or better schools—will succeed in arresting the decline of child well-being and the spread of male violence. To tolerate the trend of fatherlessness is to accept the inevitability of continued societal recession.[82]

To complete the midyear cycle, if you will, compare Blankenhorn's strictures with Moynihan's 1965 warning: "[A] community that allows a large number of men to grow up in broken families, dominated by women, never acquiring any stable relationship to male authority, never acquiring any set of rational expectations about the future—that community asks for and gets chaos."[83]

Similar as the two monitions are, they are separated by three decades in which politicians, academics, journalists and other elites made reluctant progress in recognizing that which has been painfully true about fatherlessness all along. Which is another way of saying that while Blankenhorn is correct in describing "fatherhood" as a still-abridged cultural idea, that's not to say that father absence as a sociological and psychological calamity is now dismissed as quickly as it has been over most of the period.[84] Or in the words of this paper's tide, the advance—halting as it has been—nevertheless has been real, from Moynihan to "my goodness," as empirical evidence and everyday experience have grown prodigious.

Conclusion

Another way of making this last point is to acknowledge that with any complex social phenomenon, one can find almost whatever patterns and anomalies one seeks to find. By definition, in other words, the patterns and interpretations traced in a paper like this are fair game for challenge. I would hope, however, most readers would find the judgments of this essay—while animated by a definite point of view—to be fair and reasonable.

What of solutions to rampant father absence? This paper has had little to say about them so far.

Back in the discussion of The Moynihan Report, I introduced the three main approaches which have developed over the last generation for making sense of family disintegration: The economic frame, best associated with William Julius

Wilson[85]; the policy frame, best associated with Charles Murray; and the cultural tack, best associated with the likes of William Bennett, David Blankenhorn and Glenn Loury. One could also add writer Myron Magnet here. Each approach comes with a package of "solutions" (or at least angles of attack), none of which engender more than modest confidence that they might actually work or that they may be politically feasible in the first place.

Wilson, for instance, argues that the problems of the "ghetto underclass" can be best addressed by a "comprehensive program that combines employment policies with social welfare policies and that features universal as opposed to race- or group-specific strategies." More specifically, he urges tight labor markets and economic growth; fiscal and monetary policy to increase the competitiveness of American goods; and a "national labor-market strategy to make the labor force more adaptable to changing economic opportunities."[86]

With all due respect to Professor Wilson, who is one of the nation's great sociologists, this is akin to what government already does, perhaps just marginally more so. There is virtually no reason to believe that such a policy course would make significant numbers of men newly "marriageable" in the eyes of significant numbers of women. And at any rate, Wilson's analysis and prescription have little bearing on fatherlessness in middle-class and more affluent populations.

The problem with Murray's recommendations is not that they are puny, but that they are the opposite, making them politically untenable—at least for now.

"To restore the rewards and penalties of marriage," Murray writes, "does not require social engineering. Rather, it requires that the state stop interfering with the natural forces that have done the job quite effectively for millennia."[87] This entails, he continues, restoring economic penalties to single parenthood. This translates, in turn, "into the first and central policy prescription: to end all economic support for single mothers," which is to say AFDC, subsidized housing, food stamps, an so forth (though not medical care for children themselves).

"How does a poor young mother survive without government support?" Murray asks. "The same way she has since time immemorial. If she wants to keep a child, she must enlist support from her parents, boyfriend, siblings, neighbors, church or philanthropies." The objectives of this change are three, Murray writes.

First, enlisting the help of others increases the likelihood of "other mature adults" involving themselves in raising the child.

Second, "We need to raise the probability that a young single woman who keeps her child is doing so volitionally and thoughtfully. Forcing her to find a way of supporting the child does this."

The third objective is to regenerate stigma. The pressure on relatives and others to pay for the "dolly of their children" will make out-of-wedlock births the "socially horrific" act they used to be, and "getting a girl pregnant" something that boys do at the risk of a shotgun. "Stigma and shotgun marriages," Murray writes, "may or may not be good for those on the receiving end, but their deterrent effect on others is wonderful—and indispensable."

Murray goes on to urge reforms such as making adoption more possible, spending more "lavishly" on orphanages, and "once again" making marriage "the sole legal institution through which parental rights and responsibilities are defined and exercised." But his core recommendation is the cutting off of public financial support for single mothers, an idea whose political time has not yet arrived.

Finally, the problem with Blankenhorn's proposals is that, as a culturalist, he commands no effective levers for changing much of anything decisively or quickly, as the "culture"— by definition—is everywhere and elusive.

Blankenhorn concludes Fatherless America with a dozen recommendations, ranging from every man in the United States signing a pro-fatherhood pledge; to the president of the United States issuing an annual report on the state of fatherhood nationally; to building a "broad new populist movement to empower families and strengthen community life"; to ending marriage disincentives in public housing; to regulating sperm banks.[88] Fine ideas perhaps, but collectively they make up no more than a germ of counterrevolution.

(My own stock answer to what might work to rebuild families is more impalpable still. "Nothing will get better," I usually predict with dark metaphysical and theological flair, "until more people grab their heads and say, 'My God, we can't keep committing suicide anymore.'" But, then, again—and with a bow to Loury—I really don't know of a potentially more potent answer.)

Two final points.

First, it's a fair criticism to charge that middle-class (formerly divorced) observers like myself are generally more apt to focus on out-of-wedlock births rather than on divorce when writing about father absence. This, even though, there are many more "visiting fathers" than welfare mothers.[89] I don't doubt that this paper may be guilty in this way.

And last, something doubtless can be learned from the fact that while Dan Quayle is no longer vice president of the United States, "Murphy Brown" is still a top-rated comedy show. Yes, I've suggested that rank-and-file Americans are more inclined than elites to stress cultural values and spiritual notions, as well as less inclined to swallow politically correct lines about "evolving" families and the like. Paraphrasing Blankenhorn, they are less likely to view fathers as interchangeable parts.

But the uncomfortable truth is that Candace Bergen, the actress who plays Murphy Brown, seemed to finish 1992 with almost as many commercial endorsements as Quayle got votes, and she has continued apace. Surely, one ought not read too much into this tidbit of popular culture, but it is a superb reflection of the many minds with which Americans of all stations view fatherlessness.

Notes

[1]US Department of Health and Human Services, *Vital Statistics of the United States, 1991, Volume 1, Natality* (Washington, DC: Government Printing Office, 1993). Wade F. Horn, *Father Facts* (Lancaster, PA: The National Fatherhood Initiative, 1995), p. iii.

[2]David Blankenhorn, *Fatherless America: Confronting Our Most Urgent Social Problem* (New York: Basic Books, 199S), p. 19.

[3]*Father Facts.*

[4]Alisa Bums, "Mother Headed Families: An International Perspective and the Case of Austria," *Social Policy Report 6* (Spring 1992). This citation, as well as a number of others over the next several pages, can be found in the aforementioned *Father Facts* (p. 3). This new report by Horn may well be the best such up-to date collection available.

[5]Quoted by Richard Louv, in "Two Debates are Raging on Family," *San Diego Union Tribune*, February 22, 1992.

[6]For example, the kinds of arguments made by Stephanie Coontz in *The Way We Never Were: American Families and the Nostalgia Trap* (New York Basic Books, 1992).

[7]For the sake of bibliographic simplicity, all of the data in this section can be found in *Father Facts*, although original sources also are cited each time. My great thanks to Dr. Horn and his colleagues for this superb compilation.

[8]US Congress, Committee on Ways and Means, *The Green Book* (Washington, DC, 1993); see also US Department of Commerce, Bureau of the Census, "Marital Status and Living Arrangements: March 1993," by Arlene Saluter, Current Population Reports:

Population Characteristics, pp.20-478 (Washington, DC: Government Printing Office, May 1994).

[9]Frank F. Furstenberg, Jr. and Christine Winquist Nord, "Parenting Apart Patterns of Child Rearing After Marital Disruption," *Journal of Marriage and the Family* (November 1985), p.896.

[10]*Father Facts*, p. iii.

[11]Frank F. Furstenberg, Jr. and Julien O. Teitler, "Reconsidering the Effects of Marital Disruption: What Happens to Children of Divorce in Early Adulthood?" *Journal of Family Issues* 15 (1994), pp. 173-90.

[12]Barbara Dafoe Whitehead, "Dan Quayle Was Right," *The Atlantic Monthly* (April 1993), pp. 47-48; see also Nicholas Zill and Carolyn C. Rogers, "Recent Trends in the Well-Being of Children in the United States and Their Implications for Public Policy," in Andrew J. Cherlin, ed., *The Changing American Family and Public Policy* (Washington, DC: The Urban Institute, 1988).

[13]Jayne Garrison, "Seminar Summary: Sexuality, Poverty, and the Inner City" (Menlo Park, CA: Henry J. Kaiser Family Foundation, 1994).

[14]Cited in Garfinkel and McLanahan, *Single Mothers and Their Children*.

[15]Nicholas Davidson, "Life Without Father," *Policy Review* (1990); see also Karl Zinsmeister, "Crime is Terrorizing Our Nation's Kids," Citizen (Pamona, CA: Focus on the Family, August 20, 1990), p. 12.

[16]Allen Beck, Susan Kline, and Lawrence Greenfield, *Survey of Youth in Custody*, 1987, US Department of Justice, Bureau of Justice Statistics, September 1988.

[17]Dewey Comely, et al. "Characteristics of Adolescents Charged with Homicide," *Behavioral Sciences and the Law* 5 (1987, pp. 11-23.

[18]Jean Bethke Elshtain, "Family Matters: The Plight of America's Children," *The Christian Century* (July 1993), pp. 14-21.

[19]*Ibid.*

[20]Selwyn M. Smith, Ruth Hanson, and Sheila Noble, "Social Aspects of the Battered Baby Syndrome" in Joanne V. Cook and Roy T. Bowles (eds.) *Child Abuse: Commission and Omission* (Toronto: Butterworths, 1980), pp. 217-20.

[21]Nicholas Eberstadt, "America's Infant Mortality Puzzle," *The Public Interest* (Summer 1992).

[22]Louis W. Sullivan, Secretary of Health of Human Services, 1992.

[23]US Department of Health and Human Services, National Center for Health Statistics, Survey on Child Health (Washington, DC. 1993).

[24]US Congress, Committee on Ways and Means, *The Green Book*. And US Department of Commerce, Bureau of the Census, "Marital Status and Living Arrangements: March 1993."

[25]Glenn Loury has written: "Those committed to the silencing of Moynihan, and to the banishment of the topic of behavioral pathology in the ghetto from public discussion, managed to have their way. A dear price was paid for this indulgence, although it was not paid by those responsible for it." *One by One from the Inside Out* (New York: Free Press, 1995), p. 257.

[26]I am indebted, as I was more than 15 years ago when I first wrote about this subject, to *The Moynihan Report and the Politics of Controversy*, by Lee Rainwaler and William L. Yancey (Cambridge, MA: The M.I.T. Press, 196n. This analysis of aftereffects, published two years after the Moynihan Report was released, also contains a full copy of the report itself: *The Negro Family: The Case for National Action* (Washington: DC: Office of Policy Planning and Research, US Department of Labor, March 1965).

[27]*The Negro Family*, p. 5.

[28]*The Moynihan Report and the Politics of Controversy*, pp. 27-28.

[29]*The Negro Family*, p. 18.

[30]*Ibid.*, p. 8.

[31]For example, psychologist Kenneth Clark, whose work had been cited by the US Supreme Court in its 1954 Brown decision outlawing officially segregated schools, said "It's kind of a wolf pack operating in a very undignified way. If Pat is a racist, I am. He highlights the total pattern of segregation and discrimination. Is a doctor responsible for a disease simply because he diagnoses it?" *The Moynihan Report and the Politics of Controversy*, p. 263.

[32]*Ibid.*, pp. 153-54.

[33]*Ibid.*, pp. 197-98.

[34]*Ibid.*, p. 199.

[35]While many civil rights and other liberal leaders strongly disliked the Moynihan Report they were greatly enthused about a speech given by President Johnson on racial issues at a Howard University commencement that same spring. Yet not only were many of the ideas in the speech the same as in the report, Moynihan was one of the two principal writers of the speech. It would be glib—but not entirely—to say the difference was all in terms of respective set-ups and deliveries.

[36]Daniel P. Moynihan, "A Family Policy for the Nation," *America* (September 15, 1965).

[37]For example, see William Julius Wilson, *The Truly Disadvantaged: The Inner City, the Underclass, and Public Policy* (Chicago: University of Chicago Press, 1987).

[38]For example, see Charles Murray, *Losing Ground: American Social Policy, 1950-1980* (New York: Basic Books, 1984); David Frum, *Dead Right* (New Yard: Basic Books, 1994); and George Gilder, "End Welfare Reform as We Know It," *The American Spectator*, June 1995, pp. 24-27.

[39]For example, see William J. Bennett, *The Devaluing of America: The Fight for Our Culture and Our Children* (New York: Summit Books, 1992); David Blankenhorn's previously mentioned Fatherless America; and several things by Glenn C. Loury, including: The previously cited *One by One from the Inside Out*; and "Ghetto Poverty and the Power of Faith," Center of the American Experiment, Minneapolis, MN, December 1993. See also, Myron Magnet, *The Dream and the Nightmare: The Sixties Legacy to the Underclass* (New York: William Morrow, 1993). Regarding Blankenhorn's chairmanship of the National Fatherhood Initiative, a good case can be made that the 1994 creation of this new Pennsylvania-based organization —which is "dedicated to the restoration of responsible fathering"—ought to be included among the milepost events featured in this paper.

[40]Glenn C. Loury, testimony before the Human Resources Committee of the US House of Representatives' Ways and Means Committee, Washington, DC, January 20, 1995.

[41]President Carter did convene a "White House Conference on Families" in 1980 but in the words of Barbara Defoe Wbitehead, "The result was a prolonged, publicly subsidized quarrel over the definition of 'family.' No President since has tried to hold a national family conference." "Dan Quayle Was Right," p. 48.

[42]By no stretch is this is to say that everything, for example, about feminism and heightened Black consciousness was destructive. It is to say that the more fervent manifestations of these social currents were very much a problem, and remain so. For example, see Richard Bernstein's superior critique, *Dictatorship of Virtue: Multiculturalism and the Battle for America's Future* (New York: Alfred A. Knopf, 1994).

[43]"Dan Quayle Was Right," p. 61.

[44]"Families headed by single women with children are the poorest of all major demographic groups regardless of how poverty is measured." Irwin Garfinkel and Sara S. McLanahan, *Single Mothers and Their Children: A New American Dilemma*, p. 11.

[45]For example, this is what Barbara G. Cashion wrote, almost sunnily, in 1982: "The two-parent family is hierarchical with mother and father playing powerful roles and children playing subordinate roles. In the female-headed family there is no such division. Women and children forgo much of the hierarchy and share more in their relationships.... Single mothers report that they enjoy their ability to set norms and make decisions about time schedules and routines that suit their own and their children's needs. There is general lack of conflict, and decisions are made more easily and quickly, provided resources are adequate. Barbara G. Cashion, "Female-Headed Families: Effects on Children and Clinical Implications," *Journal of Marital and Family Therapy*, 8, no. 2, April 1982, p. 80. David Blankenhorn calls Cashion's qualifier, "provided resources are adequate," an "inspired touch."

[46]*Losing Ground*, pp.154-55.

[47]*Ibid.*, pp.160-61.

[48]One such critic (all things considered, an exceptionally moderate one) wrote: "The intellectual establishment, particularly the liberal intellectual establishment, has been quick to criticize Murray's work, and these attacks have cast considerable doubt on the credibil-

ity of his conclusions. But what is often missed in this frenzy is that although Murray is almost certainly wrong in blaming the social welfare system for a large part of the predicament of the poor, he is almost certainly correct in stating that welfare does not reflect or reinforce our most basic values. He is also correct in stating that no amount of tinkering with benefit levels or work rules will change that." David T. Ellwood, *Poor Support: Poverty in the American Family* (New York Basic Books, 1988), p. 6. Murray is also co-author (with the late Richard Hermstein) of the very controversial 1994 book, *The Bell Curve: Intelligence and Class Structure in American Life* (New York: Free Press).

[49]The documentary aired January 25, 1986, on CBS.

[50]*The Moynihan Report and the Politics of Controversy*, p. 376. Rainwater and Yancey describe Moyers on the same page as Johnson's "chief policy factotum."

[51]Michael Novak, "The Content of Their Character," *National Review*, February 28, 1986, p. 47.

[52]In an essay analyzing the socialization of young Black men in light of America's history of slavery and discrimination, sociologist Orlando Patterson sums up this way with brutal directness: "This, then, is what we have inherited: a lower class with gender attitudes and behaviors that are emotionally and socially brutalizing and physically self-destructive. The posturing, pathological narcissism of 'cool pose' masculinity with its predatory, antimaternal sexuality, self-healing addictions, and murderous, self-loathing displacements; the daily and nightly carnage on the streets of the inner cities; the grim statistics on child and spousal abuse, rape, poverty, illiteracy, and suicide—these are the gruesome manifestations of this historically, sociologically, and psychologically engendered tragedy." "Blacklash: The Crisis of Gender Relations Among African-Americans," *Transition*, no. 62, 1993, p. 25.

[53]Bill Moyers Examines the Black Family," *Newsweek*, January 27, 1986, p. 58.

[54]Chester E. Finn, Jr., "Ten Tentative Truths," Center of the American Experiment, Minneapolis, MN, June 1990, p. 5.

[55]William A. Galston, "A Liberal-Democratic Case for the Two-Parent Family," *The Responsive Community*, Winter 1990-91, p. 14.

[56]Elaine C. Kamarck and William A. Galston, "Putting Children First A Progressive Family Policy for the 1990's," Progressive Policy Institute, Washington, DC, 1990.

[57]Galston was a leader of the Progressive Policy Institute. The Washington-based PPI might best be described as a "neoliberal" think-tank associated with the Democratic Leadership Council, the group of moderate Democratic politicians formerly led by Gov. Bill Clinton of Arkansas. Galston served as deputy assistant to the president from the beginning of Mr. Clinton's administration in January 1993 until May 1995, when he returned to the University of Maryland for family reasons of his own (i.e., he wanted to spend more time with his wife and son).

[58]"A Liberal-Democratic Case for the Two-Parent Family," pp. 16-17.

[59]As argued, I would expand this reference to read both the 1980s and 1970s.

[60]*Ibid.*, p. 17. This is how Rutgers University sociologist David Popenoe put it in a 1992 op-ed: "Of course, social science research is almost never conclusive. There are always methodological difficulties and stones left unturned. Yet in three decades of work as a social scientist, I know of few other bodies of data in which the weight of evidence is so decisively on one side of the issue: on the whole, for children, two-parent families are preferable to single-parent families and step-families.... Sure nontraditional families can be successful, and they deserve our support. But here is what social scientists call a confirmed empirical generalization: these families are not as successful as conventional two-parent families. What further confirmation? Ask any child which kind of family he or she prefers." "The Controversial Truth: Two Parent Families Are Better," *New York Times*, December 26, 1992, p. 21.

[61]"A Liberal-Democratic Case for the Two-Parent Family," p. 18.

[62]*Ibid.*, p. 20.

[63]*Beyond Rhetoric: A New American Agenda for Children and Families: Final Report of the National Commission on Children* (summary), (Washington, DC: US Government Printing Office, 1991), p. 18. The commission was established by Public Law 100-203 "to serve as a forum on behalf of the children of the nation." Its 34

bipartisan members were appointed by the president, the president pro tempore of the US Senate, and the Speaker of the House of Representatives.

[64]*Ibid.*

[65]*Ibid.*

[66]While I've come to understand that members of the Rockefeller commission never actually talked about the Kamarck-Galston paper during their meetings, according to one source, the paper was nevertheless very useful in persuading the panel's majority of liberal members to subscribe to its thesis precisely because its messengers were not conservative. The commission's staff, moreover, borrowed freely from "Putting Children First" in drafting the final report. A case also can be made that Chairman Rockefeller put unusual pressure on commission members to reach unanimity insofar as he was thinking about running for president in 1992 and he saw such across-the-board agreement as helpful. Even so, the report's two-parent language was a major departure for a federal document. A final note: Then Governor Bill Clinton was a member of the commission, though he may never have attended any of its meetings from 1989 to 1991.

[67]Barbara Dafoe Whitehead, "What is Murphy Brown Saying?" *The Washington Post*, May 10, 1992.

[68]Vice President Dan Quayle, remarks delivered in San Francisco to the Commonwealth Club of California, May 19, 1992.

[69]*The Wall Street Journal* editorialized: "The day-after press coverage of the Vice President's speech was remarkably tendentious, even by current standards." May 21, 1992.

[70]John E. Yang, "Quayle Sums Up Trip: 'It Worked Out Well'." *The Washington Post*, May 22, 1992. As witness Senate Majority Leader (and presidential candidate) Bob Dole's recent criticism of the popular culture, politicians are less nervous about blasting Hollywood than they were a short time ago. Much of this credit goes to film critic Michael Medved and his 1992 breakthrough book, *Hollywood vs. America: Popular Culture and the War on Traditional Values* (Harper-Collins). Of interest, Medved, an observant Jew, frequently has been ridiculed and dismissed as a "right-wing Christian."

[71]"Dan Quayle Was Right," pp. 47-84.

[72]*Ibid.*, p. 48.

[73]*Ibid.*, p. 52.

[74]*Ibid.*, pp. 60; 79-80

[75]"The Commg White Underclass." Syndicated columnist Suzanne Fields described Murray's column as the "most faxed op-ed of the year" in a speed, in Minneapolis, sponsored by Center of the American Experiment, June 9, 1994.

[76]Blacks comprised 12.4 percent of the US population in 1991. *Statistical Abstract of the United States, 1993: The National Data Book* (Washington, DC: US Department of Commerce, 1993), p. 14.

[77]For a much briefer treatment of Blankenhorn's argument, see his oral essay, "Fatherless America," Center of the American Experiment, Minneapolis, MN, April 1993.

[78]*Fatherless America: Confronting Our Most Urgent Social Problem.*, p. 2.

[79]*Ibid.*, p. 2.

[80]*Ibid.*, p. 22.

[81]Chester E. Finn, Jr., "Where's Dad?" *Commentary*, April 1995, p. 60.

[82]*Fatherless America: Confronting Our Most Urgent Social Problem*, p. 222.

[83]"A Family Policy for the Nation."

[84]This most certianly is not to say that in my own public speaking, for example, that this message is received equally well say, by Rotarians and college students. The former understand and appreciate it nearly unanimously. I've known the latter to do so only occasionally. (Or more precisely, students have seen fit to agree with me—publicly in class—only occasionally.) Likewise, Greenhorn notes that when Hennepin County commissioners, in my hometown of Minneapolis, proposed a vision statement in 1994 which urged a community in which "healthy family structure is nurtured and fewer children are born out of wedlock," vocal "local leaders" described the notion as "exclusionary," "judgmental," "intolerant," "offensive," "stigmatizing," "degrading," and "archaic." *Fatherless America*, p. 232. To say that candor and courage on the topic have increased is not to say that candor and courage now rule the day. Or that ideologically grounded wishful thinking doesn't remain power inhibiting.

[85]Orlando Patterson cites research which argues that changing employment prospects for Black men can explain only 20 percent of the decline in marriage rates for them. "Blacklash," p. 19.

[86]*The Truly Disadvantaged*, p. 163.

[87]"The Coming White Underclass."

[88]*Fatherless America: Confronting Our Most Urgent Social Problem*, pp. 225-34.

[89]"Where's Dad?" p. 62. Having said this, Douglas J. Besharov has written: "while in 1969 there was a substantial number of widows on welfare, the mothers of the majority of children were divorced. At most, about 35 or 40 percent were the children of what the Census Bureau calls 'never-married' mothers; that is, mothers who had their first baby out of wedlock and never married afterward (to either the father or another man). Today, the figures are reversed. The majority of children on welfare now have 'never-married' mothers." Douglas J. Besharov, "Teen Sex, Welfare Reform, and the Politicians," Center of the American Experiment, Minneapolis, MN, January 1995, p. 5.

Chapter 17

HOMOSEXUAL HOUSEHOLDS AND SOCIAL STABILITY

Carl Pfluger

What is the problem?

According to Thomas Mann (in his essay on Goethe and Tolstoy) Nietzsche complains somewhere that the Germans are altogether too clumsy and undiscriminating in their use of that slippery and ambiguous conjunction, "and." It is a word, Nietzsche thought, which serves much too easily as a sloppy substitute for careful thinking, bringing together subjects which have no legitimate business in the same sentence. I thought of that remark (which obviously does not apply only to Germans) as soon as I saw the title of this chapter—which was chosen, not by me, but by the organizers of this book—"Homosexual Households and Social Stability." In how many senses, after all, can we take *this* "and?" It might serve, for instance, as a simple copulative conjunction, merely setting these two terms alongside each other in the flat and meaningless way that so irritated Nietzsche; or it might suggest a more disjunctive and antithetical relationship, implying some kind of antagonism between the very existence of homosexual households and social stability; on the other hand, it might conceivably imply a more positive correlation, so that one of these was seen as supporting the other, or that they were mutually reinforcing; and so forth.

For myself, in fact, the only immediately obvious connection between the two sides of this expression is the observable fact that social stability is threatened (at least locally, in the United States) by the vehement hostility to homosexual households—and to homosexuality generally—which has become increasingly vociferous in recent years; but since I doubted that this was consciously intended by the invitation to write this chapter, I put that thought firmly to one side—for the moment, at least. Thereafter I was tempted, for a while, simply to assume the first of the alternatives listed above; in which case the most appropriate response would have been to produce two separate and distinct essays: 1) "On Homosexual Households" and 2) "On Social Stability." But no, after still further reflection, it seemed more probable that some sort of relation is implied in the framing of this topic—even if I do not immediately perceive it myself—and that this relation is most likely assumed to be a negative one. This impression is strengthened by a perusal of the programmatic material for this conference (especially for this panel on "alternative families") where references to "the impact of non-traditional families" and so forth seem redolent of a certain atmosphere of crisis and alarm, or at least of severe foreboding: of hand-wringing, that is to say, if not quite of finger-pointing. And such expressions in our program do seem to reflect a widely-felt sense of unease and anxiety, often expressed as concern about the condition of "the traditional family"—another phrase which is itself rather questionable and problematic.

In fact, of course, there is no single and definitive model of "the traditional family," and there never has been. Rather, a multitude of diverse traditions exist on our planet, and all of them have always been changing and evolving. From a certain naive point of view, therefore, the really interesting question might be: just why has this particular problem (i.e., of homosexuality) become so excessively agitated at just this point in time? We shall return to this question in due course; but first (we have not yet finished with Reconstructing our title!) we must consider in turn those two substantives which are joined by (or separated by?) that ambiguous conjunction: "households" and "stability."

"Households" first. Over roughly the past quarter of a century individuals of same-sex orientation, both male and female, have been able to live more openly than had formerly been the case, at least in most of the countries of Western Europe and North America. Not surprisingly, some of these individuals have chosen to live in association with others of their own gender and orientation in some sort of more or less permanent domestic co-habitation, either as couples or in larger and more complex arrangements. And increasingly, over this period, many of these households have assumed for themselves the effective status of families: thereby invoking first of all the emotional and affectional connotations of "family," but also, in many cases, claiming at least some of the rights—especially custodial and proprietary rights—which have generally been part of the traditional definitions of family. These claims (of which we shall have more to say later) have met with considerable—though by no means universal—success in the courts and political bodies where they have been advanced; and it is partly these successes, I presume, which have given rise in some quarters to the concerns which have led, among other things, to the framing of the topic for this essay.

But in going this far—that is to say, in asserting for themselves the right to be called families—can homosexual households legitimately claim the support of any tradition, such as that which we invoke when we deploy the phrase "the traditional family?" Well, speaking for the only tradition in which I personally can claim any authority— the tradition of the English language and its usages—I would have to be inclined to answer: yes. Dr. Johnson—than whom there has scarcely ever been a more fervent traditionalist, and who published (in 1755) the first really authoritative dictionary of the English language—gave, as his first definition of household: "A family living together." And when we turn to look up "family" we find:

1. Those who live in the same house; a household.
2. Those that descend from one common progenitor; a race; a tribe; a generation.

Please note that it is only the secondary definition that refers to any of those "biological" relationships of "blood" or lineage which are sometimes taken as essential to the definition of a "natural" family; the primary (and thus, presumably, for Johnson at least) the most authoritative definition of family refers only to the fact of co-habitation in a common domicile: a relationship defined by proximity of physical location. In Johnson's *Dictionary*, "family" and "household" are synonymous.

Nor was the tradition substantially different on the European continent. J.L. Flandrin,[1] surveying the French dictionaries of the seventeenth and eighteenth centuries, finds that in the earlier part of this period definitions of *famille* could refer equally well *either* to senses of kinship, descent, and such "relatedness" *or* to those of common residence, location, or "household." Only toward the latter part of the eighteenth century do French lexicographers start showing a tendency to insist on combining both criteria into a single definition—and even then the idea of a common residence usually is given priority, just as it is in Johnson's *Dictionary*. In an especially striking illustration of this trend, Flandrin also notes[2] that under the heading of "the Holy Family" (a prominent and familiar theme in Christian art) the earlier dictionaries give the definition as a picture of "our Lord, the Virgin, Saint Joseph *and Saint John*." (Emphasis mine.) John only starts to drop out of the picture in the later eighteenth century, not completely disappearing until well into the nineteenth. Considering that the relationship of John ("the Beloved Disciple") to Jesus has sometimes been taken as a homosexual one[3] this fact is perhaps especially relevant to our present theme.

"Household" at least has a set of fairly concrete and specific referents; now, however, we must turn to "stability," which is much more of an abstraction—and one of those abstractions, it must be observed, which has all too often lent itself to any number of abuses when it has been applied to the lives of real, particular, flesh-and-blood human beings. I feel reasonably certain that "stability" was one of the words Robert Graves had in mind when he wrote:

> There are some words carry a curse with them:
> Smooth-trodden, abstract, slippery vocables.
> They beckon like a path of stepping stones;
> But lift them up and watch what writhes or scurries![4]

At least one of the problems with the word "stability" is the same as with the word "tradition": too many people tend much too often to think of it as something static and monolithic; but really, for human beings (or any other living things, for that matter) the only kind of stability which would be genuinely desirable—or even survivable—must be more fluid, open to change and evolving. Perhaps a phrase like "dynamic equilibrium" comes closest to describing the kind of social stability which would qualify as a real desideratum. It might be worth recalling, in this context, that the official motto of the World State in Aldous Huxley's *Brave New World* was: "Community, Identity, Stability."

Whenever I encounter this sort of problem with a word, one of my first responses is to reach for an etymological dictionary: history, even of merewords, can sometimes give us a clue to understanding how we get into the messes we always do seem to be getting ourselves into. Also, it can often, as in this case, turn up results which appeal simultaneously to those parts of myself which are conservative and tradition-minded, and those which are more ironic and playfully subversive. It had never before occurred to me, for example, that the two meanings of the English word "stable"—the adjectival correlative of "stability" and the noun denoting a shelter for horses—might actually be related. But in fact they are: both descend from the Indo-European stem* *sta* ("to stand") as do the words for those natural residents of a stable, "stallion," "steed," and "stud"; all pointing back ultimately to the meaning of "a place established for breeding horses." (For that matter, we might also reflect upon the fact that the verb "establish"—very closely related to "stability" in the sense of that word in our title—has been used so early and so often in the sense of founding a lineage, a family, a dynasty....)

Whimsical though this philological excursus might appear, I think that such linguistic ramifications may at least suggest some of the historical and psychological roots of the unease felt by so many at the prospect of what are now being called "alternative families." They may serve at any rate to remind us just how many of our traditional social and sexual rules, values and taboos have been motivated by a concern over "blood-lines"—which we would nowadays prefer to call "genetic lineages"—about "establishing" them, identifying them, and keeping them disentangled. It is also worth noting that this concern about "bloodlines" is overwhelmingly a male problem —women always know who their own children are—but it has been a recurring and powerful motif in virtually all the human cultures of which we have any reliable knowledge. It is, as we have seen, not really identical with every definition of family; but it is a powerful tradition of its own, coexisting alongside the idea of "the household."

It even shows up, most revealingly, in Plato's *Republic*. Although so much of that *ur*-Utopia is an attempt to construct a systematic alternative to the traditions of family as the basis for a social order, Plato, notwithstanding his own homosexuality, cannot keep himself from worrying about the "bloodlines" at least of his official classes. This indeed is what prompted him to endorse his notorious policy of "the Noble Lie": the "Guardians" are ostensibly not supposed to know who their own children are, but the City's rulers will secretly monitor their affairs to make sure that they "breed true."[5] In fact Plato seems to have envisioned the breeding of his "ideal" citizens along much the same lines as the breeding of dogs, or of horses: a "stable society," no doubt; in both senses of our word!

Why now?

Those last ironic reflections may conclude our examination of the wording of our title; but they also have some bearing on what (as I suggested earlier) may be the really interesting question lurking behind this topic: just why these particular anxieties about homosexual households should have become so problematic at the present time. I can think of at least three possible reasons for this.

First: The most immediate and obvious of these is one that has already been mentioned, briefly, above. Gay people have become increasingly visible, vocal, and insistent in demanding recognition of their rights to form families; and this, naturally enough, has provoked some reaction, often from people who otherwise might not have given the matter a moment's thought. In February of 1994, for instance, the Vatican was moved to issue an unusually direct condemnation of a public body when the European Parliament voted to endorse same-sex marriages; the Pope claimed that the Parliament's resolution "legitimizes a moral disorder." In Ontario, in May of 1995, gay and lesbian couples, appealing to the Canadian Charter of Rights and Freedoms, won in court the right to adopt children, which had been denied to them by the Provincial Legislature just the year before. And so it has gone, back and forth, in many jurisdictions for some time now.

Laura Benkov's book *Reinventing the Family*[6] gives a fairly comprehensive overview of the issues and possibilities involved here, with a selective summary of relevant legal cases and the arguments surrounding them, especially in the United States. Children, of course, are the usual flashpoints for strong emotions in these cases. In addition to such relatively straight-forward issues like adoption and old-fashioned custody challenges, such avenues to parenthood as surrogate mother-hood, donor insemination, joint parenting, co-parenting, primary and secondary parenting, and so forth, may offer an unfamiliar and labyrinthine prospect even to the trained legal mind, let alone to the average layperson; yet the very complex-ity of the arrangements which homosexual parents have had to make in order to secure their children at least tends to ensure (as April Martin points out in her *Lesbian and Gay Parenting Handbook*[7]) that those children will be more strongly and unequivocally wanted than is often the case with children conceived by heterosexual couples in the "traditional" (and still too often unplanned) way. And for anyone who still worries about homosexual parents "recruiting" children to their own orientation, Martin also reports[8] the experiences of lesbian parents who, not without some chagrin, have seen their daughters grow up to become "flagrantly" heterosexual—hardly a surprise to anyone who recalls that most gays and lesbians were themselves brought up by heterosexual parents.

But most of this legal and political wrangling is compara-tively superficial, the effect more than the cause of profound changes in human life. I expect that many more such institu-tional battles will occur over the next few decades. I also anticipate that, in the end, gay and lesbian parents will win most of what they have been demanding: that they will significantly widen our current definitions of family, and achieve official recognition of homosexual "households" as substantially equivalent to heterosexual "families." I do not expect this to happen quickly or easily, because opposition to these changes is still very strong and very intense; but I do expect it to come about eventually, because major changes already effected in the recent history of the family (and indeed in society at large) will increasingly tend to undermine that opposition.

Second: One of those developments is by now an old (and much discussed) story: the reduction, in recent centuries, of the formerly extended family to its presently "nuclearized" dimensions. Already in the middle of the nineteenth century, the French economist P.G.F. Le Play characterized the nuclear family as "unstable"; and whatever one may think of the rest of Le Play's theories, twentieth-century experience has borne him out on this point. The problems of the nuclear family arise from its narrowness, concentration and intensity. Too much weight is made to rest on too narrow a base: hardly surprising, then, that the human components of this extremely compressed social configuration often break (or at least become seriously bent) under that strain. And of course when such breakdowns do occur (whether or not they result in divorce) the effects on children (who literally have nowhere else to escape to) are much more severe than they would be under some wider and looser familial arrangements, where children might at least have a greater number, and a wider variety, of care-giving relatives among whom they could seek protection.

The present condition of the now almost unbearably stressed nuclear family contributes substantially to the general sense of unease and anxiety about the family which we have already mentioned several times as a psychological impulse behind the questions implicitly raised in the prescription of this essay's topic. The most inflammatory of these anxieties, of course, is the concern about child abuse, which has been raised so often against homosexual parents - most unfairly, I must insist, as the majority of sexual abuse has always been hetero-sexual, and will likely remain so as long as heterosexuality remains the majority orientation. (Moreover, if sexual abuse were the real problem, it could be dealt with quite easily by imposing this simple rule: that homosexual households should only adopt children of the gender which does not interest them sexually. Needless to say, I have no serious expectation of ever seeing such a rule imposed; but that is merely because—as far as I can see—abuse is really not the issue actually motivating the opposition to gay or lesbian parents.) But since it is those very stresses intrinsic to the nuclear family which have certainly aggravated for children the burden of such abuse (and probably contributed heavily to its cause) this is in fact a weak reason for opposing the widening of our definition of the family. Rather, that formidable array of stresses constitutes one of the stron-gest sets of reasons for seeking to open it up, or at least to explore the possibilities of some more generous and expansive alternative. And so, paradoxically, the more our current cohort of "family values" campaigners succeed (by their own legal and political maneuvers) in "strengthening the family" only in its restrictively nuclearized dimensions, the more will they succeed in increasing the very pressures that threaten, eventually, to blow that frail container apart.

Third: At one time, homosexuality was called "the infertile passion"—I believe this phrase is Jeremy Bentham's. In other words, it was assumed as the defining feature of this whole set of sexual behaviors that it could not produce children—as opposed, of course, to "normal" heterosexual intercourse, which was generally valued more positively as the fertile passion. (Somehow, another Nietzschean expression sounds more apt in the closing years of this overpopulated twentieth century: might we not now prefer to call it the "all-too-fertile" passion...?) In those days, this may actually have afforded homosexuality a certain degree of protection; even, one might almost say, of privilege. As one form of sexual activity exempt from the risks of pregnancy, it was in all respects less threatening to the really core values of "the traditional family" than was heterosexual fornication or adultery: at least it could not complicate those sacred "bloodlines" (sperm lines, really) which have been so central at least to the more dynastic dimensions of "family values." At the same time, however, this also meant that, strictly with respect to family issues, homosexual activities were almost literally marginal: not important enough to be worth much excitement or attention, one way or another. (For instance, it is a noteworthy fact about the Bible—which has been invoked so often in the homophobic rhetoric of recent times—that it actually has so little to say about the subject at all.) This seems to have been true of most pre-modern cultures, even of those cultures in which homosexual relations played a significant role in public civic life (as in the pederastic pedagogy of ancient Greece) or in collective religious activities (as in the temple prostitution so prominent in most of the ancient Middle East, including early Israel.) From a "family point of view" such activities were simply irrelevant: non-issues, whether they involved exclusively homosexual attachments formed by a distinct minority of the population, or a part-time recreational diversion engaged in occasionally by a majority even of the heterosexually married.

But if, under this dispensation, homosexuality could not be seen as a threat to the traditional family, neither could it easily serve as a basis for family life itself: not as long as a central function of the family was seen as the *propagating* of children —as well as raising them, caring for them and educating them—to prepare a new generation to take over the family's inheritance. (It is true that adoption has always been a theoretical option, open perhaps to some of the same-sex unions that John Boswell wrote about in his last book; but then, even among heterosexual families adoption has been, for most of past history, so much the exception that perhaps it too should be called "marginal" for the purposes of this discussion.) And obviously propagation necessitated some sort of heterosexual union, which itself could *almost* inevitably be expected in fact to "produce" children.

All that, of course, is what has changed so dramatically in our time. The general availability of reasonably safe and reliable contraception, which has altered so much else in our traditional sexual mores and family-related expectations, has also had a profound, if indirect, effect on the relations between homosexuality and heterosexuality. To put it as concisely as possible: it has tended to equalize them with respect to the reproductive function of sex. By severing (or at any rate substantially loosening) the necessary connection between heterosexual intercourse and pregnancy, it has made less tenable than ever before those invidious distinctions which some traditions have made between sex for "mere" pleasure and sex as a "conjugal duty," allegedly only legitimated by fulfilling its "natural" function of reproduction. From *that* traditional perspective, the majority of heterosexual acts performed in the modern world are now no less "unnatural" than are homosexual acts—that is, of course, according to a theory of "Nature" which is itself highly questionable, selective, restrictive, arbitrary and, I might argue, also "unnatural" in the extreme.[9]

Contraception, then, has helped to legitimate sexual pleasure as an end in itself, decoupled from reproduction, equally for heterosexual and homosexual behavior—a major achievement, one might have thought, for a comparatively simple and limited set of technological developments. And more recently, of course, a host of other, far more sophisticated, technologies has begun to change even more profoundly the entire ambiance surrounding the processes of human reproduction. All such developments have contributed further

458

to the blurring of those value-laden distinctions which formerly had been drawn so sharply on the basis of those older feelings about "the infertile passion"—and we have every reason for expecting these trends to continue. We might then anticipate that we are heading toward a more general acceptance of sexual and reproductive diversity, which would include some recognition of homosexual households as a legitimate form of family. And as I said above, I do anticipate this—eventually. But the immediate future is likely to see a great deal of turbulence en route. Having lost most of the "functional" basis for their traditional discrimination against homosexuality, some people have taken to re-asserting that discrimination more irrationally, and therefore more vehemently, than ever before. Which is, I suppose, hardly surprising. We are, after all, dealing here with human passions of all sorts—including the fears and anxieties awakened by the very loosening of old and familiar prejudices—and that is the strongest reason, I fear, that this whole subject is still being (and will continue for some time to be) contested and agitated with so much venom and bitterness. Human beings are rarely so energetic as when they are striving to defend the indefensible.

The possible future of carnal knowledge

The prospect of completely separating sexual activity from reproductive activity suggests the speculation that some possible futures may—at least psycho-sexually, in the realm of human subjectivities—bear a closer resemblance to the lives of our remote hominid ancestors than to any condition our species has experienced since the invention of culture as we know it, since the discovery of what still may be called (if somewhat quaintly) "carnal knowledge"—that is to say, of the connection between sex and childbirth—and the consequent discovery (or "invention," if one prefers to take a strong social constructionist line here) of paternity. Certainly, so much of the social structuring of all subsequent human culture has been organized around that one phenomenon (all that agitation over "bloodlines," "seed," and so forth, seeking either to enforce the responsibility of males for their children, or to establish their rights over them…) that we have virtually forgotten that this is not the only possible way to organize a society; that, for millions of years before some unascertainable point in the past, those primates from whom we are descended— who certainly knew something about sex, and knew something about children, and who instinctively grouped themselves into at least some kind of social entity for which we can scarcely find a better word than "family"—lived quite "naturally" without bothering about the connections between them.

And so a future in which sex and reproduction are again disconnected (not through ignorance this time, but through a new kind of knowledge: less carnal but more technical) is certainly possible, and not even necessarily "unnatural." Rather, it might be seen (as technology at its best can always be seen) as liberating us from the abject condition of having to use our own bodies as "living tools"—which was, we might do well to remember, Aristotle's definition of a slave[10]—that is to say, in this case, of having to think of our bodies (in their sexual dimension at least) as having value only as instruments of reproduction.

But of course, exactly how we respond to this new/old dimension of freedom is what matters most. There are, as always, choices to be made, and responsibilities commensurate with the power our new technologies offer us. One extreme vision was offered by Aldous Huxley's *Brave New World*, in which all reproduction was completely artificial and all sexual activity was a sterile (and compulsory) promiscuity, which had itself become virtually mechanical in its dreary uniformity. More recent technologies suggest possibilities even more extreme than Huxley's. One could imagine, for example, a society in which every "individual" was a genetically identical clone. Such a society might well be highly conducive to a certain kind of "social stability"; but it would (I hope!) hardly seem a desirable option to most of us for all that.

I do not seriously expect such dystopias actually to come about; I bring them up here merely as extreme limiting cases of what conceivably could happen. Against such trends toward monolithic uniformity (which, incidentally, could also be driven, possibly to even further extremes, by religious, ideological or macro-economic forces, even more than by the impetus of technology alone) the family certainly can stand as a possible counterforce. But if it is to be really effective in such a role, if it is to serve truly as one of the primary vehicles of particularity, of diversity, and of the irreducibly stubborn varieties of flesh-and-blood "special relationships," then "the family" must be willing to embrace a definition not limited to those restrictive classifications of "blood" or genetic origin: these should now be seen as literally *superstitions* ("leftovers") from an earlier epoch. Only thus will families fulfill their potential as agents of that dynamic equilibrium which is the only truly human mode of stability. And that will mean, in this present context, protecting all forms of affectional particularism, homosexual and heterosexual equally.

Notes

[1]Jean-Louis Flandrin, *Families in former times: kinship, household and sexuality in early modern France*, Cambridge: Cambridge University Press, 1979, p. 4.
[2]*Ibid.*, p.8.
[3]John Boswell, *Same-sex unions in Premodern Europe*, New York: Villard Books (Random House), 1994, pp. 138-139; and *Christianity, Social Tolerance, and Homosexuality*, Chicago and London, University of Chicago Press, 1980, pp. 225-226.

[4]"Forbidden Words," in Robert Graves, *New Collected Poems*, Garden City, NY, Doubleday, 1977.

[5]Plato, *The Republic*, III, 413d-417b; V, 459a-461e.

[6]Laura Benkov, *Reinventing the Family: the emerging story of Lesbian and Gay Parents*, New York, Crown, 1994.

[7]April Martin, *The Lesbian and Gay Parenting Handbook: creating and raising our families*, New York, Harper Collins, 1993, pp. 15-16.

[8]*Ibid.*, pp. 210-212.

[9]I go into this argument more fully in "Claptrap and *Kulturkampf*," *The Southwest Review*, Winter 1997.

[10]Aristotle, *Politics*, I, iv, 1253b23-1254a17.

Chapter 18

RACE, GENDER, "FAMILY VALUES" AND PUBLIC POLICY

Twila L. Perry

Introduction

In recent years, the term "family values" has become a rallying cry against the increase in non-traditional families in the United States. Much of the recent public discourse about women who bear children outside of marriage seems to reflect an underlying assumption that appropriate "values" are something these women simply do not have. An alleged decline in values, often represented in the media by families headed by single mothers, especially Black single mothers, has been blamed for a myriad of social problems, including unemployment, poor health, school drop-out rates and an increase in juvenile crime.[1] Since the blame for these problems has been placed on "the breakdown of the traditional family," it is not surprising that many people have concluded that the logical solution to the "problem" is the reification of that family structure.[2] Consistent with such thinking, recent years have seen an increase in governmental programs and policy proposals at both the local and national levels aimed at bolstering the traditional family structure, or otherwise encouraging what are presumed to be "family values." Many initiatives are directed towards single mothers on public assistance—measures include: denying benefits to unmarried mothers under eighteen, conditioning the eligibility of teenagers for benefits on regular school attendance, permitting no increase in benefits for the birth of additional children, and providing small monetary incentives for women to marry their children's fathers.[3] In addition, there has been increased public discussion of subjects such as the importance of fathers to the family, the desirability of reinstituting school prayer, and the need to reinforce the value of hard work. The view is being promoted that there is a need to return America to an earlier era, the "good old days," in which the values held by individuals and the values they passed on to their children were presumably different and better.

This essay critiques the rhetoric of family values in shaping public policy toward the family. I argue that attempts by the government to shape family policy around the premise of a return to some presumed body of shared values about family structure or the values families presumably pass on to their children represents an approach to social policy that is unworkable, unwise and unjust. Family values rhetoric presumes a consensus about issues with respect to which, in reality, there is a wide diversity of views. This rhetoric also often reflects both racial and gender subordination. Finally, family values rhetoric is a poor approach to public policy because, in blaming the poor for their own problems, it encourages the larger society to feel no responsibility to seek meaningful solutions to critical social issues.

The first part of this essay will explore some general problems with focusing on private values as the solution to public problems. The middle part will examine the way in which the family values rhetoric is a reflection of both the racism and sexism that is pervasive in American society. The last part explores two very different contexts to illustrate the way in which values in American society are both subjective and relative—powerfully influenced by the statuses of individuals and groups. The first section of the last part demonstrates how one of the major values in the family values rhetoric, the value of work, is constructed in American society in accordance with racial and gender hierarchies. The second section of this last part demonstrates how it is sometimes important, desirable, or even critical for subordinated groups to embrace and teach their children values that are different from, or even in opposition to those of the majority. The essay concludes by arguing that effective family policy for the future must focus not on nostalgia for the past, but on the realities of changing demographics, economics and values and the need to achieve social and economic justice.

Private Values and Public Problems

The rhetoric of family values, in part, reflects frustration on the part of many people about some of the trends in American society. Many people see such phenomena as a high divorce rate, an increase in crime, a rise in the number of children born outside of marriage, and widespread drug use as threatening what they consider to be the stability of the nation. Some of these people have concluded that the way to address these trends is not to develop and implement more government programs, but to change the values that people have about what is important and what is right or wrong. The idea is that if you change the way individuals think, you will change the way they act, and thereby change the larger society. But focusing on private values as a solution to public concerns is an extremely problematic approach.

First, there is an assumption that there is a consensus in American society as to what the "family values" are that are deemed by some to be so threatened. Many people are deeply concerned about issues such as the increase in crime and unemployment and view these phenomena as true problems for the society. However, other changes proponents of "family values" may view as problems, may be viewed by many people as changes that are neither inherently positive nor negative. The reality is that we live in an era of change and controversy with respect to many kinds of values, including values about family life. Many people, for example, would probably agree that the values of honesty, hard work and respect for others are desirable, but there would likely be strong disagreement about issues such as the appropriate role of religion in childrearing, the effectiveness or morality of the corporal punishment of children, or the question of whether unhappily married couples should stay together in a marriage where there are minor children. Indeed, the very assumption that marriage is a prerequisite to bearing children has been challenged. Adoption, surrogate motherhood and the increase in step-families have challenged assumptions about biology and the nuclear family. Moreover, there is no obvious consensus in this country as to whether the proper role of the state is to maintain norms that are commonly shared or whether it is to protect the right of individuals to choose their own values about family.[4]

It seems clear that for *some* people, "family values" is a euphemism for the two-parent family. Indeed, the view that the two-parent family is a prerequisite to passing on "good" values was a central focus of the Republican Party National platform in the 1992 presidential election. This document vigorously took the position that "the traditional family will teach children the importance of honesty, work, responsibility and respect for others...built on a solid spiritual foundation."[5] However, recent research casts doubt on whether most Americans agree with this formulation. In a recent survey, only two percent of the women and one percent of the men questioned defined family values as being about the traditional nuclear family. Only five percent of the women and one percent of the men defined family values as being connected to religion or the Bible. Nine out of ten women defined family values as loving, taking care of, and supporting each other, knowing right from wrong and having good values, and nine out of ten said that society should value all kinds of families.[6]

Even assuming that there are *some* values that most people in the society would agree are desirable, there is no clear evidence that these values cannot be effectively transmitted in other than a traditional nuclear family. Although research purports to show that it is children raised without fathers who are disproportionately represented in statistics concerning failure in school, involvement with the criminal justice system and other problems,[7] there has been no proof that it is the presence of fathers that makes the difference between children's success or failure. A distinction must be drawn between a correlation and causation. Critical variables such as the impact of poverty, and the impact of family disruption (where that is a factor) have not been fully accounted for in empirical studies comparing children in single-parent with two-parent families. Finally, there is a growing body of research that challenges the assumption that children in single parent households inevitably suffer.[8]

Perhaps most importantly, the assumption that the solution to the problems confronting society are to be found in the private rather than the public realm is not only unrealistic—it is dangerous. It is an approach to societal problems that lets the government off the hook, permitting it to escape responsibility for developing policies to protect and improve the lives of its most vulnerable citizens. It also encourages private citizens to think selfishly—to feel no compassion for those in less fortunate circumstances and to feel no obligation to do what they can to contribute to addressing social problems.

Racism and Sexism in Family Values Rhetoric

A substantial part of the public rhetoric about family values focuses on families headed by single women. One of the main

reasons for the frequent attacks on these families is the view
that they are a burden on the rest of the society. In particular,
they are blamed for dramatic increases in the costs of welfare—in particular, the costs of the Aid to Families with
Dependent Children (AFDC) program.[9] There also seems to
be a growing belief that when people resort to AFDC it is not
a temporary situation, but instead leads to generations of
welfare dependency, crime, and low academic achievement.[10]
In other words, there is a view currently in vogue that families
on AFDC, by their very structure, are a drain on society and
are incapable of passing on good "family values."

Some of the perceptions about families on AFDC can be
addressed briefly because they are based on clear factual
misconceptions. First of all, contrary to a common perception,
the AFDC program is not a huge financial drain on American's
resources—AFDC represents only a tiny percentage of the
federal budget.[11] Similarly, the link of AFDC to non-marital
mothers is overstated. Divorced mothers constitute nearly half
of those on welfare.[12] Most mothers receiving welfare are not
teenagers, the average family on welfare has two children or
fewer,[13] and about half of all persons on AFDC are on it for
less than four years.[14] 38.9 percent of AFDC recipients are
White, 37.2 percent are Black.[15] Often ignored in the attack on
mothers on welfare is the fact that many Americans who are
not poor derive extensive benefits from social welfare programs
such as mortgage interest deductions and educational and other
loan assistance programs.[16] In such cases, there is no assumption that taking advantage of these benefits is shameful or that
it destroys the incentive of the recipients to continue striving
to improve their own lives.

Although the alleged loss of "family values," of which the
single mother family has become a symbol is posed as an issue
of ethics and to some extent, economics, it is clear that the cur-

rent rhetoric also has strong roots in two major structures of subordination in this society—racism and sexism.

Racism is implicated in a number of ways in the family values rhetoric. Although the phrase "family values" is often used to decry an alleged loss of values in society generally, the phrase also has a lurking racial subtext. The term "family values" linked, as it often is, with welfare and single mother-hood, easily becomes, like "welfare dependency," "inner city," and "the urban underclass,"[17] a code word for race. There is an implication that Black families, especially Black families headed by single mothers, do not share the values of the rest of society and do not pass on to their children the kind of values that most American believe are important.

Thus one of the ways in which the family values rhetoric is racist is that resentment against welfare mothers stems, in part, from the image of women on welfare as being Black.[18] Although there has long been hostility against Black women who receive AFDC,[19] in recent years the hostility has reached a new level. Many people feel that their hard-earned tax dollars are being snatched by the government in order to support these women, whom they believe are simply unwilling to work.[20] There is the view that many Black children born today are unlikely to become employed, productive members of society. Some proponents of family values rhetoric envision a potential situation they would deem entirely unaccept-able—working every day, at jobs that are increasingly stressful and insecure, to support a Black "underclass" of able-bodied people who do not work—a very bizarre and ironic twist in a nation with a history of Black slavery.[21]

On the other hand, some of the recent focus on "family values" is racist because it reflects a fear that in the future an increasing number of women on welfare will be White. One recurring phenomenon in American society is that a situation is often viewed as more of a problem when it affects White people. This has been true in areas ranging from the problem of drug abuse to the stresses faced by working mothers.

Part of the increased concern about welfare and single mothers is due to the fact that the phenomenon of single motherhood is growing rapidly outside of the Black community. More and more White women are now engaging in a behavior that this society typically associates with Black women, and the social policy analysts are loudly lamenting the trend. For example, the well-known conservative Charles Murray has stated that "the brutal truth is that American society as a whole could survive when illegitimacy became epidemic within a comparatively small ethnic minority. It cannot survive the same epidemic among Whites."[22] Senator Daniel P. Moynihan has also expressed concern that the birth patterns of White Americans are starting to approximate those of Blacks thirty years ago.[23] It is not clear whether these statements stem from a concern that White women may begin to lead lives that more closely resemble those of some Black women, or whether the concern is simply an economic one—that more White women on welfare will mean increased welfare costs generally. It does seem clear that one of the reasons for the recent intense focus on people on welfare is that it is becoming clear that many of the consequences of poverty often associated with single mother families cannot be internalized within the Black community.

Other concerns underlying the "family values" rhetoric also lie at the intersection of race and gender.

The formation of single mother families challenges the notion of the centrality of men to the family. The male has historically been considered the head of the family, a status which was, until recently, affirmed in the law through a whole host of legal rules.[24] Moreover, the idea of the male as the head of the family is not simply a function of the law—it is also deeply ingrained in our culture. It is a part of the pervasive nature of patriarchy that both men and women have been socialized to think of men as indispensable to the definition of a family.

In challenging the centrality of men to the family, single motherhood challenges a fundamental and longstanding social pattern: the control of men over women. A single mother on welfare may not have a great deal of power over her life, but in a sense she has more power than a woman who has no access to any money other than through a husband. Thus one consequence of the availability of public assistance is that poor women can obtain at least a small measure of economic independence from men. This can enable them to decide to have children without husbands or to leave husbands who may be physically or emotionally abusive.

The "Murphy Brown" controversy provides an illustration of the issues of centrality and control at the middle and upper middle class level.[25] Murphy, a fictional television sit-com character who was obviously well-educated, professional and economically self sufficient, decided to bear a child outside of marriage. Obviously she was unlikely to become an AFDC recipient. Why did her decision become the subject of national attention—the focus of remarks by the Vice President of the United States, and the subject of commentary in scores of newspaper articles? The answer seems clear. Murphy Brown's decision to have a child outside of marriage represented a threat to remove middle class men from centrality and control in the family. Murphy Brown was essentially saying, "I can support a child financially, and I can nurture a child without dependence on a man." She became a dangerous symbol because she posed the possibility that an attractive, affluent woman could choose to reject a powerful societal norm, decide to have a child without a man, and suffer no apparent adverse consequences.

The specific concern about the displacement of men from the center of the family implicit in the "family values" cry has implications for all men, but also has a specific racial dimension. The Black single mother family has a long history in this country.[26] While out-of-wedlock births have been traditionally associated with Blacks, the fact today is that the fastest growing group of single mothers is among White women.[27] As a result, a different group of men is now being affected by the growth in the number of single mothers. While Black female headed families have long been condemned as matriarchies, little was done to address the structures in the society that prevented Black men from being able to play the traditional role of breadwinner. The possible psychological impact on Black men of the inability to play the traditional role was obviously not considered to be a problem. However, now that it is White men who are threatened with displacement from their expected roles in the family, there is a different level of concern. This is another illustration of the way in which the "family values" rhetoric is both racist and hypocritical. It also illustrates once again the way in which issues are redefined or given a different priority when their effects are no longer limited to the Black community.

The Relativity of Values

As discussed previously, one of the problems with attempting to base public policy on the idea of "family values" is that people do not necessarily share the same values about family or about what children should be taught in their families. This section will examine the problem of the relativity and subjectivity of "values" by examining two very different contexts in American life where people may have very different views about what is and should be valued. The first area is the social construction of the value of work. The second is the need of minority groups to create alternative or even oppositional values with respect to certain aspects of American culture.

472

Family Values Rhetoric and the Value of Work

It would appear, at least from the recent obsession about forcing welfare mothers to work,[28] that one value it is assumed is passed on to children in the traditional family but not in a single-mother family is the value of work—the work ethic.[29]

The family values rhetoric on the issue of work is flawed in many ways. First of all, that rhetoric assumes that those people in the society who do not have jobs are unemployed because they simply lack the desire to work. The reality is that there are simply not enough jobs for all of the people who do want to work. This fact of life with respect to labor in America is, of course, not accidental—many scholars have noted that the stability of our capitalist society requires the existence of a certain amount of unemployment.[30] Because of racism, the pool of the unemployed remains disproportionately Black.

Contrary to the growing public image of a lazy underclass, many marginalized people in this society work at the only kinds of jobs that are available to them—jobs that are temporary, low-paying, "off-the-books" or illegal. Regina Austin has described the strength and persistence of the work ethic among some of the most dispossessed members of the society:

> ...Consider the youngsters employed in the urban crack trade. They are hardly shiftless and lazy leisure seekers. Many of them are as much Ronald Reagan's children, as much yuppies as the young urban professionals with whom the term is usually associated. Their commitment to the work ethic is incredible. They endure miserable working conditions, including long hours, exposure to the elements, beatings and shootings, mandatory abstinence from drugs and low pay relative to their superiors.[31] ...They spurn the injunctions of parents, police, teachers and other authorities, but they embrace the entrpreneurial and consumption cultures of mainstream America.[32]

Because of child care responsibilities, many single mothers on AFDC do not work. However, many do, earning unreported income in a variety of marginal jobs, often in the underground economy. They and their children survive by their ability to find ways to supplement the minimal money they receive from welfare.[33]

However, the society sees these women not as "plucky," resourceful survivors of adversity with the creativity to find ways to provide for their children. Their circumvention of the law elicits no sympathy—instead, they are denounced as "welfare cheats."

It must not be forgotten that the value we attribute to work is not, in any sense, an absolute. It is, instead, like the question of what constitutes a family, a value that is contingent upon perspective or standpoint. Work is valued in accordance with who does it and who it is done for. In a patriarchal system, the value of work is construed in accordance with what is valued under patriarchy. Thus, we have the obvious fact that in this society, market work is valued more highly than domestic labor in the home, a fact that becomes very clear when married couples divorce and women who have played the traditional role of homemaker often find themselves newly impoverished.[34]

The question of hierarchies with respect to the value of work is more complex than a mere comparison between market and domestic labor. Attitudes toward the domestic work women do in their homes are also profoundly affected by both sexism and racism. Let us take the example of two women, neither of whom has held a job in her adult life.[35] The first woman was married right out of college to a young man with a promising career. The other woman never married, but ended up having three children and receiving public assistance. Both women have been out of the workforce caring for their children for the past several years. In one case, the husband has now decided to leave the marriage. In the other case, the government has decided to take severe measures against women on public assistance in order to force them into workfare programs.[36]

It is likely that people would be sympathetic to the privileged woman. They would see it as a noble thing for an educated middle class woman to forego career opportunities in order to stay home and care for her children. They would be concerned about the likely precipitous decline in her economic circumstances and her loss of status. They would feel that she should be retrained for a job that has long-term potential for financial and personal growth. On the other hand, many people would feel that the mother on public assistance is lazy and should take any job.[37] Because we live in a patriarchal society, it is considered acceptable for women to be economically dependent, as long as that dependency is on a man.

Race also impacts upon the way in which we choose to value or not to value work. I have argued elsewhere that the work of parenting by Black mothers is devalued in the controversy over transracial adoption. In that context, the complexity of the childrearing work performed by Black parents is underappreciated. Indeed, there is frequently an underlying assumption that Black parents are inadequate to raise Black children, while Whites are assumed competent to parent both White and Black children.[38]

Dorothy Roberts has described the relationship between the devaluation of the work Black mothers perform in their own homes for their own children and the national obsession with forcing welfare mothers to work, observing that "underlying the consensus that welfare mothers should work is often the conviction that their children are socially worthless, lacking any potential to contribute to society."[39] Also, unfortunately, even feminists often fail to see the link between patriarchy and racism in thinking about the value of women's domestic labor.

It continues to be troubling that all too often upper middle class feminists devote substantial effort to developing the argument that housework should be highly valued in the context of the divorce of an upper-middle class woman, without addressing the troubling fact that successful professional women often pay low, often exploitative wages to the women, often women of color, who perform similar domestic labor for them in their homes.[40]

Black Families and Oppositional Values

Often overlooked in the "family values" rhetoric is the obvious fact that the traditional family can also be a site in which negative values can be transmitted. In the current rush to enshrine the nuclear family, it can be forgotten that traditional nuclear families have also been the place where children have seen, learned about, and been the victims of behaviors such as domestic violence, sexual abuse and incest. One would think from the focus in the rhetoric and the media on crack-addicted single mothers that alcoholism and drug abuse simply do not occur in traditional families.

One negative value that can be learned in a family whether there is one parent present or two, is racism.[41] Racism is, unfortunately, a pervasive aspect of American culture that is passed on from generation to generation. Racism complicates the work of Black parents in teaching values to their children.

While most Black parents in this country would probably agree that it is important that families teach children values such as honesty, hard work and respect for others, Black parents also understand that Black children must learn much more than the values of the White majority. In raising their children, Black parents generally employ and pass on a "double consciousness,"[42] in which the values that seem to be promoted in the larger society must be evaluated at two levels: first, a general level and then a second level which takes into account the reality of racism and minority status. An uncritical and

476

unreflective acceptance of traditional values can affect Black families differently than White families: because of racism, Blacks have less of an opportunity to live their lives in accordance with the mainstream ideal. Historian Elizabeth Pleck has argued, for example, that in northern cities in the nineteenth century, the adoption of mainstream values by Blacks often promoted marital dissolution because racial discrimination against Black men made traditional values such as the male as the economically powerful breadwinner unrealistic guides to family life.[43] This continues to be true today. A recent study indicated that the Black men most likely to leave their families when faced with unemployment were those who subscribed most firmly to the idea of the male as breadwinner.[44]

During slavery, when Black people created families that were neither acknowledged nor protected by the law,[45] Black families had to create their own "family values."[46] In a world in which they and their children were treated as sub-humans, these families had to create lives with independent moral meaning.[47] In socializing their children, they had to create values that both were consistent with but also, sometimes, in opposition to those of the larger society. Perhaps most importantly, they had to teach their children to value themselves in a society whose message was that they were not valued and had no values.[48]

The acceptance of single motherhood is one example of the ways in which Black families and communities sometimes created independent moral meaning. Thus, while the non-marital mother has long been the object of intense stigma in the larger society, many scholars have noted that Black unwed mothers have never suffered the same outcast status in Black communities as White women have in White communities.[49] Sociologist Joyce Ladner summarized the acceptance of single motherhood in Black communities as reflecting a belief that a child born outside of marriage "was a child who had a right to be cared for and reared in the community of his parents without stigmatization."[50] Through the years many Blacks have understood that society's judgment that the nuclear family is the only moral context in which to have a child was premised on a system that often did not reflect the realities and limitations that shape many Black people's lives.

The challenge of life in a racist society still requires that Black people create and pass on to their children oppositional values. Angela Harris and Patricia Hill Collins have written eloquently of the way in which Black women have to create a positive sense of self in the midst of a White world in which they are consistently devalued.[51] Although some have minimized the relevance of race in the work of parenting,[52] many Blacks agree that preparation of a Black child for life in a racist society is a major task faced by Black parents and often requires that they teach values that are different from those of the larger society.[53] Thus, while the family values rhetoric demonizes Black mothers, it ignores the challenges these mothers meet on a daily basis to instill values of pride and self-esteem that are as important to their children's survival as any other values it may be assumed enjoy widespread acceptance.

A powerful example of the challenge confronting Black parents can be found in Suzanne Carothers' study of the transmission of values between mothers and daughters in a southern Black community. One woman in the study thus describes her political socialization in a racially segregated society:

> My sister and I were somewhat awed of White people when we were growing up. We did not have to deal with them in our little environment. I mean you just didn't have to because we went to an all-Black school, an all-Black church, and lived in an all-Black neighborhood. We just didn't deal with them. If you did, it was a clerk in a store.

Grandmother was dealing with them. And little by little she showed us how. First [she taught us that] you do not fear them. I'll always remember that. Just because their color may be different and they may think differently, they are just people.

The way she did it was by taking us back and forth downtown with her. There she is, a lady who cleans up people's kitchens. She comes into a store to spend her money. She could cause complete havoc if she felt she wasn't being treated properly. She'd say things like, "If you don't have it in the store, order it." It was like she had $500,000 to spend. We'd just be standing there and watching. But what she was trying to say [to us] was, they will ignore you if you let them. If you walk in there to spend your fifteen cents, and you're not getting proper service, raise hell, carry on, call the manager, but don't let them ignore you.[54]

Although this excerpt deals with the simple, everyday family experience of shopping, it provides a powerful example of the way in which Black women teach their children a crucial value—to value themselves. It is also significant that this lesson is being taught by a person of little formal education or financial means, demonstrating that affluence and education are not prerequisites for good parenting—lessons about values and about life can be taught in many ways. Finally, in this example, the person teaching the lesson is the grandmother—a woman. This serves to remind us that the values that need to be taught can be taught regardless of the gender of the teacher—or of the learner.

Conclusion

The government needs to abandon its quest to restore the primacy of the traditional family in the hope that it will restore the "good old days." The "good old days" weren't so good for some groups in the society, including Black people and women. For many Blacks the majoritarian values of earlier days meant lynchings, riding in the back of the bus and being subject to any number of other acts of violence and indignity. For women it meant being subject to domestic violence and the denial of educational and employment opportunities. The world is clearly better now for Blacks and women, but the world is also becoming increasingly complex. Effective public policies must be developed in order to meet the challenges of changing demographics and changing values. An approach to social policy which has as its driving force a focus on the private values held by individuals is a policy doomed to be ineffective. Moreover, it is dangerous. Focusing on the family rather than the society as the source of responsibility to address social issues can also have the effect of sanctioning or even promoting racism, elitism based on class status, and other divisions between people in the society by encouraging people to feel little compassion or commitment toward those who can be easily regarded as "the other." As Stephanie Koontz has noted:

> The language of private relationships and family values
> ...leads not only to a contraction, but also to a deformation
> of the public realm. Where family relations become 'our only
> model' for defining what emotionally real relationships are
> like, we can empathize and interact only with the people
> who we can imagine as potential lovers or family members.
> The choice becomes either a personal relationship or none,
> a familial intimacy or complete alienation...using family as a
> model for public life produces an unrealistic, even destructive
> definition of community.[55]

Certainly the immediate goal of any policy that is directed toward the welfare of families must be to improve the conditions that confront children growing up in the poorest of families. This means, of course, preventing so-called "welfare reform" from taking away from poor families the economic means that ensures their very survival. In addition to providing some guaranteed income, policies must be developed and implemented to improve the health and educational access of poor children. In seeking to address racism, there must be vigorous enforcement of anti-discrimination laws as well as an reinvigoration of affirmative action. Women must be afforded opportunities that permit them to achieve levels of economic independence that will enable them to have choices about employment, marriage, children and other personal decisions.

Rather than longing for the "good old days," romanticizing the idea of family, and seeking to impose one set of values on everyone, the focus of the government should be on trying to develop policies that will create a just society where people can make their own choices about the most personal aspects of their lives.

Notes

[1] See, e.g.. Charles Murray, "No Point Fiddling With Welfare at the Margin," *Sunday Times*, July 11, 1993 (blaming births to single mothers for a rise in crime, unemployment, and a decline in the "overall civility of social interaction"); Joan Beck, "Nation Must Stem the Tide of Births Out of Wedlock," *The Times Picayune*, March 6, 1993 at B7 (blaming childbearing by unmarried women for crime, poor health and poor educational achievement among children); Andrew Rosenthal, "After the Riots, Quayle Savs Riots Sprang From a Lack of Familv Values." *NY Times*, May 20, 1992, at Al.

[2] See, e.g., Martha L. Fineman, "Images of Mothers in Poverty Discourses." 1991 *Duke Law Journal* 274, 289-93 [hereinafter Images of Mothers] (discussing poverty discourses as centering around the image of the missing male).

[3] See, e.g., H.R. 4605, 103rd Cong. 2d Sess.104 (1994) (amending Title IV-A of the Social Security Act to limit most households to 34 months of AFDC benefits); New Jersey, N.J.S.A. 44:10 *et seq*. (West, 1993) (the family cap—elimination of increase in benefits as a result of the birth of additional children). In addition

to this kind of family cap provision, a number of states have proposed or enacted "bridefare" provisions, and/or incentives for women on welfare to use Norplant. See generally Lucy Williams, "The Ideology of Division: Behavior Modification Welfare Reform Proposals." 102 *Yale Law Journal* 719 (1992) (discussing learnfare, bridefare and family cap provisions). Under the federal Personal Responsibility Act, states would be forbidden by the federal government from providing welfare payments to any child born to an unmarried woman under eighteen years old. The preamble to the Act states that the purpose of the Act is to "restore the American family, reduce illegitimacy, control welfare spending and reduce welfare dependence." Personal Responsibility Act, H.R. 4, 104th Cong. 1st Sess. Sect. 105.

[4]Peggy Cooper Davis, "Contested Images of Family Values: The Role of the State," 107 *Harvard Law Review* 1348 (1994).

[5]Charles Murray, "The Coming White Underclass," *Wall Street Journal* at A14 [hereinafter White Underclass]. See also, Barbara Defoe Whitehead, "Dan Quayle Was Right." *The Atlantic Monthly*, April 1993 at 47, 48-9. ("...The social arrangement that has proved most successful in ensuring the physical survival and promoting the social development of the child is the family including the biological mother and father.")

[6]"Women Are Becoming Equal Providers," *New York Times*, May 11, 1995, at A27.

[7]See Nancy E. Dowd, Stigmatizing Single Parents, 18 *Harvard Women's Law Journal* 19, 35-42 (1995) (discussing and critiquing research purporting to demonstrate that children inevitably suffer in single-parent families).

[8]For an example of research that does not jump to this conclusion see Ronald Angel and Jacqueline Angel, "Painful Inheritance: Health and the New Generation of Fatherless Families" (1993) (stating that studies of children of divorce do not tell much about the consequences for children who never had a father in the home.). See also, Barbara Bilge and Gladis Kaufman, "Children of Divorce and One Parent Families: Cross Cultural Perspectives," 32 *Family Relations,* 59, 68-69 (1983), (stating that "no single family form produces an optimal environment for a growing child").

[9]For statistics detailing the costs of AFDC between 1970 and 1990, see Staff of House Committee on Ways and Means, 103rd Cong. 2d. Sess., Overview of Entitlement Programs 325 (1994) (1994 *Green Book*) (Comm. Print 1194) [hereinafter *Entitlement Programs*].

[10]Some conservatives have begun to argue that there is a genetic component to the likelihood of certain people becoming welfare recipients. See Richard J. Herrenstein and Charles Murray, *The Bell Curve: Intelligence and Class Structure in Family Life* (1994) (arguing that higher fertility rates of groups with lower average intelligence helps to perpetuate welfare dependency).

[11]The federal share of the costs of the AFDC program is only about 1 percent of the federal budget. *Entitlement Programs*, supra note 9.

[12]*Entitlement Programs*, supra note 9, at 725.

[13]Joel Handler, "Two Years and You're Out," 26 *Conn. Law Review*, 857, 861 (1994).

[14]*Entitlement Programs* supra note 9, at 440.

[15]*Ibid.*, at 402.

[16]See Martha Fineman, *The Neutered Mother, The Sexual Family and Other Twentieth Century Tragedies*, 191 (1994). See generally. Robert E. Goodwin and Julia Legrand, *Not Only the Poor: The Middle Class and the Welfare State* (1987) (describing the ways in which the middle class has benefitted from the welfare state).

[17]See generally, Wahneema Lubiano, "Black Ladies, Welfare Queens and State Minstrels: Ideological War By Narrative Means," in Toni Morrison, ed., *Race-ing Justice, En-Gendering Power: Essays on Anita Hill, Clarence Thomas, and the Construction of Social Reality* 332 (1992) (arguing that references to women on welfare imply a whole range of words and concepts that imply racial degeneracy).

[18]See generally, Patrica Hill Collins, *Black Feminist Thought: Knowledge, Consciousness, and the Politics of Empowerment,* 77 (1991); Dorothy E. Roberts, "Racism and Patriarchy in the Meaning of Motherhood," 1 *AM. U. J. Gender and Law* 25 (1992).

[19]See Williams, supra note 3 at 723-25 (describing early policies designed to exclude Black women from receiving AFDC); See generally, Ricki Solanger, "Wake Up Little Susie: Single Pregnancy

and Race Before Roe v. Wade," 180-204 (1992) (discussing tax-payer resentment toward welfare mothers since the post-war years and the restrictive, punitive programs that resulted).

[20]See Lee Ann Fennell, "Interdependence and Choice in Distributive Justice: The Welfare Conundrum." 1994 *Wisconsin Law Review.* 235, 295 (discussing public perceptions of unfairness in confiscating money earned through work for the purpose of providing support to able-bodies individuals who do not work).

[21]Contrary to what may be a common perception, the majority of recipients of AFDC are not Black. According to 1994 statistics, 38.9 percent of recipients were White, 37.2 percent were Black. It is true that recipients of AFDC are disproportionately Black. *Entitlement Programs*, supra note 9, at 402.

[22]Charles Murray, White Underclass, supra, note 5, at A14.

[23]Daniel P. Moynihan, "Defining Deviancy Down," 62 *American Scholar* 17 (1993).

[24]See, e.g., Warren v. State, 255 Ga. 151, 336 S.E.2d 221 (1985) (abolition of marital rape exemption); Kirshberg v. Feenstra, 450 U.S. 455 (1981) (striking down as violative of equal protection the right of husbands to control and manage community property).

[25]See, e.g., John E. Yand, Ann Devroy,"'Hollywood Doesn't Get It.' Administration Struggles to Explain Attack on TV's Murphy Brown." *Washington Post*, May 21, 1992 at Al.

[26]See generally, Barabra Omolade, The Unbroken Circle: A Historical and Contemporary Study of Black Single Mothers and Their Families, 3 *Wisconsin Women's Law Journal* 239.

[27]Indeed, the fastest growing group is White college educated women. See, e.g., Amaru Bachu, Fertility of American Women, June 1992, *Current Population Reports*, US Department of Commerce, Bureau of the Census.

[28]For a collection of articles concerning the debate over forcing mothers on welfare to work, see the several articles in 26 *Connecticut Law Review* 817-913 (1994).

[29]See Mickey Kaus, "The Work Ethic State: The Only Way to Break the Culture of Poverty." *New Republic*, July 7, 1986, at 22 ("If we could rely on volunteers to end the culture of poverty by working themselves out of it, we probably wouldn't have a culture of poverty

in the first place. The point is to enforce the work ethic.") Another writer put it differently, stating that "The link between female leadership and welfare dependency in the urban underclass is well established, leading to legitimate concerns about the trans-generational transfer of poverty. At the root of the concerns is the paucity of employment among welfare mothers and how this affects attitudes of their children toward work." John D. Kassarda, "Urban Industrial Transition and the Underclass." 501 *Annals* 26, 44 (1989).

[30]Christopher Jencks, *Rethinking Social Policy: Race, Poverty, and the Underclass*, 128 (1992).

[31]Regina Austin, "The Black Community. Its Lawbreakers and a Politics of Identification," 65 *Southern California Law Review* 1769, 1786 (1992).

[32]*Ibid.*, citing Jefferson Morley, "Contradictions of Cocaine Capitalism." *The Nation*, Oct. 2, 1989 at 341, 133.

[33]See Jencks, supra note 30, at 204-221.

[34]See generally, Twila L. Perry, "No-Fault Divorce and Liability Without Fault: Can Family Law Learn From Torts?" 52 *Ohio State Law Journal* 55 (1991); Joan Williams, "Is Coverture Dead? Beyond a New Theory of Alimony," 82 *Georgia Law Journal*, 2227 (1994).

[35]I explore this hypothetical in a recent article. See Twila L. Perry, "Alimony: Race. Privilege and Dependency in the Search for Theory," 83 *Georgetown Law Journal*, 2481 , 2500-2503 (1994) [hereinafter Alimony].

[36]*Ibid.*

[37]*Ibid.*

[38]See Twila L. Perry, "The Transracial Adoption Controversy: An Analysis of Discourse and Subordination." 21 *N.Y.U. Review of Law & Social Change* 33 (1993-94) [hereinafter Transracial Adoption] (arguing that arguments in favor of transracial adoption are often premised on the assumption that Whites provide superior parenting skills).

[39]Dorothy E. Roberts, "The Value of Black Mothers' Work" 26 *Connecticut Law Review*, 871, 876 (1994), See generally, Williams, supra note 3.

[40]See Perry, Alimony, supra note 35, at 2508-2511. See gener-ally. Angela Y. Davis, *Women, Race and Class*, 96-97 (criticizing

middle class feminists for failing to put the exploitation of domestic workers on their agenda).

[41]See generally, Barry Trona and Richard Hatcher, *Racism in Children's Lives: A Study of Mainly White Primary Schools*, 131-135 (1992) (discussing the role of family, school, community and television as sources of White children's ideas about race). See also Frances Aboud, "Children and Prejudice" 88-92 (1988) (discussing actions and attitudes of parents that are associated with racial prejudice in children).

[42]This phenomenon of "double consciousness" was long ago described by W.E.B. DuBois, *The Souls of Black Folk*, 6 (1903).

[43]Elizabeth Pleck, *Black Migration and Poverty: Boston, 1865-1900*, 198, 200 (1979), cited in Stephanie Coontz , *The Way We Never Were: American Families and the Nostalgia Trap*, 250 (1992).

[44]Coontz, supra note 43, at 250.

[45]Davis, supra note 4, at 1364.

[46]See Omolade, supra note 26, at 240 ("Black resistance to social death took the form of creating viable families, whether patriarchal or female-headed, and of developing extended kinship networks along with political and protest strategies").

[47]Orlando Patterson, *Slavery and Social Death* 6 (1982).

[48]See John Blassingame, *The Slave Community* 181-191 (1979) (describing ways in which slave parents attempted to inculcate self-esteem in their children).

[49]Solanger, supra note 19, at 199-203 (describing in the era before Roe v. Wade the decisions of Black women to keep their non-marital children rather than place them for adoption and the support this decision had from families and the community); Regina Austin, "Sapphhire Bound," 1989 *Wisconsin Law Review*, 558, 558-61 (arguing that Blacks and Whites view teenage pregnancy differently because of cultural differences); Andrew Billingsley, *Climbing Jacobs Ladder: The Enduring Legacy of African-American Families* 111 (1992) (describing how even children without identifiable fathers were accepted into slave communities); Omolade, supra note 26, at 255 (noting that if Black single mothers worked hard to provide for their families, they were generally accepted into working class communities, although there was less acceptance in middle class communities)

[50]Joyce Ladner, *Tomorrow's Tomorrow: The Black Woman*, 2, 8, (1971).

[51]See Angela Harris, "Race and Essentialism in Feminist Legal Theory," 42 *Stanford Law Review*,.. 581 (1990) (discussion effect on Black women of White standards of beauty); See also Collins, supra note 18, at 91-113 (describing the importance of self-definition for Black women)

[52]This debate often occurs in the context of the controversy surrounding transracial adoption, where advocates of the practice dispute the argument that Black parents are in the best position to teach Black children the skills to survive in a racist society. See e.g., Elizabeth Bartholet, "Where Do Black Children Belong? The Politics of Race Matching in Transracial Adoption," 139 *University of Pennsylvania Law Review*, 1163, 1219-21 (1991) (arguing that the survival skills argument has little merit). Compare Perry, "Transracial Adoption," supra note 38, at 61-65 (supporting the survival skills argument).

[53]Perry, "Transracial Adoption," supra note 38, at 61-65; James S. Bowen, "Cultural Convergences and Divergences: The Nexus Between Putative Afro-American Family Values and the Best Interests of the Child." 26 *Journal of Family Law*, 487, 510 (1988).

[54]Suzanne C. Carothers, "Catching Sense: Learning from our Mothers to be Black and Female," in *Uncertain Terms: Negotiating Gender in American Culture* 232, 339-340 (Faye Ginsburg and Anna Lowenhaupt Tsing, eds., 1990).

[55]Coontz, supra note 43, at 113, 115.

Chapter 19

THE FUTURE OF THE FAMILY IN AN AGE OF CHANGE

Jerry E. Pournelle

Family Life Today

Family life is the distinguishing characteristic of the human condition, and this holds true in nearly all human societies. Obviously there are exceptions. The Ottoman Empire at one time rested on a celibate order of slave soldiers, and it would not be too much to say that Christian Western Civilization was saved by the monastic military orders of Caltrava and Santiago during the great jihad centuries following the founding of Islam. The point is that these are exceptions. Both Christian and Islamic societies are and always have been organized as families. Today the similarities of family life throughout world civilization—Christian, Muslim, Hindu, Buddhist, or officially atheist, are far more striking than their differences.

Thomas Sowell in his marvelous new book *The Vision of the Anointed*,[1] notes that despite misleading popular statistics, the family remains fairly strong. Many writers are fond of saying that half of all marriages end in divorce. Depending on the year, the number of divorces may well be half as large as the number of marriages that year; but then in a given year there may be half as many deaths as there are births, and that doesn't mean half the people died that year. The marriages counted in a year are those that happened that year; the divorces are from marriages that took place over decades.

The family is important. In the United States, average Black income is lower than White income, but Black college educated husband and wife families have incomes slightly higher than their White college educated counterparts. The poverty rate for families headed by Black married couples is about half the poverty rate among White female-headed families. Although Black Americans have about twice the infant mortality rates of whites in general, Black married women with a high school education have lower infant mortality rates than White unmarried women with a college education.[2] Despite the derision heaped on then Vice President Dan Quayle for his remarks about the example set by the television character Murphy Brown who decided to be an unwed mother, the facts are that Quayle was right: statistically, Ms. Brown was bringing her child into a situation of terrible risk, despite her education and income. Illegitimate kids start with at least two strikes against them, and I know of no studies indicating otherwise.

For whatever statistics of social pathology you care to collect—crime, poverty, squalor, poor health—the results are the same: married people are better off than unmarried, and children of married couples have a much better chance in future life than the children of divorced couples.[3] Their chances are enormously better than those of the children of women never married. This is true across all races and socio-economic status groups, and according to *The Bell Curve*[4] holds true across the IQ spectrum. For that matter, people of higher IQ have few illegitimate children to begin with. Statistically, the brighter you are, the more likely you are to get married and stay married.

The family, in a word, is the normal state of life, and family life is important in all aspects of civilization.

The War On The Family

That's today. Things may not remain that way. In the United States today, the family, at least as we know it, is under attack; and if trends continue the institution of the family will be greatly changed, greatly weakened, and may cease to exist.[5]

The United States, for good or ill, sets cultural trends. I was recently given a particularly striking instance of this on an airplane going to Seoul; one of the entertainments offered was an enormous music concert, I presume in Korea, where a vast crowd of western-dressed youths of oriental ancestry were entertained by oriental singers singing rock music. True, there were great differences between this event and a concert of the Grateful Dead or Mick Jagger. For one thing it was less frantic. Everyone including the performers seemed to be having fun, not merely enduring an assault. Still, the US origins of this cultural event, from blue jeans to the steel guitars, were unmistakable. I could cite other instances, but to what point? There is a great deal of literature about the ubiquity of American culture; it is often lamented as cultural aggression, and derisively described as MacCulture or MacWorld.

For good or ill, modern technology has accelerated this process of cultural distribution. It took decades to centuries for the Gutenberg Press to have an impact on the Russian of Moscow. Today a cultural innovation can reach the ends of the Earth in hours; indeed, with Internet, a new joke can be conceived in Oshkosh, Wisconsin and retold five minutes later in Pusan, Yakutsk, Patagonia, and Adeleaide.

As America often sets world trends, California often sets trends for the United States. California sits at the very center of the technological revolution. I can and do review engineering plans drawn up at NASA headquarters in Washington, and watch the flight of the resulting ship at White Sands Missile Test Range in New Mexico—and never leave my home office in Studio City.

California has declared war on the family as we know it. California with its no-fault divorce has ended marriage as we have known it for four thousand years. Married people in California have a cohabitation license; not much more. Neither partner has much in the way of legal rights to the continuation of the marriage. The result has been the withdrawal of the sanctions of government from the dissolution of the family. Government is no longer interested in preserving the stability of families.[6]

Marriage ceremonies may look as they always have. Couples may promise to have and to hold, in sickness and in health, for better or for worse, for richer or for poorer, until death do them part; but the law says that either one of them can get out of that promise for any reason that seems good or no reason at all; and the other partner has very few rights. The lifelong contract is meaningless. They're married until the woman meets a new personal trainer, or, far more likely, the man decides it's time for a New Cookie. Depending on which one has the better lawyers there may be some financial penalties for dumping a spouse, but no legal ones; and as the law changes, so does society.

The play *The Rainmaker* is set in Oklahoma in the early part of this century, and hinges in part on the fact that Deputy File is a divorced man; the stigma of divorce is so great that File claims to be a widower. Of course this makes the play nearly incomprehensible to modern students.

California no-fault divorce law has ended marriage as known in Western Civilization since before the Christian era; and many states are following suit. This is one threat to the family.

Meanwhile, the war on poverty has been a war on the family. It's a general truism of government that if you want less of something you tax it; if you want more, you subsidize it. The United States taxes marriage, and subsidizes illegitimacy.

The government will pay you to have a child out of wedlock, and pay you more if you have another; but if you are married your taxes will be higher than if you are not. It is clear what result must be wanted by the government.

Families traditionally control the introduction of their children to the mysteries of sex. The old and trite story of the parents having their talk with the children about the birds and the bees is illustrative of this right and duty.

No longer. Schools now have sex education from age six to age sixteen, often with explicit materials that would make us blush.[7] Children are exposed to films of homosexuals engaging in practices that are unhealthful; this is said to broaden their horizons.

Sex education is not voluntary, nor are the parents consulted. That part of family life—what children should be taught about sex, and at what age they should be taught it—has been pre-empted by the state in the person of the school system.[8] The result has been a quadrupling of abortion among teen age children and vast increases in venereal disease.

Thus it is easy to predict the future of the family in the United States of America: given present trends it will vanish, as it has been vanishing these past few years. The family as we knew it in our childhood is on the way out. The notion that one marries for life, "from this day forward, for better or for worse, for richer for poorer, in sickness and in health, to love and to cherish, till death do us part according to God's holy ordinance" is gone. Such marriages may be performed in churches but they are not enforced in the courts. They last so long as both parties feel like being married; but as soon as one decides it's no fun—when sickness, or poorer, or worse comes—or when a new lover appears on the horizon—it is no-fault divorce time.

This was not unintended. One may question whether those who proposed the war on poverty intended the destruction of the Black family—which had survived slavery, emancipation, poverty and segregation, but couldn't survive the war on poverty. One may question whether those who desired the war on poverty actually willed the horrible results it brought about; but it's pretty certain those who willed "no fault divorce" intended the end of the institution of marriage as it has been known in Western Civilization for four thousand years. Some glory in their accomplishments.

My Viking ancestors found that the only way to quiet their Irish young ladies was to make respectable women of them: to marry them. Furthermore they had to marry them according to the rites of the Catholic Church, and the Church made it very clear that there was no no-fault divorce. You married the girl for keeps. Clearly there was a quality about those Irish girls—But marry them they did.

Now imagine that they had no-fault divorce in those times. Imagine that all a Viking landholder had to do was send his wife packing, perhaps with a few thralls and some cattle.

Clearly I am distorting early Iron Age history here. But not by so very much. It really did happen that way, perhaps not precisely, but in general, and not all that rarely: Stark men married religious women, and thereby became religious, and less stark, and eventually civilized.

Ann Bolyn wouldn't sleep with Henry VIII until he married her. Henry went to great lengths to shed his wife, Catherine of Aragon, daughter of Isabella the Great. To that end he despoiled the monasteries of England, separated the Church of England from Rome, made alliance with Martin Luther, beheaded Sir Thomas More, and bequeathed his daughter Elizabeth a long war with Spain.

Nowadays he'd simply send her home to Spain. "Sorry, Catherine, but it's not your fault. No fault here. But I don't love you any more, and I have found the daughter of the Lord Mayor of London..." Why not?

And that is where we are today. The institution of the family as we have known it since Roman times is endangered by both law and the intellectuals.

What Can Be Done?

The family is under attack by elements of the social order. That's the bad news. Now, what can be done?

The glib answer is, "Not much." In order to reverse present sociological trends we would need to change the whole thrust of the century; to change the legal trends from their present emphasis on centralized power at the expense of individual and local power, to a greater emphasis on enforcement of individual contracts, and a devolution of power from the state to individual families. We would, in a word, have to give up the *Vision of the Anointed*; the notion that an enlightened few can and should micromanage the affairs of the benighted many. That may happen, but it will happen as part of a general revolution.

Of course not all are agreed that there ought to be such a revolution. Not all here agree that there is something fundamentally wrong with a society in which an enlightened few use the power of the state for social engineering, for imposing through state power their visions of a glorious future upon the masses too benighted to understand what is for their own good. Most of us, though, believe with John Adams that each man is the best judge of his own interest.

The Information Revolution

Philosophers can rule only if they tell the truth as they see it; as my grandmother would put it, tell the truth and shame the devil. This is precisely what many of our contemporaries in academia do not do.

Far from telling the truth, most contemporary social scientists—the new term for what would once have been called moral philosophers—don't much care what the truth is. Of course they wouldn't put it that way. I would.

I would go further. Most contemporary social science theory is not science, and is not worthy to be called theory. What is science? It is at least this: a series of statements about the real world that have not, so far, been shown to be false. Paradoxically that requires a certain quality to those statements: they must be falsifiable.

Without going deeply into the philosophy of science it is safe to follow Karl Popper at least this far: to be science, a theory must be capable of being falsified. A statement that cannot under any circumstances be proved false may be beautiful poetry, but it is not science. It follows that a social policy that cannot be proved to be wrong does not spring from science. The policy may express noble ambitions and pious hopes, but if it is thought "good" without regard to its effects, its origin is not science.

Much of the horror of this century comes from this confusion. Some Communists were merely opportunistic thugs, but many were idealists truly hoping to better the condition of mankind; and their confusion that what they taught was "science" and a "scientific theory of history" was one of the great tragedies of the age. Millions were sacrificed to it.

If a theory cannot be falsified, it cannot be science. Unfortunately, most social science, and the policies that spring from it, fail this test.

Thomas Sowell, among many others, gives countless examples of contemporary social theorists who have become so entangled in their theories that they totally ignore evidence of their falsity. Today when a new social policy is launched as an "experiment" you can be pretty sure there's nothing experimental about it. An experiment is an act of exploration, or should be. A modern social experiment is nothing of the kind.

Continuation or abandonment of today's social experiments are independent of their results. It doesn't matter if a social policy intended to reduce teenage pregnancy results in dramatic increases in teenage pregnancy. Those who proposed the theory either refuse to look at the results, or hasten to explain them away. It doesn't matter if a social policy intended to prevent the spread of AIDS results in more AIDS cases. The policies are judged by their *intended* results, and any embarrassing results in the real world are ignored or explained away.[9] Criticisms of such social policies are condemned as ignoble; as rejections of the noble intentions of those who proposed the policy. Lyndon Johnson launched a War on Poverty; those who opposed this "war" on whatever grounds were considered traitors to the human spirit who wished to keep mankind down, who wish to "balance the budget on the backs of the poor."

All this is well known; for details see Sowell's book, or nearly any issue of *Commentary*. Most of us know this is the situation. We don't know what to do about it. That's where the information revolution comes in.

Computers are part of that revolution; but the genuine revolution is not one of machinery but of information. Small computers enable us to gather, organize, and disseminate information in ways not dreamed of fifty years ago.

I said in 1978 that by the year 2000 every person in Western Civilization—in the free world—would be able to get the answer to any question that has an answer. That prediction was exactly on target. If anything we are, in 1995, a bit ahead of schedule—and the free world has expanded greatly. Now there are hermit kingdoms closed to the flow of information, but they are increasingly under threat, and faced with this dilemma that brought down the Soviet Union.

Military power rests today on the ability to gather and use information. Indeed, a new branch of military strategy is called

Information Warfare. One cannot wage information warfare without having both computers and people skilled in their use.

A nation without widespread use of small computers will be nearly powerless outside its own borders, and will be increasingly powerless within them. A nation that seeks military power has no choice: they have to bring in the small computers.

With small computers comes the information revolution. The very basis of information technology carries with it the means of spreading the word and disseminating truth. If it is true that "You shall know the Truth and the Truth shall make you free," then small computers are a great factor in bringing freedom; they certainly make it possible to spread the truth. Since that time much of what I predicted has happened.

The Free Exchange of Ideas

Today's world is different from that of our ancestors in many ways. First and foremost, there are now means for communications among those who care. Those interested in data and results have the means for obtaining data and results, tabulating data and results, combining the information with other sources—and for disseminating what they have learned. We can build and be part of a worldwide network of observers. We can record what we know and pass it on to others; and do that instantly and at low to no cost.

Arthur Koestler said that a necessary condition for the fall of any totalitarian society was the free exchange of ideas within that society. We now have the means for that free exchange throughout the western world, and it is being forced on all governments whether they like it or not.

Those who care about science have the means of communication; we can, if we will, make it impossible for the false scientists to hide the results of what they have done. We gather the facts; store them in databases; communicate the facts with each other; and confront them with those facts, demand that they pay attention; and while they don't have to listen, we can present the truth directly to their audience. It will still be possible to obfuscate and confuse, but it won't be possible to suppress the truth altogether.

My late mentor Stefan T. Possony used to say that either you believe in the supremacy of rational thought or you don't. If you do, you must act as if you do. You must welcome, must promote the free exchange of ideas. Possony welcomed the computer revolution precisely because it linked the intellectuals into a worldwide web, and he saw the implications of that a great deal sooner than nearly anyone else.

We also have the means for dissemination of information far beyond any particular interest group. Communication by small computer requires physical and intellectual resources; but none beyond the abilities of anyone in this room or at this conference. What it costs to be here is less than the cost of a good laptop computer complete with modem and Internet connections; and the intellectual ability to contend with modern travel and travel documents is more than is needed to use the Internet. Still that is beyond the abilities of many throughout the world, some of whom are illiterate—and we have the means to communicate with them, too.

The treasures of the world await on line. I can today tour many of the great museums of the world without leaving my home office—or for that matter, my hotel room in Seoul. I can today call up to my computer screen nearly all the great works of humankind, in their original language or in translation; and as well I can bring in commentaries, and discuss my thoughts with other experts. All this is available at trivial cost; and as the expression goes, you have not seen anything yet.

But in fact the information revolution goes well beyond the intelligentsia. The CD-ROM puts the *indexed* contents of an entire library onto a single disk costing about a dollar to produce. It can as economically produce photographs, drawings and illustrations, diagrams, cartoons, full motion video, and full spectrum sound, voice and music—all arranged in an interactive presentation on subjects as diverse as the evils of not refrigerating milk or the importance of vitamins to tips on childcare and parenting.. We can not only make a less expensive encyclopedia, it can also be more comprehensive and better—and much of it can be written and edited on line by scholars who need never travel from their offices.

I am indebted to Mrs. Pournelle for suggesting that CDROMS and the machinery for using them should be put in the waiting rooms at health clinics, unemployment centers, welfare offices—all the places that now warehouse people and waste their time as they wait to be "helped." They can be given interactive lessons in child care; on elementary hygiene, such as how milk spoils if left out of the refrigerator; an introduction to the germ theory of disease. Lessons can be in many languages, and need not require literacy. Constructing such lessons is hard work, but far less costly than the futile kinds of things we are doing now—and if the lessons are given to people bored out of their minds while waiting for government services, they are being delivered to the exact desired target population.

Impossible, you say. Not only is there the cost of equipment installation, but even the stupidest bureaucrat will come to understand that conveying the truth to the people undermines the authority and power of the bureaucracy. They will never pay for this. They don't have to. This is perfect work for volunteers; missionaries, if you will. Volunteers can begin this work today; we need not wait for government to act. Of course there will be opposition, but it is opposition that shows the opponent in a true light, that exposes the motives of those who oppose—and identifies the true saints among the bureaucracy for that matter.

Work at Home

It is now possible to do complex intellectual work at home. What are the implications for the future of the family if the mother is home but yet can earn an income? Clearly there is a great deal of opportunity for bonding; and a mother working at home at a computer terminal, even on such a "menial" task as data entry, will still have about the same amount of time for her children as a farm wife had in previous centuries.

Education at work

Opportunities for education at the work place. Large companies are discovering that providing on-site child care is economically advantageous. There is less absenteeism among employees, and far more employee loyalty. Microsoft Corporation now encourages families to get together for lunch in the company cafeteria.

I have written on this before: as the great corporations contemplate the dismal state of American education they may take a hand at educating the children of employees out of self defense. Xerox and Microsoft and General Electric and General Motors all require an educated talent pool from which to recruit their work force. What better place than among the children of employees who have some genuine reasons to feel gratitude to the company? Those concerned about the corporations "brain washing" their charges clearly haven't paid much attention to what's going on in the schools now—or have paid attention and approve, in which case their "concerns" are mendacious. The fact is that many schools now teach active hostility not only to large corporations but all employers.

There will be great implications for literacy. We have the means to teach everyone to read. Whether or not we will do that is not clear; but we know how. Xerox or Microsoft or GM or for that matter the County Janitorial Service could see that the children of every employee were given the gift of literacy.

It's not that hard to teach everyone to read. You just have to decide to do it.

The computer revolution will have great impact on education in general. We have new abilities to structure and present knowledge. We have the means to change attention spans and make use of new education methods.

In a word, there is hope.

Conclusion

By the year 2000 everyone in Western Civilization will be able, at reasonable cost, to get the answer to any question that has an answer. A corollary: By the year 2000, nearly anyone in the world will be able to get a message to nearly anyone else at trivial cost and within days. This is the information revolution.

I have shown some of the possible effects. There are many others. We have only begun to think of the implications. Some of those implications can be frightening. Some will wish to stuff this genie back in the bottle. That is impossible. There are opportunities as well. If one believes that the truth can set people free, the information revolution is the greatest opportunity for freedom in the history of the world.

Notes

[1] Sowell, Thomas *The Vision of the Anointed: Self Congratulation as a Basis for Social Policy.* (New York: Basic Books, 1995) p. 59. Sowell gives a number of examples of fallacious mathematical reasoning as well as examples of how modern social science ignores facts contrary to social theory.

[2] Sowell, op. cit. See also Thomas Sowell, *Ethnic America: A History* (New York: Basic Books, 1981) p. 198 and U.S. Bureau of the Census, *Current Population Reports*, Series P-20, No. 486

(Washington, DC: U.S. Government Printing Office, 1992).

[3]Jon Davis, George Erdos and Norman Dennis report the same results in "The Churches and the Family--Climbing aboard a Collapsing Bandwagon," *Salisbury Review*. June 1995 p.4.

[4]Herrnstein, Richard J. and Charles Murray, The Bell Curve (New York: The Free Press, 1994).

[5]It is about the same in England. See Jon Davis *et al, op cit.*

[6]John Dos Pasos said that the only thing liberation liberals actually wanted was to free men from their marriage vows. Whatever the truth of that charge, the liberal reform of marriage law has certainly accomplished that result. Prior to no-fault divorce, simply wanting out of a marriage wasn't enough, particularly if the other party disagreed. Now it is. Incidentally, the USSR tried this experiment decades ago but abandoned it when they saw the results.

[7]Administrators in many school districts instruct teachers to try to keep the sex education materials from falling into the hands of parents.

[8]See for instance Eugene Narrett, "Our Mr. Brooks: Letter from Massachusetts", Chronicles, September 1995, p.37. Narrett reports that in Brookline, Mass. a volunteer first grade tutor, having decided to become a female to male trans-sexual, became the subject of "counseling" to the first graders on the "normalcy of sex change." The school principal, Martin Sleeper, did not consult the parents before initiating the involuntary counseling sessions. Guidance Counselor Brenda Stern conducted the sessions, and is quoted as saying that since the trans-sexual lesbian was often at the school helping out four or five days a week, "We wanted them [the children] to hear it from one source, not from 18 sets of parents." Clearly it never occurred to the school authorities that the subject might be a bit complex for first graders, and might best be avoided by removing the volunteer tutor from the first grade classroom.

[9]In my C.P. Snow Memorial Lecture delivered in 1984 I pointed out that Snow hadn't quite got it right. It's not that the intelligentsia are divided into scientists who know no humanities and *literateurs* who know no science. Most scientists are well acquainted with the literary heritage of mankind, and most scholars have a working understanding of science. The problem is that on any university

campus there are hordes of so-called "social scientists" who know neither science nor humanities, but pretend--and often believe--that they know both. Alas, their knowledge of mathematics generally comes from a cookbook statistics course, and their knowledge of literature from a compulsory survey course in "multicultural studies."

In that lecture I noted that authors of fiction need only be plausible. Lawyers need evidence; it is not their task to discover and explain facts contrary to their client's interest. Scientists deal with data, which specifically includes information tending to falsify their hypotheses. Modern social scientists are almost universally content with evidence or plausibility, and almost never concerned with falsification of hypotheses.

Chapter 20

POLICY, LAW AND FAMILY STABILITY: FROM ANTIQUITY TO THE DAWN OF THE THIRD MILLENNIUM

Nicholas N. Kittrie

> It is better to debate a question without settling it than to settle a question without debating it.
> —Joseph Joubert (1754-1824)

> In the study of...[institutions] one should not exercise a vain and perishing curiosity, but ascend toward what is immortal and everlasting.
> —St. Augustine (354-430), *De Vera Religione*

It is the objective of this essay to explore the impact of public policy and law, as distinct from socioeconomic, psychological and environmental factors, upon family stability. Increasingly, what for some two millennia has been universally referred to as the "family," has become less precise and more difficult an institution to define. Unlike Humpty Dumpty's assertion that "when I use a word it means just what I choose it to mean—neither more nor less," there is an increasing discord in the popular, as well as scientific and legal, understanding as to what elements comprise the family. Although many continue to view the "family" as consisting of a nucleus made up of two parents of distinct gender (with the women being the home-makers) and their issue, such traditional families are in the minority in contemporary America. Instead, some seventy percent of the country's children and youth are raised either by two employed parents or in single parent, divorced or homo-sexual households. The definitional confusion is compounded by the growing uncertainty as to what public and private benefits are due or should be accorded to the familial entity. Recognizing these dramatic disparities in conceptual and operational terms, contemporary observers usually describe and comment on the ever-growing diversity within the institutions variously referred to as "families"—institutions ranging from traditional to unorthodox, nuclear to extended, monogamous to polygamous, heterogeneous to homosexual.

Moreover, even the keenest analysts of family structures often downplay the uniqueness of the traditional family and choose to blur the distinction between families and households. Family research, furthermore, tends to focus on economic, social, psychological, religious, cultural, and regional factors which affect familial stability and well-being. Only a few experts and students of family life have given adequate, if any, attention to the impact of public policy and legal provisions which might contribute, directly or indirectly, favorably or adversely, to the welfare and viability of the family in an ever-changing world.

This essay which directs attention to the role of the law and public policy in maintaining familial well-being, is due *in part* to my early exposure to this topic as a graduate law student, under the guidance of Max Rheinstein of the University of Chicago. While taking part in a comparative law seminar on Family Stability and the Law, I chose to assess the Egyptian scene with which I had become acquainted through my long-standing interest in Islam and the Middle East. Perceiving

506

Egypt primarily as a rural, socially and culturally conservative country, I expected that family stability would be inherent in that conservatism. Therefore, it turned out to be an unusually shocking experience for me, to learn that by the mid-1950s Egypt was among the leaders in divorce rates worldwide. After a careful scrutiny of the various explanations which were being offered for that high divorce rate, including social, economic, historical and other unique local conditions, the surprising, yet unavoidable, conclusion pointed in another direction altogether: to the extreme laxity of that nation's divorce laws.

Not surprisingly, therefore, in setting out again, several decades later, to address the question of family stability in a dramatically changed world, my attention was naturally drawn towards the interaction between the law—either through its offering of incentives or its imposition of hardships and penalties—and the various other forces (economic, psychological, sociocultural) which the modern era has unleashed, in America and world wide, on what used to be perceived as the "traditional" family.

The Family and Law: Early Foundations

The ancient origins of the family have been extensively detailed and generally acknowledged. The family, no doubt, has served as a critical societal organism long before the state and church came into power. In the well-known written verses of the Old Testament, the oral origins of which predate the beginning of recorded history, one finds numerous and colorful references to the primacy of the family. Immediately after Genesis' first chapter which recites the creation story there followed the dramatic account about the molding of Adam and Eve. It is with regard to these alleged parents of all humanity that the recorder of the text reiterates: "[t]herefore shall man leave his father and mother, and shall cleave unto his wife: and they shall be one flesh" (*Genesis* 2:25). The Judeo-Christian text thus makes it abundantly clear that the family, more than the tribe or state, was perceived not as a mere secular invention but as primarily a divine creation.

No less compelling testimony to the central role allocated to the family in ancient culture is supplied by the fact that three of the Ten Commandments deal with family safeguards, ranging from the requirements of familial fidelity ("Thou shalt not commit adultery" and "Thou shall not covet thy neighbor's...wife...."), to the admonition regarding the respect due to one's father and mother: "Honor thy father and thy mother: that thy days may be long upon the land which the Lord thy God giveth thee." (*Exodus* 20:12-17). The combination of these Commandments, dwelling on the centrality of the spousal relationship, mandating family fidelity, and conditioning communal longevity upon respectful inter-generational relationships, clearly emphasizes not only the role of the nuclear family as the core unit of social existence, but also points to the indispensable place of the smaller family within the more extended and inter-generational societal framework —be it the extended family, the clan, the tribe, or later the state.

The literature of anthropology, sociology, psychology and economics is replete with detailed descriptions and analyses of the role of the family and its changing functions from antiquity to contemporary times. While Bronislaw Malinowski[1] and Ruth Benedict[2] explored the family, the household and sexuality among those they perceived as primitive people, other scholars, such as Raphael Patai, concentrated on the Biblical and Judean communities,[3] Will Durant documented the Roman family and household,[4] Muhammad Abdul Rauf explored the Muslim family,[5] and more recently, Beatrice Gottlieb surveyed the family's four-hundred year history from the Black Death to the middle of the Industrial Age.[6] In all these widely-ranging scholarly efforts special attention was usually placed upon the family or the household as a *functional* organization: as an economic producer, as an accumulator and distributor of material resources, as a supplier of social and welfare services, as a child-nourisher and socializer, as a socio-psychological identity molder, and as a religio-spiritual shield against a chaotic, hostile and an often unpredictable world. Little attention was given, however, by these and other scholars to the impact of public policies and legal systems instituted by assorted societies throughout the diverse communities of the globe upon the stability and orderly functioning of their families or households.

Comparing the Judaic and Christian Models

In the Western World the two primary legal systems that shaped the structure and implemented the operations and well-being of the family were represented by the Semitic-Judaic and the Roman-Christian customs and codes. The Bible took both marriage and occasionally plural marriage (generally not exceeding two wives), as well as divorce, for granted. It was committed to a patriarchal hierarchy, accepted concubinage, prescribed a precise system of inheritance and succession, and dealt harshly with deviant sexual conduct (such as onanism, homosexuality, fornication and adultery) which competed with the marital relationship and its primary mission of child-bearing. The Biblical Israelites were ancestry-aware (as evidenced by the lengthy genealogical accounts in the Old Testament), and to them the nuclear couple, reinforced by the extended family and the additional membership of these families in larger kinship and tribal groups, served as the core of what was generally referred to as "*the* family".

But despite the Bible's emphasis on genealogy (particularly in Genesis and in Chronicles I), strictly legal Biblical regulations regarding the family, except in matters of sexual conduct, were few and limited in scope. The Israelite tradition, instead, placed much greater emphasis upon customs and conduct fostering family cohesion and values. Brotherly solidarity was frequently stressed, and harmony among siblings was held up as an ideal. The book of Proverbs depicts the high qualities of the ideal wife (31:10-31) and *Ezekiel* (ch. 16) supplies poetic allusions to the desirable marital relationship. It is undeniable that in the Israelites' heavily patriarchal family, the father was the head of the household and the owner of its property. Being the chief of authority, he was expected, nevertheless, to be benevolent and to show love as well as forgiveness to his family. Children were viewed as a divine trust. It was indeed the father's duty to teach his child religion, a trade, even how to swim (*Kid.* 40a). Not surprisingly, therefore, the decline of respect to parents was frequently viewed by Biblical prophets and commentators as symptomatic of the total dissolution of society (*Ezek.* 22:7; *Micah* 7:6; *Prov.* 20:20).

The *Encyclopaedia Judaica* summarizes the basic commitments of the Jewish family thusly: In Jewish social life and tradition the family constituted perhaps the most closely knit unit of society. All members of the family were considered bound by mutual ties of responsibility. Where Christianity glorified celibacy and monasticism as the highest virtues of chastity and divine devotion, Judaism extolled the institution of marriage and family. "Perhaps in nothing was the strength of the family bond more evident," the Encyclopaedia writer concludes, "than in the paradox that where in theory divorce among Jews is the easiest of all procedures, in practice it was, until recent times, a comparatively and even absolute rarity."[7]

The Roman family, less preoccupied with historical ancestry or with blood and marital bonds, and, consequently, much more open to familial enlargements and expansions through widespread resort to adoption and the inclusion of servants and slaves, can more accurately be described as a household—a societal unit in which people of diverse relationships find themselves allied. "[T]he Roman *familia*," it was observed, was "not so much a family as a household; not a kinship group but an assembly of owned persons and things subject to the old male ascendent."[8] Noting that the word family was adopted into modern European languages from Roman law, Carl Brinkman similarly defines that term as denoting in Roman culture "the community of producers and consumers formed by the largely self-sufficient household which included slaves and other servants as well as members connected by common descent or marriage."[9]

While the term family was central to Roman law, the institution, as seen above, often embraced not only one extended unit of monogamic parents, their children, and their slaves and servants, but also a conglomerate of several such units through the formation of a so-called "large" or "joint" family or household. Indeed, such external characteristic as living together in a single household was often the dividing line between what was considered an extended family group as contrasted with the "sib" or "clan," which was made up of a wider group of blood relatives and their attachments, which lived in a larger settlement consisting of several households.

In early Roman history (from about 500 to 200 B.C.) the strictly patriarchal family reached its peak. If a newly born child was deformed or a female, the father was permitted by custom to expose it to death. The power of the father was described as nearly absolute, as if the family had been organized "as a unit of an army always at war."[10] So powerful was the family institution that a wife charged with a crime was committed to the head of the family for judgment and punishment. The father had the power of life, death, and sale into bondage over his children. These extreme rights of the *paterfamilias* were subject to check to some degree, by custom, public opinion and the clan council. The effect of this comprehensive structure in early Rome was said "to cement the unity of the family as the basis of Roman morals and government, and to establish a discipline that hardened the Roman character into stoic strength."[11]

Throughout Roman history the sexual morality of the common man remained relatively the same: coarse and promiscuous. Yet these qualities are said not to have interfered seriously with successful family life. "Man married early—usually by twenty, not through romantic love but for the sound purposes of having a helpmate, rearing useful children, and a healthful sexual life. In the words of the Roman wedding ceremony, marriage was *liberum quaerendorum causa*—for the sake of getting children."[12] To carry out these communal objectives, early Roman law made marriage compulsory, and when that proved ineffective, special taxes were imposed on bachelors.

As far as divorce was concerned, it consisted of two categories: *cum manu* and *sine manu*. The first, which pertained to the divorce of partners whose marriages involved the payment of a dowry, required family agreement and participation, making divorce difficult and rare. In the second category, which applied to families which dispensed with religious marriage ceremonies as well as with family consent, divorce was available to either party at will and even without state approval. Despite, or possibly because, of the strict paternal and family authority, early Roman civilization was described as orderly, conservative, tenacious and practical. Enjoying discipline, the Roman had little interest, unlike his Greek neighbor, in liberty. The Roman, moreover, took it for granted that the community and the government had a right to look into his morals as well as his economics, and to value him primarily according to his services to the state.

Oligarchic Rome, during the first century BC, saw a great increase of wealth and a corruption in politics. The emergence of libertarianism began breaking down the discipline of the ancient family, loosening the country's general morals and weakening marriage bonds. Class differentiations grew and inter-marriage between prominent families became so customary that Cato complained that the empire had become a matrimonial agency. While some leaders continued to plead with the citizens to marry and beget children as part of their duty to the state, the wealthy sought other institutions— prostitution and homosexuality—to satisfy their sexual and social needs. It was thus said that children had become luxuries which only the poor could afford.

During the first century AD, the era of epicurean Rome, greater attention began to be directed towards the education of Rome's children. Early education was furnished by nurses, usually Greek. Further primary education was offered by private enterprise institutions. By the age of thirteen the able student, of either sex, was frequently placed in a secondary school. When the profitable private secondary education institutions grew in number, Emperor Vespasian brought them under government control, both for revenue producing reasons and for doctrinal control. For higher education, selected scholars went to Athens for the study of philosophy and to Alexandria for medical training.

The increasing decline of morality and the expansion of the plutocracy during oligarchic and epicurian Rome produced very lenient attitudes towards prostitution, which became both legalized and state regulated. Traditional marriage had to contend bravely with this and other rival sexual outlets by seeking to marry off the women at an early age, even if the matrimonial ties were not to last. At the same time, women increasingly began taking part in the work force -- in factories, trade and the professions. With women leaving the familial shelters and entering the wider community, traditional morality changed. "Pure Women," noted Ovid cynically, "are only those who have not been asked; and a man who is angry at his wife's amours is a mere rustic." This was the state of Roman society, its customs and laws, when Christianity made its first appearance.

Even a cursory comparison of the Biblical and Roman models of the family/household institutions demonstrates the centrality as well as the diversity of these units of social organization in the life of classical societies. It generally appears that the Biblical family was much more historically prone and tradition bound, due to the commitment of the Israelite leaders to tribe, nation and country-building. Using as their building blocks the mass of migrant individuals and families, these Biblical leaders sought during their peoples' long migrations (from Ur of the Chaldees, through the Egyptian slavery and the subsequent conquest of the land of Canaan) to reinforce amongst these nomads a new and prouder identity, with the family as its core. The Roman family institutions, on the other hand, being developed for already settled people and aiming at the continuation of a stable community, were more multi-functional and less focused in outlook. The primary objective of the Roman family law was not so much the building of long-lasting entities, but the practical improvement of family administration and the clarification of the familial lines of authority.

This essay's limited emphasis upon two historical strands, the Biblical and Roman, which played historically important roles in laying the foundation for Western family law, over-looks several other and equally important approaches to family laws and customs in the greater part of the Asian continent, in Africa, and among what used to be described as "primitive societies" and later "indigenous people" in the far-flung islands and territories of the Pacific and the frozen North. Still, in many of these overlooked societies one could readily discern variations or modification of the Biblical or Roman modalities, or else, a rich diversity and sometimes idiosyncratic laws and structures incapable of being described in a paper of this length.

To the previous description of the early foundations of the family institutions and laws in the Southern and Eastern Mediterranean, one should add the emerging and soon to be evidenced influence and central role of the Christian Church upon the family institution both in Europe and throughout the European dependencies around the world. Little by little the church, through its parish management and its ecclesiastic courts, began to assume not only a central role in matters of marriage, child-bearing and upbringing, but also to penetrate with its doctrines several other aspects of family life. From being a sacred institution in ancient Israel, and either a private and secular or state regulated organization in classic Rome, the family once more became church controlled in Christian Europe.

While several modern family scholars and historians have viewed the growing de-secularization of the family with a jaundiced eye and growing concerns, it should be noticed that the church's intervention in family law and practice did not originate with Christianity. In the early Biblical family, in the life of the later Muslim community, and among other ethnic communities and people, little differentiation has existed historically between the realms of religious and secular family life. So intertwined was religion in all aspects of private and public life during earlier history, that it would indeed have been impossible to draw clear lines of demarcation between the religious and secular standards and demands imposed by the community, the church and the state upon this most ancient of all human organizations—the family.

The American Family: From Rhetoric to Law

As the medieval and renaissance eras came to an end in Europe, the family, the household, and the feudal estates and manors (the latter having become the most central units of societal organization during feudalism) began to gradually relinquish some of their authority and functions both to the church, which had grown in wealth and power, and to the state—the preeminence of which had been gaining support from the writings of the new era's leading philosophers and political figures, including Niccolo Machiavelli (1469-1527), the father of modern nationalism. The emergence of the Enlightenment meant, moreover, that the ancient dogmas of the divinely anointed sovereign or the unchallenged patriarch who could never do wrong, no longer satisfied the increasingly skeptical public. In the face of the growing winds of libertarianism and egalitarianism, the authority of the traditional institutions of governance, first the state and subsequently the church and the family, required new legitimating supports. It was at that time that the doctrine of the "social contract," describing a mutually binding agreement tying the ruled to the ruler, granting rights and imposing duties upon the governed as well as on the governors, emerged in the writings of Jean Jacques Rousseau and John Locke.

It is from this perspective that one may best be able to understand the making of the 1620 Mayflower Compact. That unique and mutual agreement by the group of Pilgrims, hailing from England and seeking to establish themselves in the New World, set out in advance the principles of conduct which were to bind these travelers in their new haven. One may look in vain in the Mayflower Compact to language which either safeguards the family or protects individual rights and privileges. Instead, the Compact proclaimed the signatories' loyalty to their sovereign, King James of Great Britain, France and Ireland, and to the advancement of the Christian Faith. It further pledged the settlers' commitment to the enactment of such just and equal laws as shall be thought to "most meet the general Good of the Colony...."[13]

Having failed to specify the full or even approximate panoply of what the general good of the colony was to consist of, other than the pursuit of the king's glory and the advancement of the Christian faith, the commitment to such specific issues as family welfare and individual well-being remained unarticulated in the Compact. Whether the safeguarding of the family was taken so much for granted as to not require articulation, or whether the dominance of the Church and state so overshadowed individual and familial claims that any mention of the latter might have seemed to border on the seditious, will never be known. Yet, it is noteworthy that the two primary societal entities—the family and the individual—which ancient history considered central to the general good of society, were overlooked in America's first self-governing manifesto.

The Compact's failure to underscore the central role of the family in the governmental scheme of the newly planned American colony is not a unique omission in the history of United States jurisprudence. America's Declaration of Independence from Great Britain, dated July 4, 1776, as well as the subsequent Constitution of the United States, drafted in Philadelphia in 1787, more than a decade later, found it similarly unnecessary to dedicate to the "family" institution even one clause, phrase or word in the documents which were to become the cornerstones of the new republic.

Prior to the drafting of the Declaration and the Constitution, Alexander Hamilton wrote in 1775 that "[t]he sacred rights of mankind are not to be rummaged for among old parchments...." These rights, he asserted, were written "by the hand of divinity itself; and can never be erased or obscured by mortal power."[14] Yet the short Constitution which followed found enough space to deal with such subjects as the minimal ages of congressional representatives and senators, the weight of the voting rights of bonded servants, the prohibition of cruel and unusual punishment, the requirement of native citizenship for future presidents of the United States, the prohibition of the quartering of soldiers in private residences, and the right to keep and bear arms. Yet, this Constitution and its subsequent amendments made not a single reference to the rights and duties, or even to the very existence of the family institution. This neglect turned out to be a costly error.

In a country committed to a government by law and not by men (or women), the failure to make adequate reference to the family and any other components of the national population (free, slave, Indian, female, immigrant, or otherwise) or to specify in the constitutional documents any commonly agreed upon rights or duties, any requisite processes, objectives or priorities, is destined to produce a lacuna—a public policy and legal vacuum which might require years, decades, or even centuries to peacefully fill. Bridging the gaps in public policy and law can at times be attained peacefully through the building of a new popular consensus. More often such changes may be attained only through violent struggles. Some such struggles have manifested themselves in America's Civil War, and in other lesser instances of rebellion and mass disorder. New struggles revolving around contemporary issues related to the family and its status are now again emerging in our midst.

Despite the failure to recognize the family's primacy or even its existence in this nation's most hallowed documents, lip service, nevertheless, has continued to be paid to the family in government and non-governmental halls, in churches, musical comedies, popular songs and occasionally even in court opinions. Thus, despite their specific and official absence from the list of public or private institutions safeguarded in the founding documents of this republic, the family, like God and the Bible, have continued to be regularly alluded to in the nation's evolving ethos.

Dedicated to the identification of the family's place in the American legal order, and to an understanding of the impact of American jurisprudence upon family stability, we must introduce the reader to a fair sampling of the interactions between law and the family in contemporary America. One could well enlarge upon our sampling of the escalating, yet generally uncommented upon, conflict between American jurisprudence and familial autonomy by going back to the century and a half that transpired from the signing of the United States Constitution to the middle of the 20th century. But the limited space available for this essay makes such thorough undertaking both too ambitious and unfeasible.

We choose to begin the contemporary survey of legal-family relations in 1965, when the Supreme Court of the United States had before it the appeal of Estelle T. Griswold, the executive director of the Planned Parenthood League of Connecticut. Griswold was convicted of violating the Connecticut Statutes prohibiting the use or the assistance in the use of "any drug...article or instrument for the purpose of preventing conception...."[15] It is significant that among its many functions, the League, which Griswold directed, offered information, instruction, and medical advice to married persons "as to the means of preventing conception."[16]

In a majority opinion written by Justice William O. Douglas, the United States Supreme Court reversed the conviction of both appellants Griswold and Buxton, a licensed physician and a professor at the Yale Medical Center who also served as Medical Director of the League, for assisting, abetting, and counseling in the violations of the planned parenthood program. In what constituted, and may continue to serve as the highlight of America's legal endorsement of the family institution and its safeguarding from governmental interference, Justice Douglas wrote:

> We deal with a right of privacy older then the Bill of
> Rights—older than our political parties, older than our
> school system. Marriage is a coming together for better or
> for worse, hopefully enduring and intimate to the degree of
> being sacred. It is an association that promotes a way of life,
> not causes; a harmony in living, not political factions; a
> bilateral loyalty, not commercial or social projects.[17]

Although Justice Douglas conceded the Constitution's failure
to specifically recognize the family and its societal functions, he
stressed that "[t]he association of people is not mentioned in
the Constitution nor in the Bill of Rights. The right to educate
a child in a school of the parents' choice—whether public or
private or parochial— is also not mentioned. Nor is the right
to study any particular subject or any foreign language. Yet the
First Amendment has been construed to include certain of
these rights."[18] In reversing the conviction of the officials of the
Planned Parenthood League of Connecticut, the Supreme
Court opinion noted bitingly: "Would we allow the police to
search the sacred precincts of marital bedrooms for telltale
signs of the use of contraceptives? The very idea is repulsive to
the notions of privacy surrounding the marriage relationship."[19]

Yet this high-minded Supreme Court declaration, asserting
the protection due the sacred precincts of the family from both
government and law, has not prevented state legislatures from
continuing to prescribe for family members those methods of
sexual intercourse which are officially condoned, and to
proscribe those which are deemed against "the laws of nature."
Nor did the proclaimed respect for the ancient origins of the
family deter the drafters of American criminal law from
criminalizing polygamy, a practice prevailing in many other
human communities, or from prohibiting the voluntary marital
alliance between members of different racial groups (the laws
against miscegenation).

The early legal prohibitions against unorthodox positions and practices of sexual intercourse (which were described colorfully in Africa and in other missionary dominated colonies, as "non-missionary positions"), remain on the law books of many or our states to this day. Yet although now infrequently enforced, the fear of selective and prejudiced legal enforcement continues to threaten marital sexual practices. And while the criminal prohibition of inter-racial marriages finally came to an end in 1967,[20] in the *Loving* case, what caused the change was not so much the enhanced respect for marital privacy as the growth of the social and moral persuasion generated by the civil rights movement.

Earmarks of Modernity

As one examines the raw statistical data relating to family issues and practices in post World War II America, symptoms of familial disruption and decay emerge in alarming dimensions. In most civilizations the rate of marriages, their longevity and the size of the birth rate are considered as major indicators of familial health. In the United States, current data testifies to dramatic declines in all of these three measuring criteria. From an annual rate of 10.6 marriages per 1,000 population in 1970, the marriage rate declined to 8.9 per 1,000 in 1995. From 35 divorcees per 1,000 married persons in 1965 the rate of divorcees grew to some 130 per 1,000 married persons in 1990. Moreover, the nation's birth rate declined from 3.7 children per woman in 1960 to only 1.9 in 1989.[21]

If birth and upbringing by traditional two gender family guarantees for the newborn child, as some of the literature suggests, optimal care and a balanced preparation for future life, then the 1993 data that in Washington, D.C., the capital of the free world, some 67.8 percent of all infants were born to unwed mothers should have served as a serious warning.

521

Even more troubling are the recent disclosures by Senator Daniel Patrick Moynihan that while the capital's teenage birth rate (the number of births to 15-19 year old mothers per 1,000 teenagers) has hardly fluctuated between 1940 and 1995 (growing slightly from 54.1 births per 1,000 teenagers in 1940 to 58.9 in 1994), the ratio of out-of-wedlock teenage births in proportion to all teenage births grew from 13.5 percent in 1940 to 75.9 percent in 1994.[22] If one reasonably assumes that a youth's inculcation with constructive social values and behavior patterns depend, at least in part, upon stable homelife and parental input, the increases in divorce rates, in out-of-wedlock birth-rates, coupled with the growing hosts of latch-key children and juveniles—those whose parents are occupied out of their homes by the demands of employment or by other excusable and inexcusable absenteeism—raise serious questions as to where the next generation's lifestyle habits and customs are to be derived from.

With the growing decline of the traditional American family, with some 31 percent of all of the nation's families being made up of less than two adult and gender-distinct parents, with a similar percentage of families consisting of two-career couples, and with the increasing confinement of older and serviceable members of the extended family to distinct golden age havens, those who could most reliably be counted upon to be found at home by the very young and by their maturing siblings are those "virtual" members of the family who constantly surface on the television screen. And they, indeed, can be found there day and night, twenty four hours a day, every day of the year. It is undeniable, therefore, that the most permanent and available guardians of the young products of the American family are not necessarily the parents (single or married), or a readily accessible extended family, or the school teachers, or the scout masters, or the clergy and church youth groups. It is to the TV, in fact, to which we have surrendered the major task of establishing and reinforcing the role models for the children of America, and, increasingly, the children of many other countries.

What has the nation's legal system done in these recent years to either shore up or to undercut the foundations of the American family? Despite the Supreme Court's glowing 1965 dicta about the sacred precincts of the family which may not be invaded, and the continuing rhetoric of presidents, politicians and clergy, most governmental policy makers--executive, legislative, and judicial-- have continued, through legal enactments and the power of the purse, to slowly yet constantly institute or lend their support to programs and courses of action which tend to erode the integrity, the status, the privacy, and the well being of the nation's families.

Possibly one of the least noticed yet most adversarial governmental actions against the hallowed precincts of the family came in *Roe v. Wade*.[23] the widely known 1973 Supreme Court abortion rights decision. It is not our intent here to reopen or to escalate the "right to life" versus "the right to choice" controversy. Yet the inconsistent history of abortion in this country, and the standing of the state as contrasted with the federal role in family matters remains unexamined. Indeed, the ultimate question of how a country which has counted among its international priorities the active exporting of the doctrine, practices and instruments of planned parenthood could, until 1965, prohibit prophylactics domestically and, until 1973, continue to deny the safe and legal abortion of unwanted children to parents and despondent single mothers, is an issue too complicated and relatively removed from the central theme of this paper.

What we seek to address here, instead, is not the ultimate question regarding the morality or legality of medical abortions. What is more relevant to our inquiry into the law's impact on the family is an examination of *Roe's* implications for the autonomy of the family and its decision making process. Deliberately or negligently, some of the most important implications of the Supreme Court decision's in *Roe v. Wade* have been totally overlooked . The facts of the case can be readily summarized. Jane Roe, a single woman residing in Dallas County, Texas, petitioned in 1970 for an injunction against the District Attorney of the county. In her action she sought to restrain the officer from enforcing a state statute which made it a crime for her to attempt or to procure an abortion, except when the procedure was authorized "by medical advice for the purpose of saving the life of the mother." Alleging that she was unmarried and pregnant, Roe asserted further that she wished to terminate her pregnancy by an abortion performed by a licensed physician under safe clinical conditions, but was unable to secure such a procedure in Texas because her life "did not appear to be threatened by the continuation of the pregnancy". Failing to obtain the requested legal relief in Texas, the applicant caused the case to be brought before the United States Supreme Court.

Being unmarried, Jane Roe could not raise the *Griswold* doctrine which prohibited the state's invasion of the "sacred precincts of marital bedrooms." Instead, she based her objection to the state's criminalization of abortion on her "right to personal privacy, protected by the First, Fourth, Fifth, Ninth and Fourteenth Amendments." Following a lengthy review of ancient as well as common law doctrines regarding the nature of pregnancy in its diverse stages, and after reviewing contemporary developments in America's privacy law, Justice Blackman, writing for the Supreme Court, ruled against the constitutionality of the Texas statute on the ground that its language swept "too broadly."

The Court first pointed out that a fetus or an embryo consisted of potential life only and thus did not fall fully within the constitutional protection accorded to "persons" (a term allegedly limited by the Constitution to postnatal life). Next, weighing an abortion's possible deleterious effects upon the health of the mother, the Court concluded that advances in medicine had made early abortions relatively safe. Upholding the mother's claim of privacy, although pointing out that it was not absolute, the Court ruled that: "For the stage prior to approximately the end of the first trimester, the abortion decision and its effectuation must be left to the medical judgement of the pregnant woman's attending physician." The Court went on to hold further that during the second trimester, the state is entitled to regulate abortion procedures in the interest of the mother's health and safety, and that only during the final trimester, when the fetus becomes viable, could the state proscribe abortion altogether in order to promote the societal interest in potential of human life.

The 1973 Supreme Court decision, overturning the Texas abortion law, was hailed as a great victory by feminists and other "pro-choice" proponents, and was violently condemned by the "pro-life" forces. Verbal, legal and physical skirmishes pertaining to the *Roe v. Wade* outcome continue to this day, nearly a quarter of a century later.

What few, if any, observers took notice of, was the failure of the majority of the Supreme Court, as well as its dissenting members, to address or make even the slightest reference, in the voluminous 64-page opinion, to the role, view, consent or even mere consultation with the male parent of the about to be aborted fetus. One might offer various excuses for the Court's failure by pointing to Jane Roe's status as a single unmarried woman. Yet nowhere in the decision does the court make even the slightest reference to Ms. Roe's single status, or otherwise restrict its ruling to instances of single mothers. As a consequence, while a married or single male remains generally accountable for the support of children sired by him, the highest court of the land saw no reason to grant that very father any standing with regard to the decision whether his pre-natal issue should be permitted to reach its potentiality and be allowed a live birth, or whether that potential issue should be terminated through the joint decision of the mother and her physician.

This jurisprudential emphasis upon maternal privacy, while overlooking the autonomy of the wider family and its decision-making process, was not unique to, nor did it stop with the *Roe v. Wade* decision. What began as possibly a mere paternal oversight in 1973 was subsequently expanded into a more open and militant campaign against proposed requirements that abortions upon underage and unemancipated children be performed only after prior notice to, consultation with, and parental consent. So unbending has become the individualistic and feminist force operating under the banner of pro-choice, that any middle of the road efforts by state legislatures to involve a pregnant child's family in the abortion decision was regularly met with total hostility and legal opposition. Illustrative of the fierce battle lines between the unemancipated single child, who might be either totally committed to or unhesitatingly opposed to the continuation of her pregnancy, and her nuclear or extended family, which could possibly offer not only opposite perspectives but also such material and psychological support as might lead to a more broadly consensual conclusion, is provided by the case of *Planned Parenthood of Southeastern Pennsylvania v. Casey*.[24]

In *Casey*, the Supreme Court upheld a Pennsylvania statute's parental consent provision, under which an unemancipated woman under 18 could not obtain an abortion, except in medical emergencies, unless both she and one of her parents provided informed consent. But the statute included a "judicial bypass," by which a court could authorize an abortion without parental consent if the judge determined that the young woman had given her own informed consent *and* an abortion would be in her best interest.

Casey also addressed the issue of spousal notification. The Court struck down the provision in the Pennsylvania statute which required a married woman to sign a statement that she had informed her spouse that she intended to undergo an abortion before the procedure could be performed. The Court asserted that the requirement reflected an outmoded view of the position of women in society, stating that it "embodies a view of marriage inconsonant with the common-law status of married women but [which] is repugnant to this Court's present understanding of marriage and of the nature of the rights secured by the Constitution."[25] Furthermore, the Court recognized that "women do not lose their constitutionally protected liberty when they marry."[26]

The nation's highest judicial tribunal thus unhesitatingly overruled the familial consulting and decision-making standards, established by the state legislature, as an unreasonable intrusion on the mother's privacy rights guaranteed by *Roe v. Wade*. Showing no sympathy for the familial claim for the right to deal as an autonomous community with a difficult problem concerning the family's most sacred precincts, the Court vested absolute authority in the unemancipated child and the judicial system to override the family's counsel.

While some efforts to maintain the traditional family integrity and independence so glowingly described in the *Griswold* decision have been upheld by the courts, the war against the familial community and in favor of the privacy of the pregnant individual—however young, uninformed and hasty in her decision-making—continues vigorously to this date. Some compromises have been advanced, yet not one comprehensible enough for the resolution of this thorny issue.

While highlighting the federal and often the state's failure to uphold broader familial autonomy in the abortion arena, one must not overlook some governmental policies which arguably have been designed to strengthen the family institution. Among these one could count the liberalization of sick time, family leave provisions and similar innovations which may make it more possible for children and parents to spend time together. The Family and Medical Leave Act of 1993 allows a parent to take time off work to care for a new child. The Act also permits an employee to take time off work to care for a seriously ill child, a spouse (not including an unmarried partner), or a parent. Leave is also authorized in instances of serious health conditions, including pregnancy.

Yet one might also attribute to governmental bounty the greatest responsibility for the epidemic of out-of-wedlock births. The nation's welfare programs (particularly the one known as Aid to Families with Dependent Children, subsidized housing, food stamps, and the like), many of the critics assert, has turned the birth and rearing of out-of-wedlock children into a source of economic benefits for a host of underage as well as adult single women.

The Escalating Struggle Between Ideology and Reality

The family's struggle for a central role in societal affairs, for preeminence in the management of its internal affairs, and for control over the material means required for its survival and well-being has been affected not only by the constitutional failure to define and protect its status, and by the more contemporary legal emphasis upon individualistic as contrasted with familial interests. The family, one could argue, suffered also from its being reduced from its status as a publicly sanctioned institution to become more and more a mere contractual arrangement, a change which was dramatized some three or more decades ago by the introduction of "no fault divorce."

Initially, the new category of divorce by mutual consent seemed as a reasonable innovation designed to diffuse the tensions inherent in the traditional divorce process, and the intensified hostilities which usually accompanied it. The "no fault" approach sought to turn the divorce into a negotiated and consensual process, by freeing it of the elements of blame and guilt more common to the criminal, rather than civil, legal arena. "No-fault," by setting out to reduce the factors of blame-worthiness, saw among its objectives the diffusion, both immediately and for time to come, of intra-family hostilities, as well as the preservation of the remaining good will between the divorced couple and between them and their children.

California was the first state in the union to institute the "no-fault" divorce—or what some came to refer to as "divorce upon demand." The innovation soon turned out to be a national success. All states now permit resort to no-fault divorces, where the mere allegation and evidence of "incompatibility" (representing one of the law's vaguest terms and one least burdened with evidentiary standards) suffices to terminate a marital relation. Many family watchers therefore view this relaxation of the divorce standards as a major villain, alleging that it contributed heavily to the escalation of America's divorce rates.

The mere data of the mushrooming no-fault divorce rates is probably insufficient to support the allegations of state culpability, in bringing about a relaxed or possibly even hostile attitude towards the protection of the family institution. But a more thorough analysis demonstrates, nevertheless, a nonchalant governmental attitude towards the family as an institution deserving and requiring special public protection. The firmer and more protective public policy which is evidenced with regard to the protection of free speech, the right of assembly and the manifestation of individual privacy has certainly been absent in the case of family safeguards.

One might well argue that the legal recognition of no-fault divorce was merely the acknowledgment of existing realities. One might point out further that the widespread acceptance of the ideals of "romantic" marriage, the movement away from arranged marriages (where family background, status and material resources take precedence over individual characteristics and preferences), and the current unavailability of sound processes for the choice of suitable marriage partners, are indeed the main villains of family stability. Moreover, perpetual changes in a married individual's social, intellectual, economic, work-connected, and other interests are often productive of such growing incompatibility that strict enforcement of the marital relationship is likely to be more harmful than beneficial to all concerned. Yet we cannot ignore the fact that it was the public policy's and law's willingness to permit an easy dissolution of the marital institution which contributed to the attenuation of the stigma and the societal pressures which used to militate against family break-ups. From a state-supported, highly regarded, and widely protected institution, the family has been turned into a mere social contract, in which neither the state, the children, nor the extended family are accorded any right to intervene.

We do not argue that mere constitutional neglect, followed by several unfortunate legal and policy decisions (legislative as well as judicial) are the sole or primary forces which have driven the family to the low level of respect and stability that it currently occupies. One who peruses both the legal and non-legal literature will discover many other family related arenas in which in the absence of a consistent and coherent public policy, the law often played indirect yet important roles in shaping or tolerating new socioeconomic developments under which the American family has not fared too well. Altogether, as one examines the wide spectrum of this country's policies and laws directed towards or affecting the family institution, one cannot but acknowledge the outright contradictions, ambivalence, inconsistency, and even direct causing of harm for which government is responsible. While the nation's criminal codes, inherited in great part from England's earlier common law, keep insisting on the maintenance, at least on the books, of such family protecting measures as the criminalization of prostitution, fornication and adultery, the enforcement of these laws has fallen to such disuse as to charge the agencies responsible for the administration of justice with pretense or even outright deception. How many prosecutions for prostitution has one read about in the recent daily press? Why was Dick Morris permitted to become a best selling author instead of being prosecuted for adultery? And how serious can the law be in enforcing its prohibitions against fornication when civil rights advocates and city councils set out to discipline and penalize landlords for refusing to rent rooms and apartments to unmarried couples?

Neither has the law been supportive or consistent in other areas which might greatly impact on family well-being. The Internal Revenue laws have offered few if any incentives for family building and maintenance. The labor pay incentives developed some three-quarters of a century ago, which accorded pay enhancements to the heads of large families, have slowly been discarded. Tax deductions granted to individuals to encourage their pursuit of such education and training as are required for holding on or securing employment, are totally lacking with regard to parental expenses incurred in the education of the next generations of American workers. Contemporary individualism, which has replaced earlier eras of emphasis upon familial and communal well-being, has driven out many of the benefits long ago extended to the family in this as well as in other countries. Among the few, yet almost pathetic, instances of the old support granted to "familialism," one can count such examples as movie houses and private eating places in which underage children may be charged less for admission or allowed lesser prices for smaller portions of food.

But how many instances of significant governmental policy and deliberate legal programs can we marshal as evidence of the nation's claimed special support for the family institution? In Kuwait, the United Arab Republic, and elsewhere through the globe, governmental agencies might offer grants or low-interest loans to young people contemplating marriage. Additional benefits may become available to married couples upon the birth of children. But in this mother-land of democracy, both governmental policies, legal processes and other public practices have chosen to speak loudly about the maintenance of and even a return to the historically ideal family institution, yet have often set out (deliberately or out of ignorance or ideological prejudice) to do the very opposite.

Those believing that the family is the cornerstone of civilization,[27] must urgently call for the creation of new, positive as well as negative, reinforcing measures to restore and strengthen today's much weakened family institution. Compulsory pre-marital and pre-divorce counseling have been proposed and implemented here and abroad. There are undoubtedly many other avenues and approaches worth exploring. Yet what must come first is the public articulation and popular acceptance of national pro-family policies, capable of gaining widespread adherence. No law can be effective unless public policy and public support back it up.

The natural forces of economics, sociology and geography admittedly continue to batter the fragile ship of the family. Economic opportunities, business dislocations, downsizing, the wide geographic dispersions of business enterprises, multinational expansionism accompanied by the migration of production facilities and labor, the socioeconomic instability of many minority groups which cause disinclinations for long-term familial commitments—all serve to undercut the family and do not seem to be on the decline. Certainly one cannot hope to overcome the thrust of all these anti-familial forces merely through legislative enactments or the issuing of judicial decrees.

Observations on Familial Revival

The law is not an island. A viable law, if it is to have a meaningful and lasting effect, must be grounded in well established traditions and be backed by strong public commitments to the societal policies it seeks to implement. This article must not be misinterpreted, therefore, as a call for a flood of indiscriminate legislation unrelated to historical or existing public values. Ours is not to be viewed as a prescriptive package for legal action. Our more modest goal is, instead, to reiterate the significant, yet not sole or even primary, role that the law plays in maintaining or in modifying individual and collective conduct and societal realities. Our further objective is to call for a more proactive commitment of public policy and the law in a national effort to save the threatened family and its fragments from further decay or even virtual extinction.

If one is to distill the historical functions of the family, and follow those with observations of contemporary reality, the following conclusions cannot be avoided:

1. The primacy of the family to the well being of the nation and civilization is not a matter to be merely referred to in political campaigns and in church, synagogue, mosque and temple sermons. The primacy of the family institution must be given enforceable support in constitutional, federal, state, and local legislation;

2. Public policy and law need to approach issues pertaining to family welfare from an affirmative action perspective, seeking to meet familial needs with such special safeguards and benefits as are constitutionally permissible;

3. While the contemporary confusion, (semantic, cultural and practical) between the *family* (traditionally consisting of a two gender couple and its issue) and the *household* (which may be made up of a combination of persons of the same or diverse genders) is not likely to be readily resolved, and indeed seems to serve various ideological causes and camps, law and public policy should not contribute to the blurring of differences. Calling a household a family amounts to what is known in German as *"etickettenschwindel"* (labeling fraud). Such blurring will not serve, in the long run, the interests of any of the contesting camps;

4. The currently pressing debate as to whether persons not blood related and not traditionally married (homosexual or otherwise) living in a common household should be accorded rights and privileges similar to those extended to family members needs to be addressed separately and be resolved on the basis of equities and distinct public policies;

5. Given the forceful impact of the environmental changes on the global community and its institutions, it is not feasible, even through resort to dramatic policy changes and legal reforms, to restore to the family the original functions it was set up to perform or those it assumed over time. It is unlikely that the family will return to be an economic or employment center for its members. It is unlikely that we will see a major return to the extended family living in a joint household. It is unlikely that families will remain geographically centered.

What functions therefore remain for the family to carry out, and are families committed to such limited scope worthy of particular protection? It is our view that the family can and will continue to serve as the main inter-generational conveyor of communal values, mostly through the initiation of young members in character forming practices and reinforcing rituals. The family can and is likely to remain also as the main hot-house for bringing up children and the youth (an option preferable to the more recent orphanage proposal by United States House of Representatives' Speaker Newt Gingrich, or the older and now discarded Soviet model under which the state rather than natural parents was to assume responsibility for the creation of a New Soviet Man). No other existing societal institution can better play a central role in the crystallization of individual identity and continue serving as a life-long hub for inter-gender and inter-generational companionship and comradeship than the family.

Notes

[1]Bronislaw Malinowski, *Sex and Repression in Savage Society* (Chicago: University of Chicago Press, 1985).

[2]Ruth Benedict, *Patterns of Culture* (Boston: Houghton Mifflin Co., 1934).

[3]R. Patai, *Sex and Family in the Bible and Middle East* (1959).

[4]Will Durant, *The Story of Civilization: Caesar and Christ* (New York: Simon and Schuster, 1944), see generally, Ch. IV, VII, IX, XVII, XVIII.

[5]Muhammad Abdul Rauf, *The Islamic View of Women and the Family* (N.Y.: Robert Spelley and Sons, 1977).

[6]Beatrice Gottlieb, *The Family in the Western World: From the Black Death to the Industrial Age* (N.Y.: The Oxford University Press, 1993).

[7]"Family," in 6, *Encyclopaedia Judaica* (Jerusalem: Ketter Publishing House, 1972), pp. 1163-1171.

[8]Will Durant, III, *The Story of Civilization: Caesar and Christ* (New York: Simon and Schuster, 1944), p. 58.

[9]Family in *Encyclopedia of the Social Sciences* (New York: The Macmillan Co., 1949), p.67.

[10]Durant, p. 56.

[11]Durant, p. 57.

[12]Durant, p. 68.

[13]The Mayflower Compact (Nov. 11, 1620), *reprinted in* Nicholas N. Kittrie & Eldon D. Wedlock, Jr., *The Tree of Liberty: A Documentary History of Rebellion and Political Crime in America* (Baltimore: The Johns Hopkins University Press, 1986), p.8.

[14]Alexander Hamilton, "The Farmer Refuted" (Feb. 23, 1775), in 1 *The Papers of Alexander Hamilton* 81, 122 (H.Syrett ed. 1961).

[15]*Griswold v. Connecticut*, 381 U.S. 479, 480 (1965).

[16]General Statutes of Connecticut, 1958, § 53-32 and § 54-196.

[17]*Griswold*, 381 U.S. at 486.

[18]*Griswold*, 381 U.S. at 482.

[19]*Griswold*, 381 U.S. at 485-86.

[20]*Loving v. Virginia*, 388 U.S. 1 (1967).

[21]David Popenoe, "The Family Is in Decline," in Viqi Wagner (ed.), *The Family in America: Opposing Viewpoints* (San Diego: Greenhaven Press, 1992), pp. 17-24.

[22]Daniel Patrick Moynihan, "The Big Lie of 1996," *The Washington Post,* Jan. 28, 1997 A 13, col.

[23]*Roe v. Wade*, 410 U.S. 113 (1973).

[24]505 U.S. 833 (1992).

[25]*Planned Parenthood of Southeastern Pennsylvania v. Casey*, 505 U.S. 833, 838 (1992).

[26]*Casey*, 505 U.S. at 898.

[27]Carle C. Zimmerman, *Family and Civilization* (New York: Harper & Brothers, 1947).

ABOUT THE AUTHORS

Gordon L. Anderson is Secretary General of Professors World Peace Academy, and Editor of *International Journal on World Peace*. He earned his Ph.D. in Philosophy of Religion at the Claremont Graduate School. He is editor of *Worldwide State of the Family*, and coeditor of *Morality and Religion in Liberal Democratic Societies*. He has published numerous articles on Religion and Society.

Jon G. Davies is Senior Lecturer in Religious Studies at the University of Newcastle upon Tyne, England. He was educated in the UK and in East Africa; and attended the Universities of Oxford, England, and Brandeis, USA. He is author or editor of several books including *The Family: Is It Just Another Lifestyle?* (1993), *God and the Market Place* (1993), and *War and Religion in Twentieth Century Europe* (1994). He is currently working on books on the early Christian centuries and on contemporary religious debates about religion and capitalism.

Armando de la Torre is Professor of Sociology and Dean of the Graduate Division of Social Sciences at Francisco Maroquin University, Guatemala City, Guatemala. He studied Law at the University of Havana, Cuba, Philosophy at the University of Comillas in Spain, Theology at the Graduate School in Frankfort, Germany, and earned his Ph.D. at the University of Munich. He has taught at the university level in several countries, including the United States, and has publihed articles in the social sciences, law, philosophy, ethics, and education.

Jean Bethke Elshtain is the Laura Spelman Rockefeller Professor of Social and Political Ethics at the University of Chicago. She has also taught at Vanderbilt, Harvard and Yale Universities, the University of Massachussetts, and Oberlin College. She is author of numerous articles and books on society including *Public Man Private Woman: Women in Social and Political Thought* and *Democracy on Trial*. She earned her Ph.D. in Politics from Brandeis University.

William R. Garrett is Professor of Sociology and Chair at St. Michael's College in Colchester, Vermont, where he has taught since 1968. He earned an Mdiv. from the Divinity School of Yale University and a Ph.D. in the Sociology of Religion from Drew University. He is the author of *Seasons of Marriage and Family Life* (1982), edited *Social Consequences of Religious Belief* (1989), co-edited with Roland Robertson, *Religion and Global Order* (1991), and has written over 80 papers, book chapters and journal articles on topics ranging from religion, to social theory, family life, and globalization theory. In addition, he has served as editor of *the journal Sociological Analysis,* area editor for sociology/anthropology of religion for *Religious Studies Review;* and president of the Association for the Sociology of Religion. Professor Garrett is also an ordained Baptist minister.

Anthony J. Guerra received his BA from Georgetown University and Master's and Doctorate degrees from Harvard University. He has written extensively on religious traditions in the ancient as well as contemporaneous world with a focus on religious/cultural traditions self-understanding as well as their understanding of other religions and cultures. His most recent publication is *Paul and the Letter to the Romans* published by Cambridge University Press Before coming to the University of Bridgeport, Dr. Guerra was a tenured professor at Bard College in the Division of the Social Sciences. He is founder of Institute for the Study of Values and Ethics at the University of Bridgeport and senses as the Dean of the College of Graduate and Undergraduate Studies and Vice Provost of Academic Affairs. His current research and writing focuses on the role of religion in the development of the family and the latter's impact on the wider society.

Abdelmoneim Khattab is Director of the Islamic Center of Greater Toledo, Ohio, USA, and part-time teacher at Bowling Green State University. He was born in Egypt and received his MA in Theology at A-Azhar University in Cairo. He earned and MA in Sociology from the University of Alberta in Canada. He is Secretary General of The Council of Imams and a member of the Interfaith Roundtable.

Nicholas Kittrie is University Professor and the Edwin A. Mooers Scholar in Law at the American University, Washington, DC. He served as co-chair of the International Conference on the Family, held in Seoul, Korea, in 1995, under the auspices of the Professors World Peace Academy.

Jan Knappert is Senior Fellow, School of African and Oriental Studies at the University of London. He was born in Holland and received a classical education which included Greek and Latin. He studied Oriental languages and cultures at the University of Leyden earning four degrees: Buddhism, Sanskrit, and Hinduism; Arabic, Islamic and Semitic Studies; Southeast Asian, Malayan, and Polynesian languages and culture; and a doctorate in East African literature. He taught at nine universities: Ghent and Louvain in Belgium; Pretoria, South Africa; Kinshasa, Zaire; Kampala, Uganda; Dar es Salaam, Tanzania; Harare, Zimbabwe; Naples, Italy; and, the School of Oriental and African Studies at the University of London. He is currently writing on cultural history, anthropology, mythology, and religion.

Jean La Fontaine is Emeritus Professor of Social Anthropology at the London School of Economics and Political Science, London. She was born and had her early education in Kenya, then obtained a B.A. and Ph. D. in Social Anthropology from Cambridge University. She has done research in Uganda, Zaire and in England and written four books: *City Politics: Leopoldville 1962-63*; *What is Social Anthropology*; *Initiation, Child Sexual Abuse* and has another book in press. She is also the author of numerous articles in a variety of journals, including some for the general public.

Patricia Lança is a writer who lives in Portugal. She is the author of *Oldest Ally: A Portrait of Salazar's Portugal* (with Peter Fryer), *O Bando de Argel*, and is a regular contributor to *The Salisbury Review*, London. She served as a deputy in the Portuguese Parliament from 1987 to 1991.

Marion J. Levy, Jr. is Musgrave Professor of Sociology and International Affairs Emeritus at the Woodrow Wilson School of international Affairs at Princeton University. Professor Levy was one of the first modernization theorists. He published *The Family Revolution in Modern China* (1949); *The Structures of Society* (1952); *Modernization and The Structures of Societies* (1966); *Modernization: Late-comers Survivals*(1972) and *Maternal Influence: the Search for Social Universals* (1990).

Jaroslav Macháček is an economist and member of the Czech Academy of Sciences. He is director of the Institute of Architectural and Urban Studies in Prague. He is author of numerous research studies and articles on regional, demographic, environmental and social issues. He has also taught and conducted research projects at the University of Sussex, the University of London, the Universities of Helsinki and Tampere, the University of Pennsylvania, the State University of New York, Jackson State University, the Portuguese Academy of Sciences, and the UN Interregional Demographic Research Program in Moscow, Russia.

Gwendolyn Mikell is Professor of Anthropology and Director of the African Studies Program in the School of Foreign Service at Georgetown University. She served as Chair of the Department of Sociology there from 1992-1995. Currently she is the President of the African Studies Association and a Member of the Preparatory Committee of the National Summit on Africa. She has held a number of fellowships, including the Jennings Randolph Senior Fellowship at the United States Institute of Peace and a fellowship at the Institute for Advanced Study in Princeton NJ. Her book publications include *Cocoa and Chaos in Ghana* and *African Feminism: The Politics of Survival in Sub-Saharan Africa*, and she has other edited volumes and numerous articles on African rural development, politics and economic restructuring, women and changing family dynamics, as well as African women and peacebuiding. She received her Ph.D. in Anthropology from Columbia University.

540

Sushil Panjabi is Head of the Department of Philosophy, Shree Shikshayatan College, Calcutta University, India. Special areas of interest include social and moral philosophy. She is lexicographer for the Sindhi language part of *Jatiya Abhidhan*, The National Council of Bengal's fifty language National Directory with Bengali as the base language.

Mitchell B. Pearlstein is President, Center of the American Experiment, Minneapolis, Minnesota. Before his return to Minnesota in March 1990, he served two and one-half years in the US Department of Education. He has been editorial writer and columnist for the *St. Paul Pioneer Press*. He also has been special assistant for policy and communications to Gov. Albert H. Quie of Minnesota; a research fellow at the Hubert H. Humphrey Institute of Public Affairs, assistant to University of Minnesota President C. Peter Magrath; director of public intonation at the State University of New York at Binghamton. He did his graduate work in educational administration and higher education at the University of Minnesota, and his undergraduate in political science at SUNY-Binghamton.

Twila L. Perry is Professor of Law, Rutgers University School of Law, Newark, New Jersey. B.A., Mount Holyoke College, 1970, M.S., Columbia University, 1973, J.D., New York University, 1976. She has served as Assistant United States Attorney in the Civil Division of the Southern District of New York. She has published several articles on family law, children and the law, and transracial adoption in various law journals.

Carl Pfluger, whose essays have appeared in *Harper's*, *The Hudson Review*, *Shenandoah*, and *The Southwest Review*, among other publications, is presently writing a book (under the current title of "Arguing Nature") which will explore some of the deeper roots of Deep Ecology, the historical background of Natural Law, the unsettling questions of Sociobiology, and the generally vexed relations persisting among "the human," "the natural," and "the sacred." An active supporter of both human and environmental rights, he has also worked with such organizations as Amnesty International, Human Rights Watch, Friends of the Earth, and The Climate Institute.

Jerry E. Pournelle is a consultant, lecturer, social critic, and computer columnist from Los Angeles, California. He is a past president of Science Fiction Writers of America. He has authored more than thirty books including *Footfall, Lucifer's Hammer* and *The Endless Frontier*. Dr. Pournelle writes regularly for *Byte* and *Infoworld* magazines. He runs a BIX on-line computer forum on democracy.

Richard L. Rubenstein is President of the University of Bridgeport and formerly the Robert O. Lawton Distinguished Professor of Religion at Florida State University. He also serves as President of the Washington Institute and is a Past President of Professors World Peace Academy in the United States. He is author of seven books, including *The Cunning of History* (Harper and Row, 1975) and *The Age of Triage* (Beacon Press, 1983), and the editor of several books, including *The Politics of Latin American Liberation Theology: The Challenge to U.S. Public Policy* (1988). He received the M.H.L. degree from Jewish Theological Seminary, and a Ph.D. in history and philosophy of religion from Harvard University.

Elliott P. Skinner, former U.S. Ambassador to Upper Volta, is currently Franz Boas Professor of Anthropology at Columbia University. In granting him their Distinguished Africanist Award, the African Studies Association said "He has been an ardent and vigorous defender of the interests of both Africa as a region and African studies as a discipline. On the African continent, the field of African studies in America is as much identified with Elliott Percival Skinner as with any other American scholar." His books included *Glorious Age in Africa, African Urban Life: The Transformation of Ouagadougou,* and *Roots of Time: A Portrait of African Life and Culture,* and others.

Kate Xiao Zhou is from Wuhan, China. She received her Ph. D in political science from Princeton University. Her book, *How The Farmers Changed China*, was published by Westview Press in 1996.

542

She teaches comparative politics, political economy of East Asia and Chinese politics in the Political Science Department at University of Hawaii at Manoa. She is also interested in feminist theories.